Citizenship, Diversity, and Pluralism
Canadian and Comparative Perspectives

Citizenship has both a vertical and a horizontal dimension. The vertical links individuals to the state by reinforcing the idea that it is "their" state – that they are full members of an ongoing association that is expected to survive the passing generations. Accordingly their relation to the state is not narrowly instrumental but is supported by a reservoir of loyalty and patriotism that gives legitimacy to the state. The horizontal relationship is the positive identification with fellow citizens as valued members of the same civic community. Here citizenship reinforces empathy and sustains solidarity through its official endorsement of who counts as "one of us." Citizenship, therefore, is a linking mechanism that in its most perfect expression binds the citizenry to the state and to each other.

Citizenship, Diversity, and Pluralism assesses the transformation of these two dimensions of citizenship in increasingly diverse and plural modern societies, both in Canada and internationally. Subjects addressed include the changing ethnic demography of states, social citizenship, multiculturalism, feminist perspectives on citizenship, aboriginal nationalism, identity politics, and the internationalization of human rights.

ALAN C. CAIRNS is adjunct professor of political science at the University of Waterloo and author of *Charter versus Federalism: The Dilemmas of Constitutional Reform.*
JOHN C. COURTNEY is professor of political studies at the University of Saskatchewan and author of *Do Conventions Matter? Choosing National Party Leaders in Canada.*
PETER MACKINNNON is president of the University of Saskatchewan and has served as president of both the Canadian Association of Law Teachers and the Council of Canadian Law Deans.
HANS J. MICHELMANN is professor of political studies and acting associate dean (Academic) of the College of Arts and Science at the University of Saskatchewan.
DAVID E. SMITH is professor of political studies at the University of Saskatchewan and author of *The Republican Option in Canada: Past and Present.*

Citizenship, Diversity, and Pluralism

Canadian and Comparative Perspectives

EDITED BY
ALAN C. CAIRNS
JOHN C. COURTNEY
PETER MACKINNON
HANS J. MICHELMANN
AND DAVID E. SMITH

McGill-Queen's University Press
Montreal & Kingston · London · Ithaca

© McGill-Queen's University Press 1999
ISBN 0-7735-1888-6 (cloth)
ISBN 0-7735-1893-2 (paper)

Legal deposit fourth quarter 1999
Bibliothèque nationale du Québec

Printed in Canada on acid-free paper

This book has been published with the help of a grant
from the University of Saskatchewan.

McGill-Queen's University Press acknowledges the
financial support of the Government of Canada through
the Book Publishing Industry Development Program
(BPIDP) for its activities. We also acknowledge the support
of the Canada Council for the Arts for our publishing
program.

Canadä

Canadian Cataloguing in Publication Data

Main entry under title:
    Citizenship, diversity, and pluralism: Canadian and
    comparative perspectives
    Papers presented at a conference held in Saskatoon,
    Oct.30–Nov. 1, 1997.
    Includes bibliographical references.
    ISBN 0-7735-1888-6 (bnd)
    ISBN 0-7735-1893-2 (pbk)
    1. Citizenship. 2. Citizenship – Canada. 3. Pluralism
    (Social sciences) 4. Multiculturalism – Canada.
    I. Cairns, Alan C.
    JF801.C5734 1999   323.6   C99-900886-2

This book was typeset by Typo Litho Composition Inc.
in 10/12 Sabon.

Contents

Preface

In this volume are collected papers delivered at the conference on "Citizenship, Diversity, and Pluralism: Canadian and Comparative Perspectives" in Saskatoon, Saskatchewan, from 30 October to 1 November 1997. The conference was inspired by the familiar dictum that political science without constitutional law is blind, and constitutional law without political science is empty. It reflects the commitment of the Department of Political Studies and the College of Law at the University of Saskatchewan to interdisciplinary collaboration in promoting and advancing debate on issues of public importance. It was the fifth major event sponsored by the two departments since the series was inaugurated in 1990 by the conference (and now volume) *After Meech Lake* (Fifth House Publishers, 1991).

In addition to scholars and other participants from around the world, the audiences at our conferences have typically included large numbers of students at the University of Saskatchewan. Among our objectives was to expose students to the powerful contribution that academic discourse can make in illuminating issues and offering alternatives for policy-makers to consider. Our students represent the future, and we are pleased to dedicate this volume to them.

We want to express our appreciation to the Law Foundation Chair Endowment Committee, the College of Law Endowment Fund Committee, and the Publications Fund of the University of Saskatchewan for their assistance in sponsoring this publication and the conference on which it is based, and to McGill-Queen's University Press for publishing this volume.

We are particularly grateful to Russell Isinger for his excellent editorial assistance during the preparation of this book.

Alan C. Cairns
John C. Courtney
Peter MacKinnon
Hans Michelmann
David E. Smith

Contributors

HERIBERT ADAM is a professor of sociology at Simon Fraser University. Between 1992 and 1995 he was visiting professor at the University of Cape Town, South Africa. His most recent work is (with F. van Zyl Slabbert and K. Moodley) *Comrades in Business: Post-Liberation Politics in South Africa* (Cape Town: Tafelberg, 1997). Since 1960 he has published 120 pieces on South Africa, comparative ethnic conflicts, and other topics.

KEITH G. BANTING is a professor of political science and director of the School of Policy Studies at Queens University, Kingston. In 1997–98 he was visiting professor at the Centre for European Studies, Harvard University. His most recent works include "The Internationalization of the Social Contract," in *The Future of the Nation State in a Global/Information Era: Policy Challenges*, ed. Thomas J. Courchene (Kingston: John Deutsch Institute for the Study of Economic Policy, Queens University, 1997), as well as "Social Policy," in *Border Crossings: The Internationalization of Canadian Policy*, ed. G.B. Doern. L. Pal and B. Tomlin (Toronto: Oxford University Press, 1996).

ANTHONY H. BIRCH is Professor Emeritus of political science at the University of Victoria. He is the author of the *Concepts and Theories of Modern Democracy* (London: Routledge, 1993) and *Nationalism and National Integration* (London: Unwin, 1989). His works on British politics include *Political Integration and Disintegration in the British Isles* (London: Allen and Unwin, 1977) and *The British System of Government* (8th ed., London: Harper Collins Academic, 1991).

JOHN BORROWS is professor of law at the University of British Columbia and director of First Nations legal studies. His most recent publications include "Living Between Water and Rocks: First Nations, Environmental Planning and Democracy," *University of Toronto Law Journal* 47, no.4 (Fall 1997), and "Frozen Rights in Canada: Constitutional Interpretation and the Trickster," *American Indian Law Review* 22 (1997).

ALAN C. CAIRNS was the Law Foundation of Saskatchewan Chair, College of Law, University of Saskatchewan, at the time of the Citizenship, Diversity and Pluralism conference. During 1999 he was John T. Saywell Visiting Professor in the Faculty of Arts, York University, North York, and an adjunct professor with the Department of Political Science, University of Waterloo. His most recent works include *Reconfigurations: Canadian Citizenship and Constitutional Change*, ed. Douglas Williams (Toronto: McClelland & Stewart, 1995) and *Charter versus Federalism* (Montreal and Kingston: McGill-Queen's University Press, 1992).

WALKER CONNOR, John Reitemeyer Professor of political science at Trinity College, Hartford, Connecticut, is most recently the 1997 Sticerd Distinguished Visitor, London School of Economics, London, United Kingdom. His most recent works include *The Politics of Ethnonationalism* (Reno: University of Nevada Press, 1997), and "Ethnic Identity: Primordial or Modern?," in *Separatism* (Bergen: University of Bergen Press, 1996).

JOHN ERIK FOSSUM is currently an ARENA (Advanced Research on the Europeanization of the Nation State) research fellow at LOS-Senteret (the Leadership, Organization and Management Center) University of Bergen, Norway. His most recent works include *Executive Influence and Constitutional Change in the European Union and Canada*, ARENA working paper 18, 1996, and *Group-differentiated Citizenship – A Brief Evaluation*, LOS-Senter Notat, Bergen, Norway, December 1996.

VIRGINIA LEARY is Emeritus Professor of law at the State University of New York, Buffalo. Her recent works include (as co-editor) *Asian Perspectives on Human Rights* (Boulder: Westview Press, 1990), and (as co-author) *The Philippines: Human Rights After Martial Law*, International Commission of Jurists, Geneva, 1984.

DENISE RÉAUME is a professor in the Faculty of Law, University of Toronto. Her most recent works include "Common Law Constructions of Group Autonomy: A Case Study," *NOMOS* 39 (1997), and "The Right to Linguistic Security: Reconciling Individual and Group Claims," in *Linguistic Rights in Canada: Collusions or Collisions?*, ed. Sylvie Lèger (Ottawa: Canadian Centre for Linguistic Rights, 1995).

C. LYNN SMITH was dean, Faculty of Law, University of British Columbia, and is currently a justice of the British Columbia Supreme Court. Her most recent works include (as co-author) "The Equality of Rights," in *The Canadian Charter of Rights and Freedoms*, ed. G.A. Beaudoin and E. Mendes, 3rd ed. (Toronto: Carswell, 1996), and "Have the Equality Rights Made Any Difference?," in *Protecting Rights and Freedoms: Essays on the Charter's Place in Canada's Political, Legal, and Intellectual Life*, ed. Philip Bryden, Steven Davis, and John Russell (Toronto: University of Toronto Press, 1994).

CHARLES TAYLOR is Professor Emeritus of philosophy and political science at McGill University, Montreal. He was Chichele Professor of Social and Political Theory at Oxford, where he was also a fellow of All Souls College, and has taught at Princeton, the University of California at Berkeley, and l'Université de Montréal. His most recent books include *Sources of the Self: The Making of Modern Identity* (Cambridge, MA: Harvard University Press, 1989), and *Philosophical Arguments* (Cambridge, MA: Cambridge University Press, 1985).

JEREMY WEBBER was associate dean (graduate studies and research), Faculty of Law, McGill University, and is now dean of law at the University of Sydney, Australia. His recent works include *Reimagining Canada: Language, Culture, Community and the Canadian Constitution* (Montreal and Kingston: McGill-Queens University Press, 1994), and "Rapports de force, rapports de Justice: La genèse d'une communauté normative entre colonisateurs et colonisés," in *Le droit soluble: Contributions québécoises à l'étude de l'internormativité*, ed. Jean-Guy Belley (Paris: Libraire générale de droit et de jurisprudence, 1996).

Citizenship, Diversity, and Pluralism

1 Introduction

ALAN C. CAIRNS

A well-functioning institution attracts little attention. Equally, one that has lost its relevance is safe from prying scholarly eyes. Inertia may keep it from the graveyard, as is true of the powers of disallowance and reservation in the Canadian Constitution, which are quaintly described as having fallen into desuetude. Or an institution may be euthanized, as happened to the second chambers in the provinces that were endowed with them at Confederation. Quebec, the last province to abolish its second chamber, did so in 1968. However, an institution whose constitutional role remains significant, but which can no longer draw sustenance from old understandings and practices – a central institution of the modern state whose optimal functioning can no longer be assumed – *will* attract scholarly and political attention. Such is the case with the institution of citizenship.

The reawakening of scholarly interest in citizenship has been dramatic. Here is a subject that had patronizingly been considered a fit topic for civics courses, and had generated about the same level of intellectual excitement as the national anthem. From 1947 to 1957, "citizenship" appeared in only 24 new book titles in the University of Saskatchewan library; this number increased slowly in the next two decades to 39 and then 51, almost doubled to 90 by 1987, and then exploded in the last decade to 308. A new journal has been created to give citizenship studies a focus,[1] and existing journals have devoted special theme issues to the subject.[2] Prominent scholars such as Jürgen Habermas, Charles Taylor, and Iris Marion Young have written rigorous analyses,[3] and institutes and newsletters have emerged to direct scholarly attention to this rediscovered subject.[4] Presidential addresses to learned societies have taken citizenship as their theme,[5] and conferences on the subject have multiplied. This volume, based on a conference held at the University of Saskatchewan in the autumn of 1997, is one of the many testimonies to the fact that "citizenship" has assumed a prominent place on the academic research agenda in Canada and elsewhere.

This rush of attention is not the by-product of internecine academic battles divorced from the real world, as is sometimes the case. Scholarly attention to citizenship is a direct consequence of the challenges to existing citizenship (or of its regrettable absence) in the real world. The magnet is a troubled institution.

At one time, serious citizenship studies were thought of in terms of the progressive incorporation of more and more categories of the population into full membership in the state, and the suffrage was often the main focus.[6] Or, to use T.H. Marshall's evolutionary classification, such studies focused on the progressive expansion of the rights available to full members of the society: civil rights, political rights, and, with the development of the welfare state, social rights.[7]

These approaches, with their implicit Whiggism, are poorly adapted to research perspectives that see citizenship not in the teleological terms of a progressive unfolding, but rather as an institution whose capacity to do its job can no longer be taken for granted. The contemporary question is nothing less than whether the practice of citizenship still has the ability to link members of a society in a relation of rights and obligations to the state.

Citizenship has both a vertical and a horizontal dimension. The former links individuals to the state by reinforcing the idea that it is "their" state – that they are full members of an ongoing association that is expected to survive the passing generations. Their relation to the state is, accordingly, not narrowly instrumental, but supported by a reservoir of loyalty and patriotism that gives legitimacy to the state. The horizontal relationship, by contrast, is the positive identification of citizens with each other as valued members of the same civic community. Here, citizenship reinforces empathy and sustains solidarity by means of official statements of who is "one of us." Citizenship, therefore, is a linking mechanism, which in its most perfect expression binds the citizenry to the state and to each other.

Political parties and interest groups are also linking mechanisms. However, except in one-party states, political parties divide the public into teams vying with each other to take charge. Interest groups seeking to influence public policy recruit members in the pursuit of particular objectives. Even for its members, however, an interest group speaks for only a small segment of who they really are. Thus, although both political parties and interest groups link us to the state, and associate us with some of our compatriots, they are not substitutes for an inclusive citizenship. In fact, our capacity to digest their rivalry and competition presupposes the underlying source of unity provided by citizenship, which counteracts the centrifugal pressures that might otherwise undermine social stability.[8] Citizenship unites what the activities of parties and interest groups divide. Further, none of the other intermediaries between the state and its subjects calls forth the powerful language of patriotism, with its emotionally positive identification with the state, or underlines our solidarity with all recognized fellow citizens.

Citizenship is the institutional arrangement that makes empathy a natural fellow-feeling for all within its compass. To be excluded from citizenship by law or practice, as was true for Jews in Nazi Germany, blacks in the apartheid era in South Africa, and blacks in the American South before the dismantling of the Jim Crow legislation, is to be deprived of dignity and subjugated to the will of others. Accordingly, if the institution of citizenship is threatened, we are all potentially at risk. Attempts to strengthen citizenship, to enhance its ability to both tame the leviathan and predispose people to undertake common endeavours are therefore eminently worthwhile political goals. The scholarly task is to clarify the issues, to analyse how we got to where we are, and, in general, to contribute understandings that busy politicians lack the time to develop. This at least was the working assumption of the organizing committee that planned the conference and then arranged the publication of the papers presented there.

The purpose of this introduction is to set the stage and to introduce the authors' contributions. Accordingly, I will list and briefly assess the transformations in the domestic and international environments that require us to rethink the tasks of citizenship and its capacity to perform them, while drawing the reader's attention to the chapters that follow. I have not tried to weave the two opening chapters that follow into the preceding pages, for they too were intended to introduce the subject of this volume. I trust, however, that one observation on Anthony Birch's "Reflections on Ethnic Politics" may be allowed. His oral presentation, transcribed for this volume, displays to an extraordinary degree two qualities that many scholars – present company excepted – have managed to leave behind as they move through the professorial ranks: the blending of social science understanding with common sense and a clear jargon free language that George Orwell would have appreciated.

1 *Changed ethnic demography* The end of empire, the resultant displacement of theories of racial superiority by international norms of

racial equality, and the changed immigration policies of many Western countries that followed have transformed the ethnic demography of the West. The resultant ethnic heterogeneity generates a multicultural-ism of fact that is sometimes given official state support, as in Canada and Australia. A culturally homogeneous citizenship, which even in the past was usually a fiction, is in massive retreat throughout the Western world. At the best of times, and even in the most tolerant of societies, this galloping diversity generates misunderstandings as the number of behaviours and beliefs that can be taken for granted as a common possession of fellow-citizens diminishes. This greatly compli-cates the citizenship task of linking citizens to each other in a common fraternity of belonging.

Multicultural diversity, however, is far more easily accommodated than multinational diversity. The former may challenge the majority's understanding of their civic identity and their their peoplehood, but the latter, assuming that the nations within have a territorial base, invari-ably leads to demands for self-government and possibly secession. Mul-tinational diversity challenges the integrity of the state as well as the definition of the people.

2 *Indigenous and other internal nationalisms*   The achievement of national independence by Third World peoples has stimulated the nationalism of minority indigenous peoples within Western states. Their growing numbers, together with their more confident and asser-tive self-consciousness, generate pressures for greater self-determina-tion. Memories of their past marginalization and stigmatization may generate a desire for independence that their small numbers preclude. At a minimum, their emotional identification with country-wide citi-zenship tends to be weak or absent. In Canada, the internal national-ism of Indian, Inuit, and Metis peoples contributes to the increasing tendency to describe Canada as a multinational society that has not yet installed an institutional framework for its expression. Since the self-chosen labels "Aboriginal," "First Nations," and "Québécois nation" encourage these groups to develop an internal civic identity, an over-arching Canadian citizenship generates differential allegiance across the country. Civic country-wide nationalism encounters rivals who can, if circumstances are propitious, outdo it in nationalist appeals. Thus the reinvigoration of subnational loyalties in Canada, Britain, Belgium, Spain, and, potentially, France necessarily weakens feelings of civic solidarity with the whole. For some purposes, the "we" group shrinks. Members of internal nations seeking to reduce the control of others over their affairs are no longer seen, by themselves or others, as standard citizens.

The complexity, indeed ambiguity, of citizenship is a by-product of the fact that the coincidence of political and ethnic boundaries in the global community of states is minimal. As Walker Connor describes in Chapter 8, "National Self-Determination and Tomorrow's Political Map," the ethnically homogenous state is a rarity. Further, "most states are not just multi-ethnic, but multinational as well." The tension is profound and widespread when fewer than 200 states contain some 3000 homelands. It is alleviated by the fact that the ambitions of most homeland peoples fall short of total independence. Connor's message, therefore, is on balance hopeful, provided that sensitivity is practised toward national minorities. To ignore or repress homeland demands is counterproductive, for "there is an inverse relation between a government's willingness to grant meaningful autonomy and the level of separatist sentiment."

Concessions by the centre, coupled with the latter's capacity to socialize the population into a limited allegiance to the overall polity, can set limits to centrifugal forces. Divided identities and allegiances are both possible and essential. However, neither they nor the constitutional regime in which they are set is likely to reflect a binding, once-and-for-all solution. The problem attributed to socialism – "too many committees" – might more appropriately be attributed to the never-ending task of peacekeeping and fence-building in multinational, multi-homeland states.

The Canadian problem of "too many committees" in the last third of the twentieth century is a product of the unending introspection of the Quebec–Canada relationship, which has had the unfortunate effect of driving Canadians further apart. The possibility of the breakup of Canada inevitably weakens fellow-feeling. The Quebec sovereigntists, even while Quebec remains a part of Canada, neither see themselves nor are seen by others as ordinary Canadians *comme les autres*. Instead, their sovereigntist aspirations inevitably dilute a reciprocal civic empathy with the Canadians outside Quebec that they hope to leave behind when Quebec becomes a "real," "normal" independent country.

Canadian citizens live in the present, but they anticipate a possible future when they may live in separate countries – possibly after an acrimonious divorce. That possibility dilutes the emotional significance of the formal citizenship they continue to share. Their present civic relationship to each other is influenced by the future as well as by the past.

The civic cleavages generated by the Quebec sovereigntist project, as Jeremy Webber points out in Chapter 5, "Just How Civic Is Civic Nationalism in Quebec?," are fracturing Quebec society. That project not only divides the Quebec francophone community, but brutally exacerbates the ethnic cleavages between the sovereigntists, who are overwhelmingly francophone, and the anglophones, allophones and Aboriginal peoples who are almost unanimous in their vehement opposition to Quebec's secession. Webber elaborates the conventional distinction between ethnic and civic nationalism and then suggests that the dichotomy is simplistic and misleading because it ignores the ubiquitous presence of culture in all, including civic, nationalism. Indeed, the purpose of his analysis is to argue that too few sovereigntists have found an acceptable blend of cultural and civic considerations in their nationalist drive to create a new country – some criteria for which he discusses.

To Webber, an honourable nationalism has to recognize "the need for commonality while it embraces pluralism and individuality." The sovereigntist's failure to manage that task, signalled by their inability to define a commonality that extends beyond the francophone majority, has wreaked havoc on contemporary Quebec and increased the possibility that should an independent Quebec emerge it will commence its new life with a fractured citizenry devoid of reciprocal trust.

When a political community loses or fails to attain some positive collective sense of itself, it includes what might be called "domestic foreigners" or "fellow strangers." The latter's tug on the heartstrings of the majority is attenuated. The society is no longer common to the minority; it is no longer their society. The capacity of citizenship to sustain empathy for all members of the polity is reduced, and the capacity of the central authorities to employ citizenship as a resource is diminished. The ties of trust and allegiance are weakened or, perhaps more accurately, differentially distributed. The Quebec sovereigntist drive to leave Canada has weakened our common citizenship without ending our within-one-country togetherness. It has simultaneously eroded the sense of belonging to a common Quebec society that independence was to serve.

Aboriginal nationalism in Canada has also had a divisive impact within Aboriginal – especially status Indian – communities. In particular, many Native women have been apprehensive about self-government, fearing that it will lack protections against the abuse of women and children that anomic conditions too often encourage. Nationalism logically and usually empirically increases social distance from the society it is reacting against. Aboriginal nationalism, as is true of Quebec nationalism, is rhetorically more enthusiastic about maximizing self-government than about participation in Canadian society. Thus the recent report of the Royal Commission on Aboriginal Peoples was able to muster only nine out of more than 3500 pages to the shared-rule dimension of Canadian federalism, and was at best lukewarm about Canadian citizenship.

This political and intellectual context, supplemented by the natural inward-looking tendencies of nationalist movements, reveals by contrast the remarkably innovative nature of John Borrows' contribution to our discussions in Chapter 4: " 'Landed' Citizenship: Narratives of Aboriginal Political Participation." He anticipates some resistance from both Aboriginal and non-Aboriginal people to his argument of the need and desirability of Aboriginal peoples participating fully and wholeheartedly in Canadian public life. Self-government on a land base in small communities – while intrinsically desirable – is not enough. It denies or neglects half of the Aboriginal population that lives outside landed communities, and fails to recognize the complexity of evolving Aboriginal identities in contexts where intercultural exchanges – including high rates of intermarriage – are an everyday reality. Even "an autonomous Aboriginal nation," he writes, "would encounter a geography, history, economics, and politics that require participation with Canada and the world to secure its objectives."

His courageous analysis – courageous because it departs from the overwhelming emphasis on self-government that has recently enjoyed a virtual monopoly in First Nations' rhetoric – suggests that we may be at a turning point in Aboriginal/non-Aboriginal relations in Canada. The realities that an emphasis on self-government excludes half of the Aboriginal population, that self-government cannot respond to the career and likely lifestyle objectives of over 150 000 Aboriginal people who have or are getting post-secondary education, and that self-government unaccompanied by broad participation in the non-Aboriginal society may attract negligible support from the latter – all powerfully suggest the urgent need for the paradigm rethinking that Borrows undertakes.

Even more fundamentally, Borrows' vision of a different future reminds us that the predictive powers of the academic members of the chattering classes are limited. None of them did or could have predicted twenty or thirty years ago the realities that underpin Borrows' choice of a future.

The message of how little we know is powerfully reinforced in Heribert Adam's account in Chapter 11 of "The Purchased Revolution in South Africa." To look at South Africa today from the vantage point of apartheid's yesterday is to be confronted by one astonishment after another: that a peaceful transition to an African majority could occur; that the extent of bitterness and the desire for vengeance would be so limited; that the African majority regime would be neoliberal; and that the radicalism of so many black leaders could so easily be bought off by the perquisites of office, employment on public-service payrolls, and profitable positions in private corporations. While in the long run the

durability of the new South Africa may founder on the extreme inequalities between the emergent black bourgeoisie and the still impoverished masses, the point to be made here is simply that a remarkable and
almost completely unpredicted transition to a common citizenship has
occurred in a country whose previous race relations were universally
excoriated from the pulpits of the world.

Citizenship is a malleable and contested institution that can serve
different purposes. In apartheid South Africa, it divided the population.
In the new South Africa, it unites. In Canada, Aboriginal nationalism
leads to the idea of an Aboriginal citizenship in the self-governing
Aboriginal nations of the future, the nature of whose reconciliation
with Canadian citizenship is unclear. The Quebec–Canada contest for
the allegiance of Québécois is, at base, a contest between rival conceptions of citizenship. Within Quebec, the tension between an inclusive
territorial nationalism and an exclusive nationalism largely limited
to the francophone majority can be rephrased as a tension over the
boundaries of citizenship and the relevant community it should reflect.

3 *Identity politics*   Identity politics is one of the catchphrases of contemporary political discussion. It is not without ambiguity. Its relevance to an understanding of citizenship can best be approached by
contrasting what I will call its strong and its moderate version. Both
versions assert the necessity of representative practices that incorporate
diverse views linked to particular experiences, attributes of the person,
and ascriptive categories. For the individual, these crystallize into his or
her identity. In the contemporary era, identity politics, which also
encompasses ethnic groups and internal nations, tends to single out
women, disabled people, gays, and lesbians, as bearers of identities that
are under-represented. The argument that this under-representation
must be rectified is normally accompanied by an implicit, and sometimes explicit, claim that those who now wield power in the state and
society are not divorced from their own particularities as male, able,
and heterosexual. The claim of those who hold power that they are car-
riers of universal values and embodiments of impartiality is regarded
either as false consciousness or as a mask of self-interest and, in either
case, as unacceptable. When policy is discussed and decisions are taken
that affect the life chances of citizens, the identities that are not represented will be overlooked, misunderstood, or shabbily treated. This
much is common to both moderate and strong versions of identity
politics. Further, it comports so closely with common sense that any
attempted generalized refutation would be quixotic.

In Chapter 7, "Is Citizenship a Gendered Concept?," C. Lynn Smith
analyses citizenship in terms of Marshall's typology of civil, political,

and social rights and concludes that the progressive unfolding from civil to social is an evolution applicable to men, not to women. More generally, she systematically documents the historic exclusion of women, the price they have paid for that exclusion, the philosophies that were used to justify exclusion, the feminist critiques now employed in refutation, the progress that has been made, and the challenges that remain "to achieve meaningful, functional inclusion." One of the keys to this hoped-for transformation is equality. Smith, a legal scholar, devotes the last third of her chapter to a nuanced discussion of judicial decisions with a focus on equality. Given the role of the courts adjudicating the Canadian Charter of Rights and Freedoms and the consequent role of Charter interpretation in refining constitutional and social norms, the Supreme Court in particular becomes an important agent of social transformation. Smith concludes that, historically, citizenship was custom-tailored to fit male roles but can still be reworked to accommodate the needs of both men and women. Smith's argument clearly lies at the moderate end of the identity politics spectrum. She views the historic and contemporary version of citizenship as incomplete but capable of renewal. In a sense, this version of identity politics is simply the latest version of earlier working-class argument that the presence of the working class in political arenas was essential to counter upper-class and aristocratic bias. In its moderate expression, identity politics sensitizes society to expressions of difference that historically were suppressed, concealed, or unvoiced.

In its strong version, identity politics asserts that an "A" cannot represent a "B." You have to be one to understand one or to represent one. By linking understanding to membership in a particular category, it weakens the possibility of meaningful political discussion across the boundaries of group experience and of existentially-based self-knowledge. The strong version encourages charges of "voice appropriation" when "outsiders" express opinions about experiences they have not had, or identities they lack (which, if ascriptive, are forever beyond their reach). The resultant constraints on discussion inhibit the growth of the mutual understanding that contributes to social cohesion and supports a unifying citizenship. If carried to self-defeating extremes, the strong version of identity politics would produce a narcissistic solipsism locked in its own solitude. By contrast, in its moderate version it is appropriately thought of as a salvage operation directed to the repair of the troubled institution of citizenship.

The identity politics debate over who can understand and represent whom is repeated in the debate within the academy about the relative scholarly merits of the "outsider," whose alleged virtues are a dispassionate, disinterested objectivity in the analysis of the "other," versus the "insider," who brings an existential knowledge and therefore empathy to the analysis of his or her gender, ethnic group, and so on. The sensible resolution of this controversy is provided by Robert K. Merton in a deservedly famous article that reminds us that insiders and outsiders bring different virtues and skills to the search for understanding and that a synthesis of their contributions is the optimal solution. Merton's reminder applies with equal cogency to political discussion. Each one of us, after all, is simultaneously both an insider and an outsider.[9]

4 *Can the centre hold?*   Identity politics, ethnic diversity fed by immigration, the nationalist resurgence of indigenous peoples, and ethnonationalist movements throughout the Western world – Québécois, Scots, Welsh, Flemings, and Walloons: a list that could be much longer – all reflect the declining capacity of centres to have their views of culture, character, and identity automatically accepted by those geographically, culturally, or psychologically distanced from the core. Thus "WASP" has become a term of abuse; indigenous peoples reject assimilation; feminists seek to transform a world they see as having been constructed in the image of men; gays and lesbians challenge the normative monopoly of the traditional family and the heterosexuality that it privileges; and immigrants from non-traditional source countries are less willing than their predecessors were to accept the melting pot as an inescapable or desirable fate. Cumulatively, these challenges lead to the thesis that the values and identities formerly associated with the centre are simply another set of personal choices, the product of one among many possible backgrounds, with no special claim on the allegiance of others.

In sum, in the last forty years, perhaps commencing with the counterculture of the 1960s, there has been what might be called a process of psychological centrifugalism – displayed in a politicization of identities based on individual, ethnic, and national difference – that challenges the capacity of the centre to set standards. Further, centres within countries, as had been true of imperial centres in the period after the Second World War, lost the self-confidence to impose their views. A species of cultural relativism sapped the will of those who used to run the show. The decline of the confidence of rulers, reinforced by the decline of deference among citizens, produces a more balanced citizen–state relation than had prevailed when belief in the problem-solving capacity of government was stronger.

5 *Internationalization of rights discourse*   The preceding developments are reflected in and reinforced by the internationalization of human rights discourse examined by Virginia Leary in Chapter 12, "Citizenship, Human Rights, and Diversity." The rights revolution multiplies the

claims that individuals, both citizens and non-citizens, can make against the state and strengthens the resources they have to resist its impositions. International regimes of rights become measuring rods by which the performance of particular states is judged. Countries are ranked according to their observation and protection of human rights. Most of the latter are expected to be available even to resident non-citizens. Turkish guestworkers in Germany, in spite of their lack of citizenship, now enjoy most of the rights of their fellow German citizens.[10]

Obviously, the impact of rights declared to be universal falls short of universality. Yet it remains the case that the international legitimacy of rights – despite the opposition of those who see them (as Leary discusses) as Western rather than universal, or as impediments to development, or as incitements to instability – supports a degree of civic self-assertiveness whose source is outside the state. Even regimes that are opposed to the expression of many of the rights in question know that they have many adherents, especially in urban centres. The fear and loneliness of rights supporters in hostile environments are partly compensated for by the recognition that they have many sympathizers beyond their borders.

In an important sense, human rights propagandized by international instruments – often emanating from the United Nations – strengthen citizenship by engendering self-confidence, stimulating participation, and enhancing human dignity. However, in an obvious way the authority of the state is weakened because of the external source of these rights. As Leary notes, there is an inescapable tension between developing international human rights law "and the desire of states to protect their national sovereignty." This is most obviously the case in one-party communist states such as China, or Muslim polities such as Iran. External pressure to observe or extend rights, even where the rights themselves are not seen as alien, is not without its problems. In Europe, "even though postwar migrants are largely foreign, they are incorporated into various institutions and structures of host societies. They are formally included in state policies, share in governmental budgets, welfare schemes, educational systems, and trade unions, and are accorded many rights and privileges of citizenship."[11] The stability of such rights regimes for their non-citizen beneficiaries cannot, however, be assumed. The divorce of rights from standard citizenship and their labelling as human rights is too profound a development to be celebrated now as a triumph that has become routinized.

The idea of universal human rights leads, if only weakly, to the idea of universal citizenship. Or, to rephrase the issue, there is a growing divergence between the international source of rights and the responsibility of individual states to implement them. If one were to engage in imagining distant futures, one possibility would be a world of several hundred separate states ruling not national citizenries, but simply the universal-rights-possessing citizenry that happens to be located within their borders. Rights are more mobile than states. When rights lose their territorial specificity, a crucial component of citizenship is deterritorialized. When rights are extended without citizenship, the incentive to acquire citizenship is reduced. On the other hand, if the proportion of non-citizens in the population is large, there may be political and financial incentives for the state to cut back costly social rights, or to have second thoughts about their expansion.

International rights subject state authority to an external international climate of opinion that is available as a resource to the domestic citizenry. To an indeterminate extent, this shifts the balance of legitimacy from states to citizens and subjects. It encourages the latter to believe, when rights are at stake, that history is on their side.

6 *Globalization and social rights*   The international human rights movement is only one example of contemporary globalization. In its most elementary sense, the process of globalization refers to the increased incidence of external phenomena on domestic behaviour. Globalization weakens the capacity of the state to control its own domestic economy. The latter is subject to the instantaneous mobility of capital in global financial markets, and to various international trade liberalization regimes that reduce the capacity of the modern state to set its own economic policy.

In countries where social rights are well developed, their supporters fear that economic globalization will generate a race to the bottom. The pressures to persuade business not to move to low-wage, low-tax countries with minimal social rights will, it is feared, lead to the impairment of social citizenship as social rights are chipped away.

In a discussion framed by the thesis that our societies as well as our economies are experiencing globalization, Keith G. Banting raises in Chapter 6, "Social Citizenship and the Multicultural Welfare State," the more complex question of whether the growing heterogeneity of Western societies driven by internal nationalisms and immigration-induced ethnic diversification will weaken support for social rights. In a nuanced, careful discussion of a policy area that, he argues, needs more research, he nevertheless leans to the pessimistic conclusion that relative to other identities and community loyalties, citizenship (social and other) is losing ground. In such a world, he argues, social rights are more likely to be in retreat than to be advancing, although in favourable circumstances they may hold their own.

7 *The European Union*   Changes in community identities in established states triggered by growing ethnic diversity and by emergent internal nationalisms challenge uniform, universal domestic versions of citizenship. As society changes from below, state institutions, including citizenship, are under pressure to adapt to new realities by, for example, adopting differentiated, asymmetrical citizenship regimes,[12] or by transferring governing powers to territorially based national communities, with a consequent rearrangement of the meaning of citizenship.

A different citizenship challenge occurs when new political structures are placed over a number of established communities with their own individual identities and, if they are modern communities, their own prior sense of citizenship. The legacy of colonialism – state structures imposed over disparate tribal peoples – has left many independent African states with populations virtually devoid of a country-wide sense of citizenship.

The European Union has its own version of the discrepancy between a degree of centralized governing authority and a weak sense of European identity and citizenship. As John Erik Fossum points out, in Chapter 10, "Citizenship, Diversity, and Pluralism: The Case of the European Union," there is no consensus on what kind of constitutional animal the European Union is or where it is heading. One consequence of this ambiguity is a weak and variegated citizenship. Although there is a European citizenship, it is citizenship by aggregation in that each member state simultaneously determines who is a European citizen. As a consequence, European citizenship may be available to a resident of France but not to a resident of Germany, whose only difference is location. The diversity of citizenship, based on the power of historic nation-states in the European Union is, however, somewhat counterbalanced by decisions of the European Court of Justice, which gradually spread a uniformity of rights throughout the European Union.

The complexities of citizenship in the European Union are incisively described in Fossum's analysis. The experience of the European Union confirms that realignments of state authority upward and outward generate pressure, driven by legitimacy requirements, for a corresponding, functionally appropriate evolution of citizenship to make civic sense of the newly created political space. That evolution, however, will be profoundly affected by the varying citizenship practices of the member states, by the domestication of international norms, and by whatever consensus can be reached on the goal of the European Union, as well as by the precise nature of the latter's legitimacy requirement that a European citizenship is to serve. There is never a clean slate. Starting points influence destinations.

8 Citizenship and the breakup of the Western and Soviet empires: weak, amoral, or non-existent citizenship   The preceding comments have largely focused on citizenship in the democratic capitalist West. However, citizenship concerns of much greater gravity are widespread in the former colonies of European powers that have attained independence, and in the successor states to the former Soviet Union and its satellites in Eastern and Central Europe. Empire is a poor preparation for citizenship. To be told that one is incapable of self-rule is poor preparation for exercising it. To be forced to mouth the slogans of a vanguard that knows the route to utopia, or to risk the gulag by silence at the wrong time, makes hypocrisy the practice of the prudent. More generally, regimes that are either alien, corrupt, or tyrannical, or all three, encourage an amoral cynicism in their subjects. The closest one gets to citizen behaviour is a devious capacity to work the system for self-interest, including self-protection. These attitudes and behaviours do not depart when the imperialist – including communist – regimes that spawned them have left the stage. In the ex-communist world, the capacity for civic behaviour has been dulled by decades of submission to authorities who were obeyed without enthusiasm and often without conviction.[13]

For the newly independent countries of Asia, the Pacific, and tropical Africa – especially the latter – citizenship is not an inheritance but an often elusive achievement. In much of tropical Africa, the process of nation-building has been frustrated by the artificiality of state frontiers, and by the tenacious survival of more locally rooted community identities based on loyalties that preceded the colonial interlude. This reality led Robert Jackson to coin the phrase "quasi-states" for states that were accorded international recognition when they gained independence, but in too many cases have shown negligible capacity to provide services and leadership to those they ostensibly govern.[14] Basil Davidson, once a stalwart defender of African independence, now ruefully reports the high incidence of kleptocracies in tropical Africa – regimes that rob and exploit, as well as often brutalizing, their own subjects.[15]

For Davidson, the state form has become the "black man's burden" precisely because its borders as well as its operative assumptions accord neither with traditional conceptions of community nor with traditional practices. The resultant corruption is best described as amoral, not immoral, for the latter presupposes a norm that is being knowingly violated. The absence of citizenship not only weakens the state's legitimacy, but weakens restraints on the abuse of state power. The governors can more easily have their way with the governed without the distraction of citizenship. Citizenship links subjects and rulers in a moral relationship that polices the conscience of the latter. The absence of citizenship, often replaced by loyalty to kinfolk or to the military, shrinks the circle of obligation to friends, relatives and those whose support is necessary to remaining in power. Where tribal cleavages survive, they are exacerbated by the selective giving to one's own – natural behaviour for authorities with access to state largesse when the broader potential bonds of citizenship are nascent. Further, in such circumstances, office-holders view those who support their rivals not as "Her Majesty's Loyal Opposition," but as the enemy within, deserving of punishment appropriate to the disloyal. States without citizens have a limited capacity to do good for those they nominally govern, but an exaggerated capacity to do harm unrestrained by civic empathy.

CONCLUSION

Not surprisingly, one aspect of Canada's thirty year bout of constitutional introspection has been a proliferation of examinations of "who we are" and what does or does not hold us together. Royal commissions have reported on French–English relations, the status of women, and Aboriginal/non-Aboriginal relations. Again, not surprisingly, Canadian scholars – especially Ron Beiner, Joseph Carens, Will Kymlicka, Jane Jenson, and Charles Taylor – have been influential contributors to the contemporary analysis of citizenship in light of the burdens that are now placed on it. The Citizenship, Diversity and Pluralism conference was designed to clarify our understanding by exploring citizenship from three vantage points: Canadian, conceptual, and comparative.

We hoped for clarification of some of the complexities of citizenship in diverse settings. We were not disappointed. We did not expect to find answers to the question of how political authorities could establish solid citizenship foundations that would weaken separatist impulses, generate guilt in those who resorted to the underground economy, and facilitate transfers of loyalty to the state in return for the latter's positive recognition of the many identities clamouring for its attention. These answers will never be simple ones.

But it is important to realize that societies in the midst of a major paradigm shift concerning the fate and rehabilitation of a troubled institution such as citizenship can gain more assistance from scholars who do not profess to have found the answers than from the simplifiers who pretend to have done so. The scholarly objective of clarification differs from the politician's need to act – often without precisely knowing whether the means employed will achieve the results intended.

The above disclaimer aside, several insights from the chapters that follow, elementary though they may appear to be, deserve to be highlighted.

(1) The challenges confronting citizenship testify to its centrality in constitutional government. Unimportant institutions are ignored, not challenged. Where the substance of citizenship is lacking, as in much of tropical Africa, the state's legitimacy is limited, as is its capacity to achieve objectives that require popular compliance. The contemporary scholarly attention lavished on citizenship is therefore entirely appropriate.

(2) Most of the papers in this volume deal with citizenship writ large. Denise G. Réaume, by contrast, in Chapter 9, "The Legal Enforcement of Social Norms," drops down one level and cogently argues that there is much more room in the legal system for normative pluralism sensitive to the norms of minority cultures than is commonly understood. Through an analysis of Canadian legal cases dealing with internal disputes between members of a minority communities Réaume concludes that "there is significant room for culture-specific adjudication" sympathetic to "minority group autonomy." She holds out the possibility of a judicial elaboration of a multicultural sensitivity appropriate to a society whose cultural diversities resist disappearance. She reminds us, therefore, that at the grassroots level, where citizenship is experienced, there may be an adaptability and flexibility that could not be achieved by resorting to formal legislative change.

(3) Citizen–state relations are incomprehensible without attention to the international environment in which states and their peoples exist. Everywhere, the domestic sources of rights consciousness, of feminism, of the reinvigoration of indigenous nationalism, and of the power behind other internal nationalisms are supplemented by evolving understandings of the desirable and the attainable that flow unceasingly across state borders. The interaction of the domestic and the international spheres is more than simple contagion or imitation of the latter by the former. There is a *Zeitgeist* at work here which is, admittedly, fuzzy at the edges and not without contradiction, but which nevertheless appears to be saying "these are the directions in which the world is moving."

(4) The number of ethnic groups and nations will for any foreseeable future be vastly greater than the number of states. Coexistence of more than one ethnic group, people, or nation within the same state is, therefore, the inescapable norm. To think of citizenship as if its holders did, should, could belong to a single people who can view the state as "theirs" and turn it into an instrument to express their culture alone is to live in an imaginary world, or to be willing to sacrifice democracy for the sake of those who have gained control of the polity.

(5) Coexistence is not enough. An aggregation of separate identities does not add up to a common citizenship. Ethnic and national identities

within the same polity, therefore, should not be thought of as exhaustive. We cannot act together unless we have some basis of cohesion. Sharing values is insufficient to provide that cohesion. Francophones and anglophones in Canada are closer together in values than ever before, and further apart in identity. Finding a basis for cohesion without smothering difference is the task for coming decades. Or, beginning from the other end, finding a way to recognize difference and still preserve a basis for common action is the task for coming decades.

(6) The tension between the need for some form of country-wide community cohesion and the affirmative recognition of particular identities based on nation and ethnicity, but also on religion, gender, sexual preference, or whatever, is sensitively explored in the writings of Charles Taylor. In the final chapter "Democratic Exclusion (and its remedies?)," in this volume, Taylor stresses the pressures triggered by democracy itself for a high degree of homogeneity, that is, for the feeling that our fellow citizens are "like us," or are "our kind of people." When "our kind of people" are the only ones we need to consider in our civic behaviour, we have the immense benefit of tacit understandings that facilitate democratic co-operative action and minimize the divergence of goals that adversarial politics encourages. In such like-minded utopias, trust is natural and suspicion is abnormal. The desire to opt out would make no sense. The yearning for such a world, and the temptation to succumb to its lures is understandable. Most of the past franchise and immigration exclusions of Western nations reflected a preference for sameness over diversity in the polling booth and in the population.

Increasingly, however, as this volume makes clear, contemporary democratic societies are radically heterogeneous. This reality leads directly to the politics of recognition, analysed elsewhere by Taylor – the premise that a mature democratic polity must positively affirm different ways of being and the different goals to which they lead.

Taylor distinguishes between two kinds of diversity: first level diversity – in multiculturalism, for example – which is compatible with a common enveloping Canadianism; and "deep diversity," which he applies to Québécois and more tentatively to Aboriginal communities, in which their belonging to Canada "pass[es] through their national community."[16] The latter way of belonging necessarily involves giving up a uniform citizenship, although it is compatible with shared respect for the procedural principles of democracy.

The accommodation of tendencies toward the "politics of exclusion," the politics of recognition of deep diversity, and the politics of recognition of first-level or shallow diversity within a hoped-for viable constitutional order is not easy. The Canadian recognition of Quebec's deep diversity within Canada may be seen by anglophones, allophones, and Quebec First Nations as support for a majority francophone politics of exclusion. When a recognized deep diversity community is a minority national community within a larger federal constitutional order, and simultaneously a majority community within a province (as is true of francophones in Quebec), and is also engaged in a nationalist mobilization of that community in the pursuit of independence, it will be difficult to prevent deep-diversity recognition from slipping into the politics of exclusion. In this case, the recognition of other first-level diversities within Quebec, as well as the deep diversity of Aboriginal nations, may well founder. The hope is, of course, that the recognition of Quebec's deep diversity within Canada would moderate the tendencies toward a politics of exclusion by weakening the nationalist drive for independence that marginalizes the non-francophone "no" referendum voters.

Even in the best of circumstances, it is difficult to reconcile tendencies toward a majority-driven politics of exclusion to make citizenship comfortable for "our kind of people" inside the laager with a politics of recognition that affirms those who are "not our kind of people." ("They are black and we are white. They are gay and we are heterosexual. They came later, and we were here first. We offered them our culture, and they rejected it.") The politics of recognition seeks to ensure that those who would otherwise be outsiders also feel comfortable about their belonging. It affirms what the politics of exclusion denies: the inescapability and even the virtues of the diversities that get in the way of homogeneity.

One is tempted to say with Belloc, "The doctor smiled and took his fees, and said there is no cure for this disease," but that would be unhelpful. Taylor's recommendation is that we have to learn to share political identity space within the same polity. This must mean more than antithetical identities coexisting side by side, sharing only geography. We must share more than space. We need to find ways, Taylor suggests, to co-determine the political community's culture, which we approach from different backgrounds. We will be helped in working out a reconciliation if we recognize and indeed positively value multiple overlapping identities in each of us. Multiple identities are bridges. The exaggeration of one of our identities until it monopolizes who we are builds fences.

A nostalgic return to some mythic past when we were truly one is not in the cards. On the other hand, competing imperialisms of antagonistic single identities – "I am an 'A,' period, and you are a 'B,' period" – is a recipe for an international system, not for a shared country. However, dictation by the majority of its own values, identity, and goals is no longer a viable process for building a country. The political task, accordingly, is to devise constitutional orders that constantly remind us of the many identities we individually carry, identities that are not exhausted by knowing what nation or ethnic group or gender we belong to. If that happy day arrives, we will then look back with incredulity on the great simplifiers who feed on and magnify differences. Their goal is to blind us to the multiple points of positive contact we have with fellow citizens who are not really "other" at all. We need to search for institutional incentives so that the politics of exaggerating small differences can be replaced by a politics that recognizes the much greater similarities that we share. The politics of recognition must be Janus-faced, simultaneously affirming some of the ways in which our differences seek recognition, and reminding us that the multiple identities in each one of us link us with different fellow citizens who share some but not all of what we are.

In recent decades we have seen the end of the Western and Soviet empires. It is time to turn our attention to the imperialism of single identities. Single identities are psychologically wrong. They mislead us by ignoring our complexity. They are politically wrong because they exacerbate our divisions. They are ethically wrong because they stifle empathy and allow us to do horrible things to each other with an undisturbed conscience. They make the noble calling of citizen unattainable.

NOTES

1 *Citizenship Studies* 1 (1997).

2 "Special Issue on Recasting Citizenship," ed. Michael Hanagan and Charles Tilly, *Theory and Society* 26, no. 4 (August 1997). See also the special issue of *Nationalism and Ethnic Politics* 1, no. 3 (Autumn 1995), devoted to Canada: "Ethnicity and Citizenship: The Canadian Case," ed. Jean Laponce and William Safran.

3 Jürgen Habermas, "Citizenship and National Identity: Some Reflections on the Future of Europe," in *Theorizing Citizenship*, ed. Ronald Beiner (Albany: State University of New York Press, 1995), 255–81; Charles Taylor, "The Politics of Recognition," in *Multiculturalism and "The Politics of Recognition,"* ed. Amy Gutmann (Princeton: Princeton University Press, 1992), 25–73; Iris Marion Young, "Polity and Group Difference: A Critique of the Ideal of Universal Citizenship," in *Theorizing Citizenship*, ed. Ronald Beiner (Albany: State University of New York Press, 1995), 175–207.

4 See the quarterly newsletter of the Canadian Centre for Philosophy and Public Policy, University of Ottawa, distributed as part of its multi-year project on "Citizenship, Identity and Democracy in the Multiethnic State."

5 Jane Jenson, "Fated to Live in Interesting Times: Canada's Changing Citizenship Regimes," *Canadian Journal of Political Science* 30, no. 4 (December 1997): 627–44.

6 Judith N. Shklar, *American Citizenship: The Quest for Inclusion* (Cambridge, MA: Harvard University Press, 1991), ch. 1.

7 T.H. Marshall, *Citizenship and Social Class* (Cambridge, UK: Cambridge University Press, 1950).

8 The reason some newly independent countries initially feared competitive party politics, and sometimes still do, was the absence of the stable underlying social base provided by a country-wide taken-for-granted citizenry.

9 Robert K. Merton, "The Perspectives of Insiders and Outsiders," in *The Sociology of Science: Theoretical and Empirical Investigations*, ed. Norman W. Storer (Chicago: University of Chicago Press, 1973), 99–136.

10 Yasemon Nuhoğlu Soysal, *Limits of Citizenship: Migrants and Postnational Membership in Europe* (Chicago: University of Chicago Press, 1994), 166.

11 Ibid., 27.

12 See Young, "Polity and Group Difference."

13 Vaclav Havel, *Living in Truth*, ed. Jan Vladislav (London: Faber and Faber, 1989).

14 Robert H. Jackson, *Quasi-States: Sovereignty, International Relations and the Third World* (Cambridge, MA: Cambridge University Press, 1990).

15 Basil Davidson, *The Black Man's Burden: Africa and the Curse of the Nation-State* (New York: Times Books, 1992).

16 Charles Taylor, *Reconciling The Solitudes: Essays on Canadian Federalism and Nationalism*, ed. Guy Laforest (Montreal and Kingston: McGill-Queen's University Press, 1993), 183.

2 Empire, Globalization, and the Fall and Rise of Diversity

ALAN C. CAIRNS

The ambition behind this chapter is to provide a panoramic view of how the contemporary relationship between Western states and the peoples subject to their authority came into being. The straightforward route to this goal would probably be an account of the evolution of citizenship. I have taken a less direct route, one that leads us to consider a fundamental precursor of our present world: the rise and fall of empire. In the narrow sense, "empire" refers to the European empires that dominated much of the non-Western world until recent decades. But in this era of European hegemony no one – including those who were neither subjugated nor wielded power over others – was immune from the brooding presence of empire. The context will make it clear when my focus is on actual imperial situations and when the imperial era and its assumptions is my subject.

This focus may appear paradoxical in the context of this volume: empire is the antithesis of citizenship. Empire is about paternalism and authority, not rights and participation. However, much of the explanation of where we are now lies in the reaction against the former domination of much of humanity by the European powers: a reaction manifest in anti-colonialism, leading to independence; a reaction against the largely European international system of the imperial era, leading to the multiracial international system of the 1990s; and a reaction against immigration laws that typically defined people of colour, as "undesirable," leading to the adoption of more inclusive criteria for admission to many contemporary Western democracies. If much of the contemporary era can be summarized in terms of the politics of recognition, it is because the imperial world we are reacting against and leaving behind was one of non-recognition.

Obviously, empire's rise and fall had company in shaping the contemporary era. Two world wars, multiple genocides, the emergence of European dictators in the 1920s and 1930s, the rise and fall of the communist world, scientific and technological advances, and the emergence of democratic capitalist welfare states share some of the credit for where and who we are now. Accordingly, this chapter does not strive for completeness, but seeks only to underline the pervasive impact of empire on citizenship, diversity, and pluralism. I have confined myself to the European empires that extended overseas, thus excluding the rise and fall of the Soviet empire and what in retrospect might be called the empire of Yugoslavia and its collapse. Their inclusion would have required many intellectual detours in a chapter that is perhaps already too ambitious.

The analytical perspective adopted focuses on the interdependence of domestic and international phenomena: the link between the British control of India and Australian policy toward Aborigines, and between the end of empire and the emergence of large Asian populations in Britain, Canada, and the United States. In global terms, we have moved from an international system managed by a European oligarchy to a multicultural international system in which European states are a minority. The move from the imperial to the post-imperial era influenced not only those who lived in empires as rulers or subjects, but also countries such as Australia, Norway, and Canada. Canada never wielded imperial power over distant colonies, but its citizens and rulers breathed the air of empire nonetheless.

My thinking begins with a puzzle. On a global scale, there was much more cultural diversity in the nineteenth century than there is now, as we approach the twenty-first. However, the Western world is now much more *conscious* of diversity. Phrased differently, a diminishing phenomenon is attracting more attention. The answer to this puzzle is found by contrasting what I will call "Globalization i" with "Globalization ii" and examining the former's impact on the latter.

Globalization i and ii present themselves to the analyst as packages of interrelated policies and assumptions. Globalization i, the age of empire, encompassed not only an international state system dominated by Europe but also the "colonial" treatment of indigenous minorities in the West, restrictive immigration policies, and a hierarchical view of cultures, religions, and races.

Globalization ii, the post-imperial era, supported the independence of colonies (leading to a multicultural and multiracial international state system), reinforced the aspirations of minority indigenous peoples in the West for enhanced self-governance, led to a relaxation of immigration criteria, fostered respect for cultural differences at home, and was normatively underpinned by an international human rights movement that stressed equality as the norm of social and political relationships. Globalization II was clearly a reaction to Globalization I. Empire and its demise were, respectively, the motor of change for the cluster of policies and assumptions linked to each globalization era.

GLOBALIZATION I: THE ERA OF EMPIRE

The globe-straddling empires of the nineteenth century were established by a handful of European countries that "conquered the rest of the non-European globe with ridiculous ease. Insofar as they did not bother to occupy and rule it, the countries of the West established an even more unchallenged superiority by means of their economic and social system and its organization and technology."[1] For those on the receiving end of empire, the imperial phenomenon clearly merits the globalization label, as does the penetrative intrusion of Western civilization into societies not subjected to direct Western control. Its purpose was to draw hundreds of millions of people more fully into a global society and economy, largely under the hegemony of Europe. For its recipients, it magnified the impact of external forces on their way of life. In varying degrees, the historical path on which they had been travelling was redirected by distant elites whom they had little capacity to influence. Globalization I was a massive attack on the cultural diversity of the pre-imperial world.

Empire gave prestige to all Europeans. World maps coloured in the satisfying hues of domination drew attention to the (often thin) stratum of European rule and away from the diversity of subject peoples, ranging from ancient civilizations to small, loosely organized tribal societies, often within arbitrarily drawn colonial borders. The subjects of empire entered world politics not as full-fledged participants, but as peoples ruled by alien others on their own territories. Empire was a hierarchical system based on power imbalances, and on a ranking of cultures and civilizations – often equated with race – that gave a surplus of positive recognition to the ruling European peoples, counterbalanced by the non-recognition, misrecognition, or negative recognition of the people they ruled.

The practical meaning of imperialism for its subjects depended on a variety of considerations. An extreme yet instructive example is provided by Palau, a cluster of islands in the Carolines. Palau was under a weak and ineffective Spanish ascendancy from 1874 to 1898, followed by a German protectorate, which lasted from 1898 until the Japanese

occupation that began in 1914. In 1921, along with other islands in
the Marshalls, the Marianas, and the Carolines, it was placed under a
League of Nations mandate administered by Japan. In 1947, as a
consequence of the victory of the Western allies over Japan, Palau and
the other former Japanese islands in Micronesia were placed under a
special United Nations trust arrangement administered by the United
States.[2] In 1994 Palau became a sovereign state in free association with
the United States. Thus, in less than a century, the Palauan people were
subjected to four successive waves of alien authority, in the choosing of
which they had no say. Their treatment is only an extreme example
of how subject peoples were viewed as pawns on someone else's
chessboard.

The scramble for Africa that culminated in the 1885 Berlin Conference provides another example. Here, the European powers established colonial boundaries by drawing straight lines on maps, grouping
previously warring tribes within single colonies while dividing other
tribes down the middle. Anthropologists, missionaries, magistrates,
and district officers knew that Italian Somaliland, German West
Africa, the Belgian Congo, the Dutch East Indies, and British India
were far from homogeneous. Indeed, an important task of colonial
officialdom was to inject some systematic meaning into the mélange of
tribes and peoples whose initial coherence in a single colony was based
on coercion. The law-and-order mentality of empire, sometimes manifested in an erratic and excessive brutality, nevertheless fashioned a
peaceful, wary coexistence among tribes, religions, and nations that the
happenstance of empire had brought together. It is evident from contemporary accounts that the contrast between indigenous and European ways of life was much greater in the early days of empire than it
is now. It is also obvious that the cultural differences among indigenous tribal groups, particularly in Africa, were more pronounced than
they now are.

Anthropologists, the eyes and ears of empire, portrayed tribal societies in Africa and the Pacific as discrete entities with their own functional coherence. They often attributed to them a cultural integrity and
insularity that no contemporary anthropologists could apply to their
present-day successors. The fact that a single tribe was so often the unit
of analysis disaggregated the apparent impact of colonial rule. Missionaries justified their endeavours with reports of heathen customs and
religious "otherness" – of animist peoples and more formidable competitors such as Islam and Hinduism. Settlers in such colonies as Southern Rhodesia, the Dutch East Indies, and Kenya lived in enclaves with
their houseboys, cooks, gardeners, and farm workers. At the top of the
colonial hierarchy, an (often small) administrative class dispensed impe-

rial justice, sought to abolish some customs and change others, and generally saw itself as the agent of an expansive civilization. Missionaries, settlers, and administrators tended to believe that history was on their side and that they represented the wave of the future. These heady assumptions were shaken by the First and Second World Wars.

The diversities within colonies were often immense. Lord Hailey reported in the mid-1950s that of a possible 2000 languages in the world, between 700 and 1000 – were spoken in Africa.[3] In her classic account, *Native Administration in Nigeria*, Margery Perham wrote of "the hundreds of societies of widely different size and kind" that had to be coordinated. In the unselfconsciously imperial language of the 1930s, she described the political challenge of administering "a collection of peoples in such widely different cultural conditions, Muslims, Christians, and pagans; Europeanized, Lagosian gentlemen, demanding all the constitutional rights of British subjects, and naked savages on the Plateau requiring generations of paternal government."[4]

The Haileys, the Perhams, the ruling expatriate elite, missionaries, anthropologists, and, in some cases, settlers – all members of the governing imperial class – provided the lens through which colonial realities were viewed in the metropolitan heartlands of empire. Empire was engaged in voice appropriation before the phrase had been coined. Subject peoples were spoken for, written about, and judged as backward by European intermediaries. Imperialism was the antithesis of citizenship. It defined hundreds of millions of non-Western people as politically incapable and unworthy of self-rule. They were to be readied for a world they did not choose and for future roles that were unclear by alien rulers who, in many cases, harboured doubts about the capacities of their "charges" ever to handle the responsibilities of freedom.

The External Consequences of Imperialism

Imperialism and the reaction to it fashioned the world in which we now live. As the Globalization 1 era began, hundreds of tribal cultures existed in complete or almost complete isolation from the European world that was about to point them forcibly in a different direction. Imperialism, however, kept that diversity at a distance and reduced its visibility. To the extent that imperialists believed their own message, diverse ways of life were considered transitional, to be overcome by the imitative propensities of subject peoples who, under imperial tutelage, would recognize their own inferiority and the imperatives of survival in a world fashioned in the European image.

Imperialism was an instrument for the transmission of Western definitions of the good life and hence for the reduction of cultural diversity.

Culture encompassed religion, with the result that millions of Christians were left behind in the retreat of empire. By the mid-1990s there were more than 650 million Christians in Africa and Asia – one third of the world's Christian population.[5] Empire was a vehicle for the diffusion of modernization, of materialism, of Western science and medicine, and of individualism. By accident as well as design, imperialism reduced the diversity of governed peoples by fostering cultural and other interactions with the outside world. Moreover, imperialists were the conscious agents of change. Hobsbawm, writing more generally on the impact of the West on the non-Western world, states that "whatever the conscious or unconscious objectives of those who shaped the history of the backward world, modernization, that is to say, the imitation of Western-derived models, was the necessary and indispensable way to achieve them."[6]

Empire dug its own grave by the oppositional nationalism it generated. The logic of the civilizing mission of the imperialists was that independence would come in good time when their wards – who were regarded, especially in Africa, as living out the childhood of the human race – had attained the relevant capacities for self-government, as defined by their masters. With the exception of India, however, this was a distant goal, one almost lost from view in the day-to-day realities of colonial administration. Imperial authorities, ostensibly in control of the situation, repeatedly proved themselves incapable of predicting the future. The imperial powers that governed tropical Africa completely misjudged the growth of nationalism. Their failure to prepare Africans in the period between the two world wars for the independence that tumultuously arrived in the 1950s was due, according to a former British Governor of Uganda, to the almost universal belief that there was "indefinite time ahead."[7] This schoolmasterly tutelage assumed a degree of imperial will and capacity, and of acquiescence by the ruled, that evaporated after the Second World War.

Imperialism created opposition to its own continuation by generating a nationalist intelligentsia who resented the attribution of cultural and sometimes racial inferiority to their people. Typically, this led to a rediscovery of the indigenous past, a glorification of ancient traditional kingdoms and empires, and demands for access to the fruits of modernity by independence-seeking nationalist movements straining to transcend internal divisions in a temporary unity against the alien imperialist presence.

Imperialism was the genesis of the universalization and transformation of the modern state system. If it did not always create viable states, it at least laid the basis for their future existence by establishing frontiers, by providing an infrastructure of education, transportation, bureaucracy, and central authority, and by forging contacts with external economies.[8] Hedley Bull makes the important point that the attainment by African and Asian "political communities" of full membership in "international society was inseparable from domestic processes of political and social reform which narrowed the differences between them and the political communities of the West, and contributed to a process of convergence."[9] More generally, he argues that the emergence of a universal international society assumed that the new actors could conduct themselves as states, and thus would conform to the established criteria of statehood.[10] Sir Andrew Cohen's claim that bringing the Gold Coast (now Ghana) to nationhood in less than a century after the establishment of British control could surely not "have been done except through a colonial regime"[11] may be an exaggeration, but it is not idiosyncratic. Hobsbawm, for example, asserts that with the exception of the "great Asian empires – China, Persia, the Ottomans," and perhaps Egypt and one or two more, the basis of contemporary Third World states is a product of imperialism. "The post-colonial world," he notes, "is thus almost entirely divided by the frontiers of imperialism."[12] The end of imperialism, ushered in by an explosion of new states after the Second World War, not only overthrew the European-dominated international state system but, as I will discuss later, replaced it by a much more diversified international order. That transformed international order, in which white states were a minority, shattered the restrictive immigration policies of the Western world and changed the policy discourse concerning minority indigenous peoples in settler societies.

The Imperial Spillover

Imperialism shaped the intellectual climate of our grandparents' time, and its legacy shapes us still. Victor Kiernan summed up the world view of imperialists by describing them as the lords of humankind.[13] Imperialism was sustained by and supported a belief in the naturalness of white rule over non-Western peoples. Mussolini, a late arrival on the imperial stage, employed duplicity, braggadocio, and poison gas in pursuit of his goal "to found an empire." When Italy invaded "uncivilized Ethiopia" in 1935, the Italian people were informed that "Ethiopians were unanimously hailing the conquerors for bringing civilization, justice and the virtues of western civilization" to a backward people.[14]

Imperialism contributed to a view of the world as composed centres and peripheries. The centres were the imperial capitals whose emissaries, the self-appointed vanguard of an advancing civilization, were scattered around the globe.[15] As Edward Said has cogently argued, imperialist thought embedded itself in the culture of the imperial mother countries.[16] Even the lowliest citizen of imperialist nations gained an unearned but welcome increment of prestige from belonging to the society of those in charge. Until the First World War, according to Hedley Bull, non-Western societies viewed "the ascendancy of the West ... as a fact of nature" to be accepted.[17]

Imperialism was not just an overseas phenomenon. Its pervasive and gratifying presence in the mentalities of Europeans everywhere also shaped domestic policy toward minority indigenous peoples in settler colonies around the globe. The hierarchical assumptions behind policy toward Indian nations in Canada were informed by a spillover imperial mentality. The language of wardship, of subject peoples, of paternalism, of having to earn the right to self-government differed little between Uganda and the status Indian population of Canada.

The frequent parallels between imperial policies toward subject peoples abroad and domestic policies toward indigenous peoples are striking. For example, the Canadian policy of enfranchisement for individual Indians who had "advanced" to acceptable levels of civilization closely mirrored the policies of imperial powers. It resembled the Portuguese concept of the *assimilado*, the Spanish concept of *emancipados*, the French concept of the *citoyen* (someone subject to statutory law, as opposed to a *sujet*, someone subject to native customary law), and the Belgian concept of the indigenous person who had gone through the process of *immatriculation* and thus was no longer subject to native law. In each case, the premise was that a given individual had advanced to a higher level of civilization, had left tribal practices behind, and was now worthy of a standing that more closely approached that of the citizens of the imperial power.[18]

Succinctly, underlying domestic policies toward indigenous peoples in white-majority settler societies was the latter's knowledge of and psychological participation in European rule around the world. As Perham wrote of Nigeria, "The situation in which a handful of officials has almost complete control over the lives of millions of another race is accepted by most Englishmen as a perfectly normal situation."[19] If minority European populations, as in Algeria and Southern Rhodesia, or Perham's "handful of officials" could rule millions of non-Western peoples in Africa, Asia, and the Pacific, it seemed to follow that white European majorities should exercise unquestioned rule over vastly smaller indigenous populations in North America, Australasia, and elsewhere. To do so was simply to partake of the spirit of the times.

That spirit informed Canadian and American specialists meeting at a 1939 conference on Indian affairs held in Toronto and sponsored by the University of Toronto and Yale University. Participants asserted with virtual unanimity that the goal of Indian policy in Canada and the United States was, and could not be other than, assimilation.[20] Its inevitability and desirability were repeatedly emphasized by Diamond Jenness, perhaps the leading Canadian anthropologist in the middle decades of the twentieth century.[21] To that generation of non-Aboriginal scholars and administrators, the mere discussion, let alone possibility and desirability, of a distinct third order of Aboriginal government was beyond imagination.

Domestic paternalism and external imperialism drew support from the ubiquitous belief in Western superiority. That belief was embodied in the "old Western dominated international order ... associated with the privileged position of the white race: the international society of states was at first exclusively, and even in its last days principally, one of white states; non-white peoples everywhere, whether as minority communities within these white states, as majority communities ruled by minorities of whites, or as independent peoples dominated by white powers, suffered the stigma of inferior status."[22]

If the imperial era sustained racial and cultural hierarchies at home, its ending abroad weakened the power-holding resolve of dominant domestic majorities over indigenous minorities in Canada, the United States, Australia, New Zealand, and, ultimately, South Africa. As one author put it, non-white majorities at the United Nations, implacably hostile to white minority rule, "institutionalized with maximum publicity the conflict between South Africa and its critics."[23] Half a century of isolation and sustained ideological assault finally broke the apartheid regime.

The American anthropologist Edward Bruner has described the transformation in the assumptions that governed American Indian policy as follows: "In the 1930s and 1940s the dominant story constructed about Native American culture change saw the present as disorganization, the past as glorious, and the future as assimilation. Now, however, we have a new narrative: the present is viewed as a resistance movement, the past as exploitation, and the future as ethnic resurgence."[24] He attributes the change in domestic assumptions to "the overthrow of colonialism, the emergence of new states, the civil rights movement, and a new conception of equality"[25] that sent revised messages of the desirable and the possible to the Indian nations and to the non-Indian policy elite. Bruner writes of the United States, but his interpretation has a more general application.

His attribution of major causal significance for changing domestic paradigms to the end of empire is supported by the contrast between the justification for imperialism and the justification for its ending. Consider the trusteeship philosophy of the League of Nations mandates system when imperialism was at its height, as opposed to the United Nations General Assembly Resolution of 1960, when imperialism was in retreat. The assumption behind trusteeship was that "the colonial relationship would endure for a long time."[26] The League of Nations philosophy justified trusteeship over territories "inhabited by peoples not yet able to stand by themselves under the strenuous conditions of the modern world." In stark contrast, United Nations Resolution 1514, a Declaration on the Granting of Independence to Colonial Countries and Peoples, stated that "all peoples have the right to self-determination" and that "inadequacy of political, economic, social and educational preparedness should never serve as a pretext for delaying independence." The resolution was passed with a vote of eighty-nine to zero, with nine abstentions.[27] What had been fundamental – a capacity for self-government learned in the school of empire – was redefined as an obfuscating pretext. Gann and Duignan, contrasting the psychology of Britain's involvement in Africa in the 1890s with that of the mid-twentieth century, noted how in the former era "the intangible factor of morale" supported white rule. In the latter, the critics of colonialism felt that history was on their side. "The rulers ... were more apologetic; they wavered; they compromised and gradually became ... convinced of the necessity for their ultimate abdication."[28] The diffusion of this anti-colonial philosophy into domestic politics transformed the political, moral, and intellectual context of relations between minority indigenous peoples and white majorities in settler societies. In Canada, the five-volume Report of the Royal Commission on Aboriginal Peoples[29] not only employs the standard language of anti-colonialism but also notes the importance of changes in the international environment in supporting the struggle of Aboriginal peoples for self-government.

THE AFTERMATH OF EMPIRE:
GLOBALIZATION II

A Transformed International System

The end of empire transformed the image and reality of the international system of states and peoples. By the 1990s there were about fifty recognized independent states in Africa, whereas in the mid-1930s there had been only four. United Nations membership grew from 51 original members in 1945 to 185 in 1994 – a move from a largely European membership to one in which European nations were in the minority. The same development occurred in the British Commonwealth, from the "old days" of the "white dominions"[30] to the contemporary multiracial and multicultural Commonwealth. By 1997, only five of the fifty-one Commonwealth member states had majority European populations. A similar breakdown applies to "La Francophonie" (Agency for Cultural and Technical Cooperation), which has a large majority of non-European members: thirty out of thirty-seven.[31] The diverse ways of life that once were managed by empire now have to be accommodated in an international system of several hundred states.[32]

Statehood gives voice. It fashions international discourse and reveals diversities that formerly were suppressed and concealed. But the range of cultural diversity that became apparent with this new statehood is narrower than the global diversity that preceded empire. Discrete, isolated cultures are no more. Further, most colonies were consolidations of previously distinct peoples, even though many of them had no international presence. The approximately fifty African colonies consolidated "a far larger number of ... traditional political authorities. Thus, by and large, the scale of political administration became larger, the number of entities in Africa fewer, and above all the boundary lines were altered."[33] Further, the universal imposition of the modern state as the necessary vehicle for participation in the global community constrained the post-independence behaviour of the newcomers.[34] Cultural differences were also weakened by a widespread agreement on goals: productive economies, an improved standard of living, and, at least at the level of rhetoric, support for democracy and human rights. Admitting all the above constraints, the post-imperial international system accommodates a vastly wider range of voices than its predecessor. The cultural diversity of the new states is less than the diversities made voiceless by imperialism, but at least it possesses the profound advantage of recognition.

The post-imperial heterogeneity of the international society of states has transformed the moral, intellectual, and legal environment of global and domestic politics. Hedley Bull's summary is apposite. Third World states "have overturned the old structure of international law and organizations that once served to sanctify their subject status. The equal rights of non-Western states to sovereignty, the rights of non-Western peoples to self-determination, the rights of non-white races to equal treatment, non-Western peoples to economic justice, and non-Western cultures to dignity and autonomy" are embodied in "conventions having the force of law," although their implementation does not always follow, and their interpretation is often disputed.[35] The end of empire resulted not only in the global redistribution of power and status but also challenged domestic policies that had mirrored imperialist ideologies.

The New Immigration

Freda Hawkins, writing of the racially discriminatory immigration policies that prevailed in Canada and Australia until the 1960s and 1970s, was struck by these countries' "common strength of feeling on this subject, the unanimity with which their politicians and officials pursued the goal of a White Canada and a White Australia, and the obvious approval of their respective publics." These policies drew strength from the vast European empires and the accompanying "automatic assumption of the superiority of the white nations over all others."[36]

With empire's ending, that strength of feeling eroded, leading initially to a general relaxation of immigration criteria. For Canada, Australia, New Zealand, and the United States, some of the pressure for less restrictive policies came from the drying up of traditional sources of immigrants. More important was the increasing difficulty of defending the racial restrictions that had been customary in the imperial era. When Indian officials indicated as early as 1948 that Canadian immigration restrictions were being used in India to argue against membership in the Commonwealth, Canadian policy changed shortly thereafter to allow small numbers from India, Pakistan, and Ceylon to be eligible for permanent residence.[37] In the sixties, Canadian immigration policy moved decisively toward universalistic criteria. Senior immigration officials realized that "Canada could not operate effectively within the United Nations, or in the multiracial Commonwealth, with the millstone of a racially discriminatory immigration policy round her neck."[38] By 1987–90, only two other countries provided more immigrants to Canada than did India.[39] In 1996, the top seven source countries for immigration to Canada were Asian. From 1994–96, 80% of immigrants came from non-traditional source countries and only 20% from the United States and Europe.[40]

A global politics of empire and subject peoples, complemented by a generalized hierarchical view of the world's peoples, supported racially restrictive immigration policies in a way that the post-imperial contemporary international state system does not. Laws to exclude Asians were repealed in Australia, Canada, and the United States in response to the new international morality. The result has been a vastly transformed ethnic demography in the receiving countries. The 1965 American Immigration Act and its later modifications led to the admission of more than five million Asians in the two decades that followed. Before 1965, nine out of every ten legal immigrants to the United States came from Canada or Europe. Since 1965, less than one-sixth of legal immigrants have been of European origin.[41] The exclusion of Chinese and Japanese people before World War Two had to be weakened and then dropped in the post-war period "under the pressure of international politics."[42] Australia now seeks to position itself as an Asian country. Prime Minister Gough Whitlam explained the necessary demise of the White Australia immigration policy in 1973 with the assertion that "as an island nation of predominantly European inhabitants situated on the edge of Asia, we cannot afford the stigma of racialism."[43] Canada, which held Asian immigration to a trickle in the first half of the twentieth century, is now self-described as a Pacific country with a Pacific vision and vocation.

Post-imperialist migration has also had a particular impact on the former motherlands of empire, especially Britain and France, where the descendants of formerly subject peoples have moved in large numbers to what was the imperial centre. Yesterday's reality of Britain in India and Ceylon has been transformed into a large population of Indians, Pakistanis, Sri Lankans, and Bangladeshis in Britain – including 1.5 million Muslims and 400 000 Sikhs. Similarly, the former imperial presence of France in North Africa helps to explain why there are now approximately 2.5 million Muslims in France.[44] For the French, whose official policy fosters assimilation, "the strong identification of its North African immigrants with Islam is widely perceived as a threat to the integrity of the French nation."[45]

The diversity that was formerly kept at a distance by imperialism and restrictive immigration criteria is now a significant attribute of society in London, Vancouver, Paris, Berlin, and New York. Europe has been transformed. "All of the countries of Europe have become, willingly or not, countries of immigration where a foreigner who receives temporary authorization to live in the country for a short but undetermined period of time usually ends up obtaining either for himself or for his descendants the right to stay more or less permanently."[46] This challenges historic European conceptions of a universal, homogeneous citizenship and exerts continuous pressure for a multiculturalism of fact and, sometimes, of law.

Ethnic diversification often gives rise to angst and a sense of unease, triggers concerns about national identity, provides opportunities for racist attitudes and behaviour to surface, and is capable of translation into xenophobic social movements and parties. One result is the concept of "Fortress Europe" together with more restrictive immigration laws to implement it.[47]

However, whatever the reaction of majority groups and their governments to unaccustomed demographic heterogeneity, there is no turning back. Difference and "otherness" are now next door, not in distant continents. Although proximity will almost certainly lead to some convergence of cultural practices and lifestyles, the assertion that we are at "the end of the era of the attempted 'uniformisation' of a national culture by means of the state" in the Western world is probably correct.[48]

The diversification of the international community of states and the diversification of the populations of Western states are not discrete developments. They hang together as part of the post-imperial package.

DIVERSITY, RECOGNITION, AND CONTEMPORARY GLOBALIZATION

Agents and Subjects of Globalization: Then and Now

The impact of nineteenth- and twentieth-century empire on cultural diversity was complex and ambiguous. Empire managed, transcended, and reduced cultural diversity. Initially, imperial rule managed diversity by the exercise of authority in contexts where the question of citizenship was not an issue. As an instrument of modernization, empire transcended diversity by fostering intercourse with the external world. Empire reduced diversity in another sense by grouping many hundreds of tribes, nations, and peoples behind a much smaller number of colonies that subsequently became independent states.

Imperial globalization was much more congenial to the Western world than its post-imperial successor. The troubled Western response to Globalization II – fears that sovereignty is being eroded, that borders are disturbingly porous, that domestic populations fed by new immigrants are becoming radically heterogeneous, that the world is generally a less comfortable place – make sense only against the backdrop of the privileged position of the West during Globalization I.

The Western view of contemporary globalization as a new phenomenon is in a sense narcissistic. The phenomenon by which boundaries are eroded and exogenous influences become more common and more intense is not new. The reach of empires over distant peoples and the disruptions this triggered in religious, economic, and political realms represented a globalization whose impact was far more grave for its recipients than the impact of the second wave of globalization has been for the developed West. The globalization of empire was a culturally stigmatizing phenomenon based on the assumption that subject peoples were unfit for self-rule. What generates the perception that the current globalization of developed capitalist democracies is somehow novel is that the West is no longer simply the agent of globalization, but is now also its recipient.[49]

For some of the formerly subject peoples, the terms of economic globalization have shifted to their advantage. Singapore, Korea, Malaysia, and Indonesia presumably see the post-imperial era – in which they have achieved independence, grown in wealth, received international recognition, and successfully penetrated Western markets – as far superior to the globalization of empire to which they were formerly subjected.[50] Immigrants from former colonies whose arrival has generated minority anti-immigrant movements cannot be compared in disruptive potential to what their ancestors experienced in the imperial era. In general, exogenous factors in peoples' lives were much more pronounced and disruptive during Globalization 1, when Western countries were the agents, than they are now, when the West too feels intruded upon.

The International Politics of Recognition

Globalization, either in its past or its contemporary form, systematically awards respect and withholds it from the diverse peoples of the world. Our attitudes toward one another are conditioned by prevailing judgments that reflect the spirit of the times and transcend national boundaries: judgments about the virtues of different ways of life, about the acceptability or otherwise of slavery, and about which cultures or civilizations are ascendant and which in decline. In stable times, these judgments take on the character of conventional wisdom. Accordingly, the reputation of diaspora communities is inevitably caught up in the reputation of the homeland they have left behind, or by the more general reputation, positive or negative, of their people elsewhere. Indeed, a positive view of ourselves is much easier to sustain if the accomplishments of "our people" elsewhere are many and lauded, and much more difficult to sustain if the reverse is the case.

The significance of the external sources of many domestic judgments has been underestimated by contemporary students of multiculturalism and of the politics of recognition. Charles Taylor,[51] Axel Honneth,[52] and others, building on the work of G.H. Mead,[53] have underlined the importance of respect and positive recognition for individual and collective psychological health. Will Kymlicka makes a similar point in arguing for a state role in supporting minority cultures.[54] All three note the devastating effects of negative, stigmatic recognition.[55] The leverage to overcome disrespect, stimulate the politics of positive recognition, and provide support for minority cultures is generally assumed to be the individual state responding to its own peoples.

In playing these roles, however, the state is subjected to a barrage of judgments about the relative worth of the globe's cultures and societies. Thus the success or failure of post-apartheid South Africa will affect the status as well as the self-confidence of blacks in the United States. In this sense, Nelson Mandela is an extraterritorial Martin Luther King. David Apter reports that he began his research on nationalism in the Gold Coast in the 1950s with the knowledge that independence, "if well begun," would not only lead to the independence of additional African states, but would "help ... to stimulate black liberation in America."[56] Conversely, the bombing of Pearl Harbour had a devastating impact on the treatment of Canadian and American citizens of Japanese descent. The Ayatollah Khomeini's fatwa against Salman Rushdie at least temporarily fostered negative views toward the Muslim community in Britain.[57] During the Gulf War, British Muslims were seen as a "fifth column" whose internment was threatened.[58] To put it differently, global or external messages can shut down or open up domestic options.

The end of empire abroad transformed the dialogue about smaller indigenous nations and minorities in settler countries. In Canada, the extension of the franchise to status Indians in 1960 was a response more to the multiracial and multicultural nature of the new Commonwealth than to pressures from Indian peoples, many of whom viewed this "gift" as an instrument of assimilation. The 1992 Australian High Court's Mabo decision, which repudiated the concept of *terra nullius* (no man's land), (which had justified the disregard of the prior indigenous presence, and thus facilitated the assertion of sovereignty by the incoming Europeans) was consonant with global trends. This ruling would have verged on the unthinkable in the 1920s, when European empires and their accompanying justifications were at their height. In the age of empire, imperial and domestic attitudes toward subject peoples tended to move in tandem. Empire abroad gave sustenance to policies that marginalized indigenous minorities at home. The end of empire strengthened the latter's voice.

In the imperial era, the subjects of empire were seen as unworthy of self-rule, as backward, as culturally inferior, and so forth. These assumptions spilled out of the imperial framework and almost automatically embedded themselves in immigration policies, in the treatment of indigenous peoples, in the teaching of history, and in the basic world views of all Western peoples, even those who possessed no formal colonies across the water. Much of how we view and treat each other is a by-product of international messages and is thus only partly amenable to domestic influences.

The never-ending cultural messages that flow across porous borders provide shifting evaluations of states, nations, religions, cultural practices, economic achievements, and other markers of diversity. The consequences can be good or bad, depending on the criteria employed. The post-imperial moral climate has given rise to greater empathy for indigenous peoples in various countries who cannot aspire to independence and, to take another example, ultimately undermined apartheid in South Africa. These, however, were preceded by apartheid and by the marginalization of indigenous peoples, both of which reflected dominant trends in the global culture of earlier eras which was supportive of imperialism.

We cannot escape this intellectual and cultural barrage on how we view each other. No one looking at the sorry twentieth century record of brutality and incivility can assume that we will run out of materials for judging each other in the international sphere, nor that such judgments will have no effect on how we view each other in our heterogeneous societies at home. The politics of the domestic recognition of diversity, or response to difference, however it may be defined, is not immune to international influence. What we can do, however, and have increasingly done since the Second World War, is to increase the flow of international messages supportive of human rights. We can devise international instruments to monitor and regulate the domestic treatment of the "other." In doing so, one of our tasks is to counter pejorative views of the "other" that are products of history, of surviving "racial" stereotypes, or of contemporary judgments, fair or unfair, of the foreign kinfolk of those who have settled in our midst.

Accordingly, the contemporary politics of domestic recognition is filtered through positive, evolving international norms embodied in what Yasemin Soysal labels "the institutional rules of the global system."[59] In her brilliant recent volume, *Limits of Citizenship*, she reports a remarkable development in the Western European state system: the incorporation into state policies of what she labels the norms of universal personhood. The rights entailed in universal personhood, which derive from the international discourse of human rights following the Second World War and are found in innumerable instruments produced by international organizations, put pressures on individual states to treat resident non-citizens, often guest workers, in ways that increasingly erode the practical distinctions between citizens and non-citizens with respect to the possession of rights.[60]

The numbers involved are not trivial: about fifteen million migrants in Europe are foreigners, and there are about an additional three million undocumented foreigners. Foreign non-citizens amount to one-sixth of the Swiss population.[61] In general, guest workers,[62] the largest category, have been widely incorporated into the framework of the host society. "They participate in the educational system, welfare schemes, and labour markets. They join trade unions, take part in politics through collective bargaining and associational activity, and sometimes vote in local elections. They exercise rights and duties with respect to the host polity and the state."[63] Further, many of these foreign quasi-citizens do not seek full citizenship. They have low rates of naturalization,[64] and limited interest in obtaining it in most cases.[65] Their experience makes the possession of official national citizenship of diminishing relevance as an entitlement to a fruitful relationship with the state. National voting rights are normally withheld, but local voting participation is often permitted. The ethnic groups involved often have strong ethnic associations that speak for them, although the structure and significance of these vary, depending on the policies of the host state. The millions of individuals involved enjoy many of the benefits of citizenship without having to possess it. They experience a limited multiculturalism of fact outside the boundaries of citizenship. Particularly if they are legally present, they become enmeshed in a web of ties with the host society, which affords them additional protection.

Soysal attributes this tremendous improvement in the treatment of non-citizens to the fact that contemporary state policy is "conditioned" by global norms and rules.[66] She contrasts these norms with the assumptions prevalent when guest workers were first recruited or arrived in Western European countries in the middle of the twentieth century – i.e., that they were a form of returnable labour to be repatriated at the will of the host state – and with the attitudes toward immigrants in earlier eras, when a newcomer was either on the road to full citizenship or was subject to a host of exclusions from full membership in the host society.[67] (This practice was widespread with respect to Asian immigrants in Canada and elsewhere until after the Second World War.) There is, therefore, a contemporary, quasi-official international politics of positive recognition that pulls democratic Western polities toward a universal recognition of human dignity for all legitimately within state borders, regardless of their origin. This evolution of universal personhood, of rights that "do not change with geography, culture, or stages of development, and ... do not distinguish between race, class, sex, religion, or national origins,"[68] and that are embodied in international instruments, is transforming the relationship between Western states and those within their borders.

Globalization i was the age of hierarchy. Globalization ii is the age of rights. According to Louis Henkin, "human rights is the idea of our time, the only political–moral idea that has received universal acceptance."[69] In the Western world, the state's treatment of its non-citizen residents as well as of its citizens is now subject to scrutiny and challenge by the international discourse of human rights. At the same time, citizenship is devalued by the almost equal availability of rights to non-citizens. Incentives to naturalize are reduced, and the capacity of the state to assimilate its rights-possessing non-citizens is eroded. Non-citizen residents may have limited loyalty to their host state. For Turkish guest workers in Germany, as was the case for British missionaries in imperial India, "home" is where they come from, not where they are. Diaspora becomes a way of life and political identity is deterritorialized.[70] The symbolic centre of the imagined community that attracts one's strongest identification can be located almost anywhere.[71]

Domestic society in the EuroAtlantic community "has become a partial microcosm of the world-at-large."[72] The state in this emerging order, "if present trends continue, is in the process of becoming a territorial administrative unit of a supranational legal and political order based on human rights codes."[73] In the early stages of this development, the historical basis of the Western state's legitimacy is eroded at its margins. Its capacity to draw on reserves of loyalty and patriotism is weakened. Citizens, coexisting with non-citizen residents receiving almost the same rights, experience a sense of disorientation. Support for the welfare state, historically based on civic empathy and common membership, diminishes as its social benefits are distributed to non-citizens.[74]

The imperial politics of Globalization I removed governing powers from those it subjected for the sake of a transnational order based on Western hegemony. Globalization II, more benignly, but still effectively, although not without resistance, erodes the autonomy of Western states for the sake of a post-imperial normative order. There remains, however, a transitional (and possibly enduring) tension between the evolving international rights regimes and the historic theory and practice of state autonomy.[75]

States in the EuroAtlantic community have had to give up much of their former freedom of choice in selecting immigrants. Their capacity to apply grossly discrepant rights regimes to their citizens and resident non-citizens is diminished. They can no longer control their own borders (United States), or engage in mass deportations of illegal aliens,[76] or send guest workers home (Germany), or rigorously employ traditional assimilation policies (France).

The positive impact on Western state policies of the norms of universal personhood so glowingly described by Soysal is undeniable. Another body of literature, however, reminds us of the continuing pervasive racism directed particularly against black and Muslim minorities in Europe.[77] Clandestine immigrants, especially in Italy, distance themselves from the authorities and hence from state benefits. Further, the status of what Tomas Hammar calls "denizens" – "foreign citizens with a legal and permanent residence status ... [who] enjoy full social and economic rights"[78] – remains anomalous. Their exclusion from national elections deprives them of the capacity to influence the political composition of governing elites. Conversely, the majority society, disinclined to see "them" as part of "us," can pursue policies that deliberately or inadvertently disadvantage non-voting but legally present foreigners. Finally, this intermediate half-a-loaf status may so reinforce group boundaries that full membership in the future is even less likely.

These dilemmas and ambiguities have little relevance for most Third World states. They cling to the Westphalian notion of the sovereignty they have so recently won and resist the incursion of universal rights interventions in their affairs – partly because their actual control over their people and territory is often fragile, and partly because, they argue, the rights are in reality Western, not universal. Nevertheless, Henkin notes that the "international commitment to human rights ... helped remove Idi Amin of Uganda, Bokassa of Equatorial Africa, ... [as well as] the military junta in Argentina," and everywhere puts totalitarian governments on the defensive.[79]

The individual states in which we live are not insulated from the international community of states. Accordingly, a purely national civic identity verges on the anachronistic.

Globalization, Culture, and Identity [80]

Although contemporary international norms weaken rationales for negative second class treatment of fellow citizens or residents based on their "otherness," globalization simultaneously weakens the cultural rationales for *positive* differential treatment. It does so by eroding cultural difference. The global cultural diffusion of the imperial era, and the even more pronounced and irresistible circulation of ideas, values and lifestyles across contemporary borders, a process that is accelerated within individual states, suggest that differential treatment to respond to a claimed cultural differentiation from the host society needs to be approached with caution. Attributions of cultural integrity, distinct ways of life, and unique cultures to particular peoples in the contemporary era are often overdrawn. The successors of the early twentieth-century anthropologists who presented portraits of functionally integrated whole societies lack the materials for similar descriptions as the century draws to a close.[81]

Globalization and the interdependent coexistence within states of peoples with originally different backgrounds indicate that all societies, from the territorial national society that undergirds the state to smaller internal societies, are massively penetrated by external forces. The former Soviet Union was not immune. Neither is contemporary China. The most powerful nation in the world, the United States, has millions of illegal immigrants within its borders. All societies, even large national societies with powerful governments at their disposal, are in fact partial, incomplete societies. The individuals who live in their midst, and especially those who belong to smaller internal communities and nations, simultaneously partake of many cultural resources that are not confined to "their" culture. We might say that they live in many cultures at once, or that as individuals and communities they fashion their ongoing sense of self from the many sources, including exogenous ones, that modernity makes available. In a world in which globalizing interdependencies and cultural diffusion invade "the local and familiar," it is increasingly necessary for the "self ... to become its own 'author' – that is, the individual must be capable of generating a coherent narrative of self-identity in the face of these massive changes."[82]

Various contemporary students see the antithesis of culturally separate peoples as the very reality of the late twentieth century. "If there is a lesson in the broad shape of this circulation of cultures," writes Kwame Anthony Appiah, "it is surely that we are all already contaminated by each other, that there is no longer a fully autochthonous pure-African culture awaiting salvage by our artists (just as there is, of course, no American culture without African roots). And there is a clear sense in some postcolonial writing that the postulation of a unitary Africa over against a monolithic West – the binarisation of Self and Other – is the last of the shibboleths of the modernisers that we must learn to live without."[83] Edward Said agrees: "All cultures are involved in one another; none is single and pure, all are hybrid, heterogeneous, extraordinarily differentiated, and unmonolithic ... . Far from being unitary or monolithic or autonomous things, cultures actually assume more "foreign" elements, alterities, differences, than they consciously exclude."[84]

Intermarriage rates support Appiah and Said. Canadians with multi-ethnic backgrounds slightly outnumber those with single ethnic backgrounds. Further, Canadian data support the thesis that intermarriage leads to the erosion of ethnic identity[85] and indicate much higher inter-marriage rates among native-born than foreign-born Canadians claiming a common ethnic origin. For example, only 17.5% of Canadians born in Eastern European reported a multiple ethnic origin, compared to 61.5% of native-born Canadians of Eastern European origin. South-Asian Canadians born in this country are four times more likely to report multiple ethnic origins than are foreign-born South-Asian Canadians – 24.2% and 5.6% respectively.[86] Intermarriage rates are high for Aboriginal Canadians. In a 1992 report, Clatworthy and Smith estimated an out-marriage rate of 62% for off-reserve status Indians,

25% for the on-reserve population, and an overall out-marriage rate of 34%.[87] In the United States, nearly 60% of American Indians are married to non-Indians.[88] Further, only 22% of Americans claiming some Indian ancestry identified themselves as Indian.[89]

The argument is not that surviving cultural differences are trivial, or that they are fast disappearing residues, but simply that the rhetoric of difference should not be allowed to obfuscate the extensive interdependence between and within societies or the cultural diffusion that results from it. No one could now plausibly argue that the cultural differences between the majority francophone community in Quebec and the anglophone majority outside Quebec are as profound as they were forty years ago.[90] The Tremblay Report of the mid-1950s, which portrayed two cultural solitudes and described a Quebec culture that was classically "other,"[91] could not be written now. Equally, revitalization movements notwithstanding, the cultural differences between Aboriginal and non-Aboriginal Canadians are surely diminishing. The Report of the Royal Commission on Aboriginal Peoples foresees a future in which Aboriginal people are proportionally represented in all the prestigious professions, as "doctors, ... biotechnologists ... computer specialists ... professors, archeologists" and so forth.[92]

Surviving cultural differences coexist with extensive intercultural sharing of practices and values. To construct relationships in a democratic polity containing several peoples as if the latter interacted as cultural wholes – the billiard-ball theory of cultural contact – is to misread the contemporary condition and, effectively, to repudiate the eclectic choices that individuals and peoples have made in constructing their way of life.

The disappearance of discrete, whole cultures elicits a search for alternative indicators of cultural uniqueness. This leads to the promiscuous spread of the word "culture" to domains where its applicability is problematic. Thus we now have gay culture, lesbian culture, feminist culture, culture of the disabled, the blind, the deaf and many others.[93] These labels draw attention to a single trait, which their possessors speak of as if it encompassed the whole person. The exaggerated significance attributed to specific traits, followed by the latter's imperialistic usurpation of the overall cultural identity of the individuals who possess them, conceals what we share in common and divides us from each other. Here, as in the larger claims on behalf of culturally unique societies, culture is given a political role it cannot sociologically sustain.

We have been miseducated to believe, certainly in Canada, that our divisions are generated by differences in culture and values.[94] Thus in the lead-up to the Charlottetown Accord the federal government sought to locate our prospective togetherness in the values we shared. However, the claim of value or of cultural congruence, even if valid, is not the issue in conflicts between Quebec and the rest of Canada. Cultural convergence and identity divergence occur simultaneously.

Nationalist elites are uncomfortable with this fact, and hence try to deny it. They continue to make their claims for special treatment or unique recognition on the grounds of cultural difference. Thus, the Assembly of First Nations' constitutional document, *To the Source*,[95] laid its claim for a special place for the First Nations in the Canadian constitutional order on a litany of cultural contrasts that lent minimal justification, except regrettable necessity, to why Indian peoples and non-Aboriginal Canadians should stay together at all. Canadian nationalists adopt the same tactics and strain to maximize the cultural gap between the Canadian and American ways of life in their public statements, as if there were no other reasons for an independent Canadian existence. Quebec sovereigntists are similarly engaged in identifying divergences of culture and values between Quebec and the rest of Canada as a key reason for setting themselves apart in a country of their own. Much of this politically motivated language is clearly exaggerated. It is the way we have been taught to make claims for special treatment, possibly because cultural arguments were employed in the past to justify negative versions of special treatment. Yesterday's imperialists invoked cultural difference to justify the denial of self-government. Today's nationalists invoke cultural difference to justify self-government,[96] or secession.

It will not be easy to escape from a cultural discourse that, in part, misleads us. If we are grappling with the barriers to a common citizenship, or with claims for special recognition, or for self-government, we should focus on *identities*. With whom do we share feelings of solidarity? To what community does "we" refer? In Canada we are divided more by our identities than by our values, although this is less true of some Aboriginal peoples than of the Quebec francophone population. I suspect this is a common situation.

When I note that cultural differences are eroding, my intention is not to argue against decolonization or indigenous self-determination. My point is simply that to assume that massive cultural difference – "otherness," or incommensurable values – is the primary justification for self-government misses the point. It also gives ammunition to its enemies, who can stress cultural convergence. Identity difference, coupled with territory and capacity, is sufficient justification. Some surviving cultural difference is a helpful supplement. Further, self-government will contribute, at least at the margins, to the preservation and the stimulation of ongoing cultural diversity.

The Complexity of Identity

Distinct identities do not, apparently, require an elaborate cultural clothing of differentiation from the "other" to survive or to seek some degree of autonomy. Cultural change and the persistence of identity are compatible phenomena "precisely because each fulfills different important functions for the individual or society."[97] Identity can attach itself to territory, to language, and, most importantly, to historical memory – especially the memory of past mistreatment or injustice, which can then be mobilized by elites.[98] Identities rooted in history that are attached to rights have a special saliency. They provide the central justification for the claim of many indigenous peoples for differential treatment.

The focus on identities, accordingly, should be coupled with a focus on the role of memory in sustaining identity and on how memory is fashioned by experience and politics. R.J. Vincent argues that in Africa and Asia the "memory of inequality" and of how Europeans stressed their Europeanness generates counter-ideologies of Asianness and Negritude, which translate the claim "We are as good as you" into "We are different from you, and we do not necessarily have the same values as you."[99] Memories of the insensitive or coercive treatment of minority communities or internal nations give emotional substance to separate identities, even if cultural differences are declining.[100] To shift from culture to identities and memories as what makes fruitful cohabitation easy or difficult does not make our task any easier.[101] It does, however, I believe, more accurately define our situation.

Perhaps the best way to think of the relationship between culture and identity is not to consider cultural difference as the necessary basis for identity difference, but to accept that identity difference has many possible sources. One of the ways it will seek expression is by keeping alive or generating, if necessary, a visible indication of cultural difference to confirm the separate identity that, in the latter case, was its author. That such cultural difference may then receive elaborate attention in public discussion by its sponsors should not surprise us. Neither, however, should it mislead us into believing that this reality is the equivalent of the encompassing culture of the integrated tribal societies that anthropologists used to describe. What we see are cultural variations, not evidence of incommensurable solitudes.

Further, identities are not simple phenomena, and individuals have more than one. In fact, as Williams, following Simmel, observes, each of us is a veritable "colony of the selves," a meeting point for potential identities that we "edit" as we manoeuvre through the day's events.[102] Part of this "editing" is Goffman's distinction between backstage and front stage behaviour: backstage is where we put on our masks as we wait for the curtains to open, and front stage is where we wear them.[103] As Vaclav Havel notes, in totalitarian systems masks are not simple playthings to put on and shed in the theatre of everyday life, but instruments of survival.[104]

Sometimes, preferred facets of our identity are kept in the closet until the moment of liberation arrives. Bruce Lincoln writes of how in the early days of the Spanish Civil War, when the Republican forces triumphed, "virtually overnight the rules and habits of centuries dissolved, and a sweeping transformation in the conduct of human relations was accomplished. Suits and neckties disappeared, and overalls became the preferred dress ... . Waiters stared customers in the eye and spoke to them as equals. Bootblacks refused tips as signs of condescension and charity."[105]

We are not always allowed to be who we would like to be. The very purpose of imperialism was to persuade or coerce subject peoples to deny who they were in the interest of who they were supposed to become. In conditions of struggle, nationalist movements become enforcers of conformity on behalf of an exalted national identity. Slavenka Drakulic, describing the impact of war in the former Yugoslavia, laments that she is "pinned to the wall of [Croatian] nationhood ... . [T]he war is ... reducing us to one dimension; the Nation ... whereas before, I was defined by my education, my job, my ideas, my character – and, yes, my nationality too – now I feel stripped of all that. I am nobody because I am not a person any more ... I feel as an orphan does, the war having robbed me of the only real possession I had acquired in my life, my individuality."[106] Multiple identities, she was indirectly saying, take us out of the parochial sense of self that always threatens and tempts us. They facilitate connections and linkages. Imperialistic single identities repudiate them, usually in the interest of mobilizing us against the alien other.

CONCLUSION

The components and consequences of Globalization I and II had a certain coherence. The essence of Globalization I was the enclosure and subordination of much of the non-Western world within imperial frameworks dominated by European powers. This was supported and justified by a belief in the cultural and possibly racial superiority of the European peoples. Imperial consolidation was reflected in an international system largely, but not exclusively, dominated by an oligarchy of European powers and their offshoots in North America and elsewhere. The imperial example abroad supported the domestic marginalization of indigenous peoples in Canada, Australia, and elsewhere. The Ashanti in the Gold Coast, the Kikuyu in Kenya, the Australian Aborigines, and the Indian peoples of Canada were similarly judged as unready for full citizenship or self-government. The assumptions that provided the ideological justification for European domination over non-Western peoples also governed immigration policy.

These interdependent practices were held together by the stability of empire and its supporting norms. When the imperial centre could no longer hold, the periphery unravelled. In a few short decades after the Second World War, empires were dismantled and dozens of former colonies gained independence. The international state system, no longer a European club, expanded to encompass a plethora of new states who spoke for the former colonial peoples. The liberation of the Third World, the availability of the United Nations as a forum, the vivid memories of Nazi Germany's descent into barbarism, and the resentment of formerly colonized peoples put all beliefs of racial inequalities on the defensive, denied the legitimacy of colonialism where it still survived, and stressed, among other rights, the right to self-determination. This emergent order challenged the posture of wardship that had been taken toward indigenous minorities in Canada and elsewhere. The collapse of the external imperial model removed the props from domestic policies, which were now redefined as the instruments of an internal colonialism no longer consonant with the spirit of the post-imperial era.

At the same time, restrictive immigration policies in the Western world were put on the defensive, as the invidious distinctions they embodied appeared to parallel the imperial distinctions between the worthy and the unworthy – the rulers and the ruled – which lost legitimacy with imperialism's demise. The movement from imperial centres to colonial peripheries of administrators, missionaries, and settlers was reversed; millions of formerly excluded individuals who had shed their colonial status, along with other once-excluded groups of non-Western peoples, migrated to the West. The transformed ethnic demography within the Western world triggered the debates surrounding citizenship, multiculturalism, and race relations that are among the most contentious domestic policy issues of the post-imperial era.

Globalization II, as did its precursor, Globalization I, presents itself as a package of linked changes and challenges to how we relate to each other domestically and internationally. In the past, imperialism on the other side of the world, and its domestic counterpart for indigenous peoples, employed hierarchy and distance to manage relations between European and non-Western peoples without the complicating presence of a common citizenship. Now, imperial hierarchy is no longer available and the ideologies of superiority and inferiority that sustained it no longer have legitimacy. Colonial self-government is paralleled by pressures for and the achievement of indigenous self-government. The vast movements of migrating peoples have reduced the distance between us to next door in the neighbourhood, the domestic counterpart to the fact that colonial independence has us sitting side by side in the United Nations General Assembly.

Our chances of peaceful, even perhaps enjoyable and fruitful living together internationally and within our separate states depend on whether we can accept that we do not live in discrete, bounded cultures, and that we are the fortunate and proud possessors of multiple identities that link us to one another.

Success in living together harmoniously will not come easily, for the legacy of empire survives in the contradictory memories of the successors of the imperial generations. A stubborn residue of pride in past authority once confidently wielded clings to the successors of imperialist generations. By contrast, memories of past humiliations continue to haunt present generations whose parents and grandparents were the subjects of imperial rule. We do not meet, therefore, in the post-imperial world with a clean slate. However, empire's ending, although the memories remain, at least gives us a chance to begin anew.

NOTES

1 Eric Hobsbawm, *Age of Extremes: The Short Twentieth Century 1914–1991* (London: Michael Joseph, 1994), 199–200.
2 Roger Clark and Sue Rabbitt Roff, *Micronesia: The Problem of Palau, Report No. 63* (New York: Minority Rights Group, 1984), 6–7.
3 Lord Hailey, *An African Survey*, rev. ed. (London: Oxford University Press, 1957), 79.
4 Margery Perham, *Native Administration in Nigeria* (London: Oxford University Press [1937], 1962), xi, 344.
5 *World Almanac and Book of Facts 1997* (Mahwah, NJ: World Almanac Books, 1997), 646.
6 Hobsbawm, *Age of Extremes*, 203. In *Burden of Empire: An Appraisal of Western Colonialism in Africa South of the Sahara* (London: Praeger, 1967), 371, L.H. Gann and Peter Duignan assert that "colonial empire in Africa was one of the most efficacious engines of cultural diffusion in world history."
7 Sir Andrew Cohen, *British Policy in Changing Africa* (London: Routledge and Kegan Paul, 1959), 27–29. See also Perham, *Native Administration in Nigeria*, x, xi, 360, 362, for confirmation of Cohen's thesis with respect to Nigeria. When David E. Apter did research in Ghana, then the Gold Coast,

in 1952–53, he "was assured that it would be a long time before African territories would become independent." David E. Apter, *Ghana in Transition*, 2nd rev. ed. (Princeton: Princeton University Press, 1972), xiv. Sir Donald Cameron, Governor of Tanganyika and a staunch advocate of indirect rule through native authorities, viewed "the expression of [African] opinion through the ballot box ... as inconceivable" in the 1920s. Accordingly, the incremental adaptation of tribal institutions by the policy of indirect rule received far more attention than did building up central government institutions and preparing the emerging educated urban classes for self-government. Hailey, *An African Survey*, 201. According to Hobsbawm, not even "Marxist militants" foresaw "the universal end of colonial empires [as] ... imminent in 1939." Hobsbawm, *Age of Extremes*, 216.

8 See Gann and Duignan, "Imperial Balance Sheet: A Summing Up," ch. 22 in *Burden of Empire*.

9 Hedley Bull, "The Emergence of a Universal International Society," in *The Expansion of International Society*, ed. Hedley Bull and Adam Watson (Oxford: Clarendon Press, 1984), 122.

10 Bull, ibid., 121.

11 Cohen, *British Policy in Changing Africa*, 14. A similar claim for the British role in creating Nigeria is made by Perham in her introduction to the 1962 reissue of *Native Administration in Nigeria*, ix, xii.

12 Hobsbawm, *Age of Extremes*, 207–8.

13 V.G. Kiernan, *The Lords of Human Kind: European Attitudes to the Outside World in the Imperial Age* (Harmondsworth: Penguin Books, 1972). In the nineteenth century, impressed by their own technical and military prowess, Europeans "became increasingly convinced of the superiority of their capacities ... and also of their institutions and their moral values. Europeans and Asians alike had long regarded preliterate peoples as primitive but redeemable if civilised; now many Europeans came to regard civilised Asians as decadent. In their eyes modern civilisation was synonymous with European ways and standards, which it was their duty and their interest to spread in order to make the world a better and safer place." Adam Watson, "European International Society and its Expansion," in *The Expansion of International Society*, ed. Hedley Bull and Adam Watson (Oxford: Clarendon Press, 1984), 27.

14 Denis Mack Smith, *Mussolini* (New York: Knopf, 1982), 100, 197, 201.

15 See Edward Shils, "Center and Periphery," ch. 1 in *Center and Periphery: Essays in Macrosociology* (Chicago: University of Chicago Press, 1975), for an insightful application of these concepts to particular societies. I have extended them to the imperial situation.

16 Edward W. Said, *Culture and Imperialism* (New York: Alfred A. Knopf, 1993).

17 Hedley Bull, "The Revolt Against The West," in Bull and Watson, eds, *The Expansion of International Society*, 219.
18 See Hailey, *An African Survey*, rev. ed., 228–35 for Portuguese and Spanish colonies in Africa and *An African Survey* (London: Oxford University Press, 1938), 194–201, and 212, for French and Belgian colonies in Africa.
19 Perham, *Native Administration in Nigeria*, 353.
20 *The North American Indian Today*, ed. C.T. Loram and T.F. McIlwraith (Toronto: University of Toronto Press, 1943), 5, 7, 8, 10, 251–2.
21 See, for example, his evidence before the Special Joint Committee of the Senate and the House of Commons, appointed to examine and consider the Indian Act: *Minutes of Proceedings and Evidence*, no. 7, 25 March 1947, 307, 309, 310, 311.
22 Bull, "The Revolt Against The West," 221.
23 Jack Spence, "South Africa and the Modern World," in *The Oxford History of South Africa, 1870–1966*, vol. 2, ed. Monica Wilson and Leonard Thompson (Oxford: Clarendon Press, 1971), 526.
24 Edward M. Bruner, "Ethnography as Narrative," in *The Anthropology of Experience*, ed. Victor W. Turner and Edward M. Bruner (Urbana and Chicago: University of Illinois Press, 1986), 139.
25 Bruner, ibid., 152. See also 149. See Gann and Duignan, "The Rulers Waver," ch. 19 in *Burden of Empire*, for the erosion of support for empire.
26 Hailey, *An African Survey*, rev. ed., 202.
27 Robert Jackson, "The Weight of Ideas in Decolonization: Normative Change in International Relations," in *Ideas and Foreign Policy: Beliefs, Institutions and Political Change*, ed. Judith Goldstein and Robert O. Keohane (Ithaca: Cornell University Press, 1993), 121, 124.
28 Gann and Duignan, *Burden of Empire*, 313–4.
29 *Report of the Royal Commission on Aboriginal Peoples*, 5 vols. (Ottawa: Canada Communication Group Publishing, 1996).
30 See Alexander Brady, *Democracy in the Dominions: A Comparative Study in Institutions* (Toronto: University of Toronto Press, 1947).
31 There are also five associate members and two other participating governments, namely, those of Quebec and New Brunswick.
32 The end of the Soviet Empire and the collapse of Yugoslavia generated twenty new states and sixteen new members of the United Nations.
33 Immanuel Wallerstein, "The Colonial Era in Africa: Changes in the Social Structure," in *Colonialism in Africa, 1870–1966*, vol. 2, ed. Peter Duignan and L.H. Gann (Cambridge, UK: Cambridge University Press, 1970), 404.
34 The pressure to perform according to the criteria of the system that new states enter goes beyond institutional similarities – constitutions, legislatures, courts, foreign embassies, etc. – to include a tendency for states "to resemble each other more and more in their cultural forms ... Even in the

more particularistic arena of art forms, which country does not have its songs, its dances, its plays, its museums, its paintings, and today its sky-scrapers? ... It is almost as though the more intense the nationalist fervour in the world, the more identical seem the expressions of this nationalism"; Immanuel Wallerstein, "The National and the Universal: Can There Be Such a Thing as World Culture?," in *Culture, Globalization and the World System: Contemporary Conditions for the Representation of Identity*, ed. Anthony D. King (London: Macmillan, 1991), 93.

35 Bull, "The Revolt Against The West," 227. See also Bull and Watson, eds, "Conclusion" to *The Expansion of International Society*, 428–9.

36 Freda Hawkins, *Critical Years in Immigration: Canada and Australia Compared*, 2d ed. (Montreal and Kingston: McGill-Queen's University Press, 1991), 22, 24.

37 John W. Holmes, *The Shaping of Peace: Canada and the Search for World Order 1943–1957*, vol. 2 (Toronto: University of Toronto Press, 1982) 171–2.

38 Hawkins, *Critical Years in Immigration*, 39.

39 Elliot L. Tepper, "Immigration Policy and Multiculturalism," in *Ethnicity and Culture in Canada: The Research Landscape*, ed. J.W. Berry and J. A. Laponce (Toronto: University of Toronto Press, 1994), 112.

40 *A Stronger Canada* (Ottawa: Citizenship and Immigration Canada, 1997), 6.

41 "The Immigration Flood," *The Social Change Report 6*, no. 3 (fall 1996): 1. The article continues: "If current immigration policy continues more or less unchanged, it is likely that people of European origin will become a minority in the United States by the middle of the twenty-first century." This report also discusses the extensive illegal immigration to the United States and the difficulty of controlling it.

42 David Jacobson, *Rights Across Borders: Immigration and the Decline of Citizenship* (Baltimore: Johns Hopkins University Press, 1996), 51; see also 68. See also David M. Reimers, *Still the Golden Door: The Third World Comes To America*, 2d ed. (New York: Columbia University Press, 1992), for the American experience.

43 Hawkins, *Critical Years in Immigration*, 94. See also 103, 278.

44 Figures on Muslim populations are from Yasemin Nuhoğlu Soysal, *Limits of Citizenship: Migrants and Postnational Membership in Europe* (Chicago: University of Chicago Press, 1994), 117.

45 "The Immigration Flood," 2.

46 Patrick Weil, "Nationalities and Citizenship: The Lessons of the French Experience for Germany and Europe," in *Citizenship, Nationality and Migration in Europe*, ed. David Cesarani and Mary Fullbrook (London: Routledge, 1996), 82.

47 See Cesarani and Fullbrook, eds, *Citizenship, Nationality and Migration in Europe*, for overviews and chapters on the major European countries, and *Racism and Migration in Western Europe*, ed. John Wrench and John Solomos (Oxford: Berg, 1993).

48 Max Silverman, "The Revenge of Civil Society: State, nation and society in France," in Cesarini and Fullbrook, eds, *Citizenship, Nationality and Migration in Europe*, 146. This proposition is supported by international norms, discussed later, which reduce both the assimilative capacity of the state and the willingness of immigrants to choose that path.

49 As Ulf Hannerz notes, "The notion of the sudden engagement between the cultures of center and periphery may ... in large part be an imaginative by-product of the late awakening to global realities of many of us inhabitants of the center"; "Scenarios for Peripheral Cultures," in *Culture, Globalization, and the World System: Contemporary Conditions for the Representation of Identity*, ed. Anthony D. King (London: Macmillan, 1991), 110.

50 These sentences were written before the still ongoing economic crisis surfaced in late 1997 and early 1998 in East Asian economies. Whether the crisis is more than an interruption, remains to be seen.

51 Charles Taylor, "The Politics of Recognition," in *Multiculturalism and "The Politics of Recognition"*, ed. Amy Gutmann (Princeton: Princeton University Press, 1992).

52 Axel Honneth, *The Struggle for Recognition: The Moral Grammar of Social Conflicts* (Cambridge, UK: Polity Press, 1995).

53 George Herbert Mead, *Mind, Self, and Society* (Chicago: University of Chicago Press, 1934).

54 Will Kymlicka, *Multicultural Citizenship: A Liberal Theory of Minority Rights* (Oxford: Clarendon Press, 1995), especially ch. 5, "Freedom and Culture."

55 This was, of course, an almost universal consequence of imperial rule on its subjects, often resulting in self-hatred. On self-hatred, see Renate Zahar, *Frantz Fanon: Colonialism and Alienation* (New York: Monthly Review Press, 1974), 22, 35–6.

56 Apter, *Ghana in Transition*, xxiv.

57 See Bhikhu Parekh, "The Rushdie Affair: Research Agenda for Political Philosophy," *Political Studies* 38 (1990): 695–709.

58 David Cesarani, "The Changing Character of Citizenship and Nationality in Britain," in Cesarani and Fullbrook, eds, *Citizenship, Nationality and Migration in Europe*, 68–9. Two Swedish sociologists make the more general claim that "in France, Britain, Germany, Italy and other EC countries, Muslim communities and other minorities of Third World descent tend to be conceived as a fifth column, an inner enemy"; Alexsandra Alund and Carl-Ulrik Schierup, "The Third Road to Europe: Swedish Immigrant

Policy in Transition," in Wrench and Solomos, eds, *Racism and Migration in Western Europe*, 104.

59 Soysal, *Limits of Citizenship*, 33. See also Jacobson, *Rights Across Borders*, for concurrence with Soysal's thesis.

60 See ibid. In Italy, according to Enrico Pugliese, these rights are in fact unavailable to the large and growing population of mainly clandestine Third World immigrants who lack any regularized status. Enrico Pugliese, "Italy between Emigration and Immigration and the Problems of Citizenship," in Cesarani and Fullbrook, eds, *Citizenship, Nationality and Migration in Europe*, 119–20.

61 Ibid., 24.

62 Soysal uses the term guest worker rather expansively to include "legal temporary or permanent refugees, illegal migrants, ex-colonial citizens, and common-market citizens." Ibid., 9.

63 Ibid., 2.

64 Ibid., 24.

65 Ibid., 26–7.

66 Ibid., 33. See also 41–3.

67 Ibid., 122–3, 132–5.

68 Jacobson, *Rights Across Borders*, 76.

69 Louis Henkin, *The Age of Rights* (New York: Columbia University Press, 1990), ix.

70 Jacobson, *Rights Across Borders*, 126. Anthony King observes that "it is not just that, increasingly, many people have no roots; it's also that they have no soil. Culture is increasingly deterritorialised." Anthony D. King, "Introduction: Spaces of Culture, Spaces of Knowledge," in *Culture, Globalization, and the World System*, 6.

71 Jacobson, *Rights Across Borders*, 33.

72 Ibid., 17.

73 Ibid., 133.

74 Gary P. Freeman, "Migration and the Political Economy of the Welfare State," *Annals of the American Academy of Political and Social Science* 485 (May 1986), 51–63.

75 Henkin, *The Age of Rights*, 13, 26.

76 "A primarily Anglo society in the 1950s (in the United States), for example, tolerated mass deportations of illegal Mexican aliens. Such a move today would be considered illegitimate and politically inadvisable, to put it mildly." Jacobson, *Rights Across Borders*, 43.

77 See Solomos and Wrench, eds, *Racism and Migration in Western Europe*, and Cesarani and Fullbrook, eds, *Citizen, Nationality and Migration in Europe*.

78 Tomas Hammar, "Political Participation and Civil Rights in Scandinavia," in Solomos and Wrench, eds, *Racism and Migration in Western Europe*, 117.

79 Henkin, *The Age of Rights*, 29.
80 This and the following section have benefited immensely from Yosef
   Lapid's, "Culture's Ship: Returns and Departures in International Relations
   Theory," in *The Return of Culture and Identity in IR Theory*, ed. Yosef
   Lapid and Friedrich Kratochwil (Boulder: Lynne Rienner, 1996), as well as
   from other articles in this pioneering collection.
81 Hannerz writes: "Humankind has finally bid farewell to that world which
   could with some credibility be seen as a cultural mosaic, of separate pieces
   with hard, well-defined edges. Because of the great increase in the traffic in
   culture, the large-scale transfer of meaning systems and symbolic forms, the
   world is increasingly becoming one not only in political and economic
   terms, as in the climactic period of colonialism, but in terms of its cultural
   construction as well; a global ecumene of persistent cultural interaction and
   exchange." Hannerz, "Scenarios for Peripheral Cultures," 107. See also
   Hans-Rudolf Wicker, "From Complex Culture to Cultural Complexity,"
   in *Debating Cultural Hybridity*, ed. Prina Werbner and Tariq Madood
   (London: Zed Books, 1997), 29–45, and Marshall Sahlins, *How "Natives"
   Think: About Captain Cook, for Example* (Chicago: University of Chicago
   Press, 1995), 13–4.
82 Friedrich Kratochwil, "Is the Ship of Culture at Sea or Returning?," in
   Lapid and Kratochwil, eds, *The Return of Culture and Identity in IR
   Theory*, 221. See also Ulrich Beck, *The Reinvention of Politics: Rethinking
   Modernity in the Global Social Order* (Cambridge, UK: Polity Press, 1997),
   95–6.
83 Kwame Anthony Appiah, "The Postcolonial and the Postmodern," in *The
   Post-Colonial Studies Reader*, ed. Bill Ashcroft, Gareth Griffiths, and Helen
   Tiffin (London: Routledge, 1995), 124.
84 Said, *Culture and Imperialism*, xxv, 15. See also Hannerz, "Scenarios for
   Peripheral Cultures," 126–8, for a discussion of what he positively calls
   creole cultures that emerge "as people actively engage in making their own
   syntheses."
85 Karol J. Krótki and Dave Odynak, "The Emergence of Multiethnicities in
   the Eighties," in *Ethnic Demography: Canadian Immigrant, Racial and
   Cultural Variations*, ed. Shiva S. Halli, Frank Travato, and Leo Driedger
   (Ottawa: Carleton University Press, 1990), 417, 434.
86 Morton Weinfeld, "Ethnic Assimilation and the Retention of Ethnic
   Cultures," in *Ethnicity and Culture in Canada: the Research Landscape*,
   ed. J.W. Berry and J.A. Laponce (Toronto: University of Toronto Press,
   1994), 245.
87 Stewart Clatworthy and Anthony H. Smith, *Population Implications of the
   1985 Amendments to the Indian Act: Final Report* (Perth: Living Dimensions Ltd., 1992), ii. This was a report prepared for the Assembly of First
   Nations.

88 Russell Thornton, "Tribal Membership Requirements and the Demography of "Old" and "New" Native Americans," in *Changing Numbers, Changing Needs: American Indian Demography and Public Health*, ed. Gary D. Sandefur, Ronald R. Rindfuss, and Barney Cohen (Washington, DC: National Academy Press, 1996), 110.

89 Jeffrey S. Passel, "The Growing American Indian Population, 1960–1990: Beyond Demography," in Sandefur, Rindfuss, and Cohen, eds, *Changing Numbers, Changing Needs*, 86.

90 Marc-Adélard Tremblay, "The Identity of Francophone Quebecers," *Proceedings and Transactions of the Royal Society of Canada*, Fourth Series, XXII (1984): 3–18.

91 *Report of the Royal Commission of Inquiry on Constitutional Problems* (Quebec City, 1956).

92 *Report of the Royal Commission on Aboriginal Peoples*, vol.3, *Gathering Strength* (Ottawa: Canada Communication Group Publishing, 1996), 501.

93 See K. Anthony Appiah, "The Multicultural Misunderstanding," *New York Review of Books*, 9 October 1997, 30–6, for a criticism of this tendency.

94 This, and the remaining paragraphs in this section, are in agreement with Wayne Norman's analysis in "The Ideology of Shared Values: A Myopic Vision of Unity in the Multi-Nation State," in *Is Quebec Nationalism Just? Perspectives from Anglophone Canada*, ed. Joseph H. Carens (Montreal and Kingston: McGill-Queen's University Press, 1995), 137–59.

95 First Nations Circle on the Constitution, *To the Source: Commissioners' Report* (Ottawa: Assembly of First Nations, 1992).

96 For example, after citing the strong assertion of cultural difference by Ralph Akiwenzie, an Ojibway chief, Claude Denis stated "This blunt affirmation of cultural difference is not a mere statement of fact, for its utterance provides part of the foundation for the political claim of aboriginal self-government, which is a centre-piece of the current Canadian constitutional debate." Claude Denis, "Rights and Spirit Dancing: Aboriginal Peoples versus the Canadian State," in *Explorations in Difference: Law, Culture and Politics*, ed. Jonathan Hart and Richard W. Bauman (Toronto: University of Toronto Press, 1996), 199.

97 Thomas Fitzgerald, quoted in Lapid and Kratochwil, eds, *The Return of Culture and Identity in IR Theory*, 8.

98 Cultural differences, apparently, played only a minimal role in the murderous conflicts among Serbs, Croats, and Muslims as Yugoslavia disintegrated. Serbian allegations to the contrary, Bosnian Muslims had little sympathy for fundamentalist Islam, and were "primarily secular and sympathetic to the ways of Europe." Neil J. Kressel, *Mass Hate: The Global Rise of Genocide and Terror* (New York and London: Plenum Press, 1996), 23. See also Michael Ignatieff, *Blood and Belonging* (Toronto: Penguin Books, 1994), 22, 23, 25, 37, on how Serbs and Croats, once friends and

neighbours, became vengeful enemies, and Misha Glenny, *The Fall of Yugoslavia: The Third Balkan War,* 3d rev. ed. (New York: Penguin Books, 1996), 171–2. Cultural differences also shed little light on the Hutu-Tutsi genocide and mass slaughter in Rwanda. Kressel, *Mass Hate,* ch. 4.

99 R. J. Vincent, "Racial Equality," in Bull and Watson, eds, *The Expansion of International Society,* 250. See also 241.

100 See William Kaplan, ed., *Belonging: The Meaning and Future of Canadian Citizenship* (Montreal and Kingston: McGill-Queen's University Press, 1993), especially parts 2 and 4, for the role of historic grievances in sustaining the self-image of marginalized outsiders.

101 "It is a challenge to any polity to cope with old memories, identities, and loyalties within its domain. While it is easy to make martyrs, it is almost impossible to eradicate an old identity. In this respect the world appears a 'living museum' of identities and loyalties in which some exhibits are currently on show, some are being refurbished, and still others are in cold storage. Polities survive only if they can co-opt those old memories, identities, and loyalties – those that once supported other polities – or fit them into their own ideologies. Unless old authorities and ideologies are co-opted, they may haunt a new polity and later become the bases of rival political associations and faiths." Yale H. Ferguson and Richard W. Mansbach, "The Past as Prelude to the Future? Identities and Loyalties in Global Politics," in Lapid and Kratochwil, eds, *The Return of Culture and Identity in IR Theory* (Boulder: Lynne Rienner, 1996), 36.

102 Douglas E. Williams, "Crisis and Renewal in the Social Sciences and the Colonies of Ourselves," *International Political Science Review* 11, no. 1 (1990): 59–74. See also King, ed., *Culture, Globalization, and the World System* 16: "Each individual increasingly belongs to many cultures – an alternative way of saying perhaps ... that people have multiple cultural identities. Increasingly, one goes through life picking up identities. In this sense, identity construction is never finished."

103 Erving Goffman, *The Presentation of Self in Everyday Life* (New York: Doubleday Anchor, 1959).

104 Vaclav Havel, *Living in Truth,* ed. Jan Vladislav (London: Faber and Faber, 1989).

105 Bruce Lincoln, *Discourse and the Construction of Society* (New York: Oxford University Press, 1989), 105.

106 Slavenka Drakulic, *The Balkan Express: Fragments from the Other Side of War* (New York: W.W. Norton, 1991), 51.

3 Reflections on Ethnic Politics

ANTHONY H. BIRCH

GROUP IDENTITIES AND POLITICS

This volume is concerned with group identities and with the conflict that sometimes arises between our identities as citizens, which involve legal rights and duties, and our other group identities, which are ethnic and cultural. I would like to start with a simple generalization. We all have several group identities. We are socialists or conservatives, Christians or Jews, white or coloured, male or female, etc., and these identities are more or less salient according to circumstance. This is obviously true of ethnic and cultural identities, and, for many millions of people in the world (despite what Lucien Bouchard appears to believe about the Québécois) it is also true of national identities. In this age of mass migration, countless numbers of people have two national identities, not just one, and some have more. I have three and a half myself, being, in chronological order, English, British, Canadian, and half-European. These are, of course, different types of identity. Two of them, British and Canadian, are based on citizenship. They involve laws and authority, and in the modern world we are expected to give priority to our identities as citizens rather than to such other identities as we may have; this is, however, a very modern development that does not reflect the political reality in many parts of the world, such as tropical Africa.

My English identity is an emotional construct based on ethnicity, upbringing, and custom, and it comes to the forefront of my consciousness every Saturday morning when I watch European soccer on television. However, it sometimes becomes politically salient, and it did in the autumn of 1997, when it was established that Scotland would have its own parliament and Wales its own assembly. Although most English people are reasonably happy about a Scottish parliament, not many of them are happy about a Welsh assembly. The British Prime Minister asserted, perhaps a little rashly, that a general principle was involved: the days of the centralized nation state were on their way out, and we must look to a more varied system of government that would perhaps bring political authority nearer to the people.

These developments have raised the question as to why there is no proposal for an English parliament or assembly as well. The British government has ruled this out and has proposed instead to divide England into seven or eight as yet undefined regions, and to ask the population of each whether they would like to have a regional assembly. A national survey of 1500 teenagers in English secondary schools conducted in September 1997 asked: "Now that Scotland and Wales are going to get Assemblies would you like your region of England, Southwest, or Northeast, or whatever, would you like that to have an Assembly too?" The answer was very emphatic: 15% said yes and 71% said no.[1] The English do not want to be divided up. They have a strong sense of national identity, which is hardly surprising: England has been geographically united and self-governing since the twelfth century and has had its own parliament since 1275. The creation of special privileges for Scotland and Wales has inevitably led to the feeling that England should have privileges of a similar kind. As Alan Cairns has said, any attempt to create special privileges for one part or region of an existing state is bound to raise claims for similar privileges for other regions.[2]

I have said that I have three and a half national identities. The half arises from a supranational organization, the European Union, that gives me the rights and privileges necessary to live, work, and travel without restriction throughout most of Europe. I call it only half an identity because it does not carry with it the same sense of authority and consent that my British and Canadian identities carry with them. The European Union is in several ways a beneficial organization but, as I have explained elsewhere, its decision-making processes are far from democratic and thus fail to gain the whole-hearted support of its constituents.[3]

Although the national consciousness of many English people was raised by a political development, other kinds of events can raise people's awareness of their identities. My favourite example is what happened in Scotland in October 1974, when 840 000 people surprised the world by voting for the Scottish National Party, as against only 64 000 who had done so ten years earlier. This was not because they had suddenly realized that they were Scottish, but because of a geological finding. A vast oil field had been discovered in Scottish waters in the North Sea. Suddenly, a Scottish identity became more salient to these voters than their other identities as Britons, Socialists, Conservatives, and so forth. If we were suddenly to discover enormous deposits of diamonds and gold on the west coast of Canada, a secessionist movement might swiftly arise in British Columbia. These things happen. It was the exploitation of mineral deposits that recently led to the belated attempt of little Bougainville to secede from Papua New Guinea, and the copper mines in Katanga that led its politicians to try to secede from Zaire in the 1950s.

A second generalization is that most forms of group identity are socially constructed. For example, people may have several ethnic identities, but for political purposes governments have to decide on one method of identification. This sometimes creates problems. Two most commonly used methods of identification are by descent and by self-identification. Germany emphasizes descent as a requirement for citizenship, and this has had odd consequences. At the end of this century, tens of thousands of people who were brought up in the heart of Russia and whose families have been there for over a century suddenly turned up on the German border, claiming German citizenship. This was granted immediately because they were of German blood. At the same time, hundreds of thousands of people who have never known any other home but Germany may never be able to get German citizenship for themselves or their children because their blood is Turkish or Yugoslav.

The other main way of defining identity for the purposes of citizenship is by self-identification. This can also create problems, of which I give two brief examples. One is that the political leader of the Aborigines of Tasmania in the 1980s was a white man who had no Aboriginal blood at all but had to be recognized by law as an Aborigine because he had identified himself as an Aborigine on all government forms. Another curious situation emerged in Israel some years ago when a planeload of Ethiopian refugees arrived and claimed to be Jewish. They had no evidence to show what kind of religion they had practised, but they claimed to be one of the lost tribes of Israel. Because the Israeli government accepts self-identification as a principle, the refugees were admitted. These refugees were followed by others. This has occasionally created problems within Israel; the Ethiopians are not universally welcomed and have complained of casual and systematic discrimination.

Another problem is sometimes caused by the tendency of outsiders (such as imperial authorities or visiting social scientists) to confer on others ethnic or national identities that do not correspond with the self-identification of the people concerned. I came across this rather strikingly on my first visit to Africa, when I went to Nigeria at very short notice in 1956. Expecting to find that the people regarded themselves as Nigerians and me as British, I soon discovered that this was completely wrong. People identified themselves not as Nigerians but as Yorubas, Ibos, Ibidios, Fulanis, and so forth, and although in some sense I was recognized as British, I was quickly told that *everyone* was British in Nigeria so that did not distinguish *me*. The real distinction was between us and the people across the border in Dahomey (now Benin), who were all French. Now this showed an admirable understanding of the difference between the idea of citizenship and the idea of ethnic identity, but what was left out was the idea of a *Nigerian* identity. This had been conferred on them by the colonial administrators, who, along with visiting political scientists, had in some sense got it wrong. The greatest scholarly expert on Nigerian politics in that period was James Coleman. While British administrators saw Nigeria through imperialist spectacles, Coleman saw the country through the lens of American anti-imperialism. He believed that opposition to imperialism inevitably involved nationalism. In *Nigeria: Background to Nationalism* he described Nnamdi Azikiwe, a journalist and politician who opposed British rule, as having become by 1946 "the leader of a Nigeria-wide nationalist movement."[4] This was misleading. Azikiwe was the leader of the Ibo movement, which was based in the Ibo homeland in eastern Nigeria but also had some supporters in the western and northern regions of Nigeria to which Ibo workers had migrated. He was an Ibo nationalist, not a Nigerian nationalist. In 1949 he said that "the God of Africa has specially created the Ibo nation to lead the children of Africa from the bondage of the ages."[5] Not, it will be noticed, the Ibo people to liberate Nigeria or the Nigerian people to liberate Africa, but the Ibo nation to liberate the children of Africa. Eighteen years later, another Ibo leader, Colonel Ojukwu, led his people in an attempt to secede from the federation of Nigeria, the result being a disastrous and prolonged civil war in which over a million people died.

Nigeria is affected not only by tribal rivalries and conflicts but also by religious divisions. The northern half of the country is dominated by Muslim leaders with a centuries-old ambition of converting the peoples of the southern half to the Islamic faith. Because the northerners include about half of the population and more than half of the army, they have been able to dominate the government of Nigeria for most of time since it became independent in 1960, whether by civilian rule backed by the army or by military dictatorship. In 1993, the military rulers decided that they would hand over the country to civilian rule if a suitable civilian ruler could be found. A national election for the post of president was won by a millionaire from the southwest called Moshood Abiola. The election was immediately declared null and void, and Abiola was sent to prison, where he subsequently perished. The Western media reported and discussed this sad event as a violation of democracy and human rights, which of course it was. The point I want to examine, however, is how Abiola was characterized. In all the media reports I have seen he was described correctly but irrelevantly as a wealthy business man. What is relevant is that he was a Yoruba and a Christian from the south, and that the northern Muslims who domi-nate the army are no more prepared to accept political leadership from a person with these cultural identities in the 1990s than their predeces-sors were in the 1950s. In 1956 the Sardauna of Sokoto, a traditional Fulani chief who was the political leader of the northern Muslims at the time, told me frankly that this would never be acceptable. In 1962 he declared in his memoirs that a southern victory in a national elec-tion "would, of course, be utterly disastrous .... . It would therefore force us to take measures to meet the need. What such measures would have to be is outside my reckoning at the moment, but God would provide a way."[6] In 1993 God provided a prison.

Although from a Western liberal perspective all of this is sad, it may have been unavoidable. What I find strange, because it is entirely avoidable, is that it has been misrepresented by Western commentators who, with very few exceptions, have failed over four decades to recog-nize and discuss the importance of cultural divisions for the political process in tropical Africa. Another example among many is provided by Western reporting of the first free elections in Zimbabwe. During the 1970s, resistance to rule by white settlers came from two black resistance movements: one in Matabeleland, led by a liberal called Joshua Nkomo, and the other in Mashonaland, led by a Marxist called Robert Mugabe. When free national elections were held in 1980, with Nkomo's party and Mugabe's party as the main contenders, the con-test was seen throughout the West as a battle of ideologies. The US State Department, which looked on it in the context of the Cold War, was particularly concerned. In Zimbabwe, however, the newly enfran-chised electors voted not on ideological but on tribal lines, and, as the Mashona peoples greatly outnumbered the people of Matabeleland, Mugabe's party won fifty-seven seats to the twenty won by Nkomo's party. The result was predictable, but it came as a surprise to most Western commentators.

CULTURAL MINORITIES IN WESTERN DEMOCRACIES

I shall turn now to the political problems arising from the existence of cultural minorities in Western democracies such as Canada. There is nothing exceptional about Canada in this respect: virtually all states, except Japan, have cultural minorities within their borders, and there is nothing new about this situation apart from the increased prominence in the past three decades of claims by cultural minorities for special treatment.

This new feature of political debate and controversy is interesting because it stands in contradiction to the expectations generally shared by liberals and socialists in western societies over the previous century. From the 1860s to the 1960s these expectations were that ethnic and cultural divisions would gradually become politically insignificant over the years, leaving only economic and class issues to provide the basis of political argument. Of the various reasons for this development I will examine only one. This is the influence of television, which brings a majority culture right into the home and in so doing often causes resentment. I first realized this when I was studying Welsh nationalism. In Wales, only 20% of the population understood the Welsh language, and most of this minority lived in rural areas. In Welsh-speaking areas, young people normally spoke English, the language of necessity, at school or work. At home, they tended to speak Welsh, the language of affection and tradition. Their parents wanted them to admire Welsh poets as cultural heroes, and up to a point this worked. But, in the 1960s, when everyone got television and the heroes of the younger generation turned out to be not Welsh poets but Elvis Presley and the Monty Python gang, an active resistance movement arose. The Welsh Language Society saw television as the enemy of their culture and broke the law with forms of direct action such as holding noisy demonstrations in television studios and destroying a television transmitting station. The question for political theorists and lawyers is how these normally law-abiding people justified these breaches of their duties as citizens of a democratic society. Part of the answer is contained in the 1972 manifesto of the Welsh Language Society, which stated: "To that astonishing question, 'Why do you want to keep up the Welsh language?' the true Welshman need only to answer 'That our fathers be not shamed.' "[7]

A second general question is how we should discuss this new tendency to emphasize the claims and needs of cultural minorities. The new fashion since the 1970s has been to discuss them in terms of minority rights. As early as 1978, Ronald Dworkin asserted that "the language of rights now dominates political debate in the United States,"[8] and this language has spread from the United States to elsewhere and from the discussion of individual rights to that of minority rights. What I want to suggest is that, while this language of rights is appropriate with regard to individuals it is not generally appropriate with regard to minorities. I will outline this argument under four headings that I have used elsewhere, namely, the right to be in, the right to be out, the right to stay out, and the right to get out.

The right to be in is clearly the right to equal treatment in the wider society, the right not to be discriminated against. This is essentially an individual right, to some extent protected by the United Nations Declaration of Human Rights. However, problems arise when this right is extended to include the notion of equal opportunity and when governments are urged to adopt legal measures of positive discrimination to ensure equal opportunity. There are the problems surrounding the definition of a minority, for instance. Some years ago, the US Congress wanted to help Puerto Rican and Mexican immigrants to become more prosperous in American society and decreed that they should be given preference over other ethnic groups in job applications. It was decided that Puerto Rican or Mexican identity could be determined only by surname. The consequence of this was that the children of a wealthy Spanish surgeon or architect who migrated to America had to be given priority over the children of an impoverished Italian peasant who had made the same journey; since this was not quite what was intended, the provision has been repealed. Another problem is that of the duration of the help offered to immigrant groups and the difficulty of providing for a cut-off point. A third and most publicized problem is that the rights of members of the majority may be damaged, as in the case of admission to American law schools. I would urge that it is better in such situations not to talk about minority *rights* but to talk about a democratic *obligation* for any liberal government to help disadvantaged groups. This is an important distinction: whereas every right implies an obligation on the part of others to recognize the right, not every obligation implies a right. If I see someone drowning in the surf, I have a moral obligation to jump in and rescue that person, but he or she does not have a *right* to be rescued. I have to consider this moral obligation in the light of other moral obligations, such as to keep myself alive for the sake of my family.

To formulate the political issue in terms of democratic obligation allows for more flexibility than to do so in terms of rights; this is appropriate, given the fact that governments have numerous obligations that are not always mutually compatible. It can be argued, for instance, that because immigrants are often handicapped in the job market by a poor knowledge of the majority language, a host country that controls immigration has an obligation to ensure that language training is available for all immigrants. However, there are questions about how this can be organized, who should provide it, and how the costs should be divided between a national government that controls immigration but not education, local authorities that provide education but are not responsible for immigration policy, and the immigrants themselves. It would seem better to leave this to the democratic process than to give immigrants a right to language training, which might enable them to demand it for free and appeal to the courts if they are not satisfied.

Then there is the right to be out, which is the right for a minority to preserve its culture. This is often discussed as if it necessarily involved political authorities, but this of course is not true. The great majority of minority cultural habits and customs can be preserved without governmental help. In any non-totalitarian society, minorities can worship as they please and preserve their own marriage arrangements, cuisine, dress, music, dancing and so forth. The only issue that may necessitate political action is that of language. As we all know in Canada, this is apt to be a problem because people are not naturally bilingual and, as Jean Laponce has demonstrated,[9] in any mixed area the stronger language tends to drive out the weaker. I do not think, therefore, that a minority can reasonably claim a right for assistance in keeping its language alive, although there is clearly a stronger case for this if the language is indigenous to the area, as is Welsh within the United Kingdom, than if it is the language of immigrants.

The real difficulty in this matter arises when one asks whether there is an obligation to teach minority languages in school or to provide immersion classes in the language. This is a very complex question because five different groups have an interest in it. There are, first, sentimental parents who want their children to be taught in their mother tongue. Second, there are ambitious parents who resist this idea because they think their children will have a better chance of getting on in the world if they concentrate on the language of the majority. Third are the children themselves, often mixed in their views. In Australia, the most active immigrant group in terms of preserving its language is the Greek Australian group in Melbourne. However, an Australian anthropologist who did fieldwork among Melbourne teenagers found that, by and large, Greek Australian teenagers were careful to speak Greek within earshot of their parents but normally spoke English to one another when they were out of range. Fourth are the public service workers who may want to avoid the requirement of learning a minority language to be eligible for promotion. Some years ago, a leading member of the Welsh Language Society whom I was interviewing volunteered the opinion that the telephone operators' union was forcing its members not to speak Welsh when some of them might have been happy to do so in practice. To test this he had tried to cajole a local telephone operator into speaking just a few words of Welsh. Twice, he asked her a very simple question in Welsh, to which she twice replied, "Please speak English." The third time he added some term of casual endearment, as one might in the North of England say "Oh come on love." The operator trumped this ace by responding, "I'm very sorry, sir, but nobody at this exchange speaks Arabic."

A fifth group consists of the majority of parents, those parents – other than the sentimental and the ambitious – who have an interest in the question of language teaching. When international surveys of educational attainment were introduced in the 1950s, they showed among other things that Irish teenagers had lower academic standing than British teenagers. Educationalists concluded that the main reason for this finding was the large amount of time spent by Irish students learning Gaelic. In response to public pressure the time devoted to Gaelic studies was greatly reduced, and as a result the gap in educational attainment has diminished or disappeared. This is the sort of issue that ought to be dealt with by a process of political bargaining between the government and the five groups concerned. This is what the democratic process is all about, and it would be foolish to undermine it by agreeing that one group has a right that gives its interests a higher status than the interests of other groups.

The possible conflict between sentimental parents and ambitious parents that I have mentioned has come up in various parts of the world. When Khrushchev introduced some of his reforms he proposed to answer some objections to Russian imperialism by introducing the Uzbek language as the language of instruction in universities in Uzbekistan. This was immediately greeted by protests from ambitious Uzbekistani parents, who thought their children would have a better chance in life if they were taught in Russian. The same sort of reaction followed the proposal some years ago to use Hindi rather than English as the language of instruction in universities in some parts of India.

This brings me to the controversial topic of multiculturalism. Almost every state has cultural minorities within its borders, and national governments have to take some cognizance of this fact by deciding on one or more official languages. It can be said that multicultural policies are the norm rather than the exception. However, only two national governments, – Canada's in 1971 and Australia's two years later – have officially declared their societies to be multicultural, allocated public funds to the promotion of multiculturalism, and established an administrative body to take on this responsibility.

The Australian program has had certain advantages over the Canadian version. First, it was much more clearly set out and defended in government publications, which were readily available and inexpensive; this helped to foster a more informed public debate than seems to have occurred in Canada. Second, the Australians provide a very full program for training in English as a second language, which is free or almost free for adult immigrants as well as children. Third, the Australian government has issued two very full reports on the choice of foreign languages to be taught in schools and has recommended nine. Of these, five were chosen because they are the languages of Australia's main trading partners and three because of their cultural value; only one, Modern Greek, was selected in response to community pressure. Fourth, the Australians have introduced a telephone interpretation service for immigrants who are not certain about the contents of a letter or legal document. And fifth, they have television channels that specialize, in foreign programming with English subtitles. This has served the dual purpose of helping immigrants to improve their colloquial English and enlightening other Australians about foreign cultures.

Australian policies have not been free from controversy, but they are widely understood and accepted. In Canada, the Citizens' Forum on Canada's Future, which by one means or another consulted about 400 000 adult Canadians in 1991, found that multicultural policies were generally viewed with hostility because they were thought to reinforce cultural divisions instead of promoting Canadian unity. Most Canadians, it was reported, wanted expenditure on multiculturalism to be limited to helping immigrant orientation, reducing racial discrimination, and promoting social equality. The report noted that in the 1980s the department responsible for multicultural policies had "moved substantially in this direction ... but this new thrust of the department has not been explained to Canada's people, who believe its activities are promoting divisions between Canadians and doing so at the taxpayers' expense."[10] Although Canadian policies on multiculturalism are continuing to evolve and are no longer a major focus of public criticism, comparisons with Australia underline the importance of communication between governments and their citizens.

And now, the right to stay out. Whether indigenous peoples have a right to retain or recover their traditional lifestyles in a country dominated by incomers is a problem with which Canadians and others are grappling. We must regard the position of Canadian indigenous peoples with sympathy, and we have a moral obligation to help them insofar as we can. However, if this involves the preservation of traditional lifestyles, practical problems arise. The Indians of the prairies can no longer live by hunting buffalo. The Aborigines of Australia have mostly lost the traditional skills that enabled them to survive in the bush. Other examples abound. In British Columbia in the 1980s, any student interested in Indian affairs who asked the provincial government for advice would have be invited to look at the Sechelt Peninsula, an area north of Vancouver that was well developed in terms of local self-government. One of my graduate students asked the Sechelt chief how he would like his territory to develop in the next ten or twenty years and was disconcerted by the answer, "I would like it to become the Las Vegas of the North." I myself do not mind if it becomes the Las Vegas of the North if that is what the Sechelt people want, but I do mind the unrealistic language in which this kind of question is often discussed.

Again, a look at Australia is instructive. The Australian government has responded to claims by Aborigines who want to opt out of the modern economy by setting up "homeland centres," that is, small communities in the bush for kinship groups. I do not know how these have developed recently, but in 1990 I observed that a truck would go out to each of these centres once a week with medications, canned food, welfare payments, and a social worker. This was not exactly a traditional lifestyle, but the people in the homeland centres were apparently happier than they have been in the cities because they could settle most of their own disputes and manage their own affairs without having to be involved with white police officers, lawyers, courts, and prisons.

THE QUESTION OF SECESSION

The right to get out raises interesting theoretical questions. Secessionist leaders sometimes claim that they are morally justified in breaking the law in pursuit of the right of their group to secede from the state of which they are currently citizens. In principle, I believe that three conditions may be regarded as establishing such a right for a territorially concentrated minority. The first would be that the people in question were conquered by force and did not subsequently consent to the conquest. There are of course problems in defining consent, but a look around the world indicates four contemporary candidates for this situation. They are the people of East Timor, Tibetans, the Kurds of Turkey and Iraq, and the non-Arab and non-Muslim peoples of southern Sudan.

A second condition would be the failure of the state to protect the basic rights of a minority group, the clearest example being the case of the Ibos of Nigeria, hundreds of whom were killed in three massacres in 1966 for which units of the Nigerian army were partly responsible. In 1967 this led the Ibo leaders to try to take the Ibo heartland out of Nigeria under the name of Biafra.

A third condition would be internal colonialism, in which a sizeable group is systematically deprived of any real share of influence in the government of society. The clearest recent example of this is the case of the people of East Bengal, who were deprived of any influence in the government, bureaucracy, and army of Pakistan although they actually amounted to 56% of the population of the country. Their secession under the name of Bangladesh seems to have been amply justified, although it would probably not have succeeded without the help of the Indian army.

Allen Buchanan has suggested a fourth justification, namely, the need to preserve a culture. He says that for a right to secede to be established under this heading, it would have to be shown that the culture is actually endangered and that it cannot be preserved by measures less disruptive than secession. He discusses Quebec and expresses scepticism about whether it qualifies, a position with which it would be difficult to argue.[11]

As a guide to practical policies, the limitation of this whole line of argument is that the contemporary world contains an equal or larger number of secessionist movements with claims or grievances that do not fall under any of the headings mentioned. They include the Scots and the Welsh in Britain, the Bretons and Corsicans in France, the Basques in Spain, the Tamils in Sri Lanka, the Sikhs in India, and the Chechnians in Russia. If one adds up these candidates, the story of contemporary secessionist movements begins to look like an account of a steeplechase with fifteen or more starters in which the horses are so weak in comparison with the fences that only one starter, a horse called Bangladesh, has reached the finishing line and only one other, called Quebec, has any serious chance of getting there too.

It may be sensible to put an abstract right to secede into the background and to focus instead on the idea of a democratic obligation. Just as democratic governments have an obligation to help their poorer citizens, so they may have an obligation to give special attention to the claims of minority groups that are geographically concentrated in an area that might become a viable state of its own.

This puts the onus on national governments and parliaments to specify the conditions on which they would agree to a constitutional change. An example would be that of Scotland in the 1970s. Opinion polls showed some demand for a Scottish parliament, voters started to vote for a secessionist party, and a referendum drafted by the British parliament specified the powers that a Scottish parliament might have if the voters of Scotland showed by referendum that they clearly wanted such an institution. The British parliament added a 40% rule, saying that for a majority vote in a referendum to become binding, 40% of the electors would have to support it. In the event, 33% of Scottish electors supported a Scottish parliament while 32% did not want it; the 40% rule settled the issue, and a parliament was not established.

Nobody questioned the legitimacy of this process. The nationalists were not happy about it but they accepted it as British citizens. Now, eighteen years later, there is much clearer evidence of a demand for a Scottish parliament – over 50% of the electors voted for it – and so one has been established without much opposition from the English.

To take another example, in 1933 the government of Western Australia organized a referendum on succession from the federation. A small majority voted in favour of it. But nobody in Australia thought that this meant the breakup of the country, only that Western Australia had serious grievances that ought to be addressed. As they were. In the light of these examples, the near panic produced in Canada by the Quebec referendum of 1995 strikes a relative newcomer like myself as very sad.

CONCLUSION

I can only end in a general and rather platitudinous way. In sociological and political terms, the world is an untidy place. It contains several thousand cultural groups – between 6000 and 15 000, depending on the defining criteria adopted – and so the principle of self-determination cannot be an adequate guide to the organisation of government. The groups are too small and too intermingled for *each* to be self-governing. Any system of government has to be a compromise between the need to have units large enough to be efficient in providing services and the need for them to reflect the composition of their societies sufficiently for the great majority of citizens to consent to their authority.

To return to the example of Nigeria, the British decision to combine its forty-seven linguistic groups into a single state must be counted a failure, for the cultural divisions between the largest tribal groups were so great that they led to a disastrous civil war. A division into forty-seven states would not have been possible, but a division into three might have worked, with one large tribal group dominating each of them. Some of the minorities might have been rather unhappy, but such an arrangement would have offered more hope of stability when combined with democracy than the one that was adopted.

During the last century or two the nation–state system has worked as a tolerably good compromise in more advanced parts of the world, and it is now becoming established elsewhere. Many states are being challenged from within by the claims of cultural minorities, however, and have lost part of their independence as a consequence of globalization. They will never again have the sovereignty that they enjoyed in the first half of this century, and the world is gradually and uncertainly moving toward a more complex kind of political system. That will also be a compromise, one that offers the hope of more widespread prosperity and the avoidance of major wars at the cost of more bureaucracy and less democratic control over major issues of policy.

NOTES

1 *Sunday Times* (London), 21 September 1997.
2 Alan C. Cairns, "Constitutional Reform: The God that Failed," in *Can Canada Survive?*, Transactions of the Royal Society of Canada (Toronto: University of Toronto Press, 1996), 56.
3 See Anthony H. Birch, *The British System of Government,* 10th ed. (London: Routledge, 1998), 205, 261–3.
4 James Coleman, *Nigeria: Background to Nationalism* (Berkeley: University of California Press, 1958), 164.
5 Quoted in Ibid., 347.
6 Ahmadu Bello, *My Life* (Cambridge, UK: Cambridge University Press, 1962), 229.
7 1972 Manifesto of the Welsh Language Society (English translation), *Planet* [Tregaron, Wales] no. 26/27 1975: 82.
8 Ronald Dworkin, *Taking Rights Seriously* (Cambridge, MA: Harvard University Press, 1978), 184.
9 J.A. Laponce, *Languages and Their Territories* (Toronto: University of Toronto Press, 1987).
10 *Report of the Citizens' Forum on Canada's Future* (Ottawa: Canadian Government Publishing Centre, 1991), 129.
11 See Allen Buchanan, *Secession: The Morality of Political Divorce from Fort Sumter to Lithuania to Quebec* (Boulder: Westview Press, 1991), 61–4.

4 "Landed" Citizenship: Narratives of Aboriginal Political Participation

JOHN BORROWS

My grandfather was born in 1901 on the western shores of Georgian Bay, at the Cape Croker Indian reservation. Generations before him were born on the same soil. Our births, lives, and deaths on this site have brought us into citizenship with the land. We participate in its renewal, have responsibility for its continuation, and grieve for its losses. As citizens with this land, we also feel the presence of our ancestors and strive with them to have the relationships of our polity respected. Our loyalties, allegiance, and affection are related to the land. The water, wind, sun, and stars are part of this federation. The fish, birds, plants, and animals also share this union. Our teachings and stories form the constitution of this relationship and direct and nourish the obligations that it requires. The Chippewas of the Nawash have struggled to sustain this citizenship in the face of the diversity and pluralism that have become part of the land. This has not been an easy task. Our codes have been disinterred, disregarded, and repressed. What is required to re-inscribe these laws and once again invoke a citizenship with the land?

Close to thirty years have passed since Harold Cardinal wrote his influential book, *The Unjust Society*.[1] His work catalogued the troubling conditions Indians found themselves in during the late 1960s.[2] Writing in response to the Trudeau government's plan to eliminate Indian rights,[3] he described the denial of Indian citizenship. His message captured the feelings of Aboriginal people everywhere. He chronicled a disturbing tale of how Indians were marginalized in Canada through bureaucratic neglect, political indifference, and societal ignorance. He labeled Canada's treatment of Indians as "cultural genocide"[4] and in the process gave widespread literary presence to the absence of Indian rights. In convincing tones he outlined thoughtful solutions to overcome threats to our underlying citizenship, organized around the central theme of Indian control of Indian affairs. Here was an approach to protect special connections with the land. He advocated the strengthening of Indian organizations,[5] the abolition of the Department of Indian Affairs,[6] educational reform,[7] restructured social institutions,[8] broad based economic development[9] and the "immediate recognition of all Indian rights for the re-establishment, review and renewal of all existing Indian treaties."[10] Cardinal's ideas resonated within Indian country and parallel proposals became the mainstay of Indian political discourse for the next three decades.[11] He articulated a revolutionary message in a transformative time.

Fast forward to the massive five-volume report of the Royal Commission on Aboriginal Peoples, released in 1996.[12] The story is unchanged. The report describes violation of Aboriginal rights and calls for their immediate recognition and renewal. It records the continued excision of Aboriginal relationships with their lands and demonstrates that the problems Cardinal profiled stubbornly remain. Despite some notable achievements in the intervening years, such as the recognition and affirmation of Aboriginal rights, it illustrates how Indigenous citizenship with the land is increasingly tenuous. In their broad outlines, Cardinal's and the Commission's messages are notable for their similarity. Aboriginal people are suffering, their rights are being abrogated, and the answer to this challenge is Aboriginal control of Aboriginal affairs. Like Cardinal, although to a more elaborate and expansive degree, the report recommends a series of legislative and policy goals: the strengthening of Aboriginal nations,[13] the abolition of the department of Indian Affairs,[14] educational reform,[15] restructured social institutions,[16] broadly based economic development,[17] and the immediate recognition of all Aboriginal rights for the re-establishment, review, renewal, and creation of treaties.[18] Same story, same solutions. A revolutionary message in a reactionary time.

Why the same approach? If the message did not have the desired effect the first time, why repeat it? Does the call for Aboriginal control of Aboriginal affairs stand a greater chance now than it did in the late 1960s? Although there has been some reason for hope,[19] there is also cause for concern.[20] Despite the wisdom of its message, so far the reaction to the Commission has been as feeble as the response to Cardinal. All the while, Aboriginal citizenship with the land is being slowly diminished. The disenfranchisement of our people (and our spirits) from the land, water, animals, and trees continues at an alarming rate.

Do we need a new story, new solutions? We do. We need a transformative message in a reactionary time.

To preserve and extend our participation with the land, it is time to talk also of Aboriginal control of Canadian affairs. We need an Aboriginal prime minister, an Aboriginal Supreme Court judge, and numerous Aboriginal chief executive officers. We need people with steady employment, good health and entrepreneurial skill. They should be joined by Aboriginal scientists, doctors, lawyers, and educators, and coupled with union leaders, social activists, and conservative thinkers.[21] We need these people to incorporate Indigenous ideologies and perspectives into their actions, including ideas about the federation we should enjoy with the earth. They should stand beside Aboriginal elders, chiefs, grandmothers, aunts, hunters, fishers, and healers as bearers and transmitters of culture. For too long the burden of cultural transmission has been placed on these reserve-based teachers and leaders. Although their knowledge will always remain vitally important in the expansion of ideas, other Aboriginal people in different settings within Canada also have to shoulder some of this responsibility. Aboriginal people must transmit and use their culture in matters beyond "Aboriginal affairs." Aboriginal citizenship must be extended to encompass other people from around the world who have come to live on our land.

After all, this is *our* country. Aboriginal people have the right, and the legal obligation of a prior citizenship, to participate in its changes. We have lived here for centuries and will for centuries more. We will continue to influence its resource utilization, govern its human relationships, participate in trade, and be involved in all of its relations – as we have done for millennia. Fuller citizenship requires that this be done in concert with other Canadians – as well as on our own, in our own communities. Aboriginal control of Aboriginal affairs is a good message that has to be strengthened, but it only gets us so far. It is not consistent with holistic notions of citizenship, which must include the land and all beings upon it. When we speak of Aboriginal control of Aboriginal affairs it is evident that Canadians feel they do not have much of a stake in that message,[22] except, perhaps, with regard to what "they" think "we" take from "them" in the process.[23] Canada's stake in Aboriginal peoples, and in the land, has to be raised at radical, liberal, and conservative levels.

Our world is bigger than the First Nation, reserve, or settlement. Approximately one-half of the Aboriginal population of Canada live outside these boundaries.[24] Certainly our traditional lands and relationships lie outside these boundaries. Even if the reserve is where we live, national and international forces influence even the most "remote" or seemingly local time-honoured practice. In fact, an autonomous Aboriginal nation would encounter a geography, history, economics, and politics that requires participation with Canada and the world to secure its objectives. Aboriginal control through Canadian affairs is an important way to influence and participate with our lands. Without this power we are excluded from the decision-making structures that have the potential to destroy our lands. This is a flawed notion of citizenship. Canadians must participate with us and in the wider view of polity that sustained our forebears for thousands of years.

If we pursue this notion of citizenship, what will its new narrative be? How will its constituent stories be arranged? How will they relate to the old narrative? What will be lost, and what gained? These questions need to be taken very seriously. The development of a new narrative may severely undermine the interests of those who have invested their aspirations and energies in the earlier one, even if the two messages are complementary. Some people have spent a tremendous amount of time and effort promoting an exclusive citizenship and measured separatism for Indians through a form of self-government. But this approach, however appropriate and helpful, is not rich enough to encompass the range of relationships we need to negotiate the diversity, displacement, and positive potential that our widening circles represent.[25] The extension of Aboriginal citizenship into Canadian affairs is a developing reality, given the increasingly complex social, economic, and political relationships we are entering into. Intercultural forces of education, urbanization, politics, and intermarriage all have a significant influence in drawing Indigenous people into closer relationship with Canadian society.[26] The impulse behind the call for this refocused narrative is suggested by these changing dynamics in the Indian population. Since 1961 our populations have quadrupled,[27] rates of urban residency have climbed to 50% of the total Aboriginal population, and one in every two Aboriginal people has married a non-Aboriginal person.[28] Moreover, our health has improved[29] and incomes have expanded.[30] From where I stand this change has been enormous. Although I am worried that these indicators hide the continuing individual and collective pain of Aboriginal people, I also participate with numerous other Aboriginal people who more frequently interact with Canadians in a significant way.

An increasing number of Aboriginal people are graduating from Canadian universities prepared to contribute at the First Nation, provincial, national, and (in some cases) international level. Over 150 000 Aboriginal people now have or are pursuing post-secondary education.[31] This is a significant development: in 1969 there were fewer than 800 Aboriginal post-secondary graduates.[32] When 150 000 is measured against our overall population of approximately one million it is apparent that Aboriginal citizenship is expanding, and that Aboriginal control of Aboriginal affairs, while necessary, is not enough to reflect the simultaneous cultural participation that is occurring. I have directly supervised and watched 100 Aboriginal law students graduate and have spoken to and visited with hundreds more. I have watched them fill jobs as entrepreneurs, managers, lawyers, teachers, politicians, researchers, and public servants. In the wider university setting I have witnessed a similar phenomenon. In May 1997 the top medical student at the University of British Columbia (UBC) was an Ojibway woman. A few months earlier I was an external reviewer of the Native Indian Teacher Education program at UBC and discovered that some of the province's most respected educators and a good number of principals graduated from this program. UBC's programs for Aboriginal students in forestry, business, health, engineering, and arts have enjoyed a similar success. These deep changes, which can be documented statistically and anecdotally, show that Aboriginal narratives of citizenship have to be transformed.

Yet I have also witnessed the struggles of some of these same students. Racism,[33] cultural alienation, family tragedies, poor academic preparation, insensitive teachers, and unresponsive curricula conspire to rob many Aboriginal people of the benefits of education. Furthermore, many who could be participating are not – some by choice, but most because of the colonial pathologies that continue to resonate in our communities. The backdrop of these and other continuing challenges may generate a cool reaction to assertions of Aboriginal control of Canadian affairs, and I anticipate that the account I am suggesting will meet with some resistance.

For example, it may be thought that I am advocating assimilation. I am not. Assimilation implies a loss of political control, culture, and difference. I submit that Aboriginal control of Canadian affairs, by changing contemporary notions of Canadian citizenship, has the potential to facilitate the acquisition of political control, the continued development of culture, and respect for difference.[34] Aboriginal values and traditions could help shape these changes and reframe the relationships within our polity. Tradition can be the dead faith of living people, or the living faith of dead people.[35] If Indigenous traditions are not regarded as useful in tackling present concerns then they are the dead faith of living people. On the other hand, if our people, institutions and ideologies are relevant to participation beyond our boundaries, they mark the living faith of our ancestors – the living traditions of dead people. When my great-great-grandfather placed his name and totemic symbol on a treaty that surrendered one and a half million acres in southern Ontario, he did not assent to assimilation.[36] He sought control over his life amidst changing cultural circumstances. He knew that Chippewa culture could benefit from the non-Aboriginal education, employment, housing, and medicine that were pledged in return for the participation of newcomers in citizenship with our land. We have fulfilled our part of the agreement. Other people enjoy our land; it is now time for the promises made to us to be fulfilled. This is not to extinguish Aboriginal culture, but to enrich it. There is contemporary worth in Indigenous traditions that consider all the constituent parts of the land to be related.[37] Although I regard this knowledge as imperfect and incomplete, it is also insightful and wise. There is much to be gained by applying this knowledge within Aboriginal communities and within Canada. Our intellectual, emotional, social, physical, and spiritual insights can simultaneously be compared, contrasted, rejected, embraced, and intermingled with those of others. In fact, this process has been operative since before the time that Indians first encountered others on their shores.[38]

Concerns about assimilation may not be the only grounds on which others may object to a narrative of Aboriginal control of Canadian affairs. Participation within Canada may not seem "Aboriginal" enough. It may be seen to violate sacred treaties and to compromise traditional cultural values.[39] Yet it should be asked: What does it mean to be Aboriginal or traditional? Aboriginal practices and traditions are not "frozen." Identity is constantly undergoing renegotiation. We are traditional, modern, and postmodern people. Our values *and* identities are constructed and reconstructed through local, national, and sometimes international experiences. "Aboriginality" is not confined to some pristine moment before the arrival of Europeans in North America.[40] Similarly, "Canadianism", or any other cultural identifier, is not fixed.[41] As Edward Said observed about identity and culture:

No one today is purely *one* thing. Labels like Indian, or woman, or Muslim or American are no more than starting-points, which if followed into actual experience for only a moment are quickly left behind. Imperialism consolidated the mixture of cultures and identities on a global scale. But its worst and most paradoxical gift was to allow people to believe they were only, mainly, exclusively, white, or Black, or Western, or Oriental. Just as human beings make their own history, they also make their cultures and ethnic identities. No one can deny the persisting continuities of long traditions, sustained habitations, national languages and cultural geographies, but there seems no reason except fear and prejudice to keep insisting on their separation and distinctiveness, as if that was all human life was about.[42]

As Said implies, the formation of culture and identity is contingent on our interactions with others. This insight makes it difficult to object to the point that an assertion of Aboriginal control of Canadian affairs is not "Aboriginal." The values and identity of Aboriginal people develop in response to their own practices, customs and traditions *and* those within other cultures.[43] As such, "Aboriginality" is extended by Aboriginal control of both Canadian *and* Aboriginal affairs. Because important aspects of Aboriginal identity are influenced by Canada, Aboriginal control of Canadian affairs is one way to assert more control over what it means to be Aboriginal. In the process, such assertions may even shape what it means to be Canadian.

Some, however, may not be impressed with this more fluid notion of what it means to be Aboriginal. They may object that I have gone too far, and that the idea that Aboriginal citizenship could include non-Aboriginal people inappropriately stretches tradition. For example, it might be claimed that Aboriginal control of Canadian affairs violates sacred cultural traditions such as the two-row wampum belt. The Gus Wen Tah, as the belt is called, was first adhered to by my people, the Ojibway, in 1764 when the British made an alliance with the Indians of the upper Great Lakes.[44] The belt consists of three parallel rows of white beads separated by two rows of purple. To some, the belt suggests a separate nation-to-nation relationship between First Nations and the Crown that prohibits Aboriginal participation in Canadian affairs. This interpretation flows from a focus on the purple rows. One purple row symbolizes the British going down a river, navigating their ship of state, while the other purple row represents the Indians going down their river, controlling their own ship of state. Some have said "these two rows never come together in that belt, and it is easy to see what that means. It means that we have two different paths, two different people."[45] This reading of the belt centres on the autonomy of each party, as the parallel purple lines are thought to signify that neither party was to interfere in the political organization of the other. In this symbolism is rooted the idea of Aboriginal control of Aboriginal affairs. In fact, according to this description, Aboriginal control of Canadian affairs would violate a fundamental tenet of the Gus Wen Tah.

In considering the potential of the Gus Wen Tah to embrace a notion of citizenship that includes non-Aboriginal people, two important observations deserve attention. First, the Gus Wen Tah contains more than two purple rows. The three rows of white beads represent a counterbalancing message that signifies the importance of sharing and interdependence. These white rows, referred to as the bed of the agreement,[46] stand for peace, friendship, and respect. When these principles are read together with those depicted in the purple rows it becomes clear that ideas of citizenship have to be rooted in notions of mutuality and inter-connectedness. The ecology of contemporary politics teaches us that the rivers on which we sail our ships of state share the same waters. There is no river or boat that is not linked in a fundamental way to the others; that is, there is no land or government in the world today that is not connected to and influenced by others. This is one reason for developing a narrative of Aboriginal citizenship that speaks more strongly to rela-tionships that exist beyond "Aboriginal affairs." Tradition, in this case represented by the Gus Wen Tah, can support such an interpretation.

A second observation that speaks to the Gus Wen Tah's potential to encompass Aboriginal control of Canadian affairs is that its interpreta-tion must be made by reference to other belts exchanged in the same period. The Gus Wen Tah cannot be read in isolation from these other instruments, which clarify the meaning of the two-row wampum. Just as one should not read a treaty according to its written words alone, one should not interpret the Gus Wen Tah solely according to its woven characters. For example, at the time the Gus Wen Tah was exchanged at Niagara in 1764, an accompanying belt emphasized the interdepen-dence between the Indians of the Great Lakes and the nascent settler population. A ship was woven into one end of the belt with its bow facing toward Quebec. At the other end of the belt is an image of Michilimackinac, a place in the centre of the Great Lakes regarded as the heart of the Chippewa homelands. Between the two objects were woven twenty-four Indians holding one another's hands. The person furthest to the right is holding the cable of the ship, while the one on the extreme left has his foot resting on the land at Quebec. Representa-tives of the twenty-two First Nations assembled at Niagara in 1764 touched this "Belt of Peace" as a symbol of friendship and as a pledge to become "united."[47] This strong imagery conveys the connection between Aboriginal and non-Aboriginal peoples and the lands they occupied. In fact, in this belt the Indians are pulling the ship over to receive and participate in the benefits from the non-Indigenous popula-tion. These wider understandings demonstrate that tradition can sup-port a notion of citizenship that unifies and connects us to one another and to the lands we rely on.

Concerns about Aboriginal control of Aboriginal affairs, however, will probably not end at the borders of Indian reserves and Metis settlements. The idea may also cause some concern among the wider Canadian public. Some may wonder about the potentially wrenching effects of this radical approach to Aboriginal control of Canadian affairs. The participation of Aboriginal people in Canadian and global politics will require a great deal of change within the country. An asser-tive and aggressive stance for control may bring to mind ethnic and racial strife in other countries where groups are attempting to seize control of the state. However, more conciliatory liberal or conservative approaches could also create difficulties, as some within the current establishment will not be prepared to cede or share power. There is a need to overcome this near exclusivity. The chairs, corridors, and halls of legislatures, along with universities, courts, law societies, unions, and corporate boards of directors have been sluggish in responding to the influx of Aboriginal people. To my knowledge, there are approximately ten Aboriginal legislators, twenty tenured Aboriginal professors, sixteen Aboriginal judges, one law society bencher, no national Aboriginal union executives, and no Aboriginal members of boards of directors in Canada's twenty-five largest corporations. These levels of representation must change. Indeed, it is required if Canada is ever to enjoy an inclusive citizenship.

However, a narrative of Aboriginal control of Canadian affairs does not end with a greater representation of Aboriginal people within existing Canadian institutions. Perhaps the most profound concern in adopting the discourse outlined in this essay is the multi-dimensional nature of the power imbalance Aboriginal peoples experience. Control in Canada is not exercised merely through people and institutions. Both are governed by deeply rooted global and national tenets that animate and direct the "acceptable" bounds within which people and institutions can exercise power. Aboriginal notions of citizenship with the land are not among these accredited ideologies. Assertions of Aboriginal control of Canadian affairs will encounter a matrix of power that works to exclude notions of "land as citizen." This will be especially evident when its economic implications are understood. In some cases the application of indigenous traditions might require that Aboriginal people share the wealth of the land with other Canadians; in others, it may mean that a proposed use would have to be modified or terminated. A reorientation of this magnitude is not likely to occur without substantial opposition from those who currently benefit from the prevailing ideologies. To surmount this challenge Aboriginal people must employ many complementary discourses of control. This is the reason that Aboriginal control of Canadian affairs must join prevailing narratives of Aboriginal control of Aboriginal affairs in preserving and extending citizenship with the land.[48]

There exists a "special bond" between Aboriginal peoples and the lands they have traditionally occupied.[49] These bonds should be reflected in discourses of Aboriginal citizenship. To speak only of Aboriginal control of Aboriginal affairs would disenfranchise most Aboriginal people from their traditional lands. Measured separatism would separate many from places they hold dear. Why should an artificial line drawn around my reserve prevent me from participating with the vast areas my ancestors revered? This focus could prevent the acknowledgment and strengthening of the continuing Aboriginal reliance, participation, and citizenship with the lands they use outside these lines. Aboriginal peoples still honour the places made meaningful by an earlier generation's encounters. They still travel through these places and rely on them for food, water, medicine, memories, friends, and work. Many are hesitant to relinquish their relationship with them in the name of Aboriginal self-government merely because non-Aboriginal people now live there and also rely on this land. Aboriginal control of Canadian affairs provides a discourse that simultaneously recognizes the meaningful participation of Aboriginal people with one another and with their non-Aboriginal neighbours. It contains a deeper commitment to preserve and extend the special relationship Aboriginal peoples have with the land. It does not abandon age-old territorial citizenships merely because non-Aboriginal people are now necessary to preserve the land's ancient relations.

In 1976 my grandfather died on the same shores he was born on 75 years earlier. He did not live his whole life there, however. His life's experiences were not completely bounded by the artificial borders of a colonial department's Indian reserve. As a young boy he hunted with his father in traditional territories recently made into rich, fertile farmlands. As a young man he worked in Wiarton, Owen Sound, Windsor, and Detroit as a plasterer and labourer. At the same time he fished in the waters of Georgian Bay and Lake Huron (and, in later years, taught me about this practice when I was growing up). He then went on to Hollywood, where he acted in hundreds of films and married a non-Aboriginal woman. As a middle-aged man he came back to the reserve when Pearl Harbor was bombed and resumed his practice of working off-reserve as a labourer, and hunting off-reserve to support his family. He received an honorary doctorate from the University of Kentucky because of his knowledge of plants and medicines throughout the one and a half million acres of land his grandfather signed over by treaty. Everywhere he went, including California, there were people around with whom he could speak Ojibway fluently. During the last 25 years of his life he alternately lived on the reserve with my grandmother in their old cabin, on our hunting grounds north of the reserve, and with some of his eight children who lived off the reserve in non-Aboriginal towns throughout the traditional territory. Discourses of Aboriginal citizenship must be enriched to reflect this fuller range of relationships with the land. Aboriginal culture is not static and, at least in southern

Ontario, develops and redevelops through a wider variety of interactions than is recognized in conventional narratives of citizenship.
Narratives of Aboriginal political participation should be transformed
to reflect this fact.

NOTES

1 Harold Cardinal, *The Unjust Society: The Tragedy of Canada's Indians*
   (Edmonton: Hurtig, 1969).
2 For a description of these conditions see *A Survey of the Contemporary
   Indians of Canada: A Report on Economic, Political, Educational Needs
   and Policies in Two Volumes*, ed. H.B. Hawthorn (Ottawa: Indians Affairs
   Branch, 1966).
3 The government set out this plan in a 1969 White Paper. See *Statement of
   the Government of Canada on Indian Policy, 1969* (Ottawa: Department of
   Indian Affairs and Northern Development, 1969). The White Paper was a
   policy designed to reduce and minimize political and "lawful obligations"
   owed to Indian people. The leading work examining the White Paper is
   Sally Weaver's *Making Canadian Indian Policy: The Hidden Agenda
   1968–1970* (Toronto: University of Toronto Press, 1981).
4 Cardinal, *The Unjust Society*, 139.
5 Indian organizations were to "restore and revitalize a sense of direction,
   purpose and being for Indians" and to "work to weld communities together
   into dynamic, growing forces that can participate in their twentieth century
   environment." Ibid., 162–5.
6 Ibid., 163.
7 Cardinal observed: "Since the introduction of formal white education to
   the Indians of Canada, their original educational processes have either been
   shunted completely aside or discouraged. The only purpose in educating the
   Indian has been to create little brown white men, not what it should have
   been, to help develop the human being or to equip him for life in a new
   environment." Ibid., 166.
8 On the restructuring of social institutions, Cardinal wrote: "[T]here must
   be created, within these communities, structures that attack the problem at
   their source. Ideally, most of the services within a community should be
   provided by the community itself. Before this can happen, huge sums of
   money must be provided, aimed at community problems. No outside
   bureaucracy, whether in Ottawa or in a provincial capital, is flexible
   enough." Ibid., 168.
9 Economic development was to require "huge sums of money ... to enable
   Indian groups to take advantage of ... opportunities on our own reserves."
   Ibid., 169.

10 On securing Indian rights through existing and renewed treaties, Cardinal suggested: "The negotiations for this must be undertaken in a new and different spirit by both sides. The treaties must be maintained. The treaties must be interpreted in light of needs that exist today ... . The Indian simply cannot afford to allow the government to renege on its obligations because, if he does, he commits cultural suicide." Ibid., 166.

11 Writing representative of this approach can be found in Leroy Little Bear, Menno Boldt, and J. Anthony Long, eds, *Pathways to Self-Determination: Canadian Indians and the Canadian State*, (Toronto: University of Toronto Press, 1984); Menno Boldt and J. Anthony Long, eds, *The Quest for Justice: Aboriginal Peoples and Aboriginal Rights*, (Toronto: University of Toronto Press, 1985); J. Anthony Long and Menno Boldt, *Governments in Conflict: Provinces and Indian Nations in Canada* (Toronto: University of Toronto Press, 1988); Boyce Richardson, *Drumbeat: Anger and Renewal in Indian Country* (Toronto: The Assembly of First Nations and Summerhill Press, 1989); Frank Cassidy, ed. *Aboriginal Self-Determination*, (Lantzville, BC: Oolichan Press, 1991).

12 *Report of the Royal Commission on Aboriginal Peoples,* 5 vols. (Ottawa: The Commission, 1996), hereinafter RCAP *Report.*

13 Recommendation 2.3.27 of the RCAP *Report* calls on:
"The Parliament of Canada [to] enact an Aboriginal Nations Recognition and Governance Act to
a) establish the process whereby the government of Canada can recognize the accession of an Aboriginal group or groups to nation status and its assumption of authority as an Aboriginal government to exercise its inherent self-governing jurisdiction;
b) establish criteria for the recognition of Aboriginal nations, including ... [there follows a list of six criteria]
c) authorize the creation of recognition panels under the aegis of the proposed Aboriginal and Lands Tribunal to advise the government of Canada on whether a group meets recognition criteria;
d) enable the federal government to vacate its legislative authority under section 91(24) of the *Constitution Act, 1867* with respect to core powers deemed needed by Aboriginal nations and to specify which additional areas of federal jurisdiction the Parliament of Canada is prepared to acknowledge as being core powers to be exercised by Aboriginal governments; and
e) provide enhanced financial resources to enable recognized Aboriginal nations to exercise expanded governing powers for an increased population base in the period between recognition and the conclusion or reaffirmation of comprehensive treaties.

14 Recommendation 2.3.45 of the RCAP *Report* calls on The government of Canada to "present legislation to abolish the Department of Indian Affairs and Northern Development and replace it by two new departments: a

Department of Aboriginal Relations and a Department of Indian and Inuit Services."

15 See recommendations 3.5.1 to 3.5.44, *RCAP Report*.

16 See recommendations 3.2.1 to 3.4.15, *RCAP Report*.

17 See recommendations 2.5.1 to 2.5.52, *RCAP Report*.

18 See recommendations 2.2.2. to 2.2.17, *RCAP Report*.

19 For instance, in early January 1998 the Minister of Indian Affairs responded to some of the *RCAP Report* recommendations regarding residential schools. She stated that the government of Canada "expresses profound regret" for past actions that have contributed to some of the difficulties Aboriginal people currently experience.

20 For example, see *R. v. Pamajewon* [1996] 2 S.C.R. 1025, where the Supreme Court of Canada refused to consider broad rights to self-government under s. 35(1) of the Constitution.

21 The problem is not that the message of greater participation within Canada did not appear in Cardinal's book or in the Commission's proposals, but that it was not emphasized or pursued to the same degree as "Aboriginal control of Aboriginal affairs."

22 See Brian Schwartz, "A Separate Aboriginal Justice System?," *Manitoba Law Journal* 28 (1990): 78–80, where he argues that "separatism leads to indifference from the larger community instead of supportive interaction."

23 A survey conducted by Southam News and Compas Poll asked: "Do you feel the federal government should put more money in the following areas?" It then listed sixteen categories and elicited a response that gave national defence and Aboriginal people the lowest priority. See Giles Gherson, "Defence, Native Programs Get Least Support," *Vancouver Sun*, 12 December 1997, A1.

24 *RCAP Report*, vol. 1, 17–20.

25 An excellent compilation that addresses the issues surrounding simultaneous cultural participation is Bill Ashcroft, Gareth Griffiths, and Helen Tiffin, eds, *The Post Colonial Studies Reader* (New York: Routledge, 1996).

26 The intercultural nature of Canadian society has been examined in James Tully, *Strange Multiplicity: Constitutionalism in an Age of Diversity* (Cambridge, MA: Cambridge University Press, 1995).

27 *RCAP Report*, vol. 1, 14. In 1961 the Aboriginal population was estimated to be 220 000.

28 *RCAP Report*, vol. 1, 17–20.

29 "Although the life expectancy of Aboriginal people throughout North America as measured from birth is significantly lower than that for non-Aboriginal people, it has improved since the Second World War"; *RCAP Report*, vol. 3, 119.

30 However, this expansion in income did not keep pace with that experienced by non-Aboriginal people. See James Frideres, *Native Peoples in Canada:*

Contemporary Conflicts (Scarborough: Prentice Hall, 1993, 159–62. Also disturbing is the fact that rates of unemployment among Aboriginal people increased in this period. RCAP *Report*, vol. 2, 804.

31 *Aboriginal Education: The Path To Empowerment* (Ottawa: Department of Indian and Northern Affairs, 1994).

32 *Aboriginal Education: The Path to Empowerment.*

33 RCAP *Report*, vol. 2, 817.

34 The potential for the narrative of Aboriginal control of Canadian affairs to effect these changes will be strengthened as the notion of Aboriginal control of Aboriginal affairs remains strong and vibrant. I am not advocating that Aboriginal control of Aboriginal affairs be neglected.

35 For a general discussion of this issue see Jaroslav Pelikan, *The Vindication of Tradition* (New Haven: Yale University Press, 1984).

36 John Borrows, "A Genealogy of Law: Inherent Sovereignty and First Nations Self-Government," *Osgoode Hall Law Journal* 30 (1992): 291.

37 John Borrows, "Living Between Water and Rocks: First Nations, Environmental Planning and Democracy," *University of Toronto Law Journal* 47 (1997): 422.

38 The Supreme Court of Canada failed to recognize and protect as rights any practices that developed from the interaction of Aboriginal and non-Aboriginal peoples in *R. v. Vanderpeet* [1996] 2 S.C.R. 723. A critique of this test is found in Russel Barsh and James Y. Henderson, "The Supreme Court Vanderpeet Trilogy: Native Imperialism and Ropes of Sand," *McGill Law Journal* 42 (1997): 993.

39 It is first important to note that what is "traditional" or constitutes a central cultural value differs between First Nations. These differences make it difficult to anticipate which precise issues may be of concern in Aboriginal control of Canadian affairs.

40 John Borrows, "Frozen Rights in Canada: Constitutional Interpretation and the Trickster," *American Indian Law Review* 22 (1998): 1.

41 Although cultural identity is not fixed – see, for example, Eric Wolf, *Europe and the People Without History* (Berkeley: University of California Press, 1982), 387 – neither is it infinitely fluid. People's interpretation of the meaning of their culture is restrained by their sense of "how we do things here." See Charles Taylor, "The Politics of Recognition" in *Multiculturalism and the Politics of Recognition*, ed. Amy Gutman and Charles Taylor (Princeton: Princeton University Press, 1992).

42 Edward Said, *Culture and Imperialism* (New York: Vintage Books, 1993), 336. I would like to thank Natalie Oman for bringing this quotation to my attention in her PhD dissertation: *Sharing Horizons: A Paradigm for Political Accommodation in Intercultural Settings* (Montreal: McGill University 1997).

43 For a discussion of how identity is formed through this interactive, dialogical process, see M.M. Bakhtin, "Discourse in the Novel," in *The Dialogical*

Imagination: Four Essays, ed. Michael Holquist (Austin, Tex.: University of Texas Press, 1981), 354.

44 John Borrows, "Wampum at Niagara," in *Aboriginal and Treaty Rights in Canada: Essays on Law, Equality and Respect for Difference*, ed. Michael Asch (Vancouver: University of British Columbia Press, 1997). The principles found in the two-row wampum belt were over one hundred years old by the time they were received in this area. The principles represented by the belt were first established by the Haudenausanee with the Dutch in 1664, and with the English not too many years later.

45 Haudenausanee Confederacy, oral presentation, *Minutes and Proceedings and Evidence of the Special Committee on Indian Self-Government*, issue 31 (31 May – 1 June 1983), 13.

46 Ibid.

47 Thomas G. Anderson, "Report on the Affairs of the Indians of Canada, Section III," Appendix No. 95, in Appendix T of the *Journal of the Legislative Assembly of Canada*, 1847 vol. 6.

48 Aboriginal control through Canadian affairs also has the potential to check the nepotism, abuse, and disregard for women that can occur within communities. Enough of our people have now raised these concerns to necessitate a response to them. Of course, nepotism, abuse, and disregard of women's rights occur in wider Canadian society, and Aboriginal people taking control in Canadian affairs will not bring them to an end. But it may alleviate their most poignant effects if alternatives for shelter, participation, and criticism lie within both Aboriginal and wider Canadian circles. Although the potential for criticism on these issues may trouble some Aboriginal leaders, this may not be a bad result if these reproaches result in greater attention and accountability. For further discussion see Emma Laroque, "Re-examining Culturally Appropriate Models in Criminal Justice Applications," in Michael Asch, ed., *Aboriginal Treaty Rights in Canada: Essays on Law, Equality and Respect for Difference*, (Vancouver: University of British Columbia Press, 1997).

49 *Delgamuukw v. The Queen*, File no. 23799 at paragraph 128, per Lamer CJ.

5 Just How Civic Is Civic Nationalism in Quebec?

JEREMY WEBBER

Quebec nationalism is now an entirely civic movement. That, at least, is the view of most sovereigntist intellectuals.[1] But how accurate is it? How civic *is* Quebec nationalism?

In this chapter I explore the ambiguities of Quebec's nationalist movement. My objective is not to demonstrate that all Quebec nationalists are disguised ethnonationalists. I accept that most sovereigntist intellectuals genuinely want an open and pluralistic society, one that is consistent with civic nationalist aspirations. But I do question whether the civic nationalists' position provides an accurate picture of the movement as a whole. In this chapter I explore the extent to which the very struggle for separation tends to undermine the movement's civic character. And, above all, I explore tensions and ambiguities at the heart of civic nationalism, tensions that go some way toward explaining the slippage that often occurs even in ostensibly civic nationalist discourse in Quebec, in which open and pluralist aims often slide into language and assumptions that look decidedly less than civic. The civic nationalists' contributions are extremely valuable as exhortation, but they are considerably less so as description.

In large measure, these ambiguities flow from a lack of clarity regarding the relevance of culture to political life. The problem of culture is central to civic nationalism, which has been developed in deliberate contrast to forms of nationalism in which political membership is defined largely in terms of an individual's ethnic or cultural heritage. Rejecting such exclusive and narrow definitions, civic nationalism tries to capture citizens' attachment to the specific character of their society – their concern for its distinctive institutions, its history, its traditions, and perhaps also its linguistic or cultural makeup – while maintaining a firm commitment to cultural and ideological pluralism. It attempts to describe and justify a sense of identification without imposing a limited and constraining definition of citizenship. This is often done by characterizing the nation in other than ethnic or thickly cultural terms. The "nation" is not a monocultural, comprehensive, and quasi-natural unity, but a more limited and more open forum, defined perhaps by its "public culture" (the dimensions of culture associated specifically with public life), or by its laws and institutions, or by its fundamental constitutional principles.[2]

Intimately connected with this concept of nation is a theory of political membership. Citizens are defined not by characteristics such as ancestry, mother tongue, and place of birth but by factors that in principle are accessible to all, regardless of personal origin, i.e., presence on the state's territory, willing adherence to the country's institutions, or (usually) some combination of the two.

This is where the trouble begins. Civic nationalism tries to abstract from cultural characteristics in its definition of nation and citizenship precisely to maintain its openness toward people of different backgrounds. This abstraction can be quite extreme, denying all relevance of culture so that the nation is defined, ostensibly, in purely institutional or territorial terms. But, as I will sketch here and have more fully explored elsewhere,[3] culture is inevitably relevant to our structures of political engagement. These cultural factors inevitably slip back into the analysis. And unless we are very clear about the appropriate role of culture and the specific justifications for drawing criteria for citizenship from it, it can covertly play a substantial role, one that may undermine an ostensible commitment to an open and pluralistic polity.

I do not mean to suggest, on the one hand, that the civic nationalist aspiration toward openness is misconceived or, on the other, that we can escape dilemmas by embracing an atomistically liberal, rigorously acultural political theory. Neither of these simple options is available. The tensions of civic nationalism are general. Culture is inevitably implicated in political organization, political engagement occurs in specific, not blandly generic, societies, and our task therefore is to understand the proper role of cultural factors in political life, including the reasons why and the extent to which political institutions should attempt to abstract from cultural concerns. The commitment to openness – the need to abstract, to some degree, from cultural features in defining political community – is one that I share. But it has to be pursued with a clear sense of the ways in which culture is necessarily implicated in patterns of political engagement.[4] Otherwise, we are likely to fall into unhelpful, possibly illiberal, and at times foolish confusion.

I have two examples of the latter from the recent popular debate in Quebec. These will serve as useful points of departure for the discussion that follows. The first involves Gérald Larose, president of the influential Quebec labour central, the Confédération des syndicats nationaux. Speaking at the launch of a coalition sponsored by the Quebec government against the partition of Quebec in the event of secession, Larose said that partitionists were racist. When asked why, he responded: "Cutting up a territory, wherever it's done in the world, is a racist project. They cut according to the backyards and sidewalks of people, according to their race. This is a racist project." When asked why the same did not go for Quebec's secession, Larose noted that there are two peoples in Canada, not one, and that Quebec, as a territory inhabited by a single people, was indivisible.[5] He offered no explanation of why the Québécois constituted a "nation" whereas the James Bay Crees, for example, did not. But it seems that in this context the civic nationalist discourse plays a strange role: partition is damned as racist because it draws upon culture (if not expressly, at least in its pattern of support) to dismember a territorially defined Quebec. But Quebec sovereigntists themselves escape the racist epithet, presumably because their nation is defined in purely territorial terms. Quebec's secessionists are civic; the others are racist.

The second example involves someone who is emphatically not a Quebec nationalist: Gerry Weiner, president of the Equality Party and a former minister of Immigration in the Mulroney government. In August 1997, Weiner attacked Quebec's immigration policy, arguing that it was racist because it gave preference to immigrants who spoke French.[6] But is this comment not just as confused as Larose's remarks, and for remarkably similar reasons? If Quebec's policy of preferring French-speaking immigrants is racist, then presumably so too is be the federal government's policy, which prefers immigrants who speak English or French.[7] I doubt Weiner intended this implication. He simply lost sight of the fact that some cultural attributes, especially language, are inevitably relevant to political life. His apparent commitment to linguistic neutrality is, I suspect, really a commitment to a very particular kind of linguistic hegemony: a bilingual hegemony in which English and French (but no other languages) are given equal weight.

The kind of slippage evident in these two examples, between ostensible neutrality and unacknowledged cultural commitments, is common in Quebec's civic nationalism. That slippage is the focus of this chapter.

QUEBEC NATIONALISM AS CIVIC NATIONALISM

To what extent does Quebec nationalism conform to a civic ideal? To begin, it is important to realize that the nationalist movement is a coalition. Some members of that coalition do cling to the patently ethnic nationalism of the past. My concern is not, however, with these unreconstructed elements. They are present, have not been disowned by the Parti Québécois, and cannot be ignored in any adequate evaluation of the movement as a whole.[8] But it is clear that they no longer set the tone of nationalist discourse in Quebec. My concern is with the dominant strain of Quebec nationalist discourse, which claims a more modern nationalism. When that strain is scrutinized closely, Quebec nationalism reveals a more thickly culturalist character than Alain Gagnon or François Rocher would have us believe.[9] There are points of slippage toward a nationalism that is not quite so civic.

This is evident, first, in the implicit definition of those who constitute what one might call the "natural" members of the nationality – the citizens to whom the state should, most directly, belong. Concerted attempts have been made in recent years to broaden the term "Québécois" to include all residents of Quebec, regardless of linguistic or ethnic origin. Although these efforts have been and remain worth while, there is good reason to question their success. "Québécois" often seems to have an implicit and more restricted meaning.

In one sense it certainly does have and must retain a more limited meaning. "Québécois" is not merely a term of political membership. It also denotes, in some contexts, a genuinely ethnic membership. How else can one describe French Canadians who are not recent francophone immigrants but descendants of long-term residents – the *Québécois de souche* – who generally do share a distinctive cultural heritage and sense of group identity typical of ethnic groups? The term inevitably does double duty, referring both to ethnic and to political membership. The problem arises when there is slippage between the two, so that political identity is taken to be implicit in ethnic identity.

This slippage is frequent and by no means marginal. It is most clear in the phrase that is still the chant of choice at sovereigntist rallies: "Le Québec aux Québécois." This slogan retains its connotation of francophone Quebecers taking control of their own political destiny and cannot, without drastic and implausible contortions, be given a civic reinterpretation. The same goes for the catchphrase of the Quiet Revolution, "maîtres chez nous," and the concern of many Quebec nationalists with being "a minority in our own country."[10]

Indeed, the slippage in Quebec nationalism's "civic" character is evident in the very choice of nation. If Quebec nationalism were purely civic – if it truly were neutral with regard to culture – then Canada would be just as appropriate a country as Quebec. To choose Quebec, Quebec nationalism must, at the very least, be conjoined with a linguistic preference – a preference, that is, for building a polity in which French is the only, or at least the predominant, common public language.[11] How can that preference be justified in purely civic terms? I suspect that inevitably a high degree of national precommitment enters the calculation. Civic nationalism makes most sense when one takes the boundaries of the community as given; it is not very meaningful when the boundaries themselves are up for grabs.

Many prominent nationalists appear to question the viability of a multilingual nation, a stance that brings them close to the conventional nationalism that sees linguistically defined peoples as the only proper custodians of states. This is especially evident in the assumption that a multilingual or multinational country is not a "real" country. One has to be careful with such language, because there is a sense in which a country's "reality" can be seen to depend on the extent to which it has secured the willing assent of its people. It is in this sense that Robert Bourassa spoke, at his press conference on the collapse of the Meech Lake Accord, of Canada being merely a "legal" country when it might have been a "real" one. This usage is compatible with civic nationalism. But there are many other contexts in which the claim that Canada is not a "real" or "normal" country clearly refers to the fact that it is not a single-nation state, the concept of "nation" implicitly bearing a large cultural or linguistic component.[12] That meaning is much more difficult to justify within a purely civic framework.[13]

There are, moreover, a number of ways in which the content of Quebec nationalism reflects cultural commitments that go well beyond the civic realm. This is true, for example, of the emphasis on a particular historical *mémoire* in the constitution of Quebec's nationhood, a *mémoire* that is asymmetrically distributed among Quebec's ethnic and linguistic groups. The British Conquest, the struggle for *survivance* in an increasingly anglophone North America, conflicts over the Riel Rebellion, French-language schooling in Manitoba, Ontario and New Brunswick, conscription, the retaking of economic control during the 1960s – all serve as landmarks on the path to Quebec nationhood. This history's importance is reflected in the motto emblazoned on all Quebec licence plates: "Je me souviens."[14]

The significance of language in Quebec nationalism also goes well beyond a republican affirmation of French as a common language of interaction in the public sphere and certainly beyond a suggestion that French should serve merely as one of a range of linguistic options available to Quebecers. The maintenance of French is valued for the rich cultural heritage that it bears and for the sense of collective identity bound up with that language. This, after all, is the significance of *survivance*, which still colours public policy designed to promote the use of French.[15] Indeed, language is seen by some nationalists as a marker of a broader, highly desirable cultural solidarity, so that their policy toward anglophone and allophone Quebecers aspires well beyond the adoption of French as the *common* language of the public sphere to its adoption as the *only* language of general interaction, inside and outside the home.[16]

Finally, Quebec nationalists' concern with immigration, while closely related to anxieties over language, sometimes slides into a concern not so much with immigrants' linguistic capacity but with their linguistic origin. This runs the risk of losing sight of the genuinely republican interest in the preservation of a common public language to focus instead on a factor that is, in effect, merely a double for ethnic origin. The very terms "anglophone," "allophone," and "francophone" are typically used to refer neither to linguistic capacity nor to language commonly used in public interaction but, rather, to mother tongue (or, at best, language habitually used at home). The potential impact of this slippage is most evident in the concern of many nationalists that "francophones" might soon become a minority on Île de Montréal. Quite apart from the fact that there is no such likelihood in the larger metropolitan area, this anxiety takes no account of the adoption of French by allophones and anglophones in the workplace, in public interaction, or even in the home.[17]

I do not suggest that state concern with language, history and cultural heritage is inappropriate. Quite the contrary. The attempt to build a conception of nation that draws entirely upon cultural characteristics may do more to reveal the inadequacies of a purely civic model than to impugn the policies of a particular government. But it does suggest that more is involved in Quebec nationalism than the civic nationalists would have us believe. The claim that Quebec nationalism is civic should not close our eyes to the richer cultural significance that remains within the movement or to the difficult issues of adjustment and accommodation that result. Furthermore, there are instances in which ostensibly civic nationalists adopt positions that are, on any reading, illiberal and uncivic. Any serious engagement with the issues has to consider and guard against that possibility.

In recent years, the most patent departure from civic nationalist virtue has been the suggestion that, in the decision over Quebec's secession, the opinions of francophone Quebecers count more than those of anglo-phones or allophones. This view is more common than one might think. It is reflected in the emphasis given to the fact that a majority of franco-phones voted Yes in the referendum of October 1995. It is apparent in invocations of the "will of the majority" or the "decision of the major-ity," when what is meant is only the will of a majority of a majority – the decision, in other words, of a majority of francophones (which is then imputed, magically, to francophone Quebecers as a group), when a majority of all Quebecers rejected the option.[18] In its grosser manifesta-tions, it is evident in the outright denigration of the ethnic vote[19] and, on occasion, in suggestions that allophones and anglophones should not vote on such questions.[20] And of course, it was his opinions as to whose votes really counted that made Jacques Parizeau's referendum night comments so offensive.[21]

Are such comments representative, or should we agree with Quebec's civic nationalists that they are voiced only by a fringe? It is certainly true that the grosser examples, such as Parizeau's speech, were repudi-ated by other sovereigntists. That repudiation was laudable, but the fact remains that the examples are taken from much more than the fringe. At the time he made his comments, Parizeau was premier of the prov-ince and head of the Parti Québécois. Roughly similar remarks were made by Bloc Québécois members of parliament and by prominent sovereigntist intellectuals in the lead-up to the referendum. They show the possibility of slippage and the instability of sovereigntist discourse, especially when it is under stress.

THE EFFECT OF THE CAMPAIGN FOR INDEPENDENCE ON THE CHARACTER OF QUEBEC NATIONALISM

Many have remarked on Quebecers' dual allegiances to both Canada and Quebec.[22] The sovereigntist project is all about forcing a choice between those allegiances. It is about undermining Quebecers' commit-ment to a bilingual and multinational country in order to focus citizens' allegiance exclusively on a polity in which French would be the only language of public interaction. It is about the rejection of Canada and the rejection of bilingualism, not merely the affirmation of Quebec and the affirmation of French. That has consequences that make it more difficult to push, simultaneously, for openness and pluralism.

First, the intrinsic interest of the sovereigntist project is asymmetri-cally distributed. Its appeal is almost exclusively directed toward fran-cophones. Although Quebecers of other origins may feel strongly attached to Quebec, they almost unanimously see the abandonment of

Canada and the movement toward a unilingual society as a loss, not a gain. After all, their attachments would be severed and their options limited by a project that, even in its mildest forms, expressly rejects varieties of linguistic pluralism that have traditionally been important to them (for anglophone Quebecers, the language rejected is, of course, their own). Moreover, this rejection occurs even in the forms of nationalism most open to cultural difference: many Quebec nationalists (perhaps most) embrace a variety of republican citizenship on the French model that is much less open to cultural accommodation – one that would vigorously reject, for example, any strong form of Aboriginal self-government.[23] It is no wonder that members of cultural minorities are suspicious of a project that is necessarily built on the rejection of at least some forms of cultural and linguistic pluralism. The only constituency in which the sovereigntist project can have resonance is that of francophone Quebecers – although even here there is reason to doubt the appeal of sovereignty in the absence of partnership with the rest of Canada. In pursuing sovereignty the state can only act in the interest of one linguistic group, if indeed it acts in any group's interest. The project is, inevitably, culturally specific.[24]

Many nationalists have striven to open the movement to Quebecers of other origins. Although in some cases this effort is strategic, rather than sincere (Parizeau's comments on referendum might made it clear that this was true of him),[25] in others there is no doubt that the proponents seek to create a new Quebec that is as open to cultural difference as Canada now is.[26] This effort is extremely important, and one hopes that it will continue. But it cannot overcome the fact that, whatever the aspirations for an independent Quebec, the struggle now involves, objectively, the rejection of a multicultural and bilingual state, in part because those very characteristics are seen as threatening.[27] It is difficult to reject those features at the level of Canada and affirm them at the level of Quebec. The drive to open the movement to cultural pluralism, while frequently sincere, ultimately can only mitigate the effects of a policy that is, in its essence, profoundly unattractive to members of cultural minorities.

As a result, the movement elicits the almost unanimous opposition of non-francophone Quebecers. This is not, in itself, a reason for considering the sovereigntist movement as one of illiberal nationalism (as some have argued).[28] The movement has to be judged by its aspirations (as I have attempted to do here), not by its capacity to attract anglophone and allophone support. But minority opposition in turn generates a sense of frustration among sovereigntists – a disillusioned recognition that this is, after all, an ethnic fight. This, I believe, is the substance behind Pierre Bourgault's bitter affirmation that the anglophones' virtually unanimous rejection of sovereignty was "carrément raciste."[29]

Finally, the ethnicization of the debate is pushed by the need for simplicity – for simple causes and for easily identifiable enemies – in any popular struggle. Who, according to sovereigntists, are the opponents of Quebec? "English" Canadians. What are the grievances and the humiliations driving the struggle? The emotional undertones rarely observe the tenets of civic nationalist rectitude.

These undercurrents are likely to be accentuated, not reduced, if Quebec moves toward independence. The struggle for and against independence would continue throughout a referendum campaign and beyond, including the highly uncertain period after a "Yes" vote but before separation is assured and the terms negotiated. During all that time, anglophone and allophone Quebecers would strongly oppose secession. Aboriginal peoples and perhaps members of other minorities would take steps to partition Quebec. Conflict during the transition would thus be intense and strongly associated with ethnic cleavages. Even once Quebec became independent, it would be difficult for the new government to be generous to cultural minorities. The anglophone constituency would be eroded by departures. The same level of services and institutions could not be justified for a substantially smaller community.[30] There would undoubtedly be a period of insecurity, both economic and social, as Quebec attempted to establish its place in the world. Insecurity provides a poor foundation on which to build cultural accommodation. Anglophones' history of fierce opposition to independence, combined with the economic cost of their exodus, would further undermine any tendency toward generosity.

Some sovereigntists argue that the transition to independence would, of itself, push Quebec nationalism toward a more liberal character by shifting that nationalism's reference point from a culturally defined to a territorially defined community – from "French Canadians" to "Québécois."[31] This argument seems little more than a pious hope. Certainly the experience of other nationalisms (for example, the Irish, Slovakian, or Latvian) does little to bolster the view that statehood would inevitably transform Quebec nationalism from a cultural to a civic movement.

THE INHERENT TENSIONS OF CIVIC NATIONALISM

In the end, the ambiguities of Quebec nationalism are ultimately the product of tensions within civic nationalism itself. Civic nationalism, like any nationalism, is concerned with cherishing real societies, and that means cherishing those societies' particularity. Any national feeling, any patriotism, must draw upon aspects of a society's history and contemporary expression that carry cultural weight. This inevitably privileges some cultural phenomena over others. But how does one do that without overdefining the society and closing its members into a narrow and illiberal frame?[32]

The French language, for example, is necessarily crucial to any cherishing of Quebec's distinctiveness. Indeed, it is crucial to any sense of *Canada's* distinctiveness.[33] But how does one do that without slipping toward a limited definition of who really counts? To what extent should French be promoted? What degree of hegemony is appropriate? Those questions cannot be begged by asserting that one's nationalism has a civic character and that French simply forms part of the civic landscape. Indeed, they cannot be begged by eschewing nationalism altogether. The problem of culture in the state – the concern of politics with culture – is perennial. We will always be faced with determining the language or languages of government services, the courts, and parliamentary debate, and when we have finished with that, we will find that culture serves as the essential background to a host of judgments, ranging from the definition of crime to the structure of the family. And yet we also realize that, once a given culture is present, the possibility exists of slippage toward a society that is altogether too closed and constraining for individual expression. Civic nationalism lives that tension acutely, for it emphasizes the need for commonality while it embraces pluralism and individuality. The resulting ambiguity is evident in the variety of notions implicitly poured by different nationalists into the concept of French as the "common language" in Quebec, ranging from French as a language of political and commercial interaction, to French as the exclusive language of commercial and industrial life, to (ultimately) French as the language of the home (at least among immigrants).

The inescapable tensions – and they are inescapable – arise clearly in the context of the integration of immigrants. Integration in some form is a laudable goal, valued by all societies. There are, however, many measures of integration. Some of these are compatible with (and, indeed, may be fundamental to) openness and plurality, such as immigrants' participation in commerce and industry or their achievement of linguistic ability sufficient to permit involvement in public life. Others are more difficult to achieve, and their postulation seems to slip toward a less open and accessible vision of political membership. Must an anglophone or an allophone, for example, care about the Plains of Abraham or the Riel Rebellion in the same way as a

Québécois de souche? If that is required, who can pass the test? What non-francophone can accede to that society without continually playing a role? And, if patriotism is required, what form should it take before an immigrant is considered integrated? At the time of the Referendum of October 1995, several commentators bemoaned the allophones' coolness toward the independence struggle itself as a failure of integration.[34]

Indeed, the very language of integration can often be difficult to separate from the much less savoury language of ethnocentrism. We have heard the phrases before: "They keep to their own"; "They refuse to take part in our society"; "They are unassimilable." What cultural commitments should immigrants be expected to assume? In what ways are they to be permitted to reinterpret a society in their own manner?

In short, Civic nationalism has inevitable sources of instability. How can one go forward?

BEYOND THE CIVIC–ETHNIC DICHOTOMY

Any adequate response must be informed by a frank recognition that culture is relevant to political engagement, that cultural concerns are inevitably implicated in political judgment, and that if we are to care about our political communities, our concern must extend to features of those communities that are broadly cultural. Our response must also be informed by an awareness of the reasons to cherish openness and pluralism, even if we do care about our political communities – indeed, *especially* if we care about them.

I explore some of these theoretical issues elsewhere and will not repeat that discussion here. They do, however, imply the abandonment of what is in the end the simplistic and misleading dichotomy between civic and ethnic nationalism.[35] Culture – including features often associated with ethnic nationalism – is inevitably present in political life and the shaping of political communities. This is true even of those nationalists who yearn for a pluralistic and open nationalism, despite their desire to exclude cultural concerns in order to avoid slippage toward profoundly illiberal policies. That strategy of denial leaves the role of culture unexamined. A better defence is not to deny culture's relevance altogether (which only allows it to work back into the analysis, unassessed and uncontrolled, as in the examples of foolish confusion given at the beginning of this paper), but to acknowledge its presence and its importance to our attachment to political communities, and then to consider the pitfalls of culturalist nationalism with a clear eye.

That search for a more adequate nationalism has already begun, and it is not my purpose to pursue that quest in detail here.[36] I do, however, want to suggest some specific implications for nationalism in Quebec.

First, if it means anything, the aspiration to a more pluralistic nationalism must involve a relatively open definition of political membership – a concept of citizenship, in other words, that to some degree draws upon cultural membership. For this reason, the current emphasis of many Quebec nationalists on a territorial definition of citizenship is very welcome. The slippage in popular discourse toward more restrictive definitions – for example, by denigrating the right of cultural minorities to participate in the decision on sovereignty – must be strenuously resisted.

Second, a more open nationalism must involve a measure of restraint in the language of integration and the demands of allegiance (not just for immigrants, but for all members). It is useful, I believe, to think of a two-tiered structure of engagement.[37] In the first tier, there are necessary commitments in any democratic society. Public policy can be premised upon the adherence of citizens to those commitments, which therefore serve as strong considerations in, for example, the admission of immigrants. These commitments include a basic respect for political institutions, observance of the most fundamental democratic values, and the elementary requirements of democratic engagement, such as a willingness to learn the language or languages of political life (and indeed these, with French as the public language, are roughly the elements identified in 1990 by Quebec's Ministère des Communautés culturelles et de l'Immigration as fundamental principles of Quebec common public culture).[38] Even here, however, one should be careful not to exaggerate. It is essential that citizens abstain from conduct inimical to the most fundamental of the country's institutions, but perhaps not that they subjectively embrace them. For a democratic polity to remain healthy, a critical mass of the population must have a more profound attachment to democratic norms and procedures. To that end, the state should act to foster such virtues. But as long as that mass is present, democratic societies can tolerate the presence of individuals and groups who do not share that commitment. Indeed, Canada has in the past been enriched by groups some of whose members have not shared it, such as Doukhobors, old-order Mennonites, and Hasidic Jews.

This first tier of commitments should be kept analytically separate from the richer substance of allegiance: the various elements that bind individuals to a particular state and the rich constellation of features that give that state its character. This second tier of allegiance is certainly important to a country's stability. In large measure it captures what we most value about our countries, and thus why we are moved to defend them. But attempts to translate it into specific requirements of immigration, for example, are likely to be clumsy, simplistic, and ultimately self-defeating.

We are attached to our countries for a whole variety of reasons, which often differ from person to person. Even though we draw on a similar past, we see that history and our place within it in different ways. We have different ideas about what our country stands for, about what is essential, and about what is accidental. That congeries of reasons need not be arbitrated. Quite the contrary: a state's vigour often springs precisely from the vitality of its internal debates. We may want to bring newcomers (or minorities previously excluded) into those conversations. We may want to foster the conditions by which newcomers can grow to see our society as their own. This may well involve encouraging new members to see themselves against that society's history. To return to an example invoked earlier, we may want (gently) to provide the means for people to think about what the Plains of Abraham or the Riel Rebellion should say to them, in the society in which they now find themselves.[39] But that reflection cannot be compelled. And the answers newcomers give are likely to be different from those of others, just as each generation's understanding is different from that of those who came before. Such new answers are precisely the kind of contribution one should expect of a free and democratic citizen.

I should make clear that I am talking about the necessary substance of allegiance, not about all legitimate considerations in, for example, criteria for immigration. Immigration policy may take additional considerations into account, some of which may have cultural content. I accept, for example, that Quebec may give preference to French-speaking immigrants not merely for reasons of the immigrants' integration into a predominantly French-speaking polity, but also to support the continuation of a vital and dynamic French-speaking society in North America. A full discussion of these issues is beyond the scope of this chapter.

Finally, if one is entitled to cherish the particularity of nations, one should also be willing to extend a similar concern to the particularity of other cultural groups. A concern with the French language and with French-Canadian culture is appropriate and worthy, but that concern should be accompanied by policies designed to speak to minority communities. Guarantees of individual rights can go some way toward serving this role, but just as the distinctiveness of Quebec deserves institutional expression, so too may minority cultures. I am the first to admit that this platitude is hardly a solution. It is the merest beginning of an inquiry, not the end.[40] But a serious concern with the presence of minority cultures, and how those cultures should be articulated to the state, is the hallmark of a truly pluralistic nationalism.

ACKNOWLEDGMENTS

My thanks to Awanish Sinha for his able research assistance, to the Faculty of Law, McGill University, for funding that research, and to Jean-François Gaudreault-Desbiens for his comments on earlier drafts of this chapter.

NOTES

1 For examples, see Alain-G. Gagnon and François Rocher, "Présentation," in *Répliques aux détracteurs de la souveraineté du Québec*, ed. Alain-G. Gagnon and François Rocher (Montreal: vlb éditeur, 1992), 23; Anne Legaré, "La souveraineté: nation ou raison?," in *Québec: état et société*, ed. Alain-G. Gagnon (Montreal: Québec/Amérique, 1994), 41; and Intellectuels pour la souveraineté, "Quoi qu'on en dise, le nationalisme québécois n'est pas ethnique," *La Presse* (Montréal), 15 December 1995, B3. (Although this group distinguishes its position from what it terms "civic nationalism," its position falls within what I take to be civic nationalism. See note 2.) For a more sceptical assessment by a leading proponent of a sovereigntist yet pluralist position, see Guy Laforest, "Identité et pluralisme libéral au Québec," in *Identité et cultures nationales: l'Amérique française en mutation*, ed. Simon Langlois (Sainte-Foy: Les presses de l'Université Laval, 1995), 313.

2 See John Rawls, *Political Liberalism* (New York: Columbia University Press, 1993); Jürgen Habermas, "Citizenship and National Identity (1990)," in *Between Facts and Norms: Contributions to a Discourse Theory of Law and Democracy*, ed. Jürgen Habermas, trans. William Rehg (Cambridge, MA: MIT Press, 1996), Appendix II; Jürgen Habermas, "Struggles for Recognition in the Democratic Constitutional State," in *Multiculturalism: Examining the Politics of Recognition*, ed. Amy Gutman, trans. S.W. Nicholsen (Princeton: Princeton University Press, 1994); Dominique Schnapper, *La Communauté des citoyens: sur l'idée moderne de nation* (Paris: Gallimard, 1994). Specifically in relation to Quebec, see the contributions in *Libéralismes et nationalismes: Philosophie et politique*, ed. François Blais *et al.* (Quebec: Les Presses de l'Université Laval, 1995).

   Variants of what I call "civic nationalism" differ as to the extent and nature of communality required and the extent of abstraction possible. Some analysts choose to confine the term to a tightly defined subset of these. I will not try to overrefine the term, but will instead use it in a broader, more impressionistic manner, capturing within it all attempts to define nationalism in contradistinction to ethnic nationalism. This accords with general usage in Quebec. Others may prefer the term "liberal nationalism."

3 Jeremy Webber, *Reimagining Canada: Language, Culture, Community and the Canadian Constitution* (Montreal and Kingston: McGill-Queen's University Press, 1994).

4 For a valuable discussion that does take the interrelationship seriously, see Schnapper, *La Communauté des citoyens*. Schnapper, however, tends to treat the particularistic aspects of nationhood as regrettable but inescapable departures from an ideally universal nationhood. I allow them to serve a more positive role.

5 Philip Authier and Elizabeth Thompson, "Anti-partition coalition fails to take off," *The Gazette* (Montreal), 18 September 1997, A17.

6 "Quebec immigration rules are biased: Equality Party" *The Gazette* (Montreal), 29 August 1997, B11.

7 See Joseph H. Carens, "Immigration, Political Community, and the Transformation of Identity: Quebec's Immigration Policies in Critical Perspective," in *Is Quebec Nationalism Just? Perspectives from Anglophone Canada*, ed. Joseph H. Carens (Montreal and Kingston: McGill-Queen's University Press, 1995), 26, 29–30.

8 Dimitrios Karmis, "Interpréter l'identité québécoise" in *Québec: état et société*, ed. Alain-G. Gagnon (Montreal: Québec/Amérique, 1994), 305.

9 Gagnon and Rocher, *Répliques aux détracteurs*, 23.

10 See the useful, brief overview of official usage in Louise Fontaine and Danielle Juteau, "Appartenance à la nation et droits de la citoyenneté," in *Les frontières de l'identité: Modernité et postmodernisme au Québec*, ed. Mikhaël Elbaz, Andrée Fortin and Guy Laforest (Sainte-Foy: Les presses de l'Université Laval, 1996), 195–9. For the language of "minority," see, for example, André Bellemare, "Bourgault accuse les anglophones d'exercer un 'vote carrément raciste'" *La Presse* (Montreal), 27 February 1995, A2; Alain-G. Gagnon and François Rocher, "Pour prendre congé des fantômes du passé" in *Québec: état et société*, ed. Alain-G. Gagnon (Montreal: Québec/Amérique, 1994), 494.

   Sometimes the message is still more direct. Immediately before the 1995 Referendum, sociologist Pierre Drouilly stated that if the overwhelming anglophone and allophone vote turned the tide against sovereignty, "on pourra tirer la conclusion que maintenant la nation québécoise française est démocratiquement assujettie à la nation canadienne anglaise. Contre d'autres peuples sur terre on tire, contre les Québécois français on vote. D'une certaine façon, cela est plus efficace." Pierre Drouilly, "Le OUI disposera d'une majorité du vote francophone s'il dépasse les 42%," *La Presse* (Montreal), 9 October 1995, B3.

11 In "Interpréter l'identité québécoise," Karmis usefully identifies two non-ethnic strains in contemporary Quebec nationalism: a republican strain, which emphasizes immigrants' full assimilation into the dominant

francophone culture; and a pluralistic nationalism, which is much more tolerant of cultural and linguistic pluralism.

12 See, for example, the comments of Gérald Larose cited earlier. See also Laforest, "Identité et pluralisme libéral au Québec," 323–4.

13 Civic values such as broad political participation might be most easily achieved in a community with a single public language. This argument may be seen as establishing a civic justification for monolingual states, but it requires that one take a remarkably pessimistic view of the viability of multilingual states (of which, of course, there are many) and deny the efficacy of federalism as a means of dealing with linguistic difference. Indeed, it seems to put such a premium on participating in a united polity that it would be difficult to reconcile it with any form of federalism. Given their extremism, one might ask to what extent such arguments motivate the position. For a further, highly persuasive argument against this position, see Dominique Leydet, "Intégration et pluralisme: le concept de culture publique," in *Libéralismes et nationalismes*, ed. François Blais *et al.*, 124–6. For a wholehearted defence of civic nationalism within the French tradition that acknowledges the significance of language to political engagement yet has no trouble accepting the "reality" of multilingual federations such as Switzerland, see Schnapper, *La Communauté des citoyens*, 127–9.

14 For discussions that emphasize this historical dimension, see Christian Dufour, *Le défi québécois* (Montreal: l'Hexagone, 1989); Daniel Salée, "La mondialisation et la construction de l'identité au Québec," in *Les frontières de l'identité*, ed. Mikhaël Elbaz *et al.*, 111–13, drawing on work of J. Létourneau.

15 See Charles Taylor, "The Politics of Recognition," in *Multiculturalism: Examining the Politics of Recognition*, ed. Amy Gutman (Princeton: Princeton University Press, 1994), 58–9; Fernand Dumont, *Raisons communes* (Montreal: Boréal, 1995).

16 See, for example, Comité interministériel du bilan sur la situation de la langue française, "La situation de la langue française au Québec: Bilan" (draft prepared by Josée Legault and Michel Plourde, dated January 1996), 173ff, 369, and 406. Here the draft report, in its examination of immigrants' linguistic integration, professes concern with the "common language" adopted by immigrants but then goes on to use, as its principal indicator, the language most frequently spoken by immigrants at home. The retention of the immigrant's ancestral language, even at home, therefore becomes an index of incomplete integration. At 382 and 392, the discussion of the language of work emphasizes, as its principal indicator, whether French is used more than 90% of the time, the worker's capacity to work in French, or even whether he or she uses French most of the time. This draft became the subject of considerable public criticism because of features such as these and was altered before adoption. Nevertheless, the original was

strongly defended by its authors and by others within the sovereigntist movement.

17 See Legault and Plourde, "La situation de la langue française au Québec," 41ff, 403; "Notes pour une adresse à la nation du premier ministre du Québec, Monsieur Jacques Parizeau, à l'occasion de l'émission des brefs référendaires," October 1995 (unpublished), 5; Marc Termote, "Le Français langue commune: Enjeu de la société québécoise," Rapport du comité interministériel (du Québec) sur la situation de la langue française, 7 December 1995 (unpublished). See also the vagaries in the use of the term "Francophones québécois," charted by Fontaine and Juteau, "Appartenance à la nation et droits de la citoyenneté," 197–8, in one report.

18 See, for example, Jacques Brossard, *L'accession à la souveraineté et le cas du Québec: conditions et modalités politico-juridiques*, 2nd ed. (Montreal: Presses de l'Université de Montréal, [1976] 1995), 184; Denis Lessard, "Parizeau soucieux de corriger son tir," *La Presse* (Montreal), 13 September 1995, B1 (comments of Marcel Masse); Pierre O'Neill, "Parti québécois: 'Élargir l'autoroute de la souveraineté' " *Le Devoir* (Montreal), 7 November 1995, A4 (comments of Jean-Pierre Charbonneau, arguing for an enlargement of the sovereigntist constituency to include allophones, but nevertheless treating support for sovereignty among the majority of francophones as an indication that sovereignty was supported by the majority group in Quebec).

19 See the post-referendum remarks of Bernard Landry, cited in "Hotel workers claim Landry ranted about immigrants" *The Gazette* (Montreal), 3 November 1995, A1. See also Parizeau's remarks, quoted in note 21, and the comments cited in note 29.

20 See, for example, Brossard, *L'accession à la souveraineté et le cas du Québec*, 183, 185; Mario Fontaine, "Les représentants des aînés préfèrent se cantonner dans la neutralité," *La Presse* (Montreal), 21 February 1995, B1 (citing remarks of Raymond Lévesque); Pierre April, "Un député du Bloc [Philippe Paré] veut exclure les ethnies du débat référendaire," *La Presse* (Montreal), 27 February 1995, A1 (Paré's remarks were especially startling because they were made in response to interventions by representatives of immigrant communities that are among the most francophone; his comments were immediately denounced by other members of the Bloc Québécois, including Lucien Bouchard); "Jean-Marc Léger suggère l'abstention à ceux qui ne parlent pas français," *La Presse* (Montreal), 2 March 1995, B6.

These positions are not shared by a majority of Quebecers, although the minority that does share them would form a significant portion of the sovereigntist constituency. A poll published in the magazine *l'Actualité* (1 November 1995), 17–20, gives an idea of the balance of opinion. Of the respondents, 17% agreed with a statement that only francophone Quebecers should have a right to vote in a referendum on Quebec's future; 30% agreed that Quebec should have the power to declare sovereignty if a majority of *francophones* voted in favour.

21 Most accounts have focused on the portion in Parizeau's speech in which he said, "C'est vrai qu'on a été battu. Au fond, par quoi? Par l'argent puis les votes ethniques, c'est ça qui arrive." But his most chilling remarks were made toward the beginning of the speech, when he said, according to one clipping service, "on va cesser de parler des francophones du Québec, voulez-vous. On va parler de nous, à 60 pour cent, on a voté pour" (quotations taken from Medianor, Inc., "Discours du premier ministre Jacques Parizeau Référendum 1995," 30 October 1995). At the time, it was clear that Parizeau was throwing away what had been for him the convenient mask of civic nationalism, to speak now simply of "we," the francophones of Quebec, the only group whose political will mattered. There was an outcry at these remarks and Parizeau was forced to resign both as premier and as leader of the Parti Québécois, although he was not without apologists within the sovereigntist movement.

22 Dufour, *Le défi québécois*, 14; Webber, *Reimagining Canada, passim*, but especially at 258.

23 See Karmis, "Interpréter l'identité québécoise."

24 See also Jeremy Webber, "The Referendum and the Future of Anglophones in Quebec," *Choices: Québec-Canada series* [Institute for Research on Public Policy] 1, no. 9 (1995): 16.

25 See note 21.

26 See, for example, Intellectuels pour la souveraineté, "Quoi qu'on en dise, le nationalisme québécois n'est pas ethnique,"; Laforest, "Identité et pluralisme libéral au Québec," 325; André Binette, *Indépendance et liberté: Une vision du Québec souverain* (St-Rédempteur: Consultants BRAE, 1996).

27 This is true, for example, of most sovereigntists' complete rejection of the federal policy of multiculturalism as nothing more than a means used by Ottawa to counter biculturalism or, more generally, the recognition of Quebec's distinctiveness. There is no doubt that the policy was used by the Trudeau government for something like that purpose, as I have myself argued *in Reimagining Canada*, 62–6. But it is a serious error to dismiss the policy as nothing more than an anti-nationalist device invented by "English Canada." It spoke – and continues to speak – to important concerns of non-British, non-French immigrants. The same point is even more apposite with regard to the aspirations of Aboriginal peoples. It is simply foolish to treat those demands as nothing more than a federalist stalking horse, as some sovereigntists continue to do.

28 The strangest variant of this argument suggests that the simple fact that Quebec nationalists include non-francophone Quebecers within the Quebec "nation" when they do not wish to be so included is itself evidence of that

nationalism's uncivic or illiberal character. See, for example, Wayne Norman, "Les points faibles du modèle nationaliste libéral," in *Libéralismes et nationalismes*, ed. François Blais *et al.*, 91–2. This puts all too much emphasis on the success rather than the intrinsic character of a nationalist movement. All nationalisms, all patriotisms, secure varying levels of support. Their civic character cannot possibly depend upon complete and willing adherence or, in other words, on an utterly voluntaristic model of who belongs to the "nation." I agree entirely with the response of the group that calls itself "Intellectuels pour la souveraineté;": the argument ends up being too much of the form "damned if you do, damned if you don't."

29 Bellemare, "Bourgault accuse les anglophones" A1. Bourgault's remarks were denounced by the then leader of the Bloc Québécois, Lucien Bouchard (although they had been, in the words of *La Presse's* reporter, "chaudement applaudi" by the Bloc Québécois riding association meeting at which Bourgault spoke): Irwin Block and Paul Wells, "Bouchard rebukes two supporters" *The Gazette* (Montreal), 28 February 1995, A1. Almost certainly, a similar frustration was behind Bernard Landry's outburst on referendum night, cited in note 20. See also Pierre Foglia, "Le racisme, c'est personne," *La Presse* (Montreal), 2 March 1995, A5; Pierre Foglia, "Tabou," *La Presse* (Montreal), 2 November 1995, A5; Pierre Drouilly, "Un référendum exemplaire," *La Presse* (Montreal), 7 November 1995, B3.

30 Webber, "The Referendum and the Future of Anglophones in Quebec."

31 See, for example, Gagnon and Rocher, *Répliques aux détracteurs*; Daniel Latouche, *Plaidoyer pour le Québec* (Montreal: Boréal, 1995), 148. On page 23, Gagnon and Rocher slip quickly to the affirmation that Quebec's nationalism is *already* civic.

32 Schnapper, "La communauté des citoyens.".

33 See Webber, *Reimagining Canada*, 187–93, 200–12, together with the elaboration by Leydet, 124–6, which I wholeheartedly accept. Leydet emphasizes that although linguistic differences are important to the structure of a political community, they are not necessarily determinative. This indeed is my position. *Reimagining Canada* is as much a defence of the value and viability of a bilingual polity as it is an argument for Quebec's autonomy on linguistic grounds.

In other words, the importance of language in defining particular political communities does not exclude other forms of attachment that also bear a particular cultural character, at a broader level. I think in terms of a federal structure of allegiance, in which one can be strongly committed to communities within communities. This does not mean that some of these – the most extensive ones, for example – can be purely civic, utterly neutral in terms of culture, thus creating a structure of cultural nationalisms within a broader civic unity. All polities have a cultural character, and all nationalisms and patriotisms are affected by attachment to that character.

34 Gilles Normand, "Landry se porte à la défense de Jean-Éthier Blais," *La Presse* (Montreal), 13 April 1995, B4; Quebec, *Journal des débats: Commission permanente*, CC-7, 27 April 1995, 20 (comments of Bernard Landry); Marie-Claude Lortie, "Ottawa se sert des immigrants pour aider le NON, dit Landry," *La Presse* (Montreal), 14 October 1995, B9.

35 See also Schnapper, "La communauté des citoyens," especially at 168, and Fontaine and Juteau, "Appartenance à la nation et droits de la citoyenneté."

36 See Charles Taylor, "Shared and Divergent Values," in *Reconciling the Solitudes: Essays on Canadian Federalism and Nationalism*, ed. Guy Laforest (Montreal and Kingston: McGill-Queen's University Press, 1993), 172–9; Taylor, "The Politics of Recognition," 52ff (and Michael Walzer's short contribution to the same volume); Webber, *Reimagining Canada*, especially 185–93.

I do not mean to suggest that this form of nationalism (or "patriotism") is itself a new phenomenon, a product, for example, of the postmodern age. In some ways, it may recapture elements of a more tolerant "premodern" patriotism. See, for example, the description of the great Polish patriot Adam Mickiewicz's "Polishness" in Neal Ascherson, *Black Sea: The Birthplace of Civilisation and Barbarism* (London: Vintage, 1995), 145ff.

37 This analysis grew out of a discussion with Dominique Leydet at the "Séminaire de travail: Le libéralisme politique mis à l'épreuve des nationalismes contemporains," Université Laval, 14–15 October 1994, and was first discussed in print by Leydet, "Intégration et pluralisme: le concept de culture publique," 126–8. It bears some similarity to the two levels of assimilation sketched by Habermas, "Struggles for Recognition," 138, although Habermas appears to pour more content into the first level than would I.

38 See the discussions in Leydet, "Intégration et pluralisme" 121ff; and Carens, "Immigration, Political Community, and the Transformation of Identity."

39 I disagree with the notion that a society's history (its prehistory, if you will) is irrelevant to newcomers. (See, for example, Daniel Weinstock, "Le nationalisme civique et le concept de la culture politique commune," in *Libéralismes et nationalismes*, ed. François Blais *et al.*, 106–7.) That view dramatically underestimates the extent to which any current society reflects, and lives by reflecting upon, its history. Most of my immigrant ancestors arrived in Canada just before the First World War, yet consideration of the relationship between Aboriginal and non-Aboriginal Canadians, especially in the period of first contact, has been important to me both professionally and in my engagement with society. For an eloquent expression of the same sentiment, see Martin Krygier, *Between Fear and Hope: Hybrid Thoughts on Public Values* (Sydney: ABC Books, 1997).

Needless to say, that kind of relationship to a society's history is profoundly different from the chauvinism implied in Jean-Éthier Blais's comment (cited in Normand): "Jusqu'à présent, [les Québécois 'd'origine britannique ou multiraciale'] sont restés étrangers aux quelque quatre siècles d'histoire du Québec et ont signifié massivement, par des votes significatifs, leur volonté de vivre à l'écart de cette histoire et de rester attachés au Canada, leur terre constitutionnelle d'accueil."

40 I have tried to push the inquiry further in other contexts. In addition to those references that appear in notes to this chapter, see Jeremy Webber, "Individuality, Equality and Difference: Justifications for a Parallel System of Aboriginal Justice," in *Aboriginal Peoples and the Justice System: Report of the National Round Table on Aboriginal Justice Issues*, Royal Commission on Aboriginal Peoples (Ottawa: Canada Communication Group Publishing, 1993), 133; Jeremy Webber, "Multiculturalism and the Limits to Toleration," in *Language, Culture and Values in Canada at the Dawn of the 21st Century*, ed. André Lapierre *et al.* (International Council for Canadian Studies and Carleton University Press, 1996), 269.

6 Social Citizenship and the Multicultural Welfare State

KEITH G. BANTING

Contemporary politics is multicultural politics. In the past, it was perhaps feasible for students of comparative politics to distinguish neatly between, on the one hand, countries with relatively homogenous societies and, on the other, countries with pluralistic societies defined by ethnic and linguistic divisions. In the contemporary period, however, new immigration flows have altered the demographic profile of virtually every Western country, creating new forms of social difference and new patterns of social inequality. We have been living through a globalization not just of our economies but also of our societies. In addition, recent decades have witnessed the resurgence of substate nationalisms across the Western world. In defiance of the predictions of integration theory, historic cultures have taken on fresh political importance, and powerful nationalist and separatist movements have emerged in a number of countries. In a real sense, ethnolinguistic diversity is now a natural attribute of life in Western democracies.

The implications of multiculturalism for the policy agenda of governments have been powerful. Most obviously, political leaders everywhere must manage tensions between cultural minorities and majorities, and respond to demands for programs to combat discrimination and protect the rights of minorities. At a deeper level, however, cultural pluralism also shapes the frame of reference within which traditional economic and social programs are debated, and sparks intense debate about the nature of rights, citizenship, identity, and community. Social policy would seem to be particularly sensitive to this deeper politics of multiculturalism. From their inception, social programs have been influenced by prevailing interpretations of the nature of inequality. Changing images of the groups that are most disadvantaged and vulnerable have potentially powerful consequences for the definition of social problems and the discourse within which they are debated. In addition, the history of social programs has been influenced by conceptions of community. The prevailing sense of community establishes the boundaries of inclusion and exclusion, defining those who are legitimate members of the existing networks of rights and obligations, and those who are "strangers" or "others" to whom little is owed. Changing definitions of identity and community would therefore seem to be critical to the breadth of the political constituencies that support the welfare state, and to the social and territorial boundaries within which redistributive processes operate.

In particular, the politics of multiculturalism challenges the traditional view of the modern welfare state as a powerful instrument not only of social equality, but also of social integration. Post-war blueprints for the welfare state elaborated by Beveridge, Marsh, and their counterparts in other countries were premised on the assumption that citizens faced a common set of social needs, and that a common set of programs could respond equitably for populations as a whole, providing health care, education and protection from poverty during illness or unemployment or old age. But post-war theorists also believed that a set of social rights available to all citizens would strengthen a wider sense of community and social cohesion. The powerful redistributive flows inherent in major social programs would reinforce the sense that all members of the country were part of a single community, enjoying a common set of rights and shouldering a common set of obligations.

The politics of multiculturalism raises fundamental questions about this image of the post-war welfare state. On one side, cultural minorities often argue that universal social rights have been defined by the dominant culture and do not reflect the variety of needs and belief systems that exist within modern societies. On the other side, cultural majorities may retreat from a commitment to social redistribution in an increasingly multicultural context. Some analysts contend that cultural diversity is slowly eroding the sense of community on which the system of social rights was constructed, and that mainstream interests will withdraw their support as they see resources being channelled to communities that they do not recognize as their own.

The purpose of this chapter is to re-evaluate the relationship between social citizenship and the politics of multiculturalism. In so doing, it draws on two bodies of literature: the literature on citizenship and difference, and the comparative literature on the welfare state. Each of these literatures is immense, and each has distinctive characteristics.

Much of the literature on citizenship and difference is rooted in political and legal theory, and focuses on the implications of contemporary diversity for democratic theory and conceptions of justice. The political science contribution to this literature has tended to focus on the implications of cultural pluralism for conflict management and the stability of democratic political systems. In general, scholars in these areas have tended to pay relatively little attention to the substance of social policy, despite the fact that social programs represent the most frequent, day-to-day contacts between citizens and the contemporary state. In contrast, the comparative literature on the welfare state has focused primarily on the politics of class, or the implications of different systems of economic production for the social role of the state. Surprisingly little attention has been paid to the politics of cultural diversity. A thriving feminist literature has explored the gender implications of the welfare state, but the accommodation between multiculturalism and the welfare state is not well studied. The impact of social programs on the distribution of income among economic classes has been studied in detail, but few if any comparative studies have analysed the role of social programs in shaping the distribution of income and opportunities across ethnic and racial lines. There are also few comparative studies that explore the implications of multiculturalism for the scope and architecture of the modern welfare state, or for the configuration of political interests and alliances that give it shape. As a result, the intention of this chapter is primarily to formulate a research agenda rather than to draw conclusions.

The first section of the chapter sets out the traditional interpretation of the relation between social rights and social integration that underpinned policy discourse in many Western nations during the post-war construction of the welfare state. The second section examines the political challenges to this interpretation posed by growing multiculturalism and briefly surveys several streams of existing research that address the issues involved. The third section analyses in greater detail the implications of multiculturalism for the politics of social policy, paying particular attention to the impact of ethnic and racial minorities on the one hand and nationalist minorities on the other. A final section then draws together the main threads of the argument.

SOCIAL CITIZENSHIP AND SOCIAL INTEGRATION: THE POST-WAR VIEW

The dominant post-war view of the role of social rights of citizenship was most clearly articulated by the British sociologist T.H. Marshall, who wrote his most definitive work on the subject during the expansion of social programs after the Second World War. Marshall defined citizenship as the status granted to those who are full members of a community, and argued that citizenship had increasingly been invested with a formidable array of rights. These rights fell into three broad categories, which in British experience accumulated slowly over the span of centuries. In the eighteenth century, citizenship was associated with civil rights, such as liberty of the person, freedom of speech, thought and faith, the right to own property and conclude valid contracts, and the right to justice. Beginning in the nineteenth century, citizenship was extended to incorporate political rights, ensuring that all citizens could participate in the exercise of political power as a legislator or as a voter. Finally, the twentieth century saw the addition of social rights of citizenship, which for Marshall included "the whole range from the right to a modicum of economic welfare and security to the right to share to the full in the social heritage and to live the life of a civilised being according to the standards prevailing in the society."[1]

Marshall saw the expansion of citizenship as part of a powerful historical process of social integration that steadily incorporated emerging social classes into a national community. Although social rights might mitigate the gap between rich and poor, they did not eliminate the economic realities of class. Rather, a common citizenship generated a new equality of status, a symbolic moral order that would counteract the divisiveness of class inequality. For the purposes of this chapter, what is most important is that the equality of status implicit in citizenship was deeply related to the emergence of a shared sense of community. This relationship was reciprocal. In part, citizenship reflected the emergence of a national consciousness, which had began to develop even before the extension of full political and social rights in the twentieth century. But citizenship rights also reinforced this growing sense of a national community. "Citizenship," Marshall argued in an oft-quoted passage, "requires a bond of a different kind, a direct sense of community membership based on loyalty to a civilisation that is a common possession ... . Its growth is stimulated by the struggle to win those rights and by their enjoyment when won."[2] Stated in more contemporary language, Marshall's theory of social citizenship suggests two propositions. First, a common sense of community is a necessary condition for the emergence of social citizenship rights. Second, social citizenship also reinforces the sense of a common community and serves, therefore, as an instrument of social integration in divided societies.

This conception of social citizenship became deeply entwined with the expansion of social programs in Western nations during the postwar decades. Indeed, in his celebrated comparative study of welfare states, Esping-Andersen starts from the premise that "social citizenship constitutes the core idea of a welfare state."[3] Social programs that established a right to benefit were considered instruments of emancipation for the poor and vulnerable, as support no longer depended on charitable impulses or administrative discretion. In addition, the welfare state was seen as enhancing social solidarity and preserving stability in divided societies. In the late nineteenth century, Bismarck's social insurance initiatives in Germany were part of a twin agenda of class integration and the territorial consolidation of a unified state. In the middle decades of the twentieth century, the expansion and consolidation of a full range of universal social programs in Britain was not solely an effort to narrow the income differentials between rich and poor. For many, it was also a means of building a sense of "one nation" and of entrenching the social solidarity that had emerged during the Second World War.

The integrative role of social citizenship also became a powerful theme in Canadian political discourse, more so perhaps than in many other Western nations. Canadian identity is not rooted in long historical experience, or what Abraham Lincoln called "the mystic chords of memory." Rather, the formation of a pan-Canadian community was a state-led project in which major government programs, including social programs, played a crucial role. From the outset, however, the challenge of social integration was cast in territorial rather than class terms, and social programs were seen as creating a pan-Canadian network of rights and obligations. They represented spheres of shared experience in a society marked by regional diversity and tied the interests of individuals across the country to the fate of the country as a whole.

An early sign of this presumed link between social citizenship and territorial integration came in 1949, when Newfoundland joined the country. From the beginning, leaders in Newfoundland who led the campaign for union with Canada stressed the advantages that would flow from Canada's more advanced social programs, including family allowances, unemployment insurance, and old age pensions. The vote in favour of joining Canada in the final referendum was very close, however, with only 52% of islanders in support, and the federal government was concerned about how long it would take for the entire population to accept its new nationality. Federal officials operated on the assumption that the sooner Newfoundlanders experienced the benefits available to citizens elsewhere in the country the sooner they would regard themselves as Canadian, and they worked hard to ensure that family allowances and unemployment benefits were paid on time in the first month after union. The strategy was highly effective. As the cheques spread out across the new province, "Canada's newest citizens in even the remotest reaches of the province received the first visible signs that they were now Canadians ... . [T]he federal social programs were the most recognized feature of the union with Canada, and they gave the process instant credibility."[4]

Not surprisingly, the same assumptions later underpinned the response of the federal government to the pressures for decentralization that emerged in subsequent decades. A 1969 federal government document, prepared for an early round of negotiations over constitutional reform, was one of many expressing the view that social programs were part of the social glue holding the country together: "The 'sense of a Canadian community' is at once the source of income distribution between people and regions in Canada and the result of such measures. It is the sense of community which makes it possible for Parliament to tax residents of higher income regions for the purpose of making payments to persons in lower income regions. And it is the willingness of people in higher income regions to pay these taxes which gives additional meaning in the minds of those who receive the payments to the concept of a Canadian community."[5]

Thus the linkage between social citizenship and social integration has been a powerful one in the political discourse in western nations generally, and in Canada in particular. The challenge posed by the politics of diversity to the concept of social citizenship is thus a challenge not at the margins but at the heart of postwar political debate.

SOCIAL CITIZENSHIP AND MULTICULTURALISM: THE ISSUES AND EXISTING RESEARCH

Why should greater multiculturalism challenge the politics of the social citizenship and the welfare state? Analysts from a variety of disciplines point to dangers that may fragment the traditional coalitions that created and sustained the post-war settlement. First, minority groups themselves may not see the traditional welfare state as being of central importance to their most pressing problems and may give priority to an agenda focused on anti-discrimination policies, affirmative action, group rights, and greater autonomy for the expression of cultural differences. At the extreme, some minorities, especially nationalist minorities, may see universal social programs as instruments of cultural domination through which the majority culture seeks to impose its values on everyone. Even when cultural minorities remain committed to a common framework of social programs, divisions among them may undermine efforts to build a "rainbow" coalition. In countries as diverse as Canada, Spain, and Estonia, for example, there are tensions between immigrant groups on the one side and nationalist minorities on the other.[6] The second danger is the potential retreat of cultural majorities from the redistributive state. As societies become increasingly diverse, the sense of a common community emphasized by Marshall may fade. Dominant groups may abandon a sense of collective responsibility and quietly disengage, psychologically and perhaps even physically, from the wider society, shifting their allegiance to more conservative political philosophies and parties. On this increasingly rocky political terrain, vulnerable minorities might occasionally make marginal gains on their separate agendas, but they would lack the collective capacity to offset a broader drift toward a less interventionist and less redistributive ethos.

Both of these concerns find resonance in a number of streams of research. Contemporary theoretical debates over citizenship and the politics of difference confront the issues directly. Some theorists challenge the continued relevance of Marshall's interpretation of the integrative role of social citizenship. Kymlicka, for example, argues that "Marshall's theory of integration does not necessarily work for culturally distinct immigrants, or for various other groups which have historically been excluded from full participation in the national culture – such as blacks, women, religious minorities, gays and lesbians. Some members of these groups still feel excluded from the 'common culture' despite possessing the common rights of citizenship."[7] For these scholars, such diversity argues for a more variegated sense of citizenship.[8] In a similar vein, feminist scholars have challenged the ideal of a universal conception of citizenship as failing to reflect the diversities of modern life.[9] Other theorists, however, criticize this approach to social justice for ignoring the importance of a strong sense of national community to the redistributive state.[10] When Young celebrates group differences and argues that "the ideal state is composed of a plurality of nations or cultural groups," Miller replies that achieving social justice requires trust and solidarity "not merely within groups but also across them, and this in turn depends on a common identification of the kind that nationality alone can provide."[11] Wolfe and Klausen agree, arguing that "the threat to the welfare state which exists from supranational pressures towards globalization meets the threat to the welfare state from subnational group power and recognition."[12] Similarly, Taylor-Gooby fears that postmodern thought and practice represent a "great leap backwards" that can only weaken the traditional political coalition supportive of the welfare state.[13]

Although the theoretical literature on citizenship highlights central questions about social citizenship and multiculturalism, it provides no systematic empirical evidence that might help to answer them. In contrast, the comparative literature on the welfare state has a stronger empirical tradition, although it provides only hints about the politics of multiculturalism.[14] The dominant interpretation of the development of the welfare state during the post-war era emphasizes the strength of organized labour, both economically and politically, as a key determinant of the expansion of social expenditures.[15] The implication would seem to be that social heterogeneity is likely to weaken the mobilization of the working class by dividing organized labour along ethnic and linguistic lines, fragmenting political discourse, and making it more difficult to focus reformist politics on an agenda of economic inequality as opposed to inter-communal relations. Some support for this line of reasoning comes from an early study by Stephens that reaffirmed the central importance of organized labour to the expansion of the welfare state but found that ethnic and linguistic diversity was strongly and negatively correlated with the level of labour organization.[16] More recent cross-national studies of the determinants of social spending in Organization for Economic Co-operation and Development (OECD) countries have focused on a wider range of factors, extending the analysis to include the openness of the economy, the demographic profile of the population, the dominance of parties of the left and right, institutional factors such as federalism and decentralization, and so on.[17] However, these studies do not directly examine the impact of ethnolinguistic diversity on social spending.

Development economists have tackled the issue more directly, but their evidence is for a much wider range of countries, including both the richest and the poorest nations of the world. Although their findings suggest that the association between ethnic diversity and the overall size of government is weak,[18] studies that focus on the social role of the state have found more powerful relationships. For example, spending on private as opposed to public education tends to be higher in countries with considerable religious and linguistic diversity, and transfer payments tend to be lower in countries with high levels of ethnic diversity.[19] However, given the levels of ethnic diversity around the globe, these results tend to be dominated by the experience of Third World countries, and their conclusions cannot be applied directly to questions concerning the levels of social support across Western democracies.[20]

Although these bodies of literature do not come to grips fully with the interaction between multiculturalism and the welfare state in Western democracies, they do point to a variety of questions. One question is, obviously, whether higher levels of multiculturalism actually do constrain the redistributive role of the state in Western democracies, thus lowering the levels of social transfers that might otherwise be expected. A second question, which constitutes the primary focus of this chapter, is whether social citizenship retains any potential as an instrument of social integration in multicultural societies. Two issues are critical here. First, do major social programs in Western democracies still represent a regime of common benefits that incorporates new forms of diversity, as celebrated in Marshall's conception of social citizenship? Or are we seeing the emergence of more diversified policy regimes that tailor social benefits to different cultural communities and perhaps even exclude some new communities altogether? Second, to the extent that a common benefit regime exists, does it function as an instrument of social integration, reinforcing the sense of a common community and moderating the political salience of ethnolinguistic divisions? Or are common benefits at best irrelevant to divisions rooted in ethnicity and language, and at worst a source of deeper conflict? These questions do not exhaust the issues posed by multiculturalism but, as we shall see, finding answers to them remains a challenging task.

ETHNIC MINORITIES, NATIONAL MINORITIES, AND SOCIAL CITIZENSHIP

In assessing the contemporary relevance of social citizenship, it is important to recognize that multiculturalism is now a more complex phenomenon than it was in the post-war era, and that the simple dichotomy between homogeneous and pluralistic societies no longer suffices. In particular, the distinction between ethnic and national minorities seems critical.[21] Members of ethnic and racial minorities, which emerge from changing immigration patterns, tend to seek incorporation into the mainstream of society. To be sure, they normally resist full assimilation: they seek to preserve their traditions and customs, and press social institutions to be more tolerant of cultural differences; they are often unwilling to surrender their ties to their original homeland and retain dual citizenship; and they increasingly live in transnational communities. Their dominant concern, however, is to be accepted as full members of the wider society. In contrast, national minorities increasingly resist incorporation. They represent territorially concentrated, historic communities that may have been independent at some time in the past but have long since been subsumed by a larger state. In the post-war years, the political aspirations of such minorities were relatively muted, but in recent decades nationalist movements have gained strength in a number of countries. They seek to preserve their communities as distinct societies and to enhance their political autonomy, either within the context of the existing state or through the formation of a separate state altogether. The distinctive orientations of ethnic and national minorities generate very different implications for social citizenship and the welfare state.

Ethnic Minorities

The challenge to the post-war conception of social citizenship posed by ethnic and racial diversity seems to come less from minorities than from majorities. Admittedly, members of minority communities often encounter problems with important social services. Education in particular is culturally sensitive, and can become a battleground over the recognition of difference. In France, for example, *l'affaire du foulard,* which turned on the right of young Muslim women to wear traditional head scarves in school, reached the top of the national judicial system. Similar conflicts have emerged elsewhere over the language of instruction and the role of heritage studies in the curriculum. In some cases, immigrant groups seek more traditional forms of education than is available in mainstream schools; in Britain, for example, the development of some independent Muslim schools reflects a preference of parents for single-sex schools for their daughters.[22] In other cases, the response to social services may be conditioned by an underlying wariness about state organizations; undocumented migrants or those who have left countries governed by repressive regimes are often uneasy.[23]

Nevertheless, concerns about sensitivity in the delivery of public services are in principle compatible with support for the general concept of social rights and comprehensive social programs. Formal equality of status contributes to a stronger sense of social standing, and creates a firmer political position from which to assert the need for sensitivity to cultural difference. From this perspective, it seems likely that ethnic and racial minorities, especially those that are economically and socially marginal, would support a broad definition of the welfare state, in which social rights retain an important role in building social cohesion. To take the case of the best studied minority, black Americans are particularly supportive of a powerful social role for the state. The divergence of opinion between black and white Americans is enormous, not only with respect to racial policy but also with regard to social spending more generally. Although the differences are sharpest for programs with racially distinctive clienteles, such as welfare and food stamps, they are also substantial for broad social programs such as social security, Medicare and domestic social spending generally. Admittedly, there is a minority separatist strain within black political discourse. Nevertheless, "the modern American welfare state enjoys much more support among blacks than among whites," and the gap in support for federal spending is not diminished by controlling for economic class.[24] Systematic evidence of the attitudes of ethnic and racial minorities in other countries is much more limited. Undoubtedly, the views of these groups vary, reflecting distinct traditions and differences in the extent of integration into the dominant community.[25] Nevertheless, it would be surprising if the pattern in the United States proved to be highly exceptional.

The deeper tension between ethnic diversity and the welfare state seems to be rooted in the reaction of majorities. This is hardly surprising, since majorities normally carry more weight than minorities in democratic politics. Three types of majority response to new immigrant communities are possible. First, new immigrant populations might be incorporated into the existing social regime with little challenge to the underlying societal consensus on social policy. Second, vulnerable sections of the dominant culture – such as young, less educated, blue-collar workers – might be driven by a "welfare chauvinism" that supports the welfare state but rejects open immigration policies and the ready access of foreigners to social benefits.[26] Third, a political backlash against immigration and multiculturalism might help fuel a more comprehensive neo-liberal attack on the welfare state, contributing to the emergence of new radical right-wing parties, or the retreat of established parties from expansive social programs, or both.

All three of these reactions are occurring in Western democracies, but the balance among them varies considerably from country to country. One might expect that previously homogeneous countries would face the most difficulty incorporating new minorities into social citizenship regimes, and that countries with traditions as immigrant societies or long experience with ethnolinguistic diversity would have the least trouble. This is not the case. The nature of the welfare state established in the post-war period appears to be much more important. In countries with expansive welfare systems, the balance tilts toward social incorporation. In countries with more limited welfare systems, welfare chauvinism is leaving a heavier imprint.

Thus, in the expansive welfare systems of Europe, the predominant response in social policy is incorporation. Formally, immigrants enjoy social rights that differ only at the margin from those of citizens. Full benefits are denied to asylum-seekers while their claims are being processed but, once residency is confirmed, inclusion in the full regime of benefits is the norm.[27] Analysts vary in their explanation for this pattern. Soysal argues that social benefits have slowly become detached from national definitions of citizenship, and that the incorporation of immigrants reflects an increasingly transnational conception of human rights.[28] Although the underlying normative discourse may well reflect this transition, it cannot explain significant variation across different

countries and different types of welfare states.[29] Forces of a more structural nature are probably also at work. Organized labour does not
want their members to have to compete with immigrants "who would
have to accept any payment and any working conditions;"[30] within the
European Union, the mobility provisions for nationals make formal
discrimination against migrants more obvious and more difficult.

Admittedly, incorporation does not go uncontested, and European
countries do reveal some elements of welfare chauvinism. This reaction
can take two forms: restrictive immigration policy, designed to prevent
foreigners coming into the country and enjoying comprehensive social
benefits; and restrictive benefit policy, designed to deny resident foreigners access to benefits. Although both forms have figured in political
discourse in European nations, the bigger impact in policy terms has
been on immigration policy. Successive waves of restrictive legislation
have sharply reduced immigration, especially economic immigration,
to Western Europe, and regulations in the 1990s have reduced the flow
of refugees seeking asylum.[31] In comparison, denial of social benefits to
resident foreigners has been very limited. Pressures to turn social policy
into an instrument of immigration control have been resisted; for
example, a more draconian immigration policy being developed within
the French bureaucracy in 1993 initially included proposals for serious
restrictions on the access of foreigners to social security, especially
health care, but internal opposition from the social affairs minister
blocked the proposals.[32] As a result, the formal denial of social benefits
to resident immigrants has been largely limited to occasional actions at
the local level.[33] The employment-related basis of social insurance systems that predominate in these countries does implicitly disadvantage
immigrants with weak ties to the labour market, especially in the case
of pension credits, which build slowly over time. Nevertheless, welfare
chauvinism has had more impact on immigration policy than social
policy in expansive welfare systems.

Multiculturalism has also contributed to a neo-liberal strain in these
countries. Across Europe, radical right parties have combined elements
of enthnocentrism with strains of authoritarianism and neo-liberalism
or anti-state populism, France being the prototypical case. This phenomenon has led Kitschelt to worry about the essential viability of a
multicultural welfare state: "Is the rise of comprehensive welfare states
predicated on ethnic homogeneity or at least plural ethnic stability of a
country ... and will the multiculturalization of still by and large homogeneous or ethnically stable Western Europe lead to a decline of the
welfare state?"[34] Whatever the long-term potential, there is little evidence so far of serious erosion of support for the welfare state in European countries. Although radical-right parties have had a significant

impact on immigration policy, they do not appear to have seriously challenged the underlying consensus on social policy. There are ups and downs in popular support for major social programs and the welfare state generally, reflecting shifts in the partisan campaigns and other factors; but there is no evidence of a steady decline in support for the social role of the state.[35] Incorporation thus dominates in continental Europe.

In contrast, the social-policy response to new minorities has been less inclusive in countries with more limited, or "liberal" welfare systems, such as the United Kingdom, Australia, the United States and – to a lesser extent – Canada. These countries start with weaker social commitments. Most of them are immigrant societies with relatively open processes of naturalization, and closing the borders has been less of an option.[36] Moreover, liberal welfare systems rely more heavily on means-tested benefits, for which newly arrived, unemployed or poor immigrants can potentially qualify immediately. In this context, welfare chauvinism and neo-liberalism have figured more prominently.[37] In Australia, immigrants must be resident for ten years before they can receive the age pension, and for five years before they are eligible for a sole-parent or disability pension, and the required period of residency for a wide range of other allowances such as unemployment and sickness benefits has recently been extended from six months to two years.[38] In the United Kingdom, immigrants are precluded from a number of benefits, such as income support, housing benefit and council tax benefit; and this list was extended in 1996 to include attendance allowance, disability living allowance, disability working allowance, family credit, invalid care allowance and severe disablement allowance.

The United States illustrates the most potent cocktail of neo-liberalism and welfare chauvinism. Racial attitudes remain the most important source of opposition to welfare among the white population.[39] Republican electoral campaigns in the 1980s capitalized on the unpopularity of programs associated with poor black people, and the party reaped major electoral gains among white union members, urban ethnics and southerners, creating the political room for significant cuts to social programs, especially those with disproportionately minority clientele.[40] In the 1990s, the Democratic Party sought to insulate itself by embracing hard-edged welfare reform itself, promising to "end welfare as we know it." The resulting reform package replaced aid to families with dependent children (AFDC) with a block grant to the states to provide temporary assistance to needy families (TANF), eliminating the entitlement to welfare and adopting firm time limits on benefits for recipients. Recent welfare reforms have also included elements of welfare chauvinism. Indeed, the largest savings from welfare reform came from restrictions on immigrants' benefits.[41] Immigrants were denied access to food stamps and supplementary security income for the elderly until they become citizens; and other means-tested programs, such as Medicaid and social assistance, were denied to new immigrants for a period of five years.[42] In the same period, referendums in California challenged the access of immigrants' children – including those born in the United States – to education and health care. Subsequent political battles have eased some of the cuts to immigrant benefits at the national level. However, the multiracial and multicultural nature of American society has clearly helped to fragment support for the welfare system, and the political left faces a formidable task in rebuilding a multi-ethnic, multiracial coalition dedicated to redistributive policies.[43]

Canada stands as something of an exception in this group of liberal welfare states. There is a residency period for old age security, one element of the public pension system. Otherwise, legal immigrants and refugees have the same benefit entitlements as citizens and landed residents. There are muted strains of welfare chauvinism in Canadian politics, to be sure. A government review of social policy in the mid-1990s found considerable public concern about the reliance of new immigrants on social assistance and publicly-financed language training, and recommended changes in admission criteria to enhance the selection of immigrants less likely to need such support.[44] Moreover, a backlash against multiculturalism helped to launch the new Reform Party, a populist, neo-conservative party based in the western part of the country that advocates a significant reduction in the social role of the state.[45] As the party has become more established, it has struggled to mute the strains of ethnocentrism in its ranks, and its parliamentary caucus now includes a number of people of colour. However, the Reform Party remains committed to a neo-conservative approach to social issues and uses its position as the official opposition in the House of Commons to advance its agenda in national political discourse.

In summary, the primary challenge to social citizenship does not seem to come primarily from ethnic and racial minorities. The greater danger is that majorities will withdraw, denying benefits to newly arrived "strangers" or retreating to a smaller welfare system in order to minimize transfers across ethnic and racial lines. The pattern differs, however, across Western democracies. Relatively homogeneous or consociational states that established a strong social regime in the postwar era appear to have been more successful in incorporating new immigrants without eroding mass support for the welfare system. If there has been a price to be paid, it has been more restrictive immigration policies. In other countries where the welfare system has a weaker base and immigration is a strongly entrenched tradition, new forms of

cultural diversity seem to be further weakening support for redistribution generally or for inclusive definitions of social programs. Freeman
seems unduly concerned when he warns that immigration has led to
the "Americanization of European welfare politics."[46] It has, however,
accentuated the American nature of welfare politics in the United
States.

National Minorities

Countries such as Belgium, Canada, Spain, and the United Kingdom
face a second dimension of multiculturalism: the mobilization of substate nationalism. Obviously, the strength of nationalist movements varies considerably across these countries. Nevertheless, in several of them,
conflicts rooted in competing political identities pose significant challenges to a common definition of social rights. Unlike the case of ethnic
minorities, the challenge can come from minority as well as majority
communities, and the resulting political dynamics are more complex. In
common with the case of ethnic minorities, however, these cultural conflicts are played out on a field dominated by the post-war welfare state,
a reality that both stimulates and constrains intercommunal conflict.

Although the welfare state established during the post-war years was
sometimes smaller in multination states, it nonetheless represented a
form of social citizenship. These countries generally established a common framework for major income transfers and health care, and provided comparable levels of benefits to citizens across the country as a
whole, which is perhaps one indirect measure of a common sense of
political community. A variety of mechanisms was used to sustain a
country-wide framework. In the case of income transfers, such as pensions, unemployment benefits and family allowances, responsibility
was usually left with the central government; in other areas, such as
health care, broad framework legislation applied across the country
but allowed considerable scope for regional or communal discretion in
design and implementation. In these circumstances, the potential for
social policy to breathe life into the idea of a country-wide political
community remained viable.

In recent decades, the resurgence of substate nationalism has placed
intense pressure on this social framework in a number of countries.
Conflicts in these countries often centre on control over social programs, and to some extent the post-war welfare state itself helped to
create this new challenger. As governments have become more intimately involved in people's lives, national minorities increasingly wish
for a state that speaks their own language and reflects their cultural
traditions. The result has been extensive redesigning of state structures.

In Canada, a separatist movement has established a powerful position, and responsibility for several social programs has been increasingly decentralized in a series of incremental steps over the last twenty years. In formerly unitary states such as Belgium, Spain, and the United Kingdom, demands for greater national autonomy have also led to decentralization, in the form of federal, quasi-federal, or regional institutions. In addition, the intercommunal transfers that underpin the social framework have become politically controversial in several of these countries. In combination, decentralization and reduced intercommunal redistribution have the potential to fragment the common definition of social citizenship established in the post-war period.

The specifics of the challenge to social citizenship vary considerably from country to country, depending on the strength of nationalist mobilization, the level of centralization in existing political institutions, and on whether substate nationalism represents a rebellion of the rich or of the poor. Nevertheless, the experience of these countries also points to a underlying dynamic: although conflicting nationalisms tend to spark struggles over the control of social programs, the sense of solidarity embedded in a common definition of social citizenship also appears to constrain more radical nationalist agendas. Belgium, Canada, and Spain display distinctive variations on this underlying dynamic.

In Belgium, the mobilization of Flemish nationalism and the gradual transition to a federal system have unleashed powerful new political forces on the expansive welfare state built up in the post-war era. Social security, including income transfers and health care, remains the largest and most important function still lodged with the central government, and social programs involve a significant implicit transfer of resources from Flanders, the affluent Flemish-speaking region in the north of the country, to Wallonia, the poorer French-speaking region in the south. Indeed, studies completed in the early 1990s pointed to an "income paradox." Although earnings were higher in Flanders, the disposable income available to citizens after taxes and social security benefits were taken into account was actually higher in Wallonia, suggesting that redistributive mechanisms were overcompensating for intercommunal inequalities.[47] Not surprisingly, Flemish politicians increasingly attacked the transfer system, the more radical among them asserting that, in effect, Flemish taxes had bought each Wallonian family a new car in recent years.

Flemish nationalists have demanded a significant decentralization of social security in order to reduce intercommunal transfers and to gain more political control over their social destiny. The Flemish government has carefully laid the groundwork for an assault on the centralized system: in 1992, the government commissioned a substantial research program to document more fully the size of the transfers from Flanders to Wallonia and to propose a new regime; in 1994 the research group issued its report, which recommended the decentralization of health care and family benefits;[48] in 1996 the Flemish government endorsed the proposal; and in 1997 the State Reform Commission of the Flemish parliament adopted the same position virtually unanimously. More recently, the Flemish government has raised the issue of greater fiscal autonomy for community and regional governments, which currently depend heavily on transfers from the central government, raising less than 10% of their budgets from own-source revenues. A government discussion paper recommends a significant increase in own-source revenues and suggests that personal income taxes be decentralized. Separately and in combination, decentralization and fiscal reform would have a major impact on the Belgian welfare state. Unless they are accompanied by a common policy framework, which is not anticipated in the Flemish proposals, they would end a common social citizenship in health and family benefits; and unless they are accompanied by substantial interregional transfers, they would result in weaker social programs in Wallonia.

Although the social citizenship model obviously generates conflict in contemporary Belgium, the ties of solidarity implicit in its social security system also constrain more radical forms of the Flemish agenda. Not surprisingly, the decentralization of social security is rejected completely by the Walloons, who insist on the importance of social solidarity across communal lines. In addition, the full nationalist agenda meets some resistance in Flanders as well. The Flemish Socialist Party, which is part of the Flemish government, supports the general decentralization initiative but insists that it be done in ways that preserve social solidarity. In part, the socialists are concerned about links across the linguistic division. But they are also concerned about opening up the finances of social programs completely, fearing that they might end up with a less generous system even in the north. As a result, they tend to favour retaining the current funding mechanisms, including the intercommunal transfers embedded in them.[49]

Changes in the Belgian constitution require a two-thirds vote in parliament. The Flemish government hopes that another round of constitutional reform will begin after elections in 1999, and that the main issues will be resolved during negotiations over the formation of a new government. Because the Wallonian community does not have its own agenda for constitutional reform in this round of negotiations, the prospects for a compromise package are considerably reduced, and change may well be blocked. Such an outcome, however, would severely strain inter-community relations. In the words of one observer, "failure to reach an acceptable compromise on this issue would be regarded by some in Flanders as a signal that no more could be achieved through inter-community dialogue. At that point, some would seek to put separatism on the agenda."[50] A compromise that is acceptable to both major linguistic groups and that answers to the different ideological tendencies in the north is therefore likely. Thus in centralized Belgium, social citizenship plays a contradictory role: nation-wide social programs are a source of intercommunal conflict, but the ties of social solidarity embedded in those programs also constrain radical change.

Canada reveals another version of the same dynamic. The details differ from the Belgian cases in many ways. Quebec nationalism represents a challenge from a less affluent, minority community. Although there has been considerable convergence in the standard of living of anglophones and francophones over the last generation, the population of Quebec is still a net beneficiary of the transfers embedded in the Canadian welfare state. In addition, Canada is already a relatively decentralized federation. Although the federal government has considerable responsibility for pensions and unemployment insurance and still sets the broad parameters for health care delivery, the provincial governments have the exclusive or predominant role in education, health care, social assistance, and social services.

Despite these differences, the same contradictory pattern appears. Nation-wide social programs both stimulate conflict and constrain radical change. There has been a protracted struggle between the federal government and Quebec, supported at times by other provinces, for control over social programs. Both the federal and Quebec governments have long recognized the potential of social programs as instruments of statecraft that can be harnessed to nation-building objectives. The Quebec government has insisted that social programs are central to the preservation and enhancement of a distinctive francophone culture in North America and has struggled to capture programs that still operate at the federal level. The federal government has resisted, convinced that social policy is critical to sustaining a pan-Canadian political community. For many Canadians, especially in the English-speaking parts of the country, social programs are seen as part of the social glue holding together an otherwise divided society.[51]

A number of commentators have questioned whether social programs can serve an integrative role across the deep linguistic divide in the country, arguing that social programs cannot link Quebec more firmly to Canada.[52] However, public opinion polls suggest that social programs are one of a number of factors that contribute to a sense of attachment to Canada, making some Quebecers – especially soft nationalists – more ambivalent about the separatist project than they might otherwise be.[53] This attachment has emotional and instrumental dimensions. At the emotional level, francophone Quebecers take pride in the Canadian system of health care and other social programs. These programs, which stand in sharp contrast to social policy south of the border, represent a historical accomplishment which French- and English-speaking Canadians built together. As such, they reinforce a sense of engagement with the wider country. At the instrumental level, the question of whether social programs are more effectively protected inside or outside Canada remains an important one, especially for less nationalist Quebec voters.

This concern was highlighted in the referendum campaigns held on whether Quebec should separate from Canada. During the first campaign in 1980, federalist leaders argued that a sovereign Quebec would not be able to sustain the social programs that Quebecers enjoyed as citizens of Canada. The Parti Québécois protested the legitimacy of such tactics, but was on the defensive. In 1995, the pattern was reversed. The federal government was in the midst of a drive to balance its budget, and cuts to federal programs made it difficult for federal ministers to pose as defenders of social benefits. In the early weeks of the campaign, the Parti Québécois argued vigorously that only sovereignty could save social programs. Their message was targeted especially at less educated, female francophone voters, a group with a high level of concern about economic insecurity and a tendency to support the federalist side. The strategy was effective, and the gender gap closed noticeably in the referendum vote. The outcome was very close: the sovereignty option was defeated by only 0.7% of the votes cast in a record turnout. Obviously, the shift from a decisive federalist win in 1980 to a near loss in 1995 cannot be attributed solely or even primarily to differences in the debates over social policy. However, the two battles confirm the importance of the security of social policy for the Quebec population. Moreover, as memories of federal retrenchment began to fade in the months after the 1995 referendum, and as the Quebec government's drive to balance its own budget led to cuts in the province's own programs, polls once again found that a solid majority of francophone voters agreed with the proposition that a united Canada is better able to protect social programs.

The ability of social rights to serve as an instrument of social cohesion, even on the rocky terrain of Canada–Quebec relations, is no guarantee that common social programs will remain vibrant. The fiscal weakness of the federal government in recent years substantially reduced its leverage in the system, and there are powerful wider pressures for further decentralization not only from both Quebec but also from the rest of Canada. Decentralist steps have recently been taken in labour-market training and social assistance programs, and there are similar demands in the case of the universal medicare program.[54] In addition, opposition to interregional transfers, although not as marked as in Belgium, is growing in the rest of the country. Once again, this sentiment is strongest in the Reform Party, whose support among voters is also strongly correlated with anti-Quebec feelings. During the 1997 federal election campaign, Reform proposed a revision in the equalization grants program, which supports the revenue capacity of poorer provinces. If adopted, the proposal would have the effect of removing Quebec from the list of recipient provinces.[55] A continuing decentralization of responsibility for social programs, unaccompanied by some mechanism for sustaining a pan-Canadian approach to social policy and a substantially enhanced interregional equalization, would end the post-war experiment in a common social citizenship.

Spain represents a third configuration of the nationalist dynamic. As in Canada, the Catalan and Basque nationalists represent minority communities; but, like the Flemish in Belgium, they come from relatively affluent regions that are net contributors to interregional fiscal flows. Spain is at a different phase of the developmental cycle, however, and is still developing its version of the welfare state and of federalism. In theory, the emerging distribution of power in the quasi-federal system resembles the post-war pattern of most multi-nation federations. Major income security programs are designed and delivered by the central government; the basic parameters of health insurance are set centrally through an organic law; but program design and delivery in services such as health care and education are decentralized.[56] In practice, however, the balance between the central and regional governments is still highly asymmetrical; only seven of the eighteen autonomous communities have assumed responsibility for major programs such as education and health. Moreover, Spain has still not fully come to grips psychologically with the regional diversity implicit in a federal state. When the Basque regional government established a *salario social*, a minimum income for the poor designed to combat social exclusion, the central government reacted strongly against the initiative on the grounds that the benefit "might violate the constitutional right to equality of treatment for all Spanish citizens."[57]

Spain is also still finding its equilibrium in intergovernmental fiscal relations. The autonomous regions have recently been ceded greater capacity to raise their own revenues, and 45% of the 1998 budget of the autonomous region of Catalonia comes from own-source revenues. However, grants from the central state still constitute the most important revenue source, and interregional redistribution embedded in the system of central transfers means that the Catalan government has less total revenue per person than do poorer regions.[58] One consequence is that Catalonia is amassing a significant deficit in its health care program. This pattern is unlikely to be stable. Given the relative balance between the contributor and beneficiary regions, it would hardly be surprising if interregional fiscal solidarity is politicized in the years to come. So far, however, the claims of solidarity implicit in country-wide social programs has constrained a radical challenge to social citizenship, even in Catalan debates.

In summary, the political challenge to common social rights inherent in substate nationalism clearly differs from the dynamics generated by ethnic diversity. National minorities as well as majorities may disengage from a common social citizenship, generating much more complex political patterns. During the post-war period, cross-country social programs stood as a visible symbol of a common political community. In the contemporary period, the relationship between social rights and substate nationalism seems contradictory. The expansion of the welfare state contributed to the nationalist resurgence and generated intercommunal conflict over the control of social programs. At the same time, however, common social rights have also shown some capacity to mute nationalism's full force: they have helped to constrain, if only narrowly, Quebec separatism; and the claims of social solidarity may yet block more radical Flemish aspirations. Nevertheless, the future of the multination welfare state remains problematic. Resistance to interregional transfers and the pressures for decentralization are growing visibly in several of these countries. Unless decentralization were accompanied by some form of cross-country framework and enhanced interregional transfers, the long-term result would be a more variegated social landscape.

CONCLUDING REFLECTIONS

No general theory of multiculturalism and the welfare state flows from this discussion. The full implications of the politics of diversity for contemporary social policy remain to be mapped, and there is a compelling research agenda here.

Nevertheless, this survey does suggest that the concept of social citizenship retains relevance in a world of multicultural diversity. As Young has observed, "group differences are not 'natural facts'. They are made and constantly remade."[60] In that ongoing process of constructing identities and communities, social policy remains a potent instrument. However, the role of social citizenship as an instrument of cohesion varies considerably with respect to different dimensions of multiculturalism. The emergence of new immigrant minorities seems to pose the least formidable challenge to the integrative role of social rights. Admittedly, conflicts between immigrant communities and major public services are commonplace, and direct evidence on the views of ethnic minorities in Western democracies is especially limited. Nevertheless, the evidence that does exist suggests that the equality implicit in the concept of social citizenship is important to these groups. For ethnic minorities, especially those who are newly arrived or marginalized, strong social rights seem to be a stepping stone to fuller acceptance within the wider community. The primary challenge comes from majorities rather than minorities. Even here, however, the dominant story across Western democracies is one of incorporation. Countries that established a comprehensive welfare state in the post-war era have incorporated new forms of multicultural diversity without turning majority groups against the redistributive functions of the state, albeit perhaps at the price of more restrictive immigration policies. The politics of ethnicity and race have proven less benign in liberal welfare states, such as Australia, the United Kingdom, and, especially, the United States, where the post-war welfare state is less well rooted. Nevertheless, the predominant pattern across Western democracies remains incorporation in the regime of social benefits.

Substate nationalism poses a more compelling challenge to a common social citizenship. Here minorities as well as majorities can, for different reasons, withdraw. The current accommodation between the multination state and social citizenship reveals a contradictory syndrome. On the one hand, the expansion of the social role of government was one of the factors contributing to the mobilization of nationalist minorities in the post-war era, and control over social programs has been a durable source of political struggle in multination states. On the other hand, the inter-communal ties and solidarity inherent in common social programs can also help to constrain more radical nationalist agendas, as illustrated by the Belgian, Canadian, and Spanish cases. Such integrative ties may not ensure the actual survival of a common social model in several multination countries. Wearying of the struggle between conflicting internal nationalisms, these countries may surrender a common definition of social rights and devolve the definition of citizen-state relations onto constituent units without the pan-country framework and intercommunal transfers essential to preserving equal benefits for all citizens. Nevertheless, experience to date underscores the integrative potential of social citizenship, even on the challenging terrain of the multination state.

Thus, in the end, this survey suggests that the concepts of social rights and social citizenship remain relevant in a world of growing cultural diversity. They are, however, chastened concepts, and expectations of their integrative potential have considerably tempered the early optimism expressed by Marshall. Citizenship represents a less complete understanding of identity and community than in the post-war era. People in Western countries increasingly inhabit a world of multiple identities and diverse communities, all of which make separate claims on their imagination and energies. The status of citizen represents only one of these identities, one of the communities within which people find meaning and meet their social needs. In a world of multiple communities and loyalties, citizenship takes on a certain thinness.[60] Nevertheless, it is important to remember that citizenship has important advantages in a world of multiple communities. Its abstract nature and legal definition makes it potentially more inclusive than forms of community and social cohesion defined in purely cultural terms. Perhaps the case for a universal conception of social rights becomes more compelling, not less, as societies become more culturally diverse.

ACKNOWLEDGMENTS

Earlier versions of this paper were presented at the University of Saskatchewan, the Center for European Studies at Harvard University, and European University Institute in Florence. The paper has benefited from the research assistance of Peter Ciganik and Frieda Fuchs, and was strengthened by comments from Erich Bleich, Pepper Culpepper, Torben Iversen, Andrew Martin, Paul Pierson, Richard Simeon and Yasemin Soysal.

NOTES

1 T.H. Marshall, "Citizenship and Social Class," in *Citizenship and Social Class*, ed. T.H. Marshall and T. Bottomore, (London: Pluto Press, [1950] 1992), 8.
2 *Ibid.*, 24–5.
3 G. Esping-Andersen, *The Three Worlds of Welfare* (Princeton: Princeton University Press, 1990), 21.
4 R. Blake, *Canadians at Last: Canada Integrates Newfoundland as a Province* (Toronto: University of Toronto Press, 1994), 93. See also P. Neary, "Ebb and Flow: Citizenship in Newfoundland, 1929–1949," in *Belonging: The Meaning and Future of Canadian Citizenship*, ed. W. Kaplan, (Montreal and Kingston: McGill-Queen's University Press, 1993).
5 *Income Security and Social Services* (Ottawa: Information Canada, 1969), 68.
6 G. Shaifir, *Immigrants and Nationalists: Ethnic Conflict and Accommodation in Catalonia, the Basque Country, Latvia and Estonia* (Albany: State

University of New York Press, 1995); D. Conversi, *The Basques, the Catalans and Spain: Alternative Routes to Nationalist Mobilization* (Reno: University of Nevada Press, 1997); and Y. Abu-Laban and D. Stasiulis, "Ethnic Pluralism Under Siege: Popular and Partisan Opposition to Multiculturalism," *Canadian Public Policy* 17, no. 4 (1992): 365–86.

7 W. Kymlicka, *Multicultural Citizenship: A Liberal Theory of Minority Rights* (Oxford: Oxford University Press, 1995), 180.

8 See also C. Taylor, "Shared and Divergent Values," in *Options for a New Canada*, ed. R. Watts and D. Brown, (Toronto: University of Toronto Press, 1991); C. Taylor, "The Politics of Recognition," in *Multiculturalism and the 'Politics of Recognition'*, ed. A. Gutmann, (Princeton, Princeton University Press, 1992); and J. Barbalet, *Citizenship: Rights, Struggle and Class Inequality* (Milton Keynes, UK: Open University Press, 1988).

9 I. Young, "Polity and Group Differences: A Critique of the Idea of Universal Citizenship," *Ethics* 99, no. 2 (1989): 250–74; I. Young, *Justice and the Politics of Difference* (Princeton, Princeton University Press, 1990); and A. Phillips, "Whose Community? Which Individuals?" *Reinventing the Left*, ed. D. Miliband, (London: Polity Press, 1994).

10 D. Miller, *Market, State and Community: Theoretical Foundations of Market Socialism* (Oxford: Oxford University Press, 1989) and D. Miller, *On Nationality* (Oxford: Oxford University Press, 1995).

11 Young, *Justice and the Politics of Difference*, 179–80; Miller, *On Nationality*, 140.

12 A. Wolfe and J. Klausen, "Identity Politics and the Welfare State," *Social Philosophy & Policy* (1997): 231–55.

13 P. Taylor-Gooby, "Postmodernism and Social Policy: A Great Leap Backwards?," *Journal of Social Policy* 23, no. 3 (1994): 385–404. For more optimistic views, see S. Penna and M. O'Brien, "Postmodernism and Social Policy: A Small Step Forwards?," *Journal of Social Policy* 25, no. 1 (1996); also R. Plant, "Social Rights and the Reconstruction of Welfare," in *Citizenship*, ed. G. Andrews, (London: Lawrence and Wishart, 1991); and R. Plant, "Citizenship and Political Change," in *Reinventing the Left*.

14 In his early study of the determinants of social spending, Wilensky offers off-setting hypotheses on the implications of ethnolinguistic diversity, but only limited empirical analysis. H. Wilensky, *The Welfare State and Equality: Structural and Ideological Roots of Public Expenditure* (Berkeley: University of California Press, 1975). See also S. Gould and J. Palmer, "Outcomes, Interpretations, and Policy," in *The Vulnerable*, ed. J. Palmer, T. Smeeding, and B. Torrey, (Washington, DC: The Urban Institute Press, 1988).

15 W. Korpi, *The Democratic Class Struggle* (Boston: Routledge and Kegan Paul, 1983); W. Korpi, "Power, Politics and State Autonomy in the Development of Social Citizenship," *American Sociological Review* 54

(1989): 309–28; G. Esping-Andersen, *Politics Against Markets: The Social Democratic Road to Power* (Princeton: Princeton University Press, 1985); and Esping-Andersen, *The Three Worlds of Welfare*.

16 J. Stephens, *The Transition from Capitalism to Socialism* (Urbana: University of Illinois Press, 1979). For a discussion of the fears of some left-wing commentators in Europe that ethnic diversity will erode the capacity of the social-democratic welfare state to manage conflicts and that multiculturalism has usually been a rhetoric that disguises inequality, see J. Rex, "Ethnic Identity and the Nation State: The Political Sociology of Multi-Cultural Societies," *Social Identities* 1, no. 1 (1995): 21–34; and J. Rex, "Multiculturalism in Europe and America," *Nations and Nationalism* 1, no. 2 (1995): 243–59.

17 E. Huber, C. Ragin, and J. Stephens, "Social Democracy, Christian Democracy, Constitutional Structure, and the Welfare State," *American Journal of Sociology* 99, no. 3 (1993): 711–49; A. Hicks and D. Swank, "Politics, Institutions and Welfare Spending in Industrialized Democracies, 1960–82," *American Political Science Review* 86, no. 3 (1992): 658–74; A. Hicks and J. Misra, "Political Resources and Growth of Welfare in Affluent Capitalist Democracies, 1960–1982," *American Journal of Sociology* 99, no. 3 (1993): 668–710; and D. Rodrik, *Has Globalization Gone Too Far?* (Washington, DC: Institute for International Economics, 1997).

18 D. Mueller and P. Murrell, "Interest Groups and the Size of Government," *Public Choice* 48 (1986): 125–45.

19 E. James, "The Public/Private Division of Responsibility for Education: An International Comparison," *Economics of Education Review* 6, no. 1 (1987): 1–14; E. James, "Why Do Different Countries Choose a Different Public/Private Mix of Education Services?," *Journal of Human Resources* 28, no. 3 (1993): 531–92; T. McCarty, "Demographic Diversity and the Size of the Public Sector," *KYKLOS* 46, no. 2 (1993): 225–40; W. Easterly and R. Levine, "Africa's Growth Tragedy: Policies and Ethnic Divisions," *Quarterly Journal of Economics* 112, no. 4 (1997): 1203–50.

20 However, economists have completed comparable studies of the provision of public services at the municipal level in the United States and have found evidence that ethnic diversity is associated with reduced provision of services such as roads, schools, garbage collection and libraries. A. Alesina, R. Baqir and W. Easterly, "Public Goods and Ethnic Divisions," *NBER Working Paper Series*, no. 6009, Cambridge, MA, 1997.

21 This definition of the differences between ethnic and national minorities follows Kymlicka, *Multicultural Citizenship*, Miller, *On Nationality*, and many others.

22 Fully private Muslim schools in Britain have faced financial difficulties, however, and the primary pressure has been for support for Muslim schools

within the state system, as in the case of Anglican and Catholic schools. The issue had been contentious for a number of years, and several applications have been rejected. However, the first such school was approved in 1998.

23 On the attitudes of East European migrants to Western Europe, see E. Morawska, "Structuring Migration in a Historical Perspective: The Case of Traveling East Europeans," Working Paper Series EUF 98/3, European University Institute, Florence, 1998.

24 D. Kinder and L. Sanders, *Divided by Colour: Racial Prejudices and Democratic Ideals* (Chicago: University of Chicago Press, 1996), 29, 299.

25 For a thorough analysis of the attitudes of different ethnic and racial minorities in Britain, see T. Madood *et al.*, *Ethnic Minorities in Britain: Diversity and Disadvantage* (London: Policy Studies Institute, 1997).

26 On the concept of "welfare chauvinism," see J. Andersen and T. Bjørklund, "Structural Changes and New Cleavages: The Progress Parties in Denmark and Norway," *Acta Sociologica* 33, no. 3 (1990): 195–217; J. Andersen, "Denmark: The Progress Party – Populist Neo-Liberalism and Welfare State Chauvinism," in *The Extreme Right in Europe and the USA*, ed. P. Hainsworth, (New York: St. Martin's Press, 1992); and H. Kitschelt, *The Radical Right in Western Europe: A Comparative Analysis* (Ann Arbor: University of Michigan Press, 1995).

27 R. Bank, "Europeanization of the Reception of Asylum Seekers: The Opposite of Welfare State Politics," paper presented to the Conference on Migration and the Welfare State in Contemporary Europe, European University Institute, Florence, May 1998.

28 Y. Soysal, *Limits of Citizenship: Migrants and Postnational Membership in Europe* (Chicago: University of Chicago Press, 1994). See also R. Brubaker, *Citizenship and Nationhood in France and Germany* (Cambridge, MA: Harvard University Press, 1992).

29 Nor does an emphasis on a transnational commitment to human rights explain the continued exclusion of immigrants from full political rights in many of the countries that provide the fullest social benefits. For discussions of this difference, see R. Brubaker, "Citizenship and Naturalization: Policies and Politics," in *Immigration and the Politics of Citizenship in Europe and North America*, ed. R. Brubaker, (Latham: University Press of America, 1989); Brubaker, *Citizenship and Nationhood in France and Germany*; and V. Guiraudon, "The Marshallian Triptych Re-ordered? Institutional Pre-conditions for an Inclusive Regime for Migrants Welfare Benefits," paper presented to the Conference on Migration and the Welfare State in Contemporary Europe, European University Institute, Florence, Italy, May 1998.

30 F.O. Radtke, "Multiculturalism in Welfare States: The Case of Germany," in *Nationalism, Multiculturalism and Migration*, ed. M. Guibernau and J. Rex (London: Polity Press, 1997), 251.

31 A. Messina, "Political Impediments to the Resumption of Labour Migration to Western Europe," *West European Politics* 13, no. 1 (1990): 31–46; A. Messina, "The Not So Silent Revolution: Postwar Migration to Western Europe," *World Politics* 49 (1996), 30–45; J. Hollifield, *Immigrants, Markets and States: The Political Economy of Postwar Europe* (Cambridge, MA: Harvard University Press, 1992).

32 J. Hollifield, "Grand Bargain Strategies for Immigration and Immigrant Policy," paper presented to the Conference on Migration and the Welfare State in Contemporary Europe, European University Institute, Florence, Italy, May 1998.

33 For example, in the French town of Vitrolles, the National Front government began giving special "birth allowances" to families that have children, but not to immigrant families. National authorities asked the administrative courts to strike down the measure as unconstitutionally discriminatory. C. Whitney, "Chirac Puts Regional Allies on Spot after Deals with Far Right," *New York Times*, 25 March 1998, A5.

34 Kitschelt, *The Radical Right in Western Europe*, 258–59; see also H.-G. Betz, *Radical Right-Wing Populism in Western Europe* (New York: St. Martin's Press, 1994).

35 O. Borre and E. Scarborough, eds, *The Scope of Government*, vol. 3 of *Beliefs in Government*, (Oxford: Oxford University Press, 1995).

36 Brubaker, "Citizenship and Naturalization."

37 This paragraph relies heavily on information from the Organization for Economic Co-operation and Development.

38 These residency requirements can be waived if disability or lone parenthood takes place after immigration, or if adverse economic circumstances result from factors beyond the individual's control, such as the death of a financial sponsor.

39 M. Gilens, "Racial Attitudes and Opposition to Welfare," *Journal of Politics* 57, no. 4 (1995): 994–1014; M. Gilens, "Race Coding and White Opposition to Welfare," *American Political Science Review* 90, no. 3 (1996): 593–604.

40 L.F. Williams, "Race and the Politics of Social Policy" in *The Social Divide: Political Parties and the Future of Activist Government*, ed. M. Weir, (Washington, DC: Brookings Institution, 1998); and T. Skocpol, "Targeting Within Universalism: Politically Viable Policies to Combat Poverty in the United States," in *The Urban Underclass*, ed. C. Jencks and P. Peterson, (Washington, D.C.: Brookings Institution, 1991). On the role of race in the politics of social policy during the 1960s and 1970s see J. Quadagno, "Race, Class and Gender in the United States Welfare State: Nixon's Failed Family Assistance Plan," *American Sociological Review* 55 (1990): 11–28; and J. Quadagno, *The Color of Welfare: How Racism Undermined the War on Poverty* (New York: Oxford University Press, 1994).

41 K. Weaver, "Ending Welfare As We Know It," in *The Social Divide: Political Parties and the Future of Activist Government*, ed. M. Weir, (Washington, DC: The Brookings Institution, 1998).

42 State jurisdictions do have the flexibility to provide Medicaid and TANF to new immigrants within the five-year period from their own funds, but it unclear how many states are doing so.

43 W. Wilson, *When Work Disappears: The World of the New Urban Poor* (New York: Random House, 1996).

44 *Into the 21st Century: A Strategy for Immigration and Citizenship* (Ottawa: Ministry of Supply and Services, 1994).

45 The 1993 Canadian Election Study found that opposition to immigration and multicultural policy was especially concentrated in the support base of the Reform Party. As I discuss later, the party's electoral support is also correlated strongly with anti-Quebec feelings.

46 G. Freeman, "Migration and the Political Economy of the Welfare State," *Annals of the American Academy of Political and Social Science* 485, 51–63.

47 A. Alen et al., *Vlaaderen Op Een Kruispunt: Sociologische, Economische en Staatsrechtelijke perspectieven* (Leuven: Lannoo, 1990), 141–51. The "income paradox" disappeared after the early 1990s, but the intercommunal transfers remain significant.

48 The research group issued a lengthy list of reports on the social security system. However, their proposals for the future are set out in D. Pieters, *Federalisms Voor Onze Sociale Zekerheid* (Leuven: Acco, 1994); and J. Bertels, D. Pieters, P. Schoukens, and S. Vansteenkiste, *De Vlaamse Sociale Zekerheid in 101 Vragen En Antwoorden* (Leuven: Acco, 1997).

49 Based on interviews with officials of the Flemish parliament, May 1998.

50 J. Fitzmaurice, "Diversity and Civil Society: The Belgian Case," unpublished manuscript, 1998.

51 K. Banting, *The Welfare State and Canadian Federalism*, 2d ed. (Montreal and Kingston: McGill-Queen's University Press, 1987); K. Banting, "The Welfare State as Statecraft: Territorial Politics and Canadian Social Policy," in *European Social Policy: Between Fragmentation and Integration*, ed. S. Leibfried and P. Pierson, (Washington, DC: The Brookings Institution, 1995).

52 Kymlicka, *Multicultural Citizenship*, 188; and Taylor, "Shared and Divergent Values."

53 I am indebted to Matthew Mendelsohn for his insights on this issue, and for his assistance with relevant polling data. His draft note, "Evolution of Quebecers' Identity and Attachment to Quebec and Canada" was particularly helpful.

54 For a fuller discussion, see K. Banting, "The Past Speaks to the Future: Lessons from the Postwar Social Union," in *Canada: The State of the Federation 1997: Non-Constitutional Renewal*, ed. H. Lazar, (Kingston: Institute of Intergovernmental Relations, Queen's University, 1998). Some advocates of full decentralization argue that a pan-Canadian approach to

core social programs such as medicare could be sustained through a com-
pact among provincial governments, but this claim is contentious. See,
among others: T. Courchene, "ACCESS: A Convention on the Canadian
Economic and Social Systems," working paper for the Ministry of Intergovernmental Affairs, Government of Ontario (1996); Institute of Intergovernmental Relations, *Assessing ACCESS* (Kingston: Queen's University,
Institute of Intergovernmental Relations, 1997); and S. Kennett, *Securing
the Social Union: A Commentary on the Decentralized Approach* (Kingston: Queen's University, Institute of Intergovernmental Relations, 1998).

55 Reform Party of Canada, *A Fresh Start for Canadians* (Calgary: Reform
Party of Canada, 1997); Reform Party of Canada, *Blue Sheet: Principles &
Policies of the Reform Party of Canada – 1996–97* (Calgary: Reform Party
of Canada, 1997).

56 R. Agranoff, "Federal Evolution in Spain," *International Political Science
Review* 17, no. 4 (1996): 385–401; A. Guillén, "Welfare State Development in Spain," in *Comparing Social Welfare Systems in Southern Europe*,
ed. U. Ascoli *et al.* (Paris: MIRE, 1997); A. Rico, "Regional Decentralization and Health Care Reform in Spain (1976–1996)," in *Comparing Social
Welfare Systems in Southern Europe*, ed. U. Ascoli *et al.*.

57 M. Laparra and M. Hendrickson, "Social exclusion and minimum income
programs in Spain," in *Comparing Social Welfare Systems in Southern Europe*, ed. U. Ascoli *et al.* (Paris: MIRE, 1997), 528. Other regions have since
established *salario social* programs, but there remains significant regional
variation: "some regions have established important programs that reach
most of the severely poor population, while in other cases the programs
barely exist." Laparra and Hendrickson, 528.

58 J. Solé-Vilanova, "The Political Economy of Fiscal Federalism in Spain: Following the Canadian Way?" Unpublished manuscript, 1998. The Basque
Country and Navarre are not part of the general regime of intergovernmental financial relations. In their cases, a separate regime is determined
through private negotiations between the central government and the regional governments.

59 Young, "Polity and Group Difference," 133; also B. Anderson, *Imagined
Communities: Reflections on the Origins and Spread of Nationalism*, rev.
ed. (London: Verso, 1991).

60 See the discussion of "high citizenship" and "low citizenship" in R. Flatham,
"Citizenship and Authority: A Chastened View of Citizenship," in *Theorizing Citizenship*, ed. R. Beiner, (Albany: State University of New York, 1995);
and R. Beiner, "Why Citizenship Constitutes a Theoretical Problem in the
Last Decade of the Twentieth Century," in *Theorizing Citizenship*, ed. R.
Beiner, (Albany: State University of New York, 1995). See also J. Habermas,
"Struggles for Recognition in the Democratic Constitutional State," in *Multiculturalism: Examining the Politics of Recognition*, ed. A. Gutmann, (Princeton, Princeton University Press, 1994).

7 Is Citizenship a Gendered Concept?

C. LYNN SMITH

Is citizenship a gendered concept? The cultural and legal shift that ended the formal exclusion of women from citizenship took place within living memory, the presence of women in political life is still slight, yet the gender dimension is absent from many discussions of citizenship. Before exploring the connection between gender and citizenship, I will address the meaning of those two terms. In his Introduction to this volume, Alan Cairns talks about a new emphasis on "identities and memories." The first question we ask about a baby – "Is it a boy or a girl?" – reflects the importance of gender as a socially constructed identity. As for memories, in this chapter I will remind the reader, through a fairly standard feminist critique of citizenship, that women's memories about citizenship are different from those of men. They are about relentless exclusion for most of the time that citizenship has existed as a concept, followed by formal inclusion only after a long battle, and by the current ongoing struggle to achieve meaningful, functional inclusion.

WHAT DOES "GENDERED" MEAN?

By a "gendered" concept I mean one that is connected with differential roles for men and women and that carries connotations arising from a history of being applied to only one sex. My reference point is the Western European cultural tradition and political theory of citizenship and gender. In Ruth Lister's phrase, "one does not need to be a signed up post-modernist to accept that it is no longer good enough to adopt a one-dimensional gender analysis based on an understanding of women and men as unitary categories."[1] However, a one-dimensional gender analysis did play a central role in the development of "citizenship" in the Western European tradition, as I will describe. Further, to quote Nancy Harstock:

> Why is it, exactly at the moment when so many of us who have been silenced begin to demand the right to name ourselves, to act as subjects rather than objects of history, that just then the concept of subjecthood becomes problematic? Just when we are forming our own theories about the world, uncertainty emerges about whether the world can be adequately theorized? Just when we are talking about the changes we want, ideas of progress and the possibility of "meaningfully" organizing human society become suspect?[2]

Thus, I will refer to "women" and "men" and "citizenship," trying to avoid unitary categories but perhaps not always succeeding.

I also mean to ask, by phrasing the question this way, whether the role of "citizen" is "male shaped" such that it fits women uneasily, in the same way that the role of "leader" has been tailored to fit the men who have been leaders throughout history and who are still overwhelmingly the political and business leaders in our time. (The connection between "citizen" and "leader" is a strong one in a democracy. Our political leaders, at least, are drawn from the pool of citizens; to some extent, good citizens are thought to require some characteristics of good leaders, and vice versa.) An extreme case of a "male-shaped" role would be "Pope." "Leader of a Group of Seven country" is close. An extreme case of a "female-shaped" role would be – what? Interestingly, it is difficult to think of one that is unrelated to biological reproduction (e.g., "mother") or to sexuality (e.g., "whore.")[3] The closest approximations outside those categories have clear cultural connections to them: "nursemaid," "kindergarten teacher," "secretary," "exotic dancer." The first question, then, is whether the concept of "citizenship" (and thus, "citizen" and "potential leader in a democracy") is gendered in the sense that it has been tailored to fit men and men's life experiences and still retains that shape in a way that matters.

WHAT DOES "CITIZENSHIP" MEAN?

In T. H. Marshall's terms, citizenship has three aspects: civil, political, and social. These can be seen as referring to different bundles of rights. The civil bundle includes the rights "necessary for individual freedom – liberty of the person, freedom of speech, thought and faith, the right to own property and to conclude valid contracts, and the right to justice

... [i.e.,] the right to defend and assert all one's rights on terms of equality with others and by due process of law." The political bundle holds the "right to participate in the exercise of political power, as a member of a body invested with political authority or as an elector of the members of such a body." The social bundle comprises "the whole range from the right to a modicum of economic welfare and security to the right to share to the full in the social heritage and to live the life of a civilised being according to the standards prevailing in the society."[4]

Marshall sets these rights out in this order to reflect the sequence in which they were developed: first civil, then political, then social. However, what he describes is the sequence in which the various bundles of rights were conferred upon *men*. As Barbara Marshall points out, liberal conceptions of citizenship such as T.H. Marshall's see "women's rights as part and parcel of the inevitable extension of citizenship to an increasingly wider circle of individuals. What this account fails to capture is the manner in which the exclusion of some groups from citizenship has been, from the start, integral to the entitlement of other groups." With respect to women, the history of rights was different, and T.H. Marshall's "periodisation of the evolution of citizenship rights is faulty." There were first some elements of social citizenship, through benefit programs aimed at poor women and children, then some aspects of political citizenship as a result of the suffrage movement, and finally (likely only because of the successful campaign for political citizenship embodied in the extension of the franchise) the conferral of the major civil aspects of citizenship:

Women's relationship to the welfare state has always been, and remains, contradictory. At the same time that it has regulated and shaped the gender-specific parameters of social life, the welfare state has provided a basis for women's social citizenship. This paradoxical relationship of women to the welfare state is strengthened as the latter comes under attack – the women's movement has, as Banting ... puts it, emerged as "one of the political bulwarks of the social role of the state." Few feminists, despite their criticisms, would wish to see the welfare state dismantled.[5]

Although the legal definition of citizenship provides only one dimension, it is a starting point for an analysis of the concept. Legal citizenship relates to formal membership in the nation-state, membership that carries with it a bundle of rights along with certain duties and responsibilities. These may fall within all three of Marshall's categories: civil, political and social. It is one of a pair of opposites: "citizen" and "alien." Anglo-American law defines any natural person as either one or the other, and this determination is made by the country whose citizenship is at issue. Constitutionally, citizenship is matter of federal responsibility in Canada, exercised since 1947 through the Citizenship Act.

What we think of as the law of citizenship addresses topics such as acquisition of citizenship through birth or naturalization, the loss of citizenship (for example, if fraud was involved in an application for citizenship), and the consequences of citizenship (right to apply for a passport, right to return to the country, eligibility for public office and the franchise). In *Winner v. S.M.T. (Eastern) Ltd.*, the Supreme Court decided that it is Parliament, not the provincial legislatures, that can legislate on matters of citizenship. It said: "The first and fundamental accomplishment of the constitutional Act was the creation of single political organization of subjects of His Majesty within the geographical area of the Dominion, the basic postulate of which was the institution of a Canadian citizenship. Citizenship is membership in a state; and in the citizen inhere those rights and duties, the correlatives of allegiance and protection, which are basic to that status."[6]

In a later case, *Re Citizenship Act; Re Noailles*, the Federal Court of Canada said: "Canada has the right to protect itself by denying the privilege of citizenship to someone who does not meet the criteria legitimately established by an Act of Parliament."[7]

Citizenship and personhood are related concepts; only natural persons can be citizens (except metaphorically, as in "good corporate citizen"), and citizenship is an aspect of personhood. In the words of Mr Justice LaForest in *Andrews v. Law Society of British Columbia*: "The characteristic of citizenship is one typically not within the control of the individual and, in this sense, is immutable. Citizenship is, at least temporarily, a characteristic of personhood not alterable by conscious action and in some cases not alterable except on the basis of unacceptable costs."[8]

CITIZENSHIP AND PERSONHOOD

The "persons case"[9] of 1928 illustrates the relationship between citizenship and personhood. The question was whether women (who, if they were non-Aboriginal and non-Oriental, were at least partly "citizens" in the sense that they had the franchise and were British subjects with Canadian nationality) were eligible to be called to the Senate of Canada under the British North America Act of 1867, Section 24, which specified that "qualified Persons" could be so summoned.[10] The Supreme Court said that they could not. Its reasons are instructive. Chief Justice Anglin, beginning with a disclaimer ("In considering this matter we are, of course, in no wise concerned with the desirability or the undesirability of the presence of women in the Senate, nor with any political aspect of the question submitted"[11]), went on to say that they must give the provisions of the British North America Act the same meaning in 1928 as they would have in 1867. At that time, women were under a legal incapacity to hold public office. The rationale for that exclusion was stated to be, in the cases cited by the Supreme Court, "motives of decorum, and ... a privilege of the sex."[12] The problem was not so much the word "person" as the qualifier, "qualified." The Supreme Court commented that the word "person," standing alone, included women: "It connotes human beings – the criminal and the insane equally with the good and the wise citizen, the minor as well as the adult." The conclusion was nevertheless that women were ineligible for the Senate. However, on appeal, the Judicial Committee of the Privy Council disagreed, and offered near the outset of their reasons the following comment:

The exclusion of women from all public offices is a relic of days more barbarous than ours, but it must be remembered that the necessity of the times often forced on man customs which in later years were not necessary. Such exclusion is probably due to the fact that the deliberative assemblies of the early tribes were attended by men under arms, and women did not bear arms.[13]

Thus, the Supreme Court of Canada said the rationale for the exclusion of women from public life was decorum and privilege (a benefit to women), while the Privy Council said that it was the (outmoded) connection between citizenship and warlike skills.[14]

THE PUBLIC AND PRIVATE SPHERES

Underlying both rationales stated by the Supreme Court is the notion that women's nature is unsuited for public life, and that there are separate spheres of life (public and private) that are very clearly gendered. Beginning with Aristotle, influential political theorists argued that women's reproductive function destined them for the private (domestic) sphere, while men (initially, only subsets of men – free, property owning, white men) were destined to participate in public life and to represent their households, including "their" women and children, in the external world. Will Kymlicka, referring to Okin's work, summarizes this view in his survey of the liberal and socialist traditions in political theory:

In any event, the reform which is perhaps most needed has not been adequately addressed by either tradition – namely, the critique of gender. Throughout both traditions, while men are viewed as having (autonomously chosen) ends, women are viewed as having (biologically given) functions. While liberals from Locke through Mill to Rawls have officially proclaimed that their theories are based on the natural equality of individuals, they have in fact taken the male-headed family as the essential unit of political analysis; women's interests are defined by, and submerged in, the family, which is taken to be their "natural" position.[15]

The dictates of destiny were clear: not only were women *best* suited for domestic pursuits, they were suited *only* for them. Participation of women in public life would be a bad thing for society because of women's incapacity to rise above the "particular" and to consider matters of the "public good."[16] (An interesting echo of this perception is found in the persistent description of women who raise issues affecting women primarily, such as child care or the gender imbalance in decision-making positions, as advocating "special interests" rather than the "public good".) Of course, the record to date of women's performance in public life does not support the proposition that they are less able than men to pursue the "public good." Further, political theorist Iris Marion Young points out that the proposition that "all citizens should assume the same impartial, general point of view transcending all particular interests, perspectives and experiences" in exercising their citizenship is problematic. Because people "necessarily and properly consider public issues in terms influenced by their situated experience and perception of social relations," such an "impartial general perspective is a myth":

Different social groups have different needs, cultures, histories, experiences, and perceptions of social relations which influence their interpretation of the meaning and consequences of policy proposals and influence the form of their political reasoning. These differences in political interpretation are not merely or even primarily a result of differing or conflicting interests, for groups have differing interpretations even when they seek to promote justice and not merely their own self-regarding ends. In a society where some groups are privileged while others are oppressed, insisting that as citizens persons should leave behind their particular affiliations and experiences to adopt a general point of view serves only to reinforce that privilege; for the perspectives and interests of the privileged will tend to dominate this unified public, marginalizing or silencing those of other groups.[17]

Young argues that, so long as there are disadvantaged and oppressed groups, measures should be taken to provide mechanisms for the effective recognition and representation of their distinct voices and perspectives. This can be part of what she calls "differentiated citizenship."

Although the franchise and the removal of the legal incapacity to hold public office (which, in Canada, took place in a long series of steps beginning in the nineteenth century and ending in the mid-twentieth century) was an important milestone in the progress of women toward full citizenship, that change did not automatically bring about an end to the notions that underpinned women's exclusion. Jean Bethke Elshtain describes "mainstream political science" as studying power under this definition: "X has power over Y if he can get Y to do something Y would not otherwise do." She writes that within this definition

women got construed as apolitical beings ... . The argument was really quite simple. Women and men have different social roles. The social role of women promotes a value-system based upon women's "life experiences" inside non-political areas of social relations – marriage, the family, religious and communal associations. Not occupying decision-making roles and arenas, women are severed from the give and take of interest-group politics and its rule-governed power brokerage. Women are neither the X's with power-over nor the Y's whose behaviour is compelled. Women do not figure in the geometry of power relations. Even voting by women is essentially an apolitical activity, a means whereby women, who tend to be moralists hence conservative, support those political parties that appear to confirm their values rather than promote their interests. Promoting interests is a political activity; preserving values is non-political.[18]

Her comments, and those of others such as Lister and Pateman, remind us that the story is complex. Women were both powerless and powerful in earlier societies. A theme in most cultures is the "unofficial" power of women, through which they exercise considerable control over many aspects of life. Elshtain argues that this was more the case when the home was not only a centre of human reproduction but also of economic production, of treatment of the sick and dying, and of education. She writes:

We cannot return to pre-secular, pre-modern ways of life. But we can see that secular male dominance is most visible in societies in which complementarity of powers has given way to an enhancement and expansion of institutionalized male authority accompanied by a simultaneous diminution of women's domestic, sacral and informal authority. As the world of female power recedes, the sphere of male power encroaches, absorbing more and more features of social life into the orbit of the juridicopolitical, the bureaucratised, the "legitimately" powerful: the state.

Under such circumstances, Elshtain concludes, women are left with few apparent options. Among their choices are:

to acquiesce in their historic loss of symbolic-domestic authority; to manipulate their diminished social role as mothers inside increasingly powerless families;

or to join forces with the men, assuming masculine roles and identities and competing for power on established, institutionalized terms. For if one embraces a strong version of the teleology of historic progress we have inherited from the Enlightenment, with its attendant ontology that locates "women" on the negative side of the ledger along with nature, emotion and passion, one has little choice but to leap into the arms of the hegemonic discourse and to embrace the already established vision of the free, rational, wholly independent male self and his powers and power.[19]

THE NEED FOR TRANSFORMATION OF CITIZENSHIP

There is sometimes an assumption that those who fought for political citizenship did not understand, as our much wiser generation does, that it is partial and gendered, and that of course they did not understand the risks of "leaping into the arms of the hegemonic discourse." (How many of us do?). However, as Carol Pateman argues,

[a] common interpretation of the history of women's struggle for citizenship, and especially for the suffrage, is that it was simply a campaign for equality, for the "rights of men and citizens" to be extended to women. This view misunderstands the way in which our predecessors fought for citizenship. From at least 1792, when Mary Wollstonecraft's *A Vindication of the Rights of Woman* was published, women have demanded both equal civil and political rights, and that their difference from men should be acknowledged in their citizenship. Most suffragists, for example, argued that womanhood suffrage was required as a matter of justice and to make government by consent a reality, and also that the distinctive contribution that they could make to political life as women was a major reason why they should be enfranchised.[20]

In his introduction to the second edition of Catherine Cleverdon's history of the woman suffrage movement in Canada, Ramsay Cook quotes a suffrage movement leader who said:

Let no confident friend of the movement anticipate too great results from such success. That it will be followed by great disappointment to many – happy disappointment to those who fear, and unhappy to those who hope – there can be little doubt. It will effect far less change than is generally fancied; at first scarcely any. All social evils will not be voted down; nor the offices all filled with saints at the next election thereafter. It will not be found the panacea for all human, or all womanly, ills. It will scarcely be the *cure* of any. It will simply be the opening of another door – the passage into a larger freedom ... . But to work out her complete womanhood vastly more is required than the right of suffrage.[21]

Eligibility for public office and for the franchise is only one aspect of citizenship. The "civil citizenship" referred to by T.H. Marshall includes the right to invoke the process of law to maintain one's own bodily integrity, and this mattered to many more women than did ineligibility for the Senate. In this sense of citizenship, women did not become full citizens in Canada until the 1980s, when Parliament removed the legal immunity (both civil and criminal) for husbands who raped their wives[22] and when the Supreme Court of Canada confirmed the right for a woman to decide whether to carry a pregnancy to term.[23]

A still more expansive definition of citizenship looks to a community as well as to a state and incorporates the participation in and the taking of responsibility for that community. When we talk of citizenship in this way, we are often talking about rights and duties that are not limited in law to those who are formally citizens. Formal citizenship or permanent residency is an important factor in many social benefit programs and, on the other side of the coin, in the taxation system that supports them.[24] However, formal citizenship is not required for some other forms of participation or entitlement. The Canadian Charter of Rights and Freedoms is limited to "citizens" only with respect to electoral rights (Section 2), mobility rights (Section 6) and minority language education rights (Section 23). The other rights and freedoms apply to "everyone," "persons," or "individuals." The Andrews case, referred to earlier[25] was about whether it should be necessary to be a citizen to practise law; the Supreme Court of Canada said that such a requirement contravened the equality rights in the Charter. The civil courts of justice are available to anyone who wishes to invoke their process (although there are jurisdictional limits on who may be called to account to them and requirements on non-resident plaintiffs to post security for costs in some circumstances.) At the local level, formal citizenship is generally irrelevant to participation. This fact may have a bearing on the much higher participation rate of women in local politics and community organizations than in higher-level politics.

Aboriginal women and women from non-Western cultures may have a different sense about the public–private divide.[26] Many feminists have seen it as a tool to disempower women, as their centres of power (homes, communities) became less important in public life, and as the state continued to refrain from protecting women (for example, from violence) within that narrowing "private" sphere. However, from the perspective of an Aboriginal woman, the state (represented by national forces of homogenization and intervention) may be more dangerous than the traditional community. From the perspective of many women, the national state itself is becoming less important and the forces represented by the other meaning of "private" – not as in "domestic" but as in "private sector" or "the market" – now operating on a global scale, cause the most concern.

IS TRANSFORMATION OF CITIZENSHIP POSSIBLE?

A conclusion that citizenship was, and remains, a gendered concept in the sense that it was custom-tailored to fit male roles, and explicitly designed *not* to fit female roles, is hardly new or radical. Political theorists such as Carole Pateman and Susan Muller Okin have been writing about this subject for over a decade. The hard questions that remain are: (1) "What follows from this? Can the house of universal citizenship as we understand it be remodelled to meet both women's and men's needs?" and (2) "How, if at all, can a remodelling project based on gender concerns be fitted into a national agenda that also includes proposals to retrofit to meet the needs of members of different cultures, physical and mental abilities, and sexual orientations, to construct new buildings for Aboriginals and to subdivide the property as between Québécois and others by carving out a middle piece (where the family archives are found)?"

My answers to those questions are a guarded "Yes," and an equally guarded "With difficulty." I will concentrate on the first question.

The first question has been formulated in different ways. Okin, responding to a challenge posed by John Pocock, addresses the question "whether (and, if so, how) women can claim citizenship in anything like the 'classical' sense, as he construes it, or whether (and, if so, how) they should 'subvert or deconstruct the ideal itself as a device constructed in order to exclude them.'" She responds that "women can, and have every right to, claim citizenship in something like the classical sense, but ... in many respects the ideal does have to be subverted or deconstructed – not only in order to include women, but in order to be an improved ideal for men too."[27]

Pateman refers to the "familial feminism" predominant in France a century after the French revolution, in which feminists argued that "the state should support women in their duty as mothers and improve the material conditions of motherhood, and that those who performed this national task should be granted the standing and rights of citizens." Commenting that Mary Wollstonecraft had made the same argument during the period of the French Revolution, she writes:

The problem with this feminist strategy is that it remains impaled on the horns of what I have called Wollstonecraft's dilemma. The dilemma arises because, within the existing patriarchal conception of citizenship, the choice always has to be made between equality and difference, or between equality and woman-hood. On the one hand, to demand "equality" is to strive for equality with men (to call for the "rights of men and citizens" to be extended to women), which means that women must become (like) men. On the other hand, to insist, like some contemporary feminists, that women's distinctive attributes, capacities and activities be revalued and treated as a contribution to citizenship is to demand the impossible; such "difference" is precisely what patriarchal citizenship excludes.

Pateman concludes that the equal political standing of citizenship is nec-essary for democracy and for women's autonomy. She says, however, that the historical examples

should also illustrate that the heart of the matter is not sexual difference but women's subordination. "Equality," like other central political categories, is a contested term; but whereas "equality" in some of its possible meanings can encompass "difference," no sense of "equality" compatible with a genuinely democratic citizenship can accommodate subordination. By a "genuinely dem-ocratic citizenship," I mean that both sexes are full citizens and that their citi-zenship is of equal worth to them as women and men. For that to be the case, the meaning of sexual difference has to cease to be the difference between free-dom and subordination. The issue in the problem of "difference" is women's freedom.[28]

Elsewhere, Pateman has argued that "to develop a theory in which women and femininity have an autonomous place means that the pri-vate and the public, the social and the political, also have to be com-pletely reconceptualised; in short, it means an end to the long history of sexually particular theory that masquerades as universalism."[29]

Finally, Ruth Lister has addressed the question of gender and citizen-ship, beginning from the assertion by Hall and Held that there may be "an irreconcilable tension between the thrust to equality and universal-ity entailed in the very notion of the 'citizen' and the variety of particu-lar and specific needs, of diverse sites and practices which constitute the modern political subject." She characterizes the issue as "whether a concept originally predicated on the very exclusion of women can be re-formulated so as satisfactorily to include [and not simply add] them [on]; and whether, in doing so, it can give full recognition to the differ-ent and shifting identities that women simultaneously hold." Lister concludes that without the ideal of universality the concept of citizen-ship loses all political force. It is thus still worth pursuing from a femi-nist perspective, despite the difficulties. She adds "I would also argue that the deconstruction of the category 'woman' has not invalidated the project of engendering citizenship. The patterns of exclusion from citizenship are themselves sufficiently gendered to justify the exercise." She argues that "a rounded and fruitful theorization of citizenship, which can be of potential value to women, has to embrace *both* individual rights (and, in particular, social rights) *and* political participation and has also to analyze the relationship between the two." Not only formal but also informal forms of political participation (in social movements or community groups) should be encompassed, and it should be recognized that the public/private divide is an essentially contested and profoundly gendered concept. Rejecting the "dilemma," Lister argues for a conception that combines the gender-neutrality of an approach that seeks to enable women to participate with men as equals in the public sphere (suitably transformed) with a gender-differentiated recognition and valuing of women's responsibilities in the private sphere.[30]

I think that the conception of citizenship can continue to be transformed such that (to use Pateman's terms) "both sexes are full citizens and that their citizenship is of equal worth to them as women and men." Why do I think that this is possible? (Note that what is possible is not necessarily inevitable, and may not even be probable.)

The Expansion of the Practical Aspects of Citizenship to Include Women

We have seen practical aspects of citizenship – civil, political, and social – expand to include women. Unless the forces envisioned in *The Handmaid's Tale*[31] materialize, women will continue to participate and will expect to be treated as full citizens. The participation rate of women in formal political life continues to increase, although slowly, and the participation of women in community-level politics and in municipal government is relatively high. Further experience in the role will lead to increased expectations. To some extent, the very existence of the Canadian Charter of Rights and Freedoms with its equality guarantees heightens those expectations, as Alan Cairns has commented. Although I take some issue with his term "Charter citizens" (which, like "new Canadians," puts a marker in front of the term to single out the strange and the foreign) I think that he is right that the coming into being of the Charter marked a turning point in our expectations about citizen participation in national constitutional discussions.[32]

At the same time, the low rate of women's uptake of the offer of citizenship on basically men's terms, at least as measured by the less than one in five members of elected legislatures who are women, says something. The practical barriers to women's participation remain in place, and retired women politicians have described the current way of doing politics as "testosterone frenzy." Christine Boyle, pointed out that "The factor which predominated in the past has been geography, and yet it is not at all clear why it is more significant than sex, race, or economic factors ... . We lump numbers of two very different groups, men and women, together for political purposes simply because they live in close proximity to each other."[33] Expressing astonishment that the under-representation of women is not seen as more of a problem, she argues that expecting men in our current world to represent women is like expecting central Canadians to represent Newfoundlanders.

Nevertheless, I remain hopeful that women's participation will continue to increase. Similarly, I think that the presence of women will have an impact on the way politics is done and on the products of the political process.

The Relationship with Other Transformative Projects

Another reason for optimism that the concept of "citizenship" can be transformed to fully include women is that other important transformative projects are under way, as Aboriginal peoples, immigrants from different cultures, and Québécois express their discomfort with certain aspects of the citizenship currently on offer. Although it is possible that the women's project might be moved to the bottom of the list, trivialized and dismissed, it is also possible that the common elements in the various projects will be understood along with their differences. The projects all involve a critique of the homogenizing, potentially totalitarian features of a universal citizenship which, as Charles Taylor points out, is the product of a specific culture, and which, as Pateman points out, is the product of a culture whose specific goal was male dominance. The differences among the projects are many, and certainly some seem irreconcilable (the territorial issue with respect to Quebec is one such.) Nevertheless, there may be a generic aspect to the discussions about citizenship. Will Kymlicka and Wayne Norman suggest this, but also point out that a "[s]triking feature of the current debate is the timidity of proposals for public policy change to promote good citizenship."[34]

The Blurring of the "Public/Private" Line

A third reason for optimism is that, although the notion that the dichotomy between the "public" and the "private" (the "private" in the sense of "the market" and of "the domestic sphere") is strongly rooted, on closer inspection the line between the two is wavy and has always been less than clear. Many have argued persuasively that the dichotomy is a political or ideological construct. Consider the extent to which the "private" can readily become "public" when what is at stake is control of women's sexuality, whether in the context of prohibition of abortion or contraception, or in the context of pronatalist policies. On the other hand, the "public" can readily become "private" too, as in health care reforms that devolve responsibility for the care of the sick from acute care hospitals to "families" (usually women.) In sum, there may be increasingly wide acceptance (among those not at extreme ends of the political spectrum, at least) that, rather than deductive determinations based on "public" and "private," there should be case by case determinations whether government should act, or refrain from acting.

The Transformation of Other Concepts

The fourth reason for optimism is that other concepts, some of them closely related to citizenship, are undergoing a comparable transformation. Examples can be found in international human rights discourse, where the goal expressed by the slogan "women's rights are human rights" is being actively pursued with some success. It is an expression of a much more universal understanding of human rights than has previously been the case and encompasses the recognition, for example, that human rights now include the right not to be raped in the course of war. As well, there are some important examples in the jurisprudence surrounding the Canadian Charter of Rights and Freedoms.

LIBERTY

An early example of the revisiting of a concept in the Charter jurisprudence is the discussion of "liberty" in *Morgentaler*,[35] where the majority of the court found that the Criminal Code prohibition of abortion outside regulated circumstances was unconstitutional in that it infringed Section 7 ("the right to life, liberty and security of the person and not to be deprived thereof except in accordance with the principles of fundamental justice.") The court majority's conclusion that restrictions on abortion affected women's security of the person, in particular by the delays caused by the procedures that were in place, was a breakthrough in the understanding of that concept. Further, Madam Justice Bertha Wilson, in her reasons, discussed the transformation of the concept of "liberty" that will be necessary under the Charter. She began with a very traditional discussion of the individual and the state, saying that the "rights guaranteed in the Charter erect around each individual, metaphorically speaking, an invisible fence over which the state will not be allowed to trespass."[36] "Liberty," she stated, "grants the individual a degree of autonomy in making decisions of fundamental personal importance."[37] Asking whether the decision of a woman to terminate her pregnancy falls within the class of protected decisions, she concluded that it does. The history of the struggle for human rights, she wrote, has been the history of a struggle for the kinds of rights that *men* need in order to protect themselves against state interference. "Thus, women's needs and aspirations are only now being translated into protected rights. The right to reproduce or not to reproduce which is in issue in this case is one such right and is properly perceived as an integral part of modern woman's struggle to assert *her* dignity and worth as a human being."[38]

This decision attempted to take the notion of "liberty" and open it up: what would it mean if, from the outset, we had understood liberty with women's needs and experiences at the centre? Although Section 28 of the Charter was not mentioned in *Morgentaler*, this is its impact. If rights and freedoms are guaranteed equally to men and women, they are rights and freedoms understood in a way that makes them equally valuable to women. In *Winnipeg Child and Family Services (Northwest)* v. *D.F.G.*[39] the Supreme Court of Canada reached a conclusion consistent with this tendency.

EQUALITY

Since the Charter's equality rights came into effect in 1985, the Supreme Court has taken an innovative approach to their interpretation. The gender equality rights set out in Section 15 are as follows:

15(1) Every individual is equal before and under the law and has the right to the equal protection and equal benefit of the law without discrimination and, in particular, without discrimination based on race, national or ethnic origin, colour, religion, sex, age or mental or physical disability.

15(2) Subsection (1) does not preclude any law, program or activity that has as its object the amelioration of conditions of disadvantaged individuals or groups including those that are disadvantaged because of race, national or ethnic origin, colour, religion, sex, age or mental or physical disability.

28   Notwithstanding anything in this Charter, the rights and freedoms referred to in it are guaranteed equally to male and female persons.

In its first decision under Section 15 (*Andrews* v. *Law Society of B.C.*[40]) the Supreme Court rejected the existing American model, which takes the core meaning of "equality" to be "sameness" and uses a test close to the Aristotelian definition of equality: "Are similarly situated persons treated similarly?" The problem with this test is that it is tautologous, like a mathematical formula that can provide a solution only when we have identified all of the variables. (In this case, whom we will compare with whom? And at what level will we compare their treatment?) Instead, the Canadian Supreme Court has adopted an approach that looks to the rectification of substantive disadvantage. Because rectification can require differential treatment, such treatment is not only constitutionally permitted but is sometimes constitutionally mandated. An illustration of the difference between the two approaches may be found in a pair of cases: *Bliss* v. *Canada (Attorney General)*[41], and *Brooks* v. *Canada Safeway Ltd.*[42] In *Bliss*, under the Canadian Bill of Rights provision that required "equality before the law and the equal protection of the law," the Supreme Court held in 1978 that discrimination based on pregnancy was not sex discrimination. Applying the "similarly situated test," it concluded that all "pregnant persons" were treated alike, and that the discrimination was caused not by the legislation, which singled pregnant women out for lesser benefits, but by "nature." Ten years later, after the Charter had come into effect and *Andrews* had been decided, the Court overruled that decision in *Brooks*, saying:

Furthermore, to not view pregnancy in this way goes against one of the purposes of anti-discrimination legislation. This purpose ... is the removal of unfair disadvantages which have been imposed on individuals or groups in society. Such an unfair disadvantage may result when the costs of an activity from which all of society benefits are placed upon a single group of persons. This is the effect of the Safeway plan. It cannot be disputed that everyone in society benefits from procreation. The Safeway plan, however, places one of the major costs of procreation entirely upon one group in society: pregnant women.[43]

The *Andrews* approach has not been without controversy, both in the lower courts and in the Supreme Court itself. In 1995 that court showed itself to be seriously divided, with a strong minority of judges in three cases[44] favouring the adoption of what would be a model much closer to that applied in the United States: essentially, a reversal of *Andrews*. However, most recently (in three 1997 decisions) the signals suggest that the Court will maintain the essence of the *Andrews* approach.

One of the 1997 decisions directly involved citizenship and gender although it did not particularly illustrate the transformation of a concept. In *Benner* v. *Canada (Secretary of State)*,[45] the plaintiff had applied for citizenship in Canada. His mother, a Canadian, had married an American citizen, and Mr Benner was born in California in 1962. He was separated from his parents but found his mother in Canada, which he entered in 1986. In the application for citizenship he was required to produce documentation, to clear a criminal record and security check, and to swear an oath of allegiance. During the criminal-record check several charges in Canada came to light, including a murder charge. His application for citizenship was rejected. Subsequently he pleaded guilty to manslaughter and was sentenced to three years' imprisonment. If the situation had been the reverse, that is, if Mr Benner had had a Canadian father and an American mother, or if he had been born out of wedlock to a Canadian mother, he would have been entitled to citizenship upon registration of his birth without the criminal record and security check, let alone the oath of allegiance. He argued that the legislation contravened Section 15 of the Canadian Charter of Rights and Freedoms. He was unsuccessful at trial and in the Federal Court of Appeal and was deported to the United States in 1993.

In 1946, legislation was passed in Canada that provided for the acquisition and loss of Canadian citizenship. The Citizenship Act straightforwardly acted on patrilineal principles: if the parents of a child born outside Canada were married, that child's eligibility for Canadian citizenship was determined by the father's citizenship. This was consistent with the rules for becoming a British subject or acquiring British citizenship.[46] In 1976 a new Citizenship Act partly remedied the situation.[47] It conferred entitlement to citizenship on all children born abroad after 1977 provided that at least one parent – either one – was Canadian, and it allowed those (such as Mr Benner) who were born before that date outside Canada to a Canadian mother the right to apply for citizenship, subject to a prohibition against granting citizenship to an individual (such as Mr Benner) with criminal charges or convictions. It left intact the entitlement to citizenship for children born abroad before 1977 whose fathers were Canadian citizens. Thus, it created three categories of offspring: (1) all patrilineal claimants, (2) matrilineal claimants born before 1977, and (3) matrilineal claimants born after 1977.

When *Benner* reached the Supreme Court, Justice Iacobucci said that, whichever of the competing analytical approaches the Court took, the distinction between persons with Mr Benner's status (born abroad before 1977 to a Canadian mother) and persons born abroad before 1977 with a Canadian father was discriminatory: "the gender of a citizenship applicant's Canadian parent has nothing to do with the values of personal safety, nation-building or national security underlying the *Citizenship Act*."[48] The argument that it was sex discrimination, if at all, against the mother but not the son, was rejected since the gender of an applicant's Canadian parent is as completely out of his or her control as the colour of his or her skin. The argument that the differential treatment arose from "historical legislative circumstance" rather than "discriminatory stereotypical thinking" was also rejected. Justice Iacobucci said:

> For reasons never justified before a court, women were deemed incapable of passing their citizenship to their children unless there was no legitimate father from whom the child could acquire citizenship. The 1977 Act increased access to citizenship for children of Canadian mothers, but it maintained the distinction between children born of Canadian mothers and those born of Canadian fathers. By maintaining this distinction, it seems to me that the legislation maintained the stereotype.[49]

Further, the legislation did not constitute a "reasonable limit" within the meaning of Section 1 of the Charter, since there was no rational connection between the objectives (to provide access to citizenship while establishing a commitment to Canada and safeguarding the security of its citizens) and the means chosen (drawing a distinction between children born of Canadian mothers and those born of Canadian fathers).

The decision largely turns on "similarly situated" reasoning (although, illustrating that it is a tool, not a test in itself, the reasoning leads to an opposite outcome in the Supreme Court to that of the courts described later). In my view, a substantive approach would have at least adverted to the historical importance of patrilineal descent in maintaining patriarchy. Control measures in Anglo-Canadian law and policy included family organization that subsumed the legal identity of the woman in that of her husband, and an ideological division between the "public" and the "private" (in the sense of "domestic"), which relegated women to the "private" sphere alone. The pre-1977 rules for passing of citizenship mirrored the common law rules for tracing descent: legitimate children could inherit from their fathers, while an illegitimate child was *filius nullius* or "no-one's child."[50] Women had no role in establishing citizenship of their children, or even their own domicile, unless they were unmarried. The doctrine of "coverture" meant that married women were required on the whole to relate to the external world through their husbands.

Susan Moller Okin[51] points out that each of the five prerequisites for citizenship that Aristotle laid down – being male, of known genealogy, a patriarch, a warrior, and the master of the labour of others (normally slaves) – each requires that others (women and slaves) "play their non-citizenly, not fully human, role in the story." Citizens must be male, not female. To be of known genealogy in a context where only the male line of descent matters means that women's sexuality must be under the control of men. To be a patriarch, a man must be obeyed by his wives, children, and household slaves. To be a warrior, a man must have others who take care of daily life, including production and reproduction. And for there to be masters of slaves, there must be slaves. The provisions at issue in *Benner* were the descendants of Aristotle's prerequisites for citizenship.

Thus, although I agree with the conclusions reached by the Supreme Court of Canada in the Benner case, I find the discussion puzzling. The origin of the rules surrounding citizenship was in the deeply embedded set of rules about the role of women, designed to further the separate spheres ideology and the subordination of women to men. They did not flow from a concern about women being capable of passing along a commitment to Canada and to law-abidingness, or from stereotyping of women in that respect. Given that the legislation in question dealt with inheritance (of citizenship), it was just one of the elements of patriarchal control related to that central issue of inheritance through the male line, elements that are all connected to one another and that have gradually been unearthed, like a fossilized skeleton. The vestige left in the Citizenship Act and challenged in *Benner* may have been the last thighbone of a dinosaur, but it seems worthy of comment that it was that rather than a plastic pipe. Perhaps the best explanation for the approach taken in *Benner* is that it was possible to view the case as one about formal equality since it did involve explicit sex-based distinctions that now have no rational basis. Because it was possible, the Court saw that as the simplest approach to take.

In *Eldridge*,[52] the issue was whether the British Columbia Medical Services Commission and its hospitals contravened the Charter in failing to provide funding for deaf patients to have sign language interpreters when they were seeing doctors or in hospital. An initial issue was whether the Charter applied in this context. Moving away from an earlier restrictive view of the application of the Charter to private activity, the Supreme Court unanimously held that the Charter may apply to a private entity, either where that entity is itself "government" or where it is performing an activity that can be ascribed to government. This demands an investigation not into the nature of the entity whose activity is impugned but rather into the nature of the activity itself. In such cases, the quality of the act at issue, rather than the quality of the actor, must be scrutinized.

The Court decided that both the hospitals and the Medical Services Commission were carrying out governmental objectives, though neither is "government," and that their failure to provide interpretation services was subject to scrutiny under Section 15 of the Charter. The

Court also said that whichever of the competing approaches to equality analysis they followed, there would be a violation of Section 15 if the plaintiffs had not been afforded "equal benefit of the law without discrimination." Confirming earlier rulings in which the Court had established the principle that "[a] discriminatory purpose or intention is not a necessary condition of a s. 15(1) violation," but rather, "[i]t is sufficient if the effect of the legislation is to deny someone the equal protection or benefit of the law," the Court concluded that:

To argue that governments should be entitled to provide benefits to the general population without ensuring that disadvantaged members of society have the resources to take full advantage of those benefits bespeaks a thin and impoverished vision of s. 15(1). It is belied, more importantly, by the thrust of this Court's equality jurisprudence.

Section 15(1) makes no distinction between laws that impose unequal burdens and those that deny equal benefits. The government will be required … to take special measures to ensure that disadvantaged groups are able to benefit equally from government services. If there are policy reasons in favour of limiting the government's responsibility to ameliorate disadvantage in the provision of benefits and services, those policies are more appropriately considered in determining whether any violation of s. 15(1) is saved by s. 1 of the *Charter*.

The transformative aspect of the Supreme Court's decision is the adoption of a functional test for the application of the *Charter* (the nature of the activity, not the identity of the actor) and the clear endorsement of the definition of equality that goes beyond "same treatment." The requirement for governments to alleviate disadvantage in their provision of benefits and services to citizens has potentially a very long reach.

The final decision to which I will refer is also the most recent: *R. v. S. (R.D.).*[53] In this case the Supreme Court was asked whether a trial judge, a black woman, was biased or had given rise to a reasonable apprehension of bias when she made certain comments in the trial of a young black man for assaulting a police officer. Her comments were:

The Crown says, well, why would the officer say that events occurred in the way in which he has related them to the Court this morning. I am not saying that the Constable has misled the court, although police officers have been known to do that in the past. I am not saying that the officer overreacted, but certainly police officers do overreact, particularly when they are dealing with non-white groups. That to me indicates a state of mind right there that is questionable. I believe that probably the situation in this particular case is the case of a young police officer who overreacted. I do accept the evidence of [R.D.S.] that he was told to shut up or he would be under arrest. It seems to be in keeping with the prevalent attitude of the day.

At any rate, based upon my comments and based upon all the evidence before the court, I have no other choice but to acquit.[54]

The majority of the Court held that these remarks did not give rise to a reasonable apprehension of bias, though three dissenters thought that they did. The majority, however, was split as to the test to be applied and as to the requirements of impartiality for judges. Four members of the Court (in a judgment written jointly by Justices L'Heureux-Dubé and McLachlin) were prepared to take a new view of the concept. In part this was through discussion of a close cousin of "the citizen" – namely, "the reasonable person." How does the reasonable person come into it? The test for whether there is a reasonable apprehension of bias invokes that construct – indeed, it invokes a "reasonable, informed, practical and realistic person who considers the matter in some detail." L'Heureux-Dubé and McLachlin said that an understanding of the context or background to a case is essential to judging, and that this might be gained through expert witnesses, through academic studies, or from the judge's personal understanding and experience of society. They added that "This process of enlargement is not only consistent with impartiality; it may also be seen as its essential pre-condition."[55]

It is in the elaboration of the "reasonable person" construct that we see some very new ground:

The reasonable person ... is an informed and right-minded member of the community, a community which, in Canada, supports the fundamental principles entrenched in the Constitution by the *Canadian Charter of Rights and Freedoms*. Those fundamental principles include the principles of equality set out in s. 15 of the *Charter* and endorsed in nation-wide quasi-constitutional provincial and federal human rights legislation. The reasonable person must be taken to be aware of the history of discrimination faced by disadvantaged groups in Canadian society ... . The reasonable person is not only a member of the Canadian community, but also, more specifically, is a member of the local communities in which the case at issue arose (in this case, the Nova Scotian and Halifax communities.) Such a person must be taken to possess knowledge of the local population and its racial dynamics.[56]

When I went through law school, the "reasonable person" test invoked "the man on the Clapham omnibus." It is a dramatic shift to the culturally aware, committed-to-equality reasonable person, who is now, in the view of these judges, the assessor of judicial impartiality.

CONCLUSION

I have argued that citizenship in the Western European tradition is a strongly gendered – and male gendered – concept. The exclusion of women from public life was what made men's participation in it possible; the domestic and particular were taken care of, so that "citizens" could concentrate on the public and universal. The extension of universal citizenship to women has only begun to have an impact on the concept of citizenship itself, for several reasons: the strength of the connection with maleness, and the continuation of the practical barriers to women's participation in political life.

However, the promise of universal citizenship, understood as being "of equal value to men and women," is worth pursuing, so long as it is "universal" in the way that "reasonable person" is now being described by four judges in the Supreme Court, and in the way that "human rights" are now being described by feminists. It will take considerable time to accomplish, and the outcome is uncertain. I referred earlier to the fictional dystopia in *The Handmaid's Tale* (set in North America), but the actual situation of women in many parts of the world is very difficult indeed. Canada can show international leadership in this area, by virtue of the progress we have made so far toward a more inclusive citizenship.

ACKNOWLEDGMENT

Thanks to Christine Dearing, MA, for her research assistance and her thoughtful comments.

NOTES

1 Ruth Lister, "Dilemmas in engendering citizenship," *Economy and Society* 24, no. 1 (1995): 3.
2 Nancy Harstock, "Rethinking modernism: minority vs. majority theories," *Cultural Critique* no. 7 (1991): 196.
3 Of course, the pop singer Madonna has cleverly appropriated both at once.
4 T.H. Marshall, *Citizenship and Social Class* (Cambridge, UK: Cambridge University Press, 1950), 10–11.
5 Barbara L. Marshall, *Engendering Modernity: Feminism, Social Theory and Social Change* (Boston: Northeastern University Press, 1994), 133–4.
6 [1951] 4 D.L.R. 529 at 557–8.
7 [1985] 1 F.C. 852 (T.D.) at 855.
8 [1989] 1 S.C.R. 143 at 195.

9 *In the Matter of a Reference as to the Meaning of the Word "Persons" in Section 24 of the British North America Act, 1867,* [1928] S.C.R. 276; overruled by *Re Section 24 of the B.N.A. Act,* [1930] 1 D.L.R. 98 (J.C.P.C.). Hereinafter "The persons case."

10 Other qualifications of a Senator included (s. 23):

(1) He shall be of the full age of Thirty Years;

(2) He shall be either a Natural-born Subject of the Queen, or a Subject of the Queen naturalised by an Act of the Parliament of [Great Britain, or of Canada, or of one of the Legislatures of the Provinces pre-Confederation];

(3) He shall be legally or equitably seised as of Freehold for his own Use and Benefit of Lands or Tenements ... of the [net] value of Four Thousand Dollars ... ;

(4) His Real and Personal Property shall be together worth Four Thousand Dollars over and above his Debts and Liabilities ... .

11 The persons case, at 281.

12 Particularly *Chorlton* v. *Lings* L.R. 4 C.P. 374, at 392.

13 The persons case, at 99.

14 As is well known, it was in this Privy Council decision that we find the debut of the "living tree" metaphor for the Canadian constitution: "The B.N.A. Act planted in Canada a living tree capable of growth and expansion within its natural limits." The persons case, at 106–7. Interestingly, a different metaphor (for the division of powers) that follows closely behind resonates with some of the themes of this paper in its invocation of the mistress of a household: "Their Lordships do not conceive it to be the duty of this Board – it is certainly not their desire – to cut down the provisions of the Act by a narrow and technical construction, but rather to give it a large and liberal interpretation so that the Dominion to a great extent, but within certain fixed limits, may be mistress in her own house, as the provinces to a great extent, but within certain fixed limits, are mistresses in theirs." The persons case, at 107.

15 Will Kymlicka, *Liberalism, Community, and Culture* (Oxford: Oxford University Press, 1989), 91–2.

16 One of the small disappointing discoveries in the literature about the history of women's struggle for political citizenship is that some of the beloved humorous writers of the day took the opportunity to mock women who struggled for recognition of their humanity. The position of women was truly invidious – relegated to the domestic and the trivial, and strictly regulated in their sexuality, they were then ridiculed for those very things. Stephen Leacock was a strong opponent of women suffrage, as was Mark Twain, who wrote:

Think of the torchlight processions that would distress our eyes. Think of the curious legends on the transparencies: "Robins forever, vote for Sallie

Robins, the only virtuous candidate in the field." And this: "Chastity, modesty, patriotism. Let the great people stand for Maria Sanders, the champion of morality and progress, and the only candidate with a stainless reputation." And this: "Vote for Judy McGinnies, the incorruptible. Nine children at the breast." In that day a man shall say to his servant, "What is the matter with the baby." And the servant shall reply, "It has been sick for hours." "And where is its mother?" "She is out electioneering for Sally Robins." And women shall talk politics instead of discussing the fashion; and they shall neglect the duties of the household to go out and take a drink with candidates; and men shall nurse the babies while their wives travel to the polls and vote. And also in that day the man who has beautiful whiskers shall beat the homely man of wisdom for Governor, and the youth who waltzes with exquisite grace shall be chief of police in preference to the man of practical sagacity and determined energy."
Quoted by John Garner, *The Franchise and Politics in British North America 1755–1867* (Toronto: University of Toronto Press, 1969), 160, from the *British Colonist* of 27 May 1867.

17 Iris Marion Young, "Polity and Group Difference: A Critique of the Ideal of Universal Citizenship" in *Feminism and Political Theory*, ed. Cass R. Sunstein (Chicago: University of Chicago Press, 1990), 124.

18 Jean Bethke Elshtain, "The power and powerlessness of women," in *Beyond Equality and Difference: Citizenship, Feminist Politics and Female Subjectivity*, ed. Gisela Bock and Susan James (London: Routledge, 1992), 112.

19 Ibid., 116.

20 Carol Pateman, "Equality, difference, subordination: the politics of motherhood and women's citizenship" in *Beyond Equality and Difference: Citizenship, Feminist Politics and Female Subjectivity*, ed. Gisela Bock and Susan James (London: Routledge, 1992), 17–18.

21 Ramsay Cook, "Introduction," in Catherine L. Cleverdon, *The Woman Suffrage Movement in Canada*, 2d ed. (Toronto: University of Toronto Press, 1974), xiii.

22 This change to the criminal law was made through a Criminal Code amendment that reversed the common law rule: S.C. 1980–81–82–83, C.125, s. 19. The change to civil (tort) law was made earlier in some Canadian jurisdictions than in others, but the coming into effect of s. 15 of the Canadian Charter of Rights and Freedoms on April 17, 1985, provided the occasion for the last few jurisdictions to remove the spousal immunity in tort, which was a vestige of the common law doctrine of the unity of spouses in one legal person: the husband. The immunity applied both ways – that is, neither wife nor husband could sue the other in tort, including for damages for personal injuries.

23 R. v. *Morgentaler*, [1988] 1 S.C.R. 30; *Tremblay* v. *Daigle*, [1989] 2
   S.C.R. 530.
24 At the end of the day, it is striking how few rights and entitlements are
   dependent upon citizenship. This state of affairs is relatively recent. At common law, there were strong distinctions between aliens and subjects. Aliens
   could not own or inherit land, sue in the courts, etc. *Habeas corpus* did
   apply to "friendly aliens" (whose countries were not at war with Great
   Britain).
25 The persons case.
26 See, for example, Jennifer Koshan, "Sounds of Silence: The Public/Private
   Dichotomy, Violence, and Aboriginal Women" in *Challenging the
   Public/Private Divide*, ed. Susan Boyd (Toronto: University of Toronto
   Press, 1997).
27 Susan Muller Okin, "Women, Equality, and Citizenship," *Queen's
   Quarterly* 99 (1992): 56–7.
28 Okin, "Women, Equality, and Citizenship," 20.
29 Carole Pateman, "Introduction," in *Feminist Challenges: Social and Political Theory*, eds. Carole Pateman and Elizabeth Gross (Boston: Northeastern
   University Press, 1986), 9–10.
30 Ruth Lister, "Citizenship engendered," *Journal of Critical Social Policy* 11,
   no. 2 (Autumn 1991): 65–71; Lister, "Dilemmas in engendering citizenship," 1–36.
31 Margaret Atwood, *The Handmaid's Tale* (Toronto: McClelland and
   Stewart, 1985).
32 The days described (seemingly with some longing) by Brian Mulroney in his
   famous post-Meech Lake interview ("In Charlottetown, the boys arrived in
   a ship – and spent a long time in places other than the library … . This is the
   way Confederation came about. There was no public debate: there was no
   great public hearings. It became a kind of tradition.") are over. Susan Dela-
   court and Graham Fraser, "Marathon talks were all part of plan, PM says,"
   The Globe and Mail, 12 June 1990, A1 and A7.
33 Christine Boyle, "Home Rule for Women: Power-Sharing Between Men and
   Women," *Dalhousie Law Journal* 7 (1983): 799.
34 Will Kymlicka and Wayne Norman, "Return of the Citizen: A Survey of
   Recent Work on Citizenship Theory," *Ethics* 104 (January 1994): 352–81.
35 R. v. *Morgentaler*, [1988] 1 S.C.R. 30; *Tremblay* v. *Daigle*, [1989] 2
   S.C.R. 530.
36 R. v. *Morgentaler*, [1988] 1 S.C.R. 30; *Tremblay* v. *Daigle*, [1989] 2
   S.C.R. 530, at 164.
37 R. v. *Morgentaler*, [1988] 1 S.C.R. 30; *Tremblay* v. *Daigle*, [1989] 2
   S.C.R. 530, at 166.
38 R. v. *Morgentaler*, [1988] 1 S.C.R. 30; *Tremblay* v. *Daigle*, [1989] 2
   S.C.R. 530, at 172. Emphasis in original.

39 [1997] S.C.J. No. 96, 31 October 997, No. 25508. The argument put forward in the case was also consistent with some of what I have said: it urged that the best way to promote healthy babies and healthy mothers is to empower pregnant women, recognizing the circumstances of all women, and the particular situation of Aboriginal women. It did not rest solely upon the right to autonomy and self-determination.

40 The persons case.

41 *Bliss* v. *Canada (Attorney General),* [1979] 1 S.C.R. 183.

42 *Brooks* v. *Canada Safeway Ltd.,* [1989] 2 S.C.R. 1219.

43 *Brooks* v. *Canada Safeway Ltd.,* [1989] 2 S.C.R. 1238.

44 *Miron* v. *Trudel,* [1995] 2 S.C.R. 418, *Egan* v. *Attorney General,* [1995] 2 S.C.R. 513, *Thibaudeau* v. *Attorney General,* [1995] 2 S.C.R. 627.

45 [1997] S.C.R. 358.

46 See *Halsbury's Laws of England* (3rd ed.), vol. 1 at 545 fn (b), 547, paras 1047 and 1048 and at 548, para. 1050. The father had to be a British subject or citizen and the child to be a legitimate child. Up to a certain time, as well, married women automatically gained and lost citizenship with their husbands. *Halsbury's Laws of England* (3rd ed.), vol. 1 at 564–6.

47 *Citizenship Act,* S.C. 1974–75–76 C. 108, s. 3(1).

48 [1997] S.C.J. No. 96, 31 October 1997, No. 25508, at 393.

49 [1997] S.C.J. No. 96, 31 October 1997, No. 25508, at 402–3.

50 Notably, important aspects of patrilineal descent were still on the statute books and in the common law in various parts of Canada when s. 15 of the *Charter* came into effect on 17 April 1985, such as requirements that a married woman assume the surname of her husband and differentiation between legitimate and illegitimate children.

51 See Okin, "Women, Equality, and Citizenship," 56–71.

52 *Eldridge* v. *British Columbia (Attorney General)* (1997), 151 D.L.R. (4th) 577 (S.C.C.).

53 (1997), 151 D.L.R. (4th) 193 (S.C.C.).

54 Quoted by the Supreme Court of Canada,(1997), 151 D.L.R. (4th) 193 (S.C.C.).

55 (1997), 151 D.L.R. (4th) 193 (S.C.C.), at 211.

56 (1997), 151 D.L.R. (4th) 193 (S.C.C.), at 211–2.

8 National Self-Determination and Tomorrow's Political Map

WALKER CONNOR

The impact of national self-determination on yesterday's political map has been enormous. The dismemberment of the former Soviet Union and the Federal Republic of Yugoslavia are only the most recent manifestations of the challenge that ethnonationalism poses to the survival of the multihomeland state. In the 130-year period that separated the Napoleonic Era and the end of the Second World War, all but three of Europe's states either lost significant territory and population to ethnonational aspirations or were themselves newly created in the name of national self-determination. (One of the exceptions, Portugal, was ethnically homogeneous; the other two, Spain and Switzerland, while remaining intact, have not been free of ethnically inspired discord.) Ethnonational aspirations continued to challenge multihomeland political structures in the decade after, the Second World War, and, by 1965, more than half of all states had experienced significant levels of ethnonational unrest.

At the bottom this unrest is a concept of political legitimacy by which ethnicity is taken as the ultimate standard for judging legitimacy. By these terms, any ethnic group that considers itself to be a separate nation has the right to its own state. At first unnamed, later referred to as "the principle of nationalities," and more recently described as "national self-determination," this concept of political legitimacy now manifests itself universally in anti-state movements.

Significantly, no particular classification of country has proven immune. Afflicted countries are to be found in Africa (for example, Ethiopia), Asia (Sri Lanka), Eastern Europe (Romania), Western Europe

(France), North America (Guatemala), South America (Guyana), and Oceania (New Zealand). The list includes countries that are old (the United Kingdom) as well as new (Bangladesh), large (Indonesia) as well as small (Fiji), rich (Canada) as well as poor (Pakistan), authoritarian (Sudan) as well as democratic (Belgium), Marxist-Leninist (China) and militantly anti-Marxist (Turkey). The list also includes countries that are Buddhist (Burma), Christian (Spain), Muslim (Iran), Hindu (Indian), and Judaic (Israel).

The theme of this chapter is essentially a simple one and has not changed in any important regard over the three decades since my first exploration of the subject, "Self-Determination: The New Phase," appeared in *World Politics.*[1] This theme flows from the almost total lack of coincidence that still exists between political and ethnic borders. It holds that the stability of today's states will come under increasing pressure to respond to the forces of ethnonationalism.

Let me begin by re-emphasizing the continuing lack of coincidence between ethnic and political borders. Of the some more than 180 states that exist in the world today, not more than 15 could qualify as essentially homogeneous: Japan, Iceland, the two Koreas, Portugal, and handful of others. Moreover, we have entered a period of unprecedented migrations that are currently altering the homogeneity of a number of these exceptions.

The multi-ethnic state is easily the most common form of country. It contains at least two significant ethnic groups. In 40% of all states there are five or more such groups. A few states – such as Nigeria and, parenthetically, the former Soviet Union – contain more than 100 groups. Perhaps the most startling statistic is that in nearly one-third of all states (31%) the largest national group is not even a majority. This is true of newly independent Kazakhstan and nearly true of newly independent Latvia. Ethnic heterogeneity, not homogeneity, characterizes the typical state.

Most states are not just multi-ethnic but comprise multiple homelands as well. With the principal exception of a few immigrant societies such as Argentina, Australia, and the United States, the land masses of the world are divided into ethnic homelands: territories whose names reflect a particular people. Catalonia, Croatia, England, (land of the Angles), Euzkadi (land of the Basques), Finland, Iboland, Ireland, Kurdistan, Mongolia, Nagaland, Pakhtunistan, Poland, Scotland, Swaziland, Sweden, Tibet, Uzbekistan, and Zululand constitute but a small sampling.

To the people who have lent their name to it, a homeland is much more than territory. Their emotional attachment is reflected in such widely used expressions as "native land," "the fatherland," "this sacred soil," "the ancestral land," "this hallowed place," "the mother-land," "land of our fathers," and, not least, "the *home*land." Territory becomes intermeshed with notions of ancestry and family. This is how Sir Walter Scott expressed it in the eighteenth century:

> Breathes there the man, with soul so dead,
> Who never to himself hath said,
> This is my own, my native land!
> ...
> Land of my sires! what mortal hand
> Can e'er untie the filial band
> That knits me to thy rugged strand.[2]

The invulnerability of such sentiments to time, place, and culture is suggested by the works of a contemporary Uzbek poet whose home-land is located in the Muslim Central Asian area of the former Soviet Union:

> So that my generation would comprehend the Homeland's worth,
> Men were always transformed to dust it seems.
> The Homeland is the remains of our forefathers
> Who turned into dust for this precious soil.[3]

This emotional attachment derives from perceptions of the homeland as the cultural hearth and, very often, as the geographic cradle of the ethnonational group. In Bismarckian terminology, *Blut und Boden*, blood and soil, have become mixed. The emotionally pregnant concept of having "roots" implies soil. The psychological associations thus made between homeland and one's people are the more, not the less, intense for being emotional and resisting exposition in rational terms.

Such psychological associations are often predicated upon a ques-tionable history. Finns and Germans, for example, are descendants of people who migrated from east of what is today perceived as Finland and Germany. As has been illustrated more recently by the Afrikaners and the Québécois, a people can come to consider as their homeland a region where they have dwelt for a relatively short time. Moreover, as a people expands its territory, so its concept of the homeland expands. Thus, though once limited to the region of Muscovy, the Russian homeland is today popularly viewed as encompassing the strip of (ethnically) Russian-dominated land stretching from the western bor-der of the Russian Federation to Vladivostok. Somewhat analogously, Poles, in their numerous references to homeland, do not appear to differentiate between traditionally Polish-dominated regions and that large western sector of the contemporary state of Poland which, before 1945, was populated principally by Germans.

Such considerations hardly negate the emotional attachment of a people to a homeland. As in other aspects of nationalism, it is not the historical truth but what people perceive as the truth that is of essence. The important point is that the populated world is subdivided into a set of perceived homelands to which, in each case, the indigenous eth-nonational group is convinced it has a profound and proprietary claim. Again, the particular words used to describe homelands are instructive. Who but the Scots could have plenary claim to Scotland, who but Germans to Deutschland, the Flemish to Flanders, Corsicans to Corsica, Basques to Euzkadi, or Welsh to Wales?

As a consequence of this sense of primal ownership, nonmembers of the ethnic group within the homeland are viewed as outsiders even if they are compatriots. They may be endured and even treated equitably. Their stay may be multigenerational. But they remain outsiders or set-tlers in the eyes of the homeland people, who reserve what they deem their inalienable right to execute a primary and exclusive claim to the homeland whenever they desire. Ethnic cleansing of the homeland was not invented in this decade by the Serbs. The bloody expulsion of Vietnamese from Cambodia under the Lon Nol government, the re-ported eradication of Cambodia's Chams under Pol Pot, the expulsion of Chinese from Vietnam during the late 1970s, the mass atrocities com-mitted against Bengalis in Assam in 1983, and periodic race riots with Chinese as targets throughout all of southeast Asia are just a few con-spicuous illustrations of this phenomenon at work. The unceremonious, forcible expulsion of millions of people from Nigeria in the early 1980s is another example. Periodic anti-Han riots within Tibet constitute yet another. Numerous other illustrations are offered by the hostilities that erupted across the entire southern Soviet Union during its last two years and that continue today. Only somewhat less violent illustrations include pressures on Europe's *Gastarbeiter* and asylum seekers to depart from one or another homeland: from England, Germany, France, Sweden, etc. Le Pen's slogan, "France for the French," accurately captures this impor-tant aspect of homeland psychology. It is echoed today in Austria, Germany, Sweden, and elsewhere throughout northern Europe. So too it is in Québec, where the slogan *le Québec aux Québécois* is often heard.

Given that the land masses of the world are divided into some 3000 homelands over which the political borders of something less than 200 countries have been superimposed, it is hardly surprising that most states are not just multinational but also multihomeland. This is of the greatest significance to the political stability of tomorrow's world, for the demands of ethnonational movements tend to be coterminous with their homeland. In terms of geography, it is for the homeland that ethnonational groups demand greater autonomy or full independence. For example, in the last stages of the Soviet Union it was greater control over their homelands – over mother Armenia, Estonia, Georgia, Latvia, Lithuania, etc. – that the non-Russian peoples demanded of Gorbachev. It is over Catalonia, Corsica, Kashmir, Nagaland, and Tibet that Catalonians, Corsicans, Kashmiris, Nagas, and Tibetans demand greater control. The principal slogan of the Québécois – *maîtres chez nous* – captures this attitude nicely. The Québécois must be masters in their own home – meaning the homeland of Quebec.

It is possible, of course, that an autonomy or independence movement may be based on regionalism rather than on an ethnic homeland. This is true of the movement that recently separated Eritrea from Ethiopia and is also true of a much weaker and non-violent movement to separate British Columbia and other western provinces from Canada. But the most bids for autonomy or secession are made by peoples who identify themselves with a homeland. It is the multihomeland state that is the target of ethnonational demands.

A number of states contain essentially one homeland; Bulgaria, Germany, Estonia, Ireland, and Japan are some examples. Because of past migration, such states may have a large ethnic minority population, but the aspirations of minority groups, denied as they are of a homeland base and often being geographically diffuse, are customarily directed to equal treatment and improved status within the society rather than to autonomy or secession.[4] As we have noted, homeland psychology in these states can lead to violence, demands for ethnic cleansing, and the like. But only the homeland psychology of the state's dominant group is involved. There are usually no demands for autonomy or for the state's dismemberment on the part of minorities.

A small number of immigrant states are essentially non-homeland states. Behaviour patterns, as reflected in much higher inter-group marriage rates, language acculturation rates, and assimilation rates, differ markedly between immigrant and non-immigrant states. As we are all aware, the United States – the immigrant state par excellence – is certainly not free of ethnic problems. But, as in the case of unihomeland states, equal rights and opportunities, not questions of autonomy or separatism, dominate relations between minority and majority groups there. Questions concerning autonomy arise within the United States only in relation to its relatively few homeland peoples: Amerindian peoples who have elected to remain on "reserved" lands and Eskimos in settled communities within Alaska.

The point is that it is the integrity of the *multihomeland* state that is challenged by ethnonationally inspired movements and that analogies should not be drawn between their problems and the experiences of unihomeland or non-homeland states. To note that homeland-dwelling minorities aspire to greater independence from the state is not to imply that they seek independence.[5] The essence of the national self-determination imperative is choice, not result. As noted, it holds that a national group has the right to secede and form its own state *if it so desires*. In the overwhelming number of cases for which we have data, a majority – usually a substantial majority – are often prepared to settle for something less than independence. Attitudinal data on the Basques indicate that the percentage of those strongly committed to separatism peaked in the late 1970s at about 36%.[6] A survey conducted in Scotland in 1995 indicated that only one third of the populace favored independence.[7] A poll conducted in mid-1996 indicated that 86% of the Corsican population were opposed to separation from France.[8] And although the Slovaks were given their independence from Czechoslovakia in the early 1990s, this had not been the goal of most; a 1990 poll indicated that only 8% of Slovakia's population desired independence.[9] In the case of Quebec, the data suggest that pro-separatists never surpassed 20% of the Franco-Canadian community before 1990.[10]

Although separatists were a minority in these cases, a preponderant percentage of those same groups favoured major alterations in their country's power structure: that is to say, they desired a much greater measure of meaningful autonomy. Among young Franco-Canadians (seventeen to nineteen years of age) polled in 1968, 13% favoured separatism, 68% favoured greater autonomy for Québec, and only 8% preferred no change in Quebec's status.[11] Although polls in Scotland showed that only a minority preferred total separation, a strong majority regularly indicated a preference for greater autonomy.[12] Similarly, the poll conducted in Slovakia showed that 71% of the population desired a major decentralization of political power, while only 16% favored no major changes.[13]

There are numerous reasons why a national group may be prepared to settle for autonomy rather than independence.[14] A major consideration is that some form of autonomy may be all that is realistically achievable. Such an assessment is most apt to be made in an authoritarian milieu. But the issue of feasibility can also exert a restraining influence within a traditionally democratic setting. In the case of the Quebec poll in which only 13% of young Franco-Canadians opted for independence, an additional 43% desired it but did not believe it feasible either immediately (37%) or ever (6%).

Another factor that can contribute to a willingness to settle for some-thing less than total independence – at least in the democratic states of western Europe and Canada – is a reservoir of good will. Members of national groups, even those that are not dominant in the state, do not necessarily perceive loyalty to their national group and loyalty to their country as incompatible. Thus, while the Québécois express a greater affinity toward Quebec than toward Canada, they nonetheless express a powerful sense of affection toward Canada.[15] Similarly, although the Basques have good historical reasons to distrust the Spanish state (most recently because of their experiences during Franco's regime), some 10% of respondents to a poll chose to identify themselves as "more Basque than Spanish" in preference to the more limited category of "Basque."[16] At least to this 10%, "Basque," while being considered the more important identity, was not perceived as excluding a significant measure of affinity for the Spanish state.[17]

That the state should enjoy a significant measure of affection is not surprising. The state has powerful means for politically socializing (pro-gramming) its citizens, not the least of which is control of education (and especially control of the manner in which history is interpreted and taught). Even if the state is viewed with only marginal sympathy, it is not incongruous that most members of a national minority might be prepared to settle for autonomy. Autonomy has the potential to satisfy the principal aspirations of the group. Devolution – the decentralization of political decision-making – has the potential to elevate a national group to the status of masters in their own home. And this may be quite enough. Ethnonational aspirations, by their very nature, are more con-cerned with *freedom from* domination by outsiders than with *freedom to* conduct relations with states. Ethnocracy need not presume indepen-dence, but it must presume *meaningful* autonomy at the minimum. To return to the Québécois, the slogan *maîtres chez nous* expresses a conviction that within the homeland they must have the ultimate power of decision-making over those matters most affecting ethnonational sensibilities and the maintenance of the Québécois nation.

Unfortunately, central authorities have tended to perceive any demand for a significant increase in autonomy as tantamount to, or an important step toward, secession. Governments have been inclined to guard their prerogatives zealously and to resist any move toward de-centralization. In doing so, they often further the very result that they ostensibly wish to avoid, for there is an inverse relation between a gov-ernment's willingness to grant meaningful autonomy and the level of separatist sentiment. For example, when the Spanish government first granted an autonomy statute to the Basques in 1979, the proportion of Basques desiring independence dropped from 36% to 12%. Recent events in Canada illustrate this same phenomenon in reverse. Denied in 1990 a request that the constitution be so worded as to recognize the French-speaking people of Quebec as "a distinct society," those Québécois in favour of separation rose dramatically from less than 20% to well over 50%.

The message therefore is clear: governments of multinational states refuse to countenance demands for decentralization at the peril of increasing separatist sentiment and increasing the likelihood of a resumption of hostilities. Switzerland, while certainly not immune to ethnically inspired dissension, demonstrates that a multinational democracy can survive if the political system is sufficiently decentralized. The confederal cantonal structure of the country, combined with its ethnic map, minimizes the possibility of domination or even the perception of domination by the numerically predominant Germanic element. In the case of the one canton within which a sizable French-speaking minority was dominated by the Germanic element, a successful secession movement was waged by the Francophones during the 1970s. But, most instructively, the secessionists aspired to secede only from the German dominated canton of Berne, not from Switzerland. Given their own ethnocracy (a canton), they considered their right to national self-determination fulfilled. Following, if somewhat haltingly, this same path, a number of Western democracies, most notably Belgium, Britain, Canada, Italy, and Spain, have at least partly assuaged ethnonational aspirations through the recent granting of substantial autonomy to ethnonational groups.

Why assuaged rather than satisfied? Although most members of a national minority are prepared to settle for meaningful autonomy, autonomy is an amorphous concept that signifies quite different things to different people. It may refer to very limited home rule or to regional control over everything other than foreign policy; that is to say, it can depict any situation on the continuum between total subordination to the centre and total independence.

A rational first step for those hoping to negotiate an agreement that will lengthen a peaceful interval is to ascertain (through referenda, attitudinal surveys, and the like) the full spectrum of popular sentiment among the homeland people concerning minimally acceptable changes in the distribution of powers. What percentage are prepared to settle for each of the options on the spectrum ranging from the status quo to independence? The maximal levels of concessions to autonomy that would be acceptable to various segments of the state's wider population should also be ascertained. Where available, such data offer guidelines for crafting an agreement of promise. Such data can discredit extremist positions held by those who claim to speak for the entire homeland people or for the entire population of the state living outside the homeland, thereby relieving negotiators for both sides from unhelpful pressures.

The pressures on both groups of negotiators are usually intense. Typically, those associated with the centre will tend to view even minimal devolution as encouraging secession and will pressure the government to concede as little as possible. Career military officers are often in the forefront of those opposed to decentralization, which they are apt to perceive as a step toward fragmentation. The overriding function of the military is the defence of the political and territorial integrity of the country. Consonant with their traditions, military leaders assume that as compared with all other elements in the society, they have a special responsibility to act as guardians of the state as presently delimited, and they are therefore very apt to perceive any significant devolution of power – any significant grant of greater autonomy to territorially defined ethnic groups – as a step toward the state's dismemberment.

The possibility of such perceptions leading to an attempted coup is often very real. Thus, an aborted coup in Spain in 1981 and another in the Soviet Union in 1991 were both inspired in large part by a perception that the government had granted too much independence to homeland-dwelling minorities. More recently, rumours that a military revolt might occur if the Chechens were permitted too much independence eddied around Moscow after the 1996 ceasefire between the Russian military and Chechen guerrillas.

The threat to an incumbent regime's tenure can emanate from non-military circles as well. Thus, the failure of John Major's Conservative government to advance, during a lengthy, seventeen-month ceasefire, any substantively new proposals for power sharing in Northern Ireland was attributable in no small part to the fact that his Twiggy-thin margin in Parliament made his prime ministership hostage to the give-no-quarter unionist MPs representing Northern Ireland.[18]

Those on the government's side of the negotiating table are therefore subject to very real pressures. So too are those on the other side.[19] Among the homeland people, those who hold a maximalist view of autonomy will perceive any manifestation of the centre's presence in the homeland as violating the spirit of autonomy. More moderate homeland leaders will be under pressure from the maximalists, to say nothing of the separatists, to squeeze more concessions from the centre if they desire to maintain their following. Simply agreeing to introduce autonomy is therefore no guarantee of peaceful accommodation. The search for adjustments in the system that will be sufficiently acceptable to both sides to isolate extremists and render them ineffectual is a daunting enterprise.

In practice, how much have governments been prepared to cede in order to maintain a peaceful status? In a few instances (e.g., Sweden and Norway in 1905, Malaysia and Singapore in 1965, and Czechoslovakia and Slovakia in 1993) central governments have voluntarily granted independence. Although we have noted that the power to conduct foreign policy, being a defining characteristic of state sovereignty, is considered beyond the confines of the most extreme definition of autonomy, the government of the province of Quebec has in fact entered directly into a number of bilateral arrangements with foreign countries. Perhaps the broadest generality that can be made concerning the specifics of autonomy in practice is that governments have been far more inclined to grant demands for autonomy in the cultural than in the political realm. In Belgium, for example, the Flemish-, French-, and German-speaking communities are constitutionally authorized to legislate in the areas of education, cultural affairs, and health and social assistance, and, more broadly, to formulate "socio-economic policies." As to minority languages, a number of contemporary democracies (including Spain) have shown a willingness to permit the local language to be used in the courts and other public forums, including as the language of instruction in the schools. In Belgium and Canada (although not in Spain), the co-equal status of a homeland language has been extended throughout the country by declaring it an official state language.

Internal security – who controls the gun within the homeland – is a much more contentious issue, particularly when a violence-prone group is operating in the name of the nation. Relations between Madrid and the Basque autonomous government were long soured by the former's reluctance to withdraw the "national" police and the paramilitary *Guardia Civil*. The realization that Basque perceptions of these forces as outsiders engendered popular sympathy for the violent ethnonational group known as ETA led Madrid in 1989 to promise to transfer all security duties to local forces within six years.

An issue of seemingly unavoidable conflict between the centre and homeland peoples involves the migration of peoples. Central governments not only control the movement of people across state borders (immigration and emigration) but also the movement of people within the country. Democratic governments customarily insist that all legal residents have the right to live wherever they choose. Typical is the wording of the Constitution Act of 1982, guaranteeing to every citizen and permanent resident of Canada, "the right (a) to move to and take up residence in any province; and (b) to pursue the gaining of a livelihood in any province." On the other hand, few if any matters will be deemed more of an exclusive prerogative by a homeland people than the issue of who is to be permitted to live within the nation's home. An influx of significant numbers of non-members of the nation can be expected to trigger resentment and a rise in separatist sentiments. This linkage between separatism and the movement of non-indigenes into the homeland holds true even if the non-indigenes are fellow citizens (for example, Frenchmen moving into Corsica or Brittany, or Castilians into the Basqueland).

Many of the prerogatives inherent in the homeland demand to be *maîtres chez nous* have a dialectical relation to the prerogatives of state sovereignty. For example, any agreement concerning migration cannot eradicate the natural tension between the notion of *le Québec aux Québécois* and the notion of the free movement of citizens within the state. An agreement does not annihilate the underlying contradictions and should not be viewed as permanently ensuring a non-violent relationship. The price of such an enduring peaceful relationship is apt to be permanent negotiation. Peace accords between independent states can endure because the parties can subsequently go their own ways, but homelands and states do not enjoy separate spheres. Working, enduring autonomy will require periodic adjustments in the interrelationship of the homeland and the centre in response to changing circumstances and perceptions.

The reference to perceptions brings up a final point. A major problem confronting designers of an accord for perpetuating a peaceful interlude in an ethnic conflict is that they are operating in a world not of fact but of perceptions of fact. Not with chronological history, but with sentient or felt history. Pointing out, for example, that the Croats and Serbs are descended from the same ancestors will not alter the intuitive conviction that each group tends to harbour concerning its own ethnic purity. Historical facts and current incidents are internalized through ethnic filters. Objective reality and ethnically processed reality are not the same.

In the fall of 1994, the Atlantic Council sponsored a meeting in Romania that brought together an impressively large number of relatively young members of the business, educational, financial, labour, media, military, and political elites of western Europe, east Asia, North America, and the former Soviet Union. The purpose was to discuss ethnic and sectarian conflict. Participants were often drawn from bitterly opposed groups. Here is the conclusion from the final report on the conference:

Ethnic conflicts cannot be entirely reduced to arguments over resources ... . Often, ethnic aims are pursued at the expense of other issues because they come from a subjective, emotional commitment the other side finds difficult to understand in objective terms ... . This theme echoed throughout almost every discussion, leading participants to one of the most simple but profound conclusions of the conference: perceptions are as important or more so than reality when it comes to ethnic issues and must be addressed before discussion can move forward.[20]

Realistic attempts to peacefully resolve ethnic conflicts necessitate an appreciation of the emotional and elusive nature of ethnic identity and homeland psychology. Probing these matters requires not a knowledge of "facts" but of commonly held perceptions of facts. Facts perceived through Israeli eyes are remarkably different from those same facts viewed through Palestinian eyes. The same holds true for Russian versus Chechen-processed facts; Irish versus Ulsterman-processed facts; or Xhosa versus Zulu-processed facts. This duality helps to explain why fact-finding commissions and mediators whose past experience has been limited to non-ethnic disputes do not achieved notable successes in resolving ethnic conflicts.

By way of summation, the quest for formulae to accommodate ethnic heterogeneity peacefully need not be a quixotic one. The principle of national self-determination need not presume a world in which each nation possesses its own state. A realistic attempt to arrive at a formula for the peaceful accommodation of heterogeneity should consider the following:

1 The segment of a homeland-dwelling people who will not be content with anything less than independence seldom represents a majority of that people.

2 However, a large majority typically desires significant changes in the distribution of powers between the centre and the homeland.

3 The specific goals of those favouring greater autonomy can range over a broad spectrum from very limited home rule to homeland control over everything other than foreign policy.

4 Ascertaining the attitudes of the homeland and state-wide peoples toward specific grants of autonomy should be a primary goal of negotiators.

5 Both centre and homeland leaders are typically under intense pressure to maximize or minimize concessions.

6 Because of the antithetical nature of state supremacy and autonomy, the specifics of any agreement concerning autonomy will be subject to periodic pressures for change.

7 A formidable handicap in seeking a formula for peacefully accommodating the aspirations of an ethnonational minority is that it is not reality but reality filtered through different ethnic prisms that influences attitudes and behaviour.

NOTES

1 Walker Connor, "Self-Determination: The New Phase," *World Politics* 20 (October 1967): 20–53.
2 Sir Walter Scott, *The Lay of the Last Minstrel*, canto I.
3 Cho Lpan Ergash, "Recognizing the Homeland," in *The Nationality Question in Soviet Central Asia*, ed. Edward Alworth (Praeger Publishers: New York, 1973), 15.
4 The group aspirations of a settler community are, of course, quite different if that community has become politically dominant, as happened to the settler community within Northern Ireland after the division of Ireland in 1920.
5 The following account draws heavily on my paper "From a Theory of Relative Economic Deprivation toward a Theory of Relative Political Deprivation," presented at the Conference on Minority Nationalism in the Changing World Order, University of Western Ontario, November 1997.
6 Robert Clark, *The Basque Insurgents: ETA, 1951–1980* (Madison: University of Wisconsin Press, 1984), 171ff. This figure would be higher, however, if it represented the sentiments of ethnic Basques only. An equivalent qualification holds true for all of the examples given here.
7 *International Herald Tribune*, 20 October 1995.
8 *International Herald Tribune*, 6 June 1996.
9 Vladimir Kusin, "Czechs and Slovaks: The Road to the Current Debate," *Report on Eastern Europe*, vol. 1 (5 October 1990): 4–13.
10 The reason for the abrupt change in 1990 is discussed later. For an analysis of earlier separatist sentiment in Quebec, see Richard Hamilton and Maurice Pinard, "The Bases of Parti Québécois Support in recent Quebec Elections," *Canadian Journal of Political Science* 11 (1976): 1–26.
11 H. D. Forbes, *Nationalism, Ethnocentrism, and Personality: Social Science and Critical Theory* (Chicago: University of Chicago Press, 1985), 200–1.
12 In 1997, some three fourths (74.3%) voted favorably on a referendum offering greater autonomy to Scotland. *International Herald Tribune*, 13–14 September 1997.
13 Kusin, "Czechs and Slovaks," 6. A 1996 poll of Okinawan opinion, conducted by the University of the Ryukyus, demonstrated the same type of pattern. While only 3.3% preferred independence, 13.2% desired homeland control over all powers other than foreign policy and defence, and 38.4% would have settled for authority over budgetary and legal matters. *Weekly News* (Okinawa), 26 February 1996. (Only 570 of a sample of 1000 agreed to be interviewed.)
14 In a number of situations for which we have no attitudinal data, the same willingness to settle for something less than separatism is often evident. See, for example, the letter to the editor of the *New York Times*, 10 February

1996, by the President of the Association of Tamils of Sri Lanka in the United States. It reads in part: "The Tamils want a space of their own where their physical security, economic welfare, and ethnic and cultural identity can be assured. All Tamil parties, including the Liberation Tigers of Tamil Eelam, are agreed on this demand. They also agree it is possible to find a solution within a united but not unitary Sri Lanka."

15 See, for example, the results of a poll in Lawrence LeDuc, "Canadian Attitudes towards Québec Independence," *Public Opinion Quarterly* 41 (Fall 1977), particularly 352–3. Canada, however, was held in lower esteem in Quebec than it was in the other provinces.

16 Richard Gunther, *A Comparative Study of Regionalism in Spain* (Toronto: Society for Spanish and Portuguese Historical Studies, 1981). See also the table in Goldie Shabad and Richard Gunther, "Language, Nationalism, and Political Conflict in Spain," *Comparative Politics* 15 (July 1982): 449.

17 It is against the backdrop of such data that the results of opinion polls conducted within the Soviet Union during its last years starkly underlined the lack of affection for that state. A poll conducted in October 1990, for example, indicated that 91% of the population of the three Baltic nations and 92% of all Georgians favoured secession. See Vera Tolz, "The USSR this Week," *Report on the USSR* 2 (26 October 1990): 30.

18 It is also possible that a highly competitive political situation at the centre may have the opposite effect of presenting ethnonational minorities with a favourable opportunity for pressing their demands. Thus, in Spain during 1996, when the elections failed to produce a clear-cut winner, the ethnonational parties desirous of greater autonomy for the Basques, Canary Islanders, and Catalans pledged their support to José Maria Azuar's Popular Party, only after wrenching away support for specific grants of power to the homeland governments. The Catalan party's election program had contained two-and- a-half pages of specific demands and described its overall position as calling for "as much autonomy as the special situation demands." See *Globe and Mail* (Toronto), 8 March 1996, and the *International Herald Tribune*, 8 March and 30 April 1996.

19 Quite characteristically, the 1996 agreement to create a new autonomous region of Muslim Mindanao came under violent attack from both Moro and non-Moro groups on the island: the former were unhappy because it did not grant enough independence, the latter because it granted too much. See the *International Herald Tribune*, 3 July and 4 September 1996, and the *New York Times*, 20 August 1996.

20 *Final Report of the Twenty-Second Young Leaders Seminar*, Atlantic Council, Bucharest, Romania / Washington, DC, Fall 1994.

9 The Legal Enforcement of Social Norms: Techniques and Principles

DENISE G. RÉAUME

In any society, multiple normative orders coexist, competing with one another for the allegiance and obedience of the individuals under their influence. This phenomenon gives rise to a challenge to the law, itself a normative order whose agents are used to thinking of it as superior to all others. To what extent should the legal system take cognizance of, and even give way to, social norms that develop independently of officially endorsed rules? To the extent that it does so, it exhibits a form of normative pluralism, the inclusion of different and in some sense competing normative frameworks under a single umbrella. Although this kind of approach has been largely foreign to Western common law, the colonial and post-colonial legal systems of the former British colonies in Africa and elsewhere were and are explicitly based on this form of pluralism. The British policy of "indirect rule" in Africa divided people and practices into those that were to be governed by British common law and statute and those that were to be regulated according to the customary rules of the indigenous populations.[1] This was intended to accommodate the cultural and religious differences between white, settler populations and indigenous Africans, and between different groups within the indigenous population. In the Western common-law tradition, the idea of pluralism has only marginally impinged upon the dominant understanding of law;[2] nor has it typically had the protection or recognition of cultural or religious difference as its focus.[3] The dominant mindset in our tradition has tended to treat law as a set of rules that apply uniformly throughout society. It follows from such a mindset that any deviation that takes account of cultural difference is to be regarded with suspicion. Hence the common objection raised against Aboriginal self-government or the recognition of "distinct society" status for Quebec is that these measures constitute "special treatment" and violate equality.

The extent to which the Canadian legal system is normatively pluralistic has been underplayed. Indeed, there are many contexts in which courts and other adjudicators are called upon to recognize the semi-autonomous nature of a form of social ordering grounded in culture. To the extent that such arguments succeed, so that instead of applying the legal rules that would be applied to any other parties embroiled in a similar dispute the adjudicator applies norms specific to a particular community, the legal system exemplifies pluralism. In doing so, it confers some degree of autonomy on minority cultural groups. If the pluralistic tendencies of existing legal doctrine have been underestimated, the potential of the system to incorporate pluralism is recognized even less. In better understanding both where we are and where we might go, we might learn something from the experience of legal systems that are explicitly pluralistic.

Claims for autonomy of minority groups usually attract attention only in extreme cases in which the norms of the minority community seem clearly wrong or have unwelcome implications for the well-being of outsiders. While the debates over these issues are important, there is also something to be learned from a detailed exploration of disputes of less operatic proportions. My focus, then, is on what I shall call "internal disputes" between members of a minority community that centre on practices involving more subtle deviations from majority norms. The cases I shall examine involve disputes with civil consequences: a group has taken an action against a member because of an alleged breach of the group's rules, and this action is legally cognizable, that is, normally regulated by law. This allows the challenge to the group's action to reframe that action according to legal norms. The dispute is brought before civil adjudicators because of its civil consequences, but this also has implications for the integrity of the group's internal norms. This focuses our attention on adjudication-specific techniques for achieving normative pluralism. In situations in which the minority group's autonomy to pursue its own practices has not been institutionalized through legally constituted governance and adjudicative mechanisms, disputes are decided by ordinary judicial bodies under the rules – whether common-law or statutory – that apply to the wider society. Recognizing some autonomy for minority groups would mean that disputes between members are resolved according to the group's own norms, rather than by reference to some external body of wisdom such as the law. The outside adjudicator must first be able to determine what those norms are and then decide whether they can be incorporated into existing laws and legal doctrine. If the group has formally empowered some person or body to authoritatively identify, create, or interpret its substantive rules, the outside adjudicator may be able to defer to these decisions. In the absence of formal internal sources for identifying the group's norms, the outside adjudicator must take on this task.

Within these parameters, how much scope is there for normative pluralism? This is both a technical legal question – "*How* should one incorporate exogenous norms?" – and a question of normative justification – "*When* should one incorporate such norms?" Using three quite different legal contexts I explore two interpretive techniques for achieving normative pluralism: the use of relatively content-neutral legal tools to which minority group practices can be mapped, and the use of interpretive discretion to apply abstract legal concepts in a culture-sensitive way. The former represents a way of crystallizing the group's practices in a form recognizable to the legal system; the latter recognizes that there is very often interpretive room to manoeuvre within the vague concepts often employed in legal doctrine. Insofar as people lack the foresight to pin down all contingencies explicitly using the former, the latter fills an important residual function.

In employing these techniques, Canadian courts seem, de facto, to have adopted an approach very similar to that explicitly imposed by law in the British colonies: that of qualifying the acceptance of pluralism with the proviso that internal group norms that are repugnant to some overarching sense of natural justice or morality will not be enforced.[4] In the African context, these repugnancy clauses have given rise to a debate about the degree of ethnocentrism exhibited in their application;[5] the same questions come more clearly into focus in the Canadian context once we notice the parallels between explicit legal practice in colonial Africa and implicit legal practice in multicultural Canada. I cannot canvass all the normative arguments for and against invoking the repugnancy doctrine in each of the types of dispute I shall analyse. My objective is to create an analytical framework for thinking about them. I hope it will prove useful in illustrating some of the conditions that facilitate the adjudicative recognition of minority group autonomy and clarifying where the normative issues arise.

The first of my three examples involves expulsions of disobedient members from the Hutterian Brethren and hence from their agricultural colony. Since Hutterites hold all of their property in common, expelled members are deprived of a share of the community property. The second issue arises out of the dismissal of teachers at religious schools for breach of a religions tenet when that dismissal could otherwise be construed as wrongful dismissal or unlawful discrimination. Finally, I examine a case in which a Salish community's effort to include someone in a traditional practice provoked an action in battery and false imprisonment.

EXPULSIONS FROM THE HUTTERIAN BRETHREN

These cases involve two disputes twenty years apart over matters of discipline, and ultimately of membership status, in two Hutterite colonies. In *Hofer* v. *Hofer*,[6] four dissidents claimed that, despite their expulsion from the Church, they remained members of their agricultural colony and as such were entitled to a share of the assets of the colony. The other members countered with the argument that expulsion from the Church entailed expulsion from the colony, and since property is communally held in Hutterite colonies, loss of membership meant loss of any interest in the community's assets. For legal purposes the internal dispute was transposed into the categories of contract and trust. In this case conventional tools for private ordering were used by a minority group to structure community life in accordance with its own practices. In regulating such use, courts face the question of how far they can or should apply the normative framework of the minority community.

In *Lakeside Colony of Hutterian Brethren et al.* v. *Hofer et al.*,[7] the dispute again centred around the expulsion of certain members for disobedience. But, here, the expelled members challenged the validity of the expulsion itself. The legal argument turned not on the substantive criteria for expulsion, but on the procedural requirements for effecting it. The issue was the extent to which the court should incorporate Hutterite practices and understandings into the notion of due process. The pluralistic technique advocated was the interpretation of an abstract conventional legal concept in a way sensitive to the culturally distinct way of life that Hutterianism represents.

The Use of Content-Neutral Legal Tools

The legal doctrines of contract and trust are relatively empty vessels into which people may pour such content as they see fit. In a multicultural society we can expect to see such tools occasionally put to use by minority groups to structure relationships within their own communities. The Hutterites have done just this. Their colonies are established by articles of association signed by all adult male members. In *Hofer*, some judges[8] construed these articles as a simple contract determining the rights of members *inter se*, including the valid reasons for expulsion and its consequences. Other judges[9] used the articles to determine the terms of the trust under which they found Hutterite property to be held. Both legal techniques enabled the colony effectively to codify its rules in respect of communal ownership, thereby providing the Supreme Court with a clear and authoritative statement of its internal rules.

Through the use of the contract rubric, the Hutterites made their internal requirements mesh with a key component of the legal system: contract law and its anchor in the idea of consent as a basis of obligation. The dissenters had signed the articles and presented no evidence that their consent was not free (the Court also heard evidence that acceptance of communal property was a part of adult baptismal and wedding ceremonies as well). Given that contract law is supposed to allow people to design their own relationships, the dissidents were forced to ground their claim ultimately in the repugnancy doctrine, arguing that communal property with no right to division upon dissolution of the relationship is contrary to public policy. This argument found favour with only one judge.[10] The rest found nothing contrary to public policy in the Hutterite norms of sharing, provided individual members had agreed to them. There was therefore no impediment to incorporating them into the terms of a contract and enforcing them as such.[11]

The explicit internal rule prescribing communal ownership was equally capable of being incorporated into the terms of the trust. However, the rules governing expulsion, crucial to determining who was a beneficiary of the trust, seemed not to have been explicitly laid out but, rather, were inferred from the judges' understanding of Hutterianism. Here, the group's internal norms exhibited a more subtle influence on the Court's reasoning. To interpret the trust, the judges had to discover the religious requirements of the Hutterite way of life. In line with Hutterian belief, the colony was held to be an extension of the Church and to have been endowed by the Church for the purposes of continuing the Hutterian faith precisely because this form of life was a requirement of the religion.[12] For this reason, it made sense to interpret the trust as making Church membership a prerequisite of membership in the colony. The plaintiffs were treated as having effectively left the Hutterian Brethren[13] and, by this fact, as having lost any interest they had in the property of the colony. Thus, the loss of their membership in the colony turned on the loss of their membership in the Church rather than directly on the vote to expel them from the colony. The articles of association, however, did not specify the conditions under which membership in the Church could be lost. Having no contractual or other explicit ground for deciding that the plaintiffs had ceased to be members of the Church, these judges could only rely directly on the Church's norms.

Two different methods for determining Church membership are discernible in the judgments. The judges sometimes inquire directly into the substantive beliefs of Hutterianism, with the aim of determining whether the plaintiffs were sufficiently out of communion with the Church to be treated as having quit it; at other points, they appear to defer to an internal decision-maker on the question. The former involves identifying and directly applying the substantive rules of the group; the latter, identifying an authoritative decision-making mechanism internal to the group.[14] Apparently adopting the former approach, Justice Dickson at times enters into the internal Hutterian debate to ratify the majority's interpretation of Hutterian practices and requirements:

[B]ecause of [the plaintiffs'] repeated pronouncements ... those in authority in the Hutterian Brethren *were justified* in concluding that plaintiffs as at the dates of their respective expulsions had not only endorsed another faith but were also guilty of persistent breach of discipline. This was not simply a discussion of metaphysical subtleties but a denunciation by plaintiffs of the doctrines of their Church.[15]

The alternative approach is ambiguously evident in the judgment of Justice Ritchie. On the one hand, he explicitly says that membership should be left for the Church authorities to determine.[16] On the other hand, this apparent deferral to Church authority is called into doubt by his discussion of the differences between the beliefs of the minority and the majority.[17] This gives the impression that he is relying on his own reading of the situation to conclude that the plaintiffs deserved to be expelled. Yet, genuine deferral to another authority means accepting its decision whether or not one agrees with it substantively.

In the final analysis, the issue in *Hofer* boils down to two fairly straightforward questions: whether the communal ownership of property is acceptable, and whether the views held by the dissidents were inconsistent with their continued membership. With respect to the latter, there was little room for disagreement. Indeed, by the time of the trial the plaintiffs had been baptized into the Radio Church of God and were not claiming continued membership in the Hutterian Brethren. Second, while most of the judges held that the practice of holding all property in common was at odds with majority cultural practices, it was not deemed outside the bounds of the acceptable, provided it was consensual. Since the Hutterite's relevant practices and the dissidents' membership status were relatively unambiguous, a highly sophisticated capacity for cultural empathy was not necessary on the part of the court. This raises the question of how far courts will be willing to go down the pluralistic path of incorporating exogenous norms into the legal categories in cases that require more of an effort to understand the minority group practices because the dispute *does* turn on "a discussion of metaphysical subtleties."

The Interpretation of Abstract Legal Concepts

The issue at stake in *Lakeside Colony* was a more subtle one, and it is arguable that, in the face of a demand for greater cultural empathy, the Supreme Court faltered. First, the decision implicitly indicates a limit on judicial willingness to defer to internal decision-making authorities. Despite the talk in *Hofer* of leaving it up to groups to decide their own membership, the Court reviewed the process resulting in expulsion in *Lakeside* and found it wanting. It therefore appears that the strategy of deferral is subject to the group's ability to pass muster according to legal criteria of procedural fairness. Although the decision to subject internal decision-making procedures to any kind of review might be controversial in some situations, I want to focus here on the conception of procedural fairness imposed by the Court and to question whether it adequately takes account of the Hutterite way of life. Even if the decision to review the internal decision was appropriate, the reasoning displays a lack of openness to diversity in its interpretation of procedural justice, and this may have consequences for the Hutterites' ability to pursue their chosen way of life.

The membership dispute in this case ultimately grew out of a larger dispute about the economic management of the colony,[18] in the course of which Hofer and several supporters acted in clear defiance of the decisions taken by the leadership of the colony.[19] Ultimately, a meeting was held of the voting members (i.e., the married men) of the colony. At the meeting, Hofer behaved disruptively and was asked to leave. In his absence the rest of the members decided he should be disciplined by a mild form of shunning, being required to eat and worship separately for a time. Upon being called back to the meeting, Hofer refused to accept this discipline. He was told that such defiance constituted self-expulsion from the church, but he persisted. He was then told he was "out of the Church." Still defiant, Hofer insisted that he would appeal to a higher authority. A further meeting was held ten days later, to give Hofer a chance to repent; he refused to attend.

As a result of these meetings, the colony considered Hofer to have been expelled. For his part, Hofer and his supporters refused to acknowledge the validity of the judgment about his behaviour or the discipline offered. They refused to eat separately, requiring the others to stay away from the communal dining hall in order to avoid contact with them; they refused to follow orders with respect to the hog-farming operation they ran; indeed, they diverted the proceeds of the hog farm into separate bank accounts and purported to elect new officers for the colony, with Hofer as president. A month later, the colony filed a statement of claim seeking an order requiring the dissidents to vacate the colony and turn over colony property and assets. The dissidents continued their defiance as the action proceeded through the courts. In the meantime, the Lakeside situation was considered at two meetings of ministers of the wider Hutterian Conference, of which Lakeside was a part. Hofer was invited to attend these meetings to give his side of the story; he refused.

In deciding whether the expulsion of Hofer was valid, the Supreme Court narrowed the issue to whether he had adequate notice of the consequences of his defiance: they judged the notice inadequate. Although Justice Gonthier starts his analysis by noting that the "content of the principles of natural justice is flexible and depends on the circumstances in which the question arises,"[20] his analysis is very legalistic and more suitable to interactions in large, anonymous communities than to the circumstances of Hutterite life. Hutterite colonies are small, close communities in which everyone is required to work and live in harmony with one another. Substantively, the Hutterites have a very strict code of conduct, requiring members to "obey the rules and regulations and the officers of the congregation or community," "give and devote all [their] time, labor, services, earnings and energies to the congregation," and "do and perform the work, labor, acts and things required of [them] by the congregation" on pain of discipline.[21] When a member has misbehaved, the community decides on the appropriate discipline, ranging from mild to severe shunning. This discipline is understood as being "offered" to the wrongdoer to allow him or her to be reconciled with the community. Refusal to accept discipline is considered to result in self-expulsion, since it marks a refusal to be reconciled.[22]

There is no doubt that the Hutterite way of life requires a high degree of uniformity of belief and behaviour of its members, requiring submission to the decisions of the colony. It is not a way of life to everyone's taste, but it was a life that Hofer had accepted and then came to defy. Indeed, his defiance took essentially the form of an attempted coup. Nevertheless, the Court decided that it was inappropriate for the initial meeting to have declared Hofer "out of the Church" when he refused to accept discipline. Instead, it was argued, the appropriate procedure would have been to postpone the expulsion decision to a later meeting, giving due notice to all voting members of the colony so that Hofer would have a chance to consider his position or defend himself. The defect was not cured by the second meeting because its purpose was not to reconsider the decision to expel, merely to give Hofer a chance to repent.[23] It thus presupposed the validity of the earlier decision. This seems to me an excessively legalistic analysis. It makes perfect sense in the context of legal proceedings in a society not characterized by close social bonds between members and in which there is a great deal of room for misunderstanding between authorities and those subject to authority. These conditions may make it necessary to ensure that discipline is preceded by a carefully structured opportunity to defend oneself.

In a closely knit community, it is unclear what purpose is served by such rigid attention to procedural niceties. The Court acknowledged that Hofer's behaviour warranted discipline and that he could not help but have been aware that his behaviour would be taken up at the first meeting. This can only be because of a common understanding, of which he was a part, that his behaviour was considered out of step and therefore liable to some discipline. Instead of taking the opportunity to put his case, he disrupted the meeting, refusing to hear the complaint against him. Given the norms of obedience within Hutterite society, can it be doubted that he knew that he was in violation of the community's substantive norms? Nevertheless, when offered discipline, he refused to accept it,[24] again clearly flouting community norms. He dug himself in deeper by refusing to attend the second meeting. His behaviour reveals a consistent pattern of refusal to accept the authority of the duly constituted decision-making body of the community. Indeed, given Hofer's efforts to set himself up as president, the argument made on his behalf that he was merely challenging the technical validity of the decision to expel him has a distinctly fictional quality. The fact that he did not press his claim as president, that is, as purported spokesperson for the colony, suggests that he understood only too well where the true authority lay. In this context, how can it be doubted that he understood the consequences of outright defiance of this authority?

Thus the Court imposed on this Hutterite community a conception of natural justice that, given its internal social relations, was unnecessary. Although the Court undertook a fairly sensitive examination of the substantive norms binding Hutterite colonies, exploring the rules laid down in the articles of association and expressed in traditional customs and practices, little attention was paid to the kind of procedural framework for decision-making suitable to this kind of community. Instead, the Court simply assumed that the notice rules of procedural justice appropriate in the wider Canadian context were appropriate here. In the process it may have contributed to a weakening of discipline within Hutterite colonies. If members are given an incentive to look for technical procedural defects in communal decisions and can insist on their right to continue drawing on communal resources while disputes are resolved (especially while apparently being relieved of their obligation to otherwise abide by community norms), this is bound to have a serious impact on a way of life that requires close co-operation among members on a daily basis. The Court seems to have ignored the elementary insight that procedure affects substance, and rather blithely assumed that the law can prescribe a uniform set of procedural norms that will be suitable for every decision-making context. In doing so, it may have undermined the ability of communities like the Hutterites' to regulate their own communal lives according to a less legalistic ethos.

Generally speaking, the Hutterites have been able to use legal tools available to society at large to facilitate the structuring of their communal life. This strategy allows the Court to incorporate into those generic tools the internal norms of Hutterianism. In doing so, however, the courts become, through their interpretation of the contract or trust, the final interpreters of the group's social practices. This means that the better defined the terms of these legal instruments are, the better the group will protect itself from the effects of an interpretive mindset not fully informed by Hutterianism. The obvious corollary is that to the extent that a group's internal norms are not explicitly articulated in such instruments, it must rely upon the courts' willingness and ability to interpret vague concepts in ways that are sensitive to the group's way of life. This was precisely the difficulty encountered in *Lakeside*. The colony's internal procedural norms were much less clearly articulated in its articles of association than its substantive prescription of communal property. Judging from these two cases, to rely upon judicial discretion in a culture-sensitive context is a somewhat dangerous strategy for minority groups. The remaining examples of internal disputes will allow us to explore in further detail some of the conditions militating in favour of and against the successful deployment of this technique to achieve pluralistic outcomes.

DENOMINATIONAL SCHOOL DISCIPLINE

Denominational schools occasionally dismiss teachers for failing to live up to the tenets of the religious group concerned. To date, most cases have dealt with teachers in violation of the school's religious norms concerning marriage – getting divorced or marrying a divorced person when the religious group does not allow divorce, or living in a common-law relationship. Provincial legislation or collective agreements typically allow teachers to appeal to an arbitrator for determination of whether the dismissal was for just cause. In other cases a complaint is made under provincial human rights legislation that the teacher has been discriminated against on the basis of religion or marital status. Some disputes involve separate schools, whose existence is protected under Section 93 of the Constitution Act, 1867; others involve dismissals from private religious schools.

A careful analysis of the case law reveals, so far, a fairly high level of deference to the religiously defined needs of denominational schools. Several courts have held that schools protected under Section 93 have had the power to dismiss employees for what has come to be called "denominational cause" since before Confederation,[25] rendering the right impervious to legislative interference.[26] In fact, most human rights codes have an explicit exemption from the usual prohibition against discrimination on various grounds for certain kinds of organizations, including religious schools. Some, like Ontario, have an explicit exemption from the prohibition against, among other things, marital status discrimination if the discriminatory requirement is a reasonable and bona fide qualification given the nature of the employment.[27] It is these sorts of exemptions that have been used to find that religious schools that do not have Section 93 protection nevertheless also have at least some right to dismiss teachers for denominational cause.

The case law conveys the impression that the issue is clearly settled as a matter of positive law – constitutional or statutory – to which the courts have no choice but to submit. In fact, it turns out that the courts have a fair amount of discretion in these cases, which they have used to protect the right of religious schools to police the religious conformity of teachers. Let me illustrate this using Ontario law. To begin with, Section 93 does not itself give denominational schools any particular powers. Rather, it merely preserves whatever rights or privileges the denominational schools had by law at the time of Confederation. Hence, the ultimate legal source for the right to dismiss for denominational cause must be sought in the law as it was before 1867. But no statute governing school administration in Upper Canada before 1867 explicitly grants the power to dismiss a separate school teacher for failing to abide by Church doctrine. In fact, in *Porter*, Justice Zuber indicates that pre-Confederation rights to dismiss teachers were grounded in the common law of employment, which gave public and separate schools alike the power to dismiss for "just cause". From this he infers:

I take it to be obvious, that if a school board can dismiss for cause, then in the case of a denominational school cause must include denominational cause. Serious departures from denominational standards by a teacher cannot be isolated from his or her teaching duties since within the denominational school religious instruction, influence and example form an important part of the educational process.[28]

Since no pre-1867 case law is cited, we must infer that even if there were no actual cases settling this point, the *correct* interpretation, according to Justice Zuber, is that just cause includes denominational cause in the case of a separate school. In other words, the ultimate authority for the proposition that separate schools have this power is the courts themselves, in their role as interpreters of the common law. This takes a vague standard – "just cause" – and gives it a culture-sensitive interpretation: in the educational environment of a denominational school, it should be interpreted to include "serious departure from denominational standards."

A similar interpretive power is exercised in cases decided under human rights legislation. Many of these cases fit uneasily into the legislative exemptions from the prohibition on discrimination. The exemptions were not drafted with this type of case in mind (they are more clearly designed to permit religious schools to hire only co-religionists), and the reasoning leading to the conclusion that the exemption applies is often tortured.[29] Any Board of Inquiry that feels inclined to use its interpretive discretion to narrow the scope of these exemptions would be able to find ways to do so. For example, an adjudicator could, as has been suggested by one judge, require proof that a disobedient teacher had been formally expelled from her or his Church in order for a school to invoke the exemption in favour of allowing the exclusive employment of co-religionists. Boards have not done so, carrying on the tradition started by the common law courts of making room for religious schools to operate differently.

In addition, the Ontario exemptions do not give carte blanche to discriminate. The exemption is subject to an objective standard of reasonableness. This opens the door to arguments that a particular school rule of religious conformity is not objectively necessary to the smooth functioning of the school. Yet boards of inquiry have tended not to invoke these objective limits. For example, in *Caldwell* Justice McIntyre echoed Justice Zuber's view, which was cited earlier:

In addition to the ordinary academic program, a religious element which determines the true nature and character of the institution is present in the Catholic school. To carry out the purposes of the school, full effect must be given to this aspect of its nature and teachers are required to observe and comply with the religious standards and to be examples in the manner of their behaviour in the school so that students see in practice the application of the principles of the Church on a daily basis and thereby receive what is called a Catholic education.[30]

If religious schools are to be allowed at all, this must be right. Yet the courts have left unexplored the tension between the objective elements of the legal tests (it is the courts who must decide what counts as just cause, and the requirements imposed on a teacher must be "reasonable") and the rationale that a teacher who is not a good Catholic cannot adequately contribute to the creation of a Catholic ethos. How is an outside adjudicator to decide whether a teacher is a good Catholic or what a Catholic ethos requires, except according to the standards of the Church? From the point of view of the religious community, the violation of certain religious tenets renders a teacher unfit to teach. From the point of view of the law, the question is whether this is just cause for dismissal or whether the imposition of the rule is reasonable. If these legal terms were interpreted entirely from the religious point of view, they would not constitute *objective* constraints on the power of schools to regulate their internal operations. At best, they would test the subjective bona fides of the official who did the firing. Yet, to a large extent, courts and tribunals have simply accepted the evidence of the school that particular behaviour constitutes "a serious departure from denominational standards" or that conformity with a particular religious doctrine is a reasonable requirement.[31] Thus, in effect, courts and tribunals have recognized the autonomy of religious groups to police the religious integrity of their schools.

It may be the nature of the religious groups involved in these cases so far and the nature of the rules violated that explains the non-interventionist stance of courts and tribunals and leaves open the question of how much autonomy will ultimately be recognized. Many of the cases have involved Roman Catholic schools who fired teachers for flouting the Church's rules on divorce. It may be the obviousness and clarity of the rules about divorce in Catholicism that explains why outside adjudicators have not found it necessary to second-guess a school's claim that: (a) a teacher has violated this rule, and (b) this is sufficiently serious to justify dismissal. In a way, judicial notice has been taken of the fact that breach of the rules with respect to divorce make a Catholic teacher a bad role model for Catholic students. And whether someone has been divorced or married in a civil ceremony is readily verified, because this is a formal, legally recognized status. The importance of the rule and its application are clear. This makes it easier for an outside adjudicator to appear simply to adopt the Church's own rule in determining what constitutes just cause for legal purposes rather than making its own judgment.

Private religious schools have tended to take one further precaution, using the legal system to their advantage, just as the Hutterites have done, to incorporate their rules into their teachers' contract of employment. In this way, they help establish the authoritative status of the rule and provide one further reason for enforcing it: that the teacher agreed to it. Even this argument, however, bends the normal rules in favour of religious institutions: normally, a contract provision waiving one's rights under human rights legislation is invalid, precisely because human rights codes are designed to protect vulnerable social groups against those who have greater power. In a situation in which the bargaining power of two parties is unequal, agreement to a contractual term that disadvantages the weaker party is suspect. The implicit reliance in these cases on the teacher's agreement to abide by the religious rules of the school indicates that the adjudicators thought the usual argument invalidating such agreements carries less force within a religious community than elsewhere.

We can explore one of the challenges of this pluralism and test its limits by asking what would happen if the rule relied on by a school was either less clear, or less clearly central to its religious teaching, thus giving greater room for the exercise of the vague limitations built into the legal rules.[32] Suppose, for example, that a Catholic school were to dismiss a teacher for her outspoken advocacy of the ordination of women. Although a recent Papal encyclical on the subject has taken the position that an exclusively male clergy is official Church doctrine, this has been followed by considerable theological debate within Catholicism about whether the criteria for such a determination are in fact satisfied. At first glance, one might argue that to decide in accordance with internal norms whether the outspoken advocacy of the ordination of women is just cause for dismissal, a court should defer to the Church hierarchy on the point. But that would be to ignore the claim that there is an argument *within* Catholicism that the Papal pronouncement on the subject is, in a sense, ultra vires. To justify deference to the internal authority under these conditions, one would have to go a step further and say that within that community Papal encyclicals have validity even if they get their theology wrong, just as civil courts must be obeyed even if they interpret the law wrongly. Otherwise, to take seriously the difference of opinion within Catholicism, the court would have to make its own investigation into the theological debate to ascertain what rule binds the religious community controlling the school and whether it is important enough that its observation is necessary to the religious ethos of the school. Without the benefit of a clear, authoritative internal statement on such questions the religious community runs the risk of having a foreign understanding imposed on it in the guise of an interpretation of its own practices. Adjudicators would find themselves being called upon to make pronouncements about theological matters, those metaphysical subtleties that Justice Dickson was worried about.

If an adjudicator can conclude that internal norms do not support an employee's dismissal, he or she will have been able to bring internal and mainstream legal norms into sufficient alignment to avoid having to choose between them. Otherwise, the decision comes down to whether a religious rule is so seriously at odds with the values that otherwise inform the legal system that it should be labelled repugnant to natural justice and equity. This is the question posed by a recent case involving the dismissal of a gay teacher from a Catholic school.[33] The teacher was fired not simply for being gay, but for having undergone a public "commitment ceremony" with his lover. To the school board, this flouted the official teaching that while homosexuality per se is not wrong, homosexual behaviour is. Should an adjudicator regard an injunction against homosexual behaviour as within the bounds of what a reasonable religion may require of teachers in its schools or will this be caught by a de facto repugnancy clause? Such a case more clearly tests the depth of the commitment to pluralism. But our reaction needs to be tested against the outcome in the Hutterite expulsion cases. If Hutterite enforcement of their norms, even on pain of forfeiting one's share in the community's property, is not contrary to public policy, should not a religious school's prohibition on intimate same sex relationships be equally binding?

NONCONSENSUAL RITUAL INITIATION: *THOMAS V. NORRIS*[34]

Thomas was forcibly taken from a friend's home by a group of men to a Salish longhouse, where he was kept for four days and initiated into the Spirit Dancing tradition of the Salish. Presided over by an elder, the initiation involved fasting, loss of sleep, and flagellation. In addition, the initiate was repeatedly lifted horizontally by several men who blew on him and pressed their fingers into his sides. When Thomas' ulcer began acting up during this process, his brother was allowed to take him to the hospital. Thomas then brought suit against most of the participants in the initiation for battery, assault, and false imprisonment.

From the point of view of the defendants, Thomas was a troubled member of the community, one who had strayed from a responsible, healthy life. His initiation was sought by his common-law wife, who hoped it might improve their marital relationship. Initiation into Spirit Dancing was meant to enable the initiate to hear the call of his guardian spirit. Upon hearing his spirit, the initiate "sings" a song, one that is a unique expression of his relationship with his spirit. According to tradition, once a dancer, Thomas would enjoy a continual spiritual renewal through his participation in the annual winter dances. From the point of view of the law of tort, Thomas had been abducted against his will, forcibly confined for four days, deprived of food and water, and subjected to physical contact to which he did not consent. All this spelled an obvious violation of his personal security of the sort that tort law normally gives protection against.

Thus described, the distance between the defendants' understanding of their actions and that of the law is greater in this case than in the other situations I have examined. It is perhaps not surprising, therefore, that the judge's response most clearly relied on a de facto repugnancy doctrine. For their part, the defendants made little attempt to fit their actions into the common law,[35] preferring to defend Spirit Dancing as an Aboriginal right protected by Section 35 of the Constitution Act.[36] As a traditional practice, the defendants argued, the Spirit Dancing initiation enjoyed a form of civil immunity such that the common law of battery and false imprisonment did not apply to behaviour conducted under its auspices. In other words, the defendants were claiming that the Salish community's autonomy in respect of Spirit Dancing should be respected by others and the decisions about it left to community representatives without outside interference.

Although in the end I think the court reached the right decision – *this* initiation should not have been considered to fall under the protection of an Aboriginal right and was properly judged to be a tort – the reasons given showed little sensitivity to Salish practices in particular and the ideal of normative pluralism in general. I will return to my own analysis of the case later; for now, I want to focus on the problems with the court's analysis, for they help to illuminate some of the central tensions and challenges involved in the process of adjudication in a spirit of pluralism.

To Justice Hood this was a clear case of battery and false imprisonment; he was right in the sense that had a group of non-Aboriginal men done this to another man it would very likely have been actionable. He also rejected the Section 35 argument at each step of its analysis. He first held that there was insufficient evidence that Spirit Dancing has been in existence and practised at all material times so as to qualify as an Aboriginal right. Further, he held that even if such proof had been offered, any such practice that involves "force, assault, injury and confinement, all against the will of the initiate" cannot be an Aboriginal right. The nature and scope of Section 35 Aboriginal rights must take account of criminal and civil laws "which govern the relationships between Canadian citizens in a peaceful society in order to protect the freedoms and rights of all." In other words, only those practices consistent with laws of general application can attract the protection of Section 35. What accounts for this singularly unpluralistic analysis?

In contrast with judicial efforts in other cases to enter into the spirit of the community practices in issue, Justice Hood showed no very deep understanding of the spiritual nature of the Spirit Dancing tradition. Whereas others have waxed eloquent over the religious significance of a life governed by communal sharing and the importance of teachers' exemplification of the model Christian life, Justice Hood merely skimmed the surface of the practice of Spirit Dancing. Although he claimed that he had been able to glean the general nature of Spirit Dancing from the evidence,[37] his descriptions of the "nature" of Spirit Dancing were confined to the behavioural details of who does what to whom, when. Completely absent is any hint of understanding of the spiritual meaning of dancing within Salish traditions. The contrast between Justice Hood's interpretation of Section 35 and the courts' interpretation of Section 93 of the Constitution Act, 1867, is also instructive. Neither section confers substantive rights: each merely preserves pre-existing rights. But whereas the courts have themselves decided that the common law rights of denominational schools before 1867 included the right to dismiss teachers for denominational cause, Justice Hood argued that no Aboriginal practice inconsistent with the way the common law would ordinarily be applied can count as an Aboriginal right preserved by Section 35.

It is unclear whether this is because Justice Hood was so out of sympathy with the practice that he was incapable of entering into the Salish world view even for the purposes of accurately stating the defendants' claim, or because the evidence was genuinely inadequate to enable him to undertake such a journey of the imagination. This points to a greater challenge facing the Salish than we have seen in the other cultural claims examined here. Whereas the judges in the denominational schools cases could effectively take judicial notice of the practices of the Catholic Church in respect of divorce because they are so well known, and the judges in the Hutterite expulsion cases could rely on the relatively clear codification of Hutterite practices in their colonies' Articles of Association, Spirit Dancing is not a well-known practice, nor is there an authoritative "manual" that either articulates its spiritual meaning or outlines the correct "procedures" to be followed. The Salish have an oral tradition. The few academic writings on Spirit Dancing are themselves written from an outsider's perspective.[38] Nor, unlike in other religions, is there an internal, formal hierarchy whose evidence might be accepted as authoritative.[39] There are elders, and indeed the elder in charge of Thomas's initiation gave evidence in his own defence, but his testimony seems to have been neither offered nor received as expert evidence.[40] By contrast, a minister of the Hutterian Brethren was treated as an expert witness in *Hofer* and the court had the benefit of testimony from an academic expert. The contrast with the "judicial notice" of the rules about divorce in the Catholic Church is even more stark.

Thus the defendants may have been handicapped by the relative informality of Salish practices. They had little in the way of easily recognizable – at least to legal authorities – authoritative sources to identify the content and meaning of these practices. Or perhaps they were reluctant to reveal the internal workings of Spirit Dancing to the outside world. There seems to be some element of secrecy surrounding the tradition of Spirit Dancing, which the defendants may have been trying to preserve. Perhaps it was some combination of these factors that led to the decision to pursue a very ambitious autonomy claim, namely, that the court should simply recognize the sovereign authority of the Salish over this customary practice. But an all-or-nothing litigation strategy is always risky. The judge, not having been fully educated about Spirit Dancing, was clearly unhappy about being asked to give the community carte blanche to conduct the practice in any way they saw fit. Given the rejection of the Section 35 argument, the defendants were left extremely vulnerable to having their traditions read entirely from the outside perspective of the common law, from which perspective their behaviour appeared clearly unlawful. The result was effectively to treat *any* departure from ordinary legal standards as repugnant to natural justice and morality. This, however, renders Section 35 completely empty: it protects only those practices that need no protection.

Thus, Justice Hood's analysis was deeply flawed in that it left no room for normative pluralism. However, even if it is accepted that First Nations communities should have some autonomy over these sorts of matters – indeed, even if it is argued that they should have complete autonomy – this does not settle the issue in this case. However sympathetic one is to the idea of group autonomy, this cannot be interpreted to give each group the power to determine its own jurisdiction without very obviously leading to interminable conflict-of-laws situations as different groups contest jurisdiction in various disputes. This illustrates another dimension of the problem of designing a legal system that accommodates an appropriate degree of normative pluralism.

Quite apart from the question of whether any group should be allowed to do this sort of thing to one of its members, *Thomas* v. *Norris* can be analysed as raising the issue of whether Thomas was a member of the Salish community and therefore eligible for initiation into its spiritual practices. He clearly did not consider himself part of the spiritual community. He had not been raised within it and had no interest in it, having lived off the reserve most of the time. The defendants equally clearly considered him a member, claiming at trial that Thomas's rights as an individual must give way to those of the Aboriginal nation to which he belonged. Indeed, one can read into Justice Hood's opinion an inchoate understanding of this problem. In referring to the rights Thomas enjoyed as a Canadian, Justice Hood seemed to be claiming him as a member of Canadian society, entitled to the protections accorded all other members. This status is inconsistent with membership in the Salish community if the latter leaves him liable to treatment from which he would otherwise be entitled to protection. To make the case that Section 35 protects their spiritual practice in this instance, the defendants would first have to establish their jurisdiction over Thomas. Ideally, this question must be subject to impartial adjudication – if not by an adjudicative body that does not "belong" to either party, then at least according to impartial criteria acceptable to both groups. In this respect, Justice Hood's decision was also wanting, taking as he did, an almost proprietorial attitude toward the plaintiff. He treated membership as all-or-nothing, leaving no room for overlapping memberships unless their implications are perfectly congruent. This is antithetical to any idea of pluralism and minority group autonomy.

While the judgment does not fully articulate the basis for the defendants' claim on Thomas as a member, this claim was clearly independent of Thomas's consent. It seems likely that even had Justice Hood analysed the case in more nuanced terms he would have rejected any membership criteria that did not incorporate the member's consent. This is where *Thomas* differs significantly from the other cases. In *Hofer*, for example, consent was explicitly incorporated into the Hutterian criteria for membership: one became a member of the colony by signing the articles of association and signified one's continued acceptance of key doctrinal beliefs in baptismal and wedding ceremonies. Thus it was a relatively straightforward matter for the courts to rely on the fact that the plaintiffs had agreed to renounce private property and to forgo any claim on communal property should they leave the Church in order to deny their claim. Similarly, membership in the Catholic Church or other Christian denominations is consensual. One is free to abandon that membership, although at the cost of the entitlement to carry on teaching in a denominational school. The reliance on consent has been reinforced through the incorporation of teachers' agreement to abide by certain religious rules in contracts of employment and collective agreements. In the final analysis, *Thomas* is about a community's claim to include someone as a member with consequences for his treatment that would otherwise be prohibited by law; the other cases are about a community's claim to deny membership to someone with consequences for some benefit to which they would otherwise be able to lay claim.

CONCLUSION

The cases reviewed here suggest that if we look at such disputes through the lens of normative pluralism we can see that there is significant room for culture-specific adjudication, and that the decision to employ such adjudication directly affects the autonomy of minority groups. As far as they go, these cases indicate only timid forays into this territory and a fairly ready willingness to invoke a de facto repugnancy doctrine to require minority groups to bring their practices into line with mainstream legal values. How much autonomy to accord remains an open and largely submerged normative question. My hope is that the use of this analytical framework will bring these questions to the surface for fuller debate. One virtue of this framework is that it allows us to compare cases that otherwise would be considered to fall into quite different legal categories. This kind of comparison seems crucial to the development of a coherent and defensible approach to the incorporation of the norms of minority groups into the law.

The pluralism issue embedded in these cases gives us a hint of some of the questions that will have to be faced should normative pluralism be more vigorously pursued. The conflict in *Thomas* over which group's norms apply to a particular dispute suggests that we need to give more thought to a set of conflict-of-laws rules that could occupy a place in the domestic sphere parallel to those governing choice of rule in the private international law context. Can conventional conflicts of laws rules be adapted to this context, or must we start from scratch to develop new ones? Second, the criteria of proof for establishing the existence of an applicable custom or practice will need more systematic attention. This is particularly important for groups whose methods of codifying and recording their traditions differ most from mainstream Western methods. In addition, we must avoid rules for the recognition of cultural practices that freeze them in time rather than allowing them to grow and change organically. This is turn requires the legal system to be alert to incentives within minority communities for elite groups to attempt to appropriate community practices for their own ends. Finally, we must be attentive to the internal governance structure of minority communities in order to ascertain whether the community has a genuine internal decision-making body empowered to authoritatively pronounce upon internal rules. If so, it becomes possible for an external adjudicator to defer to the decisions of such a body; otherwise, the outsider must contend with having to enter fully into that community's practices to ascertain how the group's rules should be applied on their own terms.

However far our normative theorizing goes in justifying some degree of pluralism, I suggest that these will be worthwhile questions to pursue. The legal system already embodies some pluralistic tendencies that seem relatively entrenched. Part of the reluctance to go any further may stem less from uncertainty about whether it would be fair to do so, than from uncertainty about how to go about it and whether it can be accomplished without creating excessive confusion and complexity.

These are essentially technical questions of legal design – not in any dry, dull sense, but in a theoretically deeper sense in which we confront the task of keeping law a supple, fluid tool for regulating society, including its multicultural dimension.

ACKNOWLEDGMENTS

I am grateful to the Wright Foundation, Faculty of Law, University of Toronto, for funding that enabled me to undertake this research, and to David Wiseman and Linda Shin for finding various needles in several very large haystacks.

NOTES

1 M. Hooker, *Legal Pluralism: An Introduction to Colonial and Neo-Colonial Law* (Oxford: Clarendon Press, 1975); T.W. Bennett, "Conflict of Law – The Application of Customary Law and the Common Law in Zimbabwe," *International and Comparative Law Quarterly* 30 (1981): 59; A.N. Allott, "What is to be Done with African Customary Law?," *Journal of African Law* (1984): 56; J.N. Matson, "The Common Law Abroad: English and Indigenous Law in the British Commonwealth," *International and Comparative Law Quarterly* 42 (1993): 753.

2 It has been invoked mainly by commentators to analyse "social ordering which is ... familiar to and applied by the participants in ... everyday activit[ies]" such as the family, the corporation, and the business network. Marc Galanter, "Justice in Many Rooms: Courts, Private Ordering, and Indigenous Law," *Journal of Legal Pluralism* 19, no. 1 (1981): 17. Galanter labels this "indigenous law," not to be confused with law specifically relating to indigenous or Aboriginal peoples.

3 Insofar as Aboriginal self-government can be analysed in this light, it is the exception that highlights the rule.

4 J.D.M. Derrett, "Justice, Equity and Good Conscience" in *Changing Law in Developing Countries*, ed. J.N.D. Anderson (London: George Allan & Unwin, 1963); Matson, "The Common Law Abroad."

5 Allott, "What is to be Done With African Customary Law?", 59; Matson, "The Common Law Abroad"; L. Amede Obiora, "New Skin, Old Wine: (En)gaging Nationalism, Traditionalism, and Gender Relations," *Indiana Law Review* 28 (1995): 581; Sebastian Poulter, "African Customs in an English Setting: Legal and Policy Aspects of Recognition," *Journal of African Law* (1988): 207.

6 (1966), 59 D.L.R. (2d) 723 (Man. Q.B.); aff'd (1967), 65 D.L.R. (2d) 607 (Man. C.A.); aff'd (1970), 13 D.L.R. (3d) 1 (S.C.C.).

7 (1992), 97 D.L.R. (4th) 17 (S.C.C.).

8 Freedman J. in the Manitoba Court of Appeal, and Cartwright and Spence JJ. in the Supreme Court of Canada.

9 Dickson J. at the trial level, and Ritchie, Martland, Judson, and Hall JJ. in the Supreme Court.

10 Pigéon J., in the Supreme Court, would have declared the provisions of the articles of association holding the members to a communal property regime with no right to any share of the assets upon leaving contrary to public policy because it placed such an impediment in the way of someone wanting to leave that it effectively violated freedom of religion.

11 It would be interesting to know whether the Hutterites use the legal tool of articles of association and incorporate affirmations of communal property ownership in their ceremonies because they, independently, value the members' consent to this regime and regard it as essential to its moral foundations, or whether they have merely realized that they can fit their religious beliefs into this legal framework without distorting their beliefs (too much?) and thereby ensure their enforceability by the legal authorities.

12 For example, Dickson J. commented, "To a Hutterian the whole life is the Church. The colony is a congregation of people in spiritual brotherhood. The tangible evidence of this spiritual community is the secondary or material community around them." *Hofer* v. *Hofer* (1970) 13 D.L.R. (3d) 1 (S.C.C.) at 8, as quoted approvingly by Ritchie J. Ritchie J. concludes "the colony was merely an arm of the church and the overriding consideration governing the rights of all the Brethren was the fulfilment of their concept of Christianity." *Hofer* v. *Hofer* (1970) 13 D.L.R. (3d) 1 (S.C.C.) at 8–9.

13 *Hofer* v. *Hofer* (1970) 13 D.L.R. (3d) 1 (S.C.C.), per Dickson J., at 732 (hereinafter *Hofer*)

14 I have identified these as two complementary strategies for recognizing group autonomy in "Judicial Constructions of Group Autonomy: A Case Study", in *Ethnicity and Group Rights*, Will Kymlicka and Ian Shapiro, eds. (New York: New York University Press, 1997), 257.

15 *Hofer*, at 732, emphasis added.

16 *Hofer*, at 10: "Whether or not any member of the Colony had ceased to be a true believer in the church doctrines was a matter for the church authorities"; and at 13: "I am also of opinion that the decision as to whether or not any individual was a Hutterian Brethren so as to be entitled to continue as a member of the community was a decision which could only be made by the Hutterite Church."

17 He appears to agree with the majority that their daily tasks "are related to and an expression of their religious beliefs" and concludes that this implies that a non-Church member could not remain a member of the colony. *Hofer*, at 7.

18 The triggering event was a decision by the leadership in the colony to recognize the awarding of a patent for a hog-feeding device, similar to one designed by Mr Hofer, to another colony in which such a device had been simultaneously developed. This required Lakeside to instruct Hofer to stop making his device and required the colony to pay damages to the holder of the patent for its breach up to that time. Hofer thought the other patent should not have been recognized and that the colony should have challenged it and claimed the patent for itself. He, together with several other members of the colony, went so far as to persuade the bank – without having any authority to do so – to stop payment on the cheque issued to cover the amount settled upon for breach of the other colony's patent. He also refused to stop manufacturing his hog-feeder.

19 In what follows, I will simplify the discussion somewhat by dealing only with the question of whether Daniel Hofer Sr was properly expelled from the colony. The question of whether his various supporters were properly expelled raises further procedural complexities into which it is unnecessary to delve for my present purpose.

20 *Lakeside Colony of Hutterian Brethren et al.* v. *Hofer et al.*, (1992), 97 D.L.R. (4th) 17 (S.C.C.), at 36 (hereinafter *Lakeside*).

21 From the articles of association, reproduced in the judgment in *Lakeside*, at 24–5.

22 *Lakeside*, at 27.

23 *Lakeside*, at 56.

24 It is unclear from the evidence whether the discipline offered Hofer at that first meeting was considered to cover his defiance in respect of the hog-feeder or only his disruptiveness at the meeting. Although there was no full discussion of the hog-feeder issue, it seems fully consistent with Hutterite practices to have imposed a mild shunning simply in virtue of his behaviour at the meeting. If this is so, his refusal to accept the discipline left the colony with very little choice about what to do next. The practice of offering discipline that the offender must accept in order to be reconciled to the community seems so central to Hutterite practices that it is hard to see how Hofer could claim that he did not have adequate notice that his membership in the colony was at risk.

25 *Re Essex County Roman Catholic Separate School Board and Porter* (1978), 89 D.L.R. (3d) 445 (Ont. C.A.)(hereinafter *Porter*); *Stack* v. *Roman Catholic School Board for St. John's* (1979), 99 D.L.R. (3d) 278 (Newf. S.C. T.D.); *Caldwell* v. *Stuart* (1984), 15 D.L.R. (4th) 1 (S.C.C.) (hereinafter *Caldwell*).

26 Collective bargaining legislation and other school administration legislation as well as human rights codes have been held to be inoperative against denominational schools to the extent that they limit this power. For a

general discussion of the various provisions in force across the country, see
Walter Tarnopolsky, William Pentney, and John D. Gardner, *Discrimination
and the Law* (Toronto: Carswell, 1994), 6–34.

27 See, for example, the Ontario Human Rights Code, s. 24 (a) and (b).

28 *Porter*, at 447.

29 For example, in *Garrod v. Rhema Christian School* (1992), 15 C.H.R.R
D/477 (hereinafter *Garrod*), even though the complainant argued that she
was discriminated against on the basis of marital status, the Tribunal
dismissed the complaint on the grounds that s. 24(a) gives a religious school
the freedom to give preference to persons of the same creed. In effect, the
right of a school to discriminate on the basis of religion was used to justify
its discrimination on the basis of marital status.

30 *Caldwell*, at 13.

31 For example, the board of inquiry in *Garrod* raised the question of whether
not living in a common-law relationship was necessary to the teacher's job
as a role model and noted that no evidence was introduced to back up the
"impressions" of the school. Nevertheless, the board found that the
school's decision was covered by the exemption.

32 Tarnopolsky and Pentney asked whether human rights tribunals would be
willing to use the Code's exemptions to allow a school to refuse to hire a
teacher on the grounds of sex because of a religious belief that children
should be taught only by men, for example. The example is an interesting
one precisely because a likely response from many outsiders would be to
doubt that this kind of sex discrimination really is central to the religious
functioning of the school. This is to invoke the objective standard by which
to gauge the reasonableness of the religious requirement. But that, of
course, is an outsider's perspective, one that reflects a secular commitment
to gender equality. Nor may it be as easy for such a religious group to *prove*
the religious importance of the requirement as it is for the Catholic Church
to establish that it prohibits divorce.

33 Rosie DiManno, "Gay teacher's 'wedding' costs him job," *Toronto Star*,
6 October 1997.

34 [1992] 2 C.N.L.R. 139 (B.C.S.C.).

35 The argument that Thomas acquiesced in this treatment was given short
shrift by Justice Hood. He accepted the plaintiff's evidence that he did not
consent to being initiated. This seems incontrovertible in the face of the
testimony of one of the elders that even if Thomas had clearly asked to
leave, he would not have been released.

36 S. 35(1) reads as follows: "The existing aboriginal and treaty rights of the
aboriginal peoples of Canada are hereby recognized and affirmed."

37 This consisted of the defendants' testimony and a book on the subject:
Pamela Amoss, *Coast Salish Spirit Dancing: the Survival of an Ancestral
Religion* (Seattle: University of Washington Press, 1978). The book is an

anthropological treatment of the practice of Spirit Dancing and focuses on its practice in the late nineteenth and early twentieth centuries in the Washington State area.

38 The only academic work on Spirit Dancing that I have been able to find is the book by Amoss mentioned in the judgment. Even Amoss's book is very much an outsider's perspective on the Salish tradition.

39 Indeed, there is anecdotal evidence to suggest that there was considerable disagreement within this particular community as to whether this "grabbing" was appropriate. In the absence of an internal formal mechanism for dispute resolution it is difficult for a litigant in such a case to establish that he or she acted in accordance with the community's norms rather than as a vigilante.

40 This seems sensible, given that the elder was a defendant; an expert witness, to be credited, must not have a personal stake in the outcome of the litigation. No other expert evidence from someone with an insider's knowledge of the practices in issue was offered.

10 Citizenship, Diversity, and Pluralism: The Case of the European Union

JOHN ERIK FOSSUM

INTRODUCTION

Diversity has always been a hallmark of Europe. It is evident in all aspects of life, including language, culture, ethnicity, race, religion, social class, and social status. Diversity has also manifested itself in a broad spectrum of organizational forms, ranging from empire to city-state. These entities have sought in different ways and with widely varying degrees of success and principled sanction to elicit widely different types of allegiance and support, from the direct democracy of the Greek *polis*, all the way to the totalitarianism of Nazi Germany.

In historical terms, one of the most important unifying forces in Europe has been the nation-state. It has reduced domestic diversity and sought to instil a uniform sense of loyalty and belonging in its citizens. The particular organizational form and the type of attachment associated with the nation-state have been exported to the entire globe. As Anthony Smith has observed, "if any phenomena are truly global, then it must be the nation and nationalism."[1] In fact, it is possible to talk of the "globalization of nationalism."

The nation-state has also protected and fostered diversity. It has served as a vehicle to sustain or propagate national identity and nationally based difference in the global society of states. The model of the nation-state is premised on the mutually supporting effects of sovereign immunity, national identity, and citizenship.[2] And while the modern nation-state was established through the complex interaction of state formation and nation building, these processes were rarely complete, nor are they necessarily irreversible.[3]

In recent years, the process of globalization has deeply affected the nation-state and has sparked a debate on its future. This debate highlights changes in interstate relations, changes in internal organization and in decision-making procedures, changes in the overall capacity of the state to control and manage domestic society, and changes in the principles on which political power is legitimated.[4]

Not all of these dimensions of the phenomenon of globalization are equally prevalent in the debate. Generally, the debate on globalization tends to highlight interstate connectedness and sees this as a recent and contemporary phenomenon. It is arguable, however, whether the debate on globalization has been sufficiently inclusive (in academic disciplinary terms) to shed light on the most salient changes in the role of the state, and on how the different processes of transformation interact. What is often included under the rubric of globalization, and therefore implicitly portrayed as a contemporary phenomenon, is the long-term historical transformation that has generally been referred to as the decline of hierarchies, not only of control, but also of meaning.[5] The most prominent hierarchies that historically have provided people with a ready-made sense of meaning and belonging are religion, aristocracy, and the nation-state itself. In earlier times, society was stratified so that every person knew his or her role. Nobility and royalty were justified by reference to tradition and blood.

The nation-state itself spurred the decline of earlier cultural and religious hierarchies that had provided people with ready-made systems of meaning and a sense of belonging.[6] In the late medieval epoch, a multitude of attachments were eradicated, suppressed, transformed, or channelled into modern notions of national identity. This transition was neither uniform nor entirely complete.[7]

In this sense, the secularization, democratization, and heightened interconnectedness that weakened the hierarchies associated with religion, culture, and nobility have been transformed and now touch on the defining features of the nation-state itself. The result may be significantly altered conceptions of sovereignty, citizenship, and identity. Several analysts refer to the emergence of a more universal concept of citizenship, one that is no longer directly tied to the nation-state.[8] These changes have moral implications: people's values are affected, as are the standards by which they assess what is good and bad, and right and wrong.

It is in Western Europe, the cradle of the modern system of nation-states, that the most important transformations are taking place. Of particular interest is the role of the European Union (EU). Article 1 of the Amsterdam Treaty states that "this Treaty marks a new stage in the process of creating an ever closer union among the peoples of Europe, in which decisions are taken as openly as possible and as closely as possible to the citizen."[9] European integration, according to the architects of the Maastricht and Amsterdam treaties, does foster a process of transformation of the member states of the EU (and of other affiliated and affected states).

What kind of transformation does the EU represent? More specifically, how much of the transformation now underway in Europe is transmitted through and actually caused by the EU? Is it primarily an economic association that leaves the basic nature of the member states and of the state system unchallenged? If so, the changes in Europe must be driven by factors other than the particular type of cooperation and set of institutions that are associated with the EU. Or has the EU in fact helped to trigger a more profound transformation of the state system that has existed in Europe for the past several hundred years? In this chapter I will present and briefly assess three views of the European Union that are prevalent in the literature. The first sees the EU as an economic association. I will argue that while the EU is "incomplete" with respect to normative principles, it is clearly more than an economic association.[10] In its present form it represents an attempt to transform the existing system of states in Europe. Precisely how this transformation proceeds and what its principled and normative status can be are assessed by means of two different conceptions of the political nature of the European Union. The first of these sees it as a federation in the making, and the second sees it as a post-Westphalian community. These two conceptions differ in terms of how the EU is justified. The former is tied to conventional conceptions of state, whereas the latter represents a departure from the nation-state model. These two conceptions therefore differ in terms of the kinds of identities that they seek to promote, and in terms of the conception of citizenship that they embrace.

This chapter is organized in the following manner. Since the assumption is that the EU represents an attempt to transform the nation-state, it is necessary to develop a conceptual framework that can shed light on the nature of this transformation. I have approached the question by means of the notion of recognition as developed by Charles Taylor.

THE POLITICS OF RECOGNITION: A BRIEF OVERVIEW OF RELEVANT DIMENSIONS

The decline of hierarchies can challenge established conceptions of citizenship and identity. Charles Taylor has observed that the general decline of established hierarchies has weakened or even undermined cultures and social orders that provided the populace with ready-made sources of meaning and a sense of belonging.[11] The decline of hierarchies has strengthened the notion of society as man-made and as consisting of laws and norms that are societal and hence subject to change. This compels humans to a greater extent than before to establish the requirements for truth and validity.[12] It also forces individuals and groups to find or construct meaning and a sense of belonging. Taylor's philosophical anthropology is based on the notion of humans as self-interpreting. As he observes, "the claim is that our interpretation of ourselves and our experience is constitutive of what we are, and therefore cannot be considered as merely a view on reality, separable from reality, nor as an epiphenomenon, which can be bypassed in our understanding of reality."[13] The emphasis on humans as self-interpreting also means that emotive aspects are important and morally significant. As Grimen observes, to clarify our emotions is to articulate the evaluative assessments that the emotions entail.[14] This is done by means of "strong evaluations," which are based on morally significant visions of life and of who a we wish to be.[15] Our identity is based on conceptions of the good and closely linked to our strong evaluations. Language is important to identity, because strong evaluations are both embedded in and articulated through a given language. Thus, identities are formed, clarified, and altered through dialogue. This is also indicative of another important aspect of Taylor's philosophical stance, namely the primacy of the community over the individual. As Taylor observes, "the community is ... constitutive of the individual, in the sense that the self-interpretations which define him are drawn from the interchange which the community carries on."[16]

Taylor links the decline of social hierarchies to important changes in basic societal values. For example, the modern notion of dignity has replaced the older notion of honour. This notion of dignity has become associated with democracy in a universalist and egalitarian manner. Taylor observes that "democracy has ushered in a politics of equal recognition, which has taken various forms over the years, and has now returned in the form of demands for the equal status of cultures and of genders."[17] This "politics of recognition," as Taylor observes, was initially based on equality. However, in recent years, other changes have occurred that have given this push for equality a peculiar twist. These are the strengthened emphasis on the individual, or what Taylor terms an "individualized identity." This is the effect of both the decline of social hierarchies and the increased salience of economic factors – with a strengthened attendant emphasis on politics as rational exchange.

This focus on the individual has served to strengthen the ideal of "authenticity," which initially referred to being true to oneself and to the search for a "moral voice from within." But in recent years the moral voice has become more silent. The decline of hierarchies and the attendant weakening of ready-made systems of meaning and order have robbed the individual of contact with the "inner moral voice" while leaving the ideal of authenticity otherwise intact. Only now, the atomized individual feels a greatly enhanced need for recognition, to replace what has been lost. This need for recognition, it is assumed, has been directly linked to the identity of the individual. As Taylor observes:

[T]he thesis is that our identity is partly shaped by recognition or its absence, often by the *mis*recognition of others, and so a person or group of people can suffer real damage, real distortion, if the people or society around them mirror back to them a confining or demeaning or contemptible picture of themselves ... . What has come about with the modern age is not the need for recognition but the conditions in which the attempt to be recognized can fail.[18]

Recognition is achieved through interaction with others and is bound up with the identity of the individual. Therefore, according to Taylor, failure to obtain recognition will seriously harm the identity of the individual or the group.

The need for recognition, initially applied to individuals, has now entered into the discourse of groups. The nature of the demands has also changed and been increasingly oriented to recognition of uniqueness. They have therefore increasingly come to relate to what Taylor has termed the politics of difference. The politics apply to group-based differences based on gender, sex, race, ethnicity, language, and, of course, nationality.

Taylor therefore sees the decline of hierarchies as having triggered a politics of recognition that has profound implications for established conceptions of both citizenship and national identity. One important premise shared by everyone concerned with this phenomenon is that "practical identity-formation presupposes intersubjective recognition."[19] Taylor highlights two types of recognition. The first, the recognition of equal dignity, emphasizes identity formation as individually based and universalizable. The second type, the politics of difference, emphasizes the importance for identity formation of the life-context in which each person is placed.

These two patterns of recognition interact. In viable nation-states they can reinforce each other in such a manner as to contextualize the thrust for equal dignity and to channel and subject the quest for difference into the imperative of loyalty to the nation-state. When these two patterns of recognition are related to the process of globalization, they no longer necessarily reinforce each other within the nation-state framework but, rather, seem to pull the state in different directions.

The globalization of human rights highlights the universalizable component of citizenship and identity, for instance as embedded in the European Convention on Human Rights, whereas the politics of difference may introduce new and challenging issues that can cause states to become fragmented. Many of these problems cut across established territorial boundaries and raise profound questions as to what the new polities will look like.

To assess the character of the EU, I will seek to identify the key principles on which it is justified and to provide a brief assessment of the extent to which it is marked by struggles for recognition. The notion of recognition can be used to locate and assess assumptions about individual identities and values within the larger structure of societal beliefs and values. Identities and values can be seen primarily as entrenched in legal and institutional structures, or as expressed in cultural contexts. Struggles for recognition revolve around identities, values, and rights. Struggles for recognition therefore provide a route to understanding the "moral grammar of social conflicts" and how this changes as contextual factors change.

Although the recognition of equal dignity and the recognition of difference are both associated with modernity, they differ in how they relate to modernity. For instance, the recognition of equal dignity brings forth the democratic ideal of modernity in that it fosters a view of humans as equally worthy of respect. But Taylor is concerned not only with the democratizing potential inherent in modernization, but also with the new forms of estrangement and deprivation that modernity brings in its wake. Therefore, to Taylor, the politics of recognition – writ large – is not simply a manifestation of modernity; it is also a reaction to certain aspects of modernity. The struggle for recognition can therefore also be seen as a manifestation of how morally salient emotions seek to respond to and counteract the modern trend in which economic forces weaken the ethical and moral bases of contemporary societies.

This is a point of contention among "recognition-oriented" analysts. For instance, while Taylor does see the democratic impetus in a rights-based thrust for recognition, he is more ambivalent than discourse-centred analysts such as Axel Honneth and Jürgen Habermas with respect to the normative salience of this thrust for recognition. Because it highlights the universalizable component of personhood, Honneth and Habermas see rights-based recognition as a means to exploit the normative potential embedded in modernity Honneth conceives of rights as "depersonalized symbols of social respect." Rights provide their bearers with the reassurance of a standardized form of entitlement. This provides an opportunity "to exercise the universal capacities constitutive of personhood"[20] and offers a measure of protection against negative social evaluations. The assumption, however, is that the heightened self-reflection and inclusivity of such respect will alter the nature of affective relations. Taylor does not think that rights adequately cover the emotive aspects of human behaviour, which are so important both to identity and to ethics. Further, Taylor's notion of the politics of difference is even more explicitly a rejection of the individualization of human relations that is associated with modernity. To Taylor, the politics of difference can be seen as a defence of collective systems of belief and meaning – infused with ethical value – that various cultures erect in response to an individualizing modernity.

To address the challenges posed by the politics of difference, Taylor speaks of the need to think in terms of "deep diversity," "in which a plurality of ways of belonging would ... be acknowledged and accepted."[21] In the context of citizenship, deep diversity implies that it is necessary to abandon the notion of a uniform citizenship and instead grant culturally distinct groups special status and protections that will help to preserve their cultures over time.[22] Since Taylor is not wholly content with rights-based protections, it is not entirely clear precisely what kind of measures he feels would be necessary to ensure cultural protection over time.[23] Iris Young, from a feminist stance, goes much further than Taylor in her insistence on the need to promote and protect difference.

There are several important and relevant dimensions to this debate. One dimension relates to the sources of identity-based claims for recognition. To simplify the arguments greatly, Charles Taylor highlights language and culture, Axel Honneth highlights individual rights, and Iris Young highlights social structure and gender. One underlying set of questions relates to the moral salience and legitimacy of the law as the anchor of rights and identity.[24] Jürgen Habermas identifies two central questions in this debate. On the one hand is the philosophical and legal discourse on the legitimacy of the law; on the other is the philosophical discourse on the "relationship between morality and ethical life or the internal connection between meaning and validity," which refers to "the old question of whether we can transcend the context of our respective language and culture at all or whether all standards of rationality remain bound to specific world-views and traditions."[25] Habermas's preferred solution is a kind of "constitutional patriotism" embedded in constitutionally entrenched rights imbued with ethical content. Constitutional patriotism is ultimately anchored in the notion of individual autonomy, both public and private. Rights of communication and participation are required to ensure popular sovereignty, and classic human rights ensure the private autonomy of citizens. Together, these sets of rights enable citizens not only to be legal rights-bearing subjects but also, at least in principle, to act as the authors of the law.

Note that this debate is not confined to the relationship between citizenship and national identity. Citizenship and national identity are not conceptually linked but have become linked by the particular historical contingencies associated with the nature of the nation-state.[26] Further, the question of rights revolves around a wider range of rights, as well as a wider range of conceptions of rights, than are usually associated with citizenship rights. The question of identity is not confined to nation and nationality but refers to a wide range of identity seeking.[27] It is readily acknowledged that much of the thrust for recognition has emanated from or at least been given added momentum by non-nationally based groups and movements based on gendered, racial, and ethnic identities. These identity-based thrusts for recognition do not have a natural territorial anchoring, and many of them consist of global networks. They have also been supported by a vastly increased body of international law, which offers legal protections to groups and individuals. These developments also suggest that there are deeper and more fundamental changes on the international scene that raise questions as to the future not only of individual nation-states but also of the entire state system. With David Held, are we faced with a shift from the Westphalian state system to some variant of cosmopolitan democracy? If so, to what extent and how are these developments reflected in the EU?

THE EUROPEAN UNION

The philosophical debate on recognition sketched briefly in the previous section is relevant to the analysis of the European Union. First, it provides us with clues as to the principles on which the EU is based, i.e., whether it is based on weak or strong evaluations. Second, it enables us to discuss the salience of identity-based claims without confining the analysis to conventional notions of identity associated with the nation-state. Third, since we can assess the nature of the EU with reference to a wide range of claims and claimants, we can get a better sense of the nature of the entity and the extent to which it reflects the diversity of Europe than were we simply to consider this in relation to the nation-state. In the following pages, three different conceptions of the EU that have figured in the literature are briefly presented and assessed.

The European Union as an Economic Organization

The first conception of the European Union is of an economic association in which the cultural, linguistic, and ethnic diversity of Europe is not played out. In this view it is based foremost on pragmatic concerns and legitimated with reference to weak evaluations, i.e., with reference to its anticipated outputs, particularly economic ones. This conception has gained credence partly because of the strong influence of certain academic disciplines that have dominated the study of the EU, namely economists, political economists, and, to some extent, international relations specialists.[28] These analysts have portrayed the European integration process and the EU as informed and driven primarily by instrumental and strategic modes of rationality.

Several aspects of the EU give such a conception credence. It is marked by extensive economic co-operation, which is fostered by a comprehensive regulatory structure and through interstate and inter-institutional bargaining. It is in the realm of economic co-operation, i.e., in the internal market program, or Pillar I of the Maastricht and Amsterdam Treaties, that co-operation is most firmly entrenched. Pillar I encompasses the internal market, i.e., the "four freedoms" (freedom of movement of goods, services, capital, and labour), and European monetary union. The internal market program has an important rights-based component in that it contains the right to work and to move freely between member states. It represents a comprehensive program of state deregulation, demonopolization, and privatization within a setting in which the rules and regulations that guide economic exchange are standardized or mutually adjusted. The program for monetary union includes a common and quite independent European Central Bank; a common currency, the Euro, has come into operation in 1999. Monetary union establishes a set of strict criteria for fiscal and monetary policy and for public debt. Since the Single European Act (SEA) came into force in 1987, Pillar I has been based on qualified majority voting. Pillar I makes up the European Community, that part of the EU with the most strongly entrenched legal structure. It is this part that is protected and promoted by the Court of Justice and the supranational legal structure of the EU.

The assumption is that binding interstate cooperation in the economic realm yields considerable benefits. At least in theory, it is in the economic realm that the benefits of co-operation can most easily be discerned, and it is also an area in which, presumably at least, the loss of sovereignty is outweighed by the benefits that derive from the added economic growth that a more open and uniform common market will yield. Further, it is alleged that in those areas that are vital to state sovereignty, states are able to exercise veto. The two pillars, foreign and security (Pillar II) and justice and home affairs (Pillar III), together with Pillar I, make up the EU. Pillars II and III are formally, at least, based on unanimity; this means that each member state can exercise a veto. Member states also completely dominate the process of treaty change and are able to exercise veto. The process of treaty change is closed; it is diplomacy-driven, and there is little room for the European Parliament and for national parliaments in the process. Most national parliaments enter the process during the ratification stage. The (executive) member-state imprint on the process is also revealed by the fact that treaty changes must be ratified by each member country.

Similarly, it is alleged that whereas EU citizenship includes both political and economic rights, such rights are instrumental, i.e., they are necessary for the internal market to work. They are not really entitlements. The assumption, then, is that the rights associated with citizenship do not have strong identity-based implications. In sum, the EU is portrayed as a structure in which binding economic co-operation does not and should not seriously affect the cultural and security-based concerns of individual member states.

The basic assumption informing this conception of the EU is that the extent of co-operation is contingent on considerations of utility. These vary according to academic disciplinary bounds: economists highlight Pareto-optimal gains, whereas realists and neo-realists insist that whereas economic co-operation matters, it will always be contingent on and even dependent on the power-based considerations of state actors jealously guarding their national interests.

Recent developments have revealed that many of the assumptions on which this view of the EU is based are inadequate. The magnitude and nature of binding interstate co-operation in the EU has affected national interests and constrained the large states more than the small ones, an observation that flies in the face of the assumptions of realists and neo-realists. Further, the scope of co-operation presently at work far exceeds the economic realm; this means that the problem of identifying national interests, which has always plagued realists and neo-realists, has become far more pronounced. The structure that has been wrought is so complex that it is hard to establish its alleged benefits. Finally, with regard to citizenship, Eddie Moxon-Browne observes that "the metamorphosis of workers into persons was no semantic accident: it reflected the transformation of the Community from being a merely economic organization into one that affected, and benefited, all its inhabitants irrespective of their economic function and, indeed, irrespective of whether they had any economic function."[29]

This conception of the EU as an economic association was clearly more appropriate in the period prior to the 1990s when integration had less depth and breadth and when it was still in operational and normative terms a derivative of or an extension of the nation-state.[30] After Maastricht that was no longer the case, and the academic literature has started to question what is and should be the principled status of the entity. This reassessment is taking place, it is important to note, at a time when the international scene and how we conceive of the nation-state and the state system are being reexamined.

The European Union as a "Federation in the Making"

The second conception of the European Union posits that while it no doubt is strongly focused on economic co-operation, it is far more than an economic association. In fact, it is seen as a "federation in the making." Binding economic cooperation in Europe, it is asserted, has an obvious normative underpinning: namely, to prevent future wars. This is based on the proposition, "voiced early in the eighteenth century, ... that the expansion of commerce is incompatible with the use of force in international relations and would gradually make for a peaceful world."[31] The underlying question that has torn Western Europe in the post-war period is how much and what type of co-operation "will do" to ensure that. Is it necessary to replace the state system with a novel entity to ensure that wars will no longer happen, or is it possible to develop a structure that builds on interstate co-operation and does not replace the nation-state in its present form? Most of the original founders did not provide a firm answer to this question. Instead, as practitioners, and in light of the war experience, they proposed a set of methods that would foster co-operation. The assumption was that this would help resolve the dilemma. The most important method was the neo-functionalist notion of "spillover." Integration within a given policy area would over time spill over into other policy areas and as such foster increasingly binding co-operation. Once it spilled over into the political realm proper, it would be necessary to develop a federal-type entity to ensure its continued existence. Little was said about the particular nature of this entity, however.

The underlying assumption was obviously problematic. It was implied that a pragmatic approach to integration, one based on weak evaluations, would generate over time the sense of need, purpose, and direction that would enable decision-makers to embed this structure in an institutional setting founded on strong evaluations.

There is no doubt that the process of spillover has worked. European co-operation has both widened and deepened over the years. It has also clearly entered the political realm. The legitimacy of this structure, given the comprehensive and binding nature of co-operation, must be determined on the basis of the democratic quality of the institutions at the EU level. The EU has already developed a legal system with obvious federal features. The challenge now is to extend this into all areas and to develop an institutional structure that is commensurate with and capable of adequately controlling the legal system. But the basic problem of legitimation has only partly been addressed. Since it is widely acknowledged that the EU suffers from a "democratic deficit," the answer would have to be that it is "not yet" legitimate. It is therefore partly legitimated on the assumption that an answer will be found, a problematic stance given the closed, diplomacy-run, and elitist manner in which the process of treaty change is conducted.

Throughout the period since the SEA, a wide range of proposals has been presented to strengthen the role and decision-making powers of the European Parliament, transforming it from a largely advisory body to a decision-making body on par with the Union Council. That is, the intention has been to strengthen the supranational as opposed to the intergovernmental component of the EU. Measures have also been taken to heighten accountability of the appointed bureaucratic "motor of integration," the European Commission, and to increase transparency in the operations of the system in order to heighten institutional accountability and inter-institutional coherence. In addition, European citizenship was formally established in the Maastricht Treaty. Every person holding the nationality of a member state was declared to be a citizen of the Union. Efforts have also been made to foster a European identity, such as creating a European flag and European Anthem, and declaring the 9th of May as Europe Day.

The EU is therefore principally a political construct. In this view, it is a "polity in the making." This means that it is both concerned with the establishment of both a European identity and a European citizenship. The present weak and "incomplete" status of European citizenship and European identity, it is alleged, reflects not to the incompatibility of its components but the considerable time and effort required to develop the institutional and other supports necessary.

It is important to note, however, that the notion of spillover does *not* properly capture the process that has led the EU to its present state. For instance, it cannot account for the vital role of Franco-German cooperation, as was most recently evidenced at the Amsterdam European Summit. Franco-German cooperation is not simply based on utilitarian considerations. It is based on the need to ensure continued peaceful relations in Europe, and there is an important identity-based component involved, perhaps in particular with regard to Germany. As Joseph Weiler has observed, "European integration was always perceived as a positive element in German policy, desirable on its own terms but also as a major platform for German relegitimation after 1945."[32] Because the German state and national identity were discredited after the war, German commitment to European integration could ensure "legitimation through integration." A similar argument could be applied to Italy, Spain, and

Portugal, which all saw European integration as a means of legitimation. These countries have therefore pursued integration in a manner
consistent with the recognition of equal dignity. Through closer co-
operation, their fellow states in Europe would recognize that they were
committed to basic democratic ideals and could be trusted as equals.

European integration could also contribute to a strengthening of
national identities, as has been the case for Ireland. European integration has rendered Ireland less dependent on the United Kingdom. Part
of the dynamic of the integration process has therefore been fuelled by
the thrust for recognition of equal dignity, a process that has seen a certain convergence of certain national and European identities. But it is
also quite clear that identity-based national opposition has affected the
process of integration at several crucial junctures.

Identity-based concerns have no doubt affected the process of integration, sometimes in a complex manner. For instance, it is apparent
that even among those who are generally supportive of further integration, precisely how a European identity is envisaged varies considerably
with regard to what is desirable and feasible, and what the sources
of such an identity should be. One of the most common inclinations
among elites and populace alike has been a propensity to transpose
nationally based conceptions of citizenship and identity onto the European level. Perhaps the best such example is the German Constitutional
Court's famous Maastricht decision, which Joseph Weiler labelled "the
No-Demos thesis." This "is premised on an organic understanding of
peoplehood deriving from the European Nation-State tradition which
conflates nationality and citizenship and can, as a result, conceive of
Demos only in statal terms."[33] The German Constitutional Court supported the Maastricht Treaty but sought to justify the EU not primarily
with reference to its supranational legal structure but rather with reference to it being an association of states. This is due to the Court's conception of the vital link between Demos as *Volk*, with both common
subjective (socio-psychological) elements and common objective elements (common language, history, cultural habits and sensibilities,
ethnic origin and religion) on the one hand, and the state on the other.
The assumption was that only a nation could have a state and that the
state belongs to the nation. The implication, then, was that the EU lacks
a clearly defined Demos and will most likely not develop one. The
conundrum facing the Court, according to Weiler, is that it has legitimated a European constitutional order without furnishing it with a
principled justification. The justification is linked to the member states
but the member states are themselves subject to the constitutional order
of the EU (through the principle of supremacy of EU law over national
law and the principle of direct effect of EU law). This places the Court

in a fundamental and irresolvable dilemma. The upshot, according to Weiler, is that the "condition of Europe on this reading is not, as is often implied, that of constitutionalism without a constitution, but of a constitution without constitutionalism. What Europe needs, thus, is not a constitution but an ethos and telos to justify, if they can, the constitutionalism it has already embraced."[34] On this reading, one of the problems facing the EU is not a lack of concern with identity but rather an obvious lack of appropriate alternative models on which to construct identity and citizenship.

A viable constitutionalism requires public participation and a sense of attachment to the entity. Europe, however "was built in a St Simonian way from the beginning, this was Monnet's approach. The people weren't ready to agree to integration, so you had to get on without telling them too much about what was happening. Now St Simonianism is finished. It can't work when you have to face democratic opinion."[35] Opposition to the Maastricht Treaty was motivated by national concerns as well as democratic ones, i.e., it was a rejection of the elite-based and technocratic approach that had dominated the process of European integration in general and treaty change in particular. But while the executive elites have recognized this in the subsequent attempt to revise the Maastricht Treaty with the 1996 Intergovernmental Conference, which resulted in the Amsterdam Treaty, the process of treaty reform has not changed all that much.

The "No Demos" thesis illustrates how different the EU is from, for instance, the United States. It also reveals that it is virtually impossible, saving massive and even dramatic changes, to develop a United States of Europe.

The European Union as a Post-Westphalian Community

The third view of the European Union in the literature is that it is akin to a post-Westphalian community.[36] A post-Westphalian community is one that has effectively abandoned the unitary conception of sovereignty derived from Jean Bodin. It is not founded on pragmatic concerns or weak evaluations but on strong evaluations. But the strong evaluations are somewhat different from those normally associated with the nation-state. The normative standards required to assess it can not simply be derived from the principles and the conventional language associated with the nation-state. As Hedley Bull has observed, "one reason for the vitality of the state system is the tyranny of the concepts and normative principles associated with it."[37] A post-Westphalian community reflects the normative standards and principles that David Held has labelled "cosmopolitan democracy."[38] The post-Westphalian conception of citizenship, therefore, also differs from the conventional notion of citizenship associated with the nation-state. As Linklater observes:

Cosmopolitan democracy involves the dispersal of sovereign powers rather than their aggregation in an unchallengeable central authority. If the central bond is transformed to recognize claims for diversity then the rights of citizens need to have a flexible and varying content: the idea of an undifferentiated public which is subordinate to a single sovereign power becomes untenable. Citizenship then involves rights of access to international bodies to seek redress against abuses of sovereign power.[39]

This conception of citizenship highlights citizenship as based on consent. Various forms of exit are intrinsic to this very notion.

The EU has obvious similarities with this notion of post-Westphalian community, but it is far from a perfect match. The EU has become a relatively stable combination of interstate and supranational components, on top of a highly complex and multi-layered institutional configuration that occupies a specific territorial space but also exhibits a strong pull on its surroundings. It is also apparent, after three comprehensive bouts of treaty reform, (the SEA, the Maastricht Treaty and the Amsterdam Treaty) that while the EU is an "incomplete" entity with respect to principles, there is a structure in place that exerts a significant pull on subsequent efforts at change. Much of the change that the EU is presently undergoing is therefore path-dependent. If there is an overall trend, it seems to be in the direction of more rather than less diversity. Perhaps the best such indication is the drive toward enlargement to the East combined with the inclusion of the notion of "flexibility" in the Amsterdam Treaty (Article 40). One powerful trend is to strengthen the "core" (the states in continental Western Europe that are most willing to integrate further) and permit a degree of flexibility with regard to those states that are not willing or able to integrate so fast or so far. Therefore, the EU is not only diverse in terms of embodying widely diverse member states, but its territorial reach includes a wide range of attachments, including differences in membership status and forms of affiliation.

Notwithstanding its diversity, the EU has always been marked by a strong member state presence. And it has long been an arena in which the politics of nationally based difference has been played out.[40] The EU is culturally complex and has twelve official languages.[41] Some of the member states have at various instances seen the integration process as a threat to their national culture and identity. The most obvious and ardent defenders of nationally based difference have been Denmark and the United Kingdom (the latter in particularly during the recent Conservative regime). Both states have sought and obtained exemptions from integrationist measures, with Denmark obtaining the widest range of such exemptions, including citizenship.[42]

The EU is also an arena in which the politics of regional difference is played out, in particular regionally based nationalisms (intrastate as well as interstate ones).[43] The initial treaties did not include specific recognition of the regional level; this has emerged in the last decade. The EU has established a Committee of the Regions "whose birth reflects Member States' strong desire not only to respect regional and local identities and prerogatives but also to involve them in the development and implementation of EU policies."[44] This relatively new institution is a weak manifestation of what amounts to a quite dramatic revival of regionalist sentiment and regionally based identities in contemporary Europe. Many regions have established regional representations.[45] What is noteworthy is that this regional sentiment is not channelled through the nation-states. And while it is not clear how much of this regional revival is driven by economic motives and how much of it amounts to an identity-based rejection of the nation-states of which the regions are part, this development has the potential to alter profoundly the nature and salience of the nation-states in Europe. Note that the most profound transformation will be if they do not reject their respective states outright, i.e., if Scottish devolutionists are not swayed by the Scottish National Party to seek full independence but settle for devolution. As Hedley Bull has observed, "if nationalist separatist groups were content to reject the sovereignty of the states to which they are at present subject, but at the same time refrained from advancing any claims to sovereign statehood themselves, some genuine innovation in the structure of the world political system might take place."[46]

The principle of subsidiarity is not premised on the vocabulary associated with the nation-state and may be construed as a means to foster a more complex governance structure based on a more complex view of sovereignty. In a Europe based on the Althusian principle of subsidiarity, nationalist movements would not need to seek independence. In such a Europe, there would not be one overarching identity but rather scope for a wide range of identity-based thrusts to self-expression. The principle of subsidiarity reflects the notion of the EU as a multi-layered governance structure that does not privilege the national level. It is premised on multiple identities and overlapping memberships and could be said to be based upon the following central tenets:

The first is linked to the idea of inviolate and inalienable rights. Not only individuals but also communities have such rights. There are some rights a higher level under no circumstances can revoke, or a lower level give away ...

The second proposition is that a higher level has a duty to support a lower level to the degree that this helps the lower level to fulfil its true potential ...

The third proposition is that "the principle of subsidiarity governs the burden of proof." The higher level is obliged, through arguments, to make it clear why a decision should be taken at a higher level.[47]

This principle, initially derived from Catholic thought and closely related to, for instance, the political thought of Johannes Althusius, highlights the individual as a social being. Social justice is therefore a central concern.[48]

But while the original content of the principle of subsidiarity highlights social justice, the EU has embraced a more narrow reading of the principle. Article 3b of the Maastricht Treaty states that "In areas which do not fall within its exclusive competence, the Community shall take action, in accordance with the principle of subsidiarity, only and in so far as the objectives of the proposed action cannot be sufficiently achieved by the Member States and can therefore, by reason of the scale or effects of the proposed action, be better achieved by the Community." This article privileges the member states, rather than the wide range of actors – state and societal – that the original principle of subsidiarity addresses. Further, Article 3b provides a set of more explicit criteria for how the principle is to be applied. These criteria are quite constraining and are not explicitly linked to social justice. The principle of subsidiarity as presently entrenched in the EU is primarily a means for reallocating tasks among levels of governance within the EU. Article 3b explicitly refers to member states, but the principle of subsidiarity is also often mentioned and increasingly related to regions.

The development of social rights in the EU has been somewhat stymied by a strong tension between a liberal and individualistic conception of social rights on the one hand and a communitarian notion more akin to the central tenets of the principle of subsidiarity on the other. What is ironic is that the British Conservative regime sought to use the principle of subsidiarity to weaken the thrust of the social program in the EU.

This brief assessment suggests that the principle of subsidiarity cannot be considered a blueprint for a radical restructuring of the EU in the direction of a multi-level and matrix-based entity in which power and authority are located as closely to the citizen as is possible. The principle of subsidiarity in its present form in the EU is made compatible with the protection and promotion of the common market project and the supranational legal structure.[49] This is not to deny the structural diversity of the EU. Rather, it simply affirms that the EU is not founded on one set of coherent principles or one doctrine, whether this be a set of conventional principles derived from the nation-state or one with its roots in the late Middle Ages.

What is particularly important about the principle of subsidiarity, however, is that it does compel the institutions at the EU level to justify, with reference to arguments, what tasks they should undertake and why. This is indicative of the general role of the EU as a meeting place for cultures and nations. The EU has become increasingly important as a site in which various actors must justify their claims with reference to wider and more inclusive principles. It is important to note, however, that it is still a site that privileges territorially based conceptions of identity more than, for instance, gendered ones and other non-territorially based identities.[50]

The EU is not a post-Westphalian community in the sense that it is a clear break with the nation-state. Rather, it is characterized by several competing principles of governance. As such it is also an attempt to relate to the tension between two internationally entrenched institutional principles of the global system, namely that embedded in the notion of national sovereignty and that embedded in the notion of universal human rights. This tension also colours the particular conception of citizenship that the EU has embraced. Article 6 of the Amsterdam Treaty (ex-Article F of the Maastricht Treaty) states that:

1. The Union is founded on the principles of liberty, democracy, respect for human rights and fundamental freedoms, and the rule of law, principles which are common to the Member States.
2. The Union shall respect fundamental rights, as guaranteed by the European Convention for the Protection of Human Rights and Fundamental Freedoms signed in Rome on 4 November 1950 and as they result from the constitutional traditions common to the Member States, as general principles of Community law.
3. The Union shall respect the national identities of its Member States.

The Amsterdam Treaty states that:

Citizenship of the Union is hereby established. Every person holding the nationality of a Member State shall be a citizen of the Union. Citizenship of the Union shall complement and not replace national citizenship.

The statement on citizenship in the Amsterdam Treaty is a modified version of what was written in the Maastricht Treaty, in the sense that the Amsterdam Treaty explicitly states that Union citizenship shall not replace national citizenship.

In the context of citizenship, in particular with regard to political rights, the EU appears at least on the face of it to be more similar to Taylor's "deep diversity" than to Habermas's notion of citizenship as based on a constitutionally entrenched notion of public and private autonomy. The link to Taylor's notion of deep diversity stems from the fact that citizenship in the Union is based on citizenship in a member state and is subject to and reflects the particular rules that guide citizenship in each member state. The member states differ widely with regard to how they conceive of citizenship, i.e., the principles on which citizenship is granted and how citizens are incorporated in practical terms. Therefore, the actual content of Union citizenship varies widely. As is well known, some countries such as Germany rely on a modified version of *jus sanguini,* whereas France relies on a modified version of *jus soli.*[51] But whether this really qualifies as "deep diversity" in Taylor's sense is more doubtful.

Union citizenship is not intended to replace national citizenship but provides rights in relation to other member states and in relation to the EU. Citizens can seek redress from several levels of governance, which means that they can constrain sovereign state power. Further, EU citizenship includes the right to vote in local elections, as well as the right to vote in European Parliamentary elections, and the right to move and take up work anywhere in the EU (and in the European Economic Association). The rationale for thinking of these political rights as reflective of "deep diversity" stems also from the fact that they do little in themselves to ensure recognition of equal dignity, not only because of the narrow range of rights, but also because there is no firm link between the legal structure of the EU and the participatory rights of citizens. This means that citizens cannot be conceived of as the ultimate authors of the law. The legal structure is left with fewer constraints to develop principles based upon its internal logic. There are also wide differences in the administrative implementation of the material content of legal provisions.[52]

But it is doubtful as to whether Union citizenship really qualifies as "deep diversity" in Taylor's sense. There are outer limits to the range of diversity in the EU that emanate from the particular manner in which national sovereignty and universal human rights are embedded in this structure. Therefore, the EU is a far more important site for the thrust for recognition of equal dignity than is apparent simply from the provisions on citizenship. The EU – in particular the European Court of Justice – has continuously strengthened its commitment to harmonize its rules and practices with the growing body of international human rights such as those associated with the United Nations and with the European Convention on Human Rights. This is indicative of a strong commitment to a more universalist conception of the rights of persons, in particular civil rights but also social and work-based rules and protections. As such, it is reflective of what Yasemin Soysal has termed the global transformation of citizenship, which highlights an international rights-based discourse founded on personhood. But while this international body of conventions and this international discourse serve to legitimate universal human rights, these rights are still administered by states. This to a large extent also applies to the EU. The European Court of Justice appeals to and applies the constitutional traditions of the member-states, many of whom have incorporated international conventions into their own constitutions. The point is that member states, represented by national courts, are vital in the administration of community law. Individuals often take their claims to national courts that give preliminary rulings but then ask the European Court of Justice for advice or a final ruling. This way, the national courts, and lower courts, have entered into a symbiotic relationship with the European Court. The legitimacy of the Court and indeed of European law is therefore contingent on this vital working relationship, which is also a reflection of the particular manner in which state sovereignty and international human rights are tied together in the EU.

The Union is able to sustain a commitment to certain universalizable principles while retaining a notion of Union citizenship in which political rights are far less uniform. The universalist thrust is underlined by the fact that the EU "may impose suitable political and economic sanctions on Member States that seriously and systematically flout fundamental rights." The introduction of Union Citizenship has enabled the EU to extend its commitment to principles and values to would-be members who are compelled to justify their national traditions – not simply with reference to established ways of life but also with regard to more universalist conceptions of human dignity, as exemplified in the commitment to basic human rights in the European Convention on Human Rights: "A State that is applying to join the Union will not be admitted if it does not guarantee enjoyment of these rights."[53] In a similar manner, certain rights and entitlements are gradually extended to non-nationals of the Union, such as migrant workers from non-EU states. These are entitlements precisely because they have been legitimated on the basis of personhood.[54] What is also interesting is that migrants have also sought to justify claims for cultural protection, not with reference to the need to protect culturally based difference, but with reference to universal human rights and dignity.[55]

The EU is a complex entity that seeks to reconcile civil, economic, political, and social rights at several levels of governance and amid deeply divergent traditions of rights exercise and rights incorporation.

The particular mode of citizenship that has been developed in the EU is based on the notion of multiple allegiances, and there is a continued strong national or member-state pull on the nature of the allegiance. Union citizenship is a weak type of citizenship not primarily because it highlights utilitarian concerns but because it is premised on the notion of respect for nationally based difference. Such respect, however, does not amount to positive legal sanctioning of culturally-based patterns of difference, as Taylor's notion of "deep diversity" implies. Nor does it seem reasonable to see European citizenship as a clear-cut and principled commitment to "deep diversity." The commitment to respect the national identities of the member states is clearly reflective of the tension between competing conceptions of what kind of political entity the EU is. As such it can be seen as a means to placate the fears of Denmark (and others) of a nascent European federal state. Some member states want a more pronounced European identity. And most states seem more comfortable with the EU as a cultural meeting ground than as a site marked by distinct national cultures. The EU has also established certain "outer bounds" for how divergent these rights and their application can be.

The relative success with which the EU can ensure the thrust in the direction of rights-based equal dignity is contingent on member state co-operation and compliance. It is also contingent on the institutional development of the EU. For instance, were the powers of the European Parliament to be further strengthened, the participatory rights embedded in European citizenship would become more important.

The political salience of European citizenship is also highly contingent on *international* legal and political developments. Global developments will affect internal EU constellations and vice versa. Insofar as the world continues to move away from the Westphalian system and toward a system founded on the principles embedded in the cosmopolitan democracy model, this thrust will be reinforced, and the various rights involved will either co-exist at different levels of governance or be mutually reinforced in an institutionally concentric manner. But if the world is to reverse this trend and move back to the Westphalian system, or to some more conflict-prone variant, it is questionable how resilient Union citizenship will be. If the latter development were to occur, the attempt to reconcile differences in a more discursive and deliberative manner will also suffer.

CONCLUSION

The European Union is more than an economic association. It is not really a conventional federation in the making. It is different, as is perhaps best reflected in the notion of the EU as a post-Westphalian community. The EU is still a faint reflection of such a community, but there is no doubt that it has taken several important steps to strengthen the normative autonomy of the entity, in particular since the introduction of the Single Economic Act. This has led it to develop a rather unique institutional structure and a unique conception of citizenship. What is apparent is that this process both spurs and is spurred within an international setting, which is itself undergoing profound changes. This indicates that the EU may incorporate such changes into its structure and operations at a faster rate than would conventional nation-states. But it is also important to note that since the EU is so dependent on contextual developments, it is also particularly fragile to reversals.

One problem related to contextual factors is that the ability of the EU to ensure recognition both of equal dignity and of difference is contingent on its ability to develop institutional means for counterbalancing the standardizing and imperialistic thrust of the utilitarian common market philosophy. The most reliable way to stem such a thrust, it seems, is to continue to strengthen the legal commitment to equal dignity while also subjecting the legal structure to closer public scrutiny and accountability. It seems that it is only through a more firmly entrenched and institutionally based system committed to the protection of equal dignity that a real commitment to protection of difference also can be ensured. This means that the EU will embody a greater tension between a more universalist system of rights on the one hand and particularistic and territorially based identities on the other. It may well be that this tension is necessary precisely to weaken the national and state-based thrusts for recognition that have been so dominant in the EU and that have completely dominated the process of treaty change. A strengthened commitment to equal rights will serve to democratize the EU further.

The sheer diversity of Europe to which the EU must relate has made it an arena not simply for interstate bargaining. It is a setting where actors are more compelled than before to justify their stances with reference to arguments. This point serves to underline that the question of citizenship and diversity in Europe is really a question of which normative standards are most appropriate. In this chapter I have discussed this question in relation to different conceptions of the EU. These conceptions are based on different theoretical perspectives and to some extent also reflect different academic disciplines. Recent developments in Europe are also interesting and important because Europe has finally become a meeting place for different academic disciplines where we are increasingly compelled to justify our disciplinary orientations with reference to more inclusive arguments.

NOTES

1 A. Smith, *National Identity*, (London: Penguin, 1991), 143.
2 The model of the Westphalian system has these characteristic features:
   1. The world consists of, and is divided by, sovereign states which recognise no superior authority.
   2. The processes of law-making, the settlement of disputes and law-enforcement are largely in the hands of individual states subject to the logic of "the competitive struggle for power."
   3. Differences among states are often settled by force: the principle of effective power holds sway. Virtually no legal fetters exist to curb the resort to force; international legal standards afford minimal protection.
   4. Responsibility for cross-border wrongful acts are a 'private matter' concerning only those affected; no collective interest in compliance with international law is recognised.
   5. All states are regarded as equal before the law: legal rules do not take account of asymmetries of power.
   6. International law is orientated to the establishment of minimal rules of coexistence; the creation of enduring relationships among states and peoples is an aim, but only to the extent that it allows national political objectives to be met.
   7. The minimisation of impediments on state freedom is the 'collective' priority.
   From D. Held, *Prospects for Democracy* (Cambridge, UK: Polity Press, 1993), 29.
3 S. Rokkan, "Dimensions of State Formation and Nation-Building: A Possible Paradigm for Research on Variations within Europe," in *The Formation of National States in Western Europe*, C. Tilly, ed. (Princeton: Princeton University Press, 1975), 562–600; G. Marks, F.W. Scharpf, P.C. Schmitter, and W. Streeck, *Governance in the European Union* (London: Sage, 1996).
4 David Held identifies three particularly salient aspects of how globalization affects the state: "first, the way processes of economic, political, legal and military interconnectedness are changing the state from above, as its 'regulatory' ability is challenged and reduced in some spheres; secondly, the way local groups, movements and nationalisms are questioning the nation-state from below as a representative and accountable power system; and thirdly, the way global interconnectedness creates chains of interlocking political decisions and outcomes among states and their citizens, altering the nature and dynamics of national political systems themselves." Held, *Prospects for Democracy*, 39.

5 J. Habermas, "Om den interne forbindelsen mellom rettsstat og demok-
rati," in *Den politiske orden*, ed. E.O. Eriksen (Bergen: TANO, 1994),
190–9; E.O. Eriksen, ed., *Deliberativ politikk*, (Bergen: TANO, 1995);
C. Taylor, "The Politics of Recognition," in *Multiculturalism*, ed.
A. Gutmann (Princeton: Princeton University Press, 1994); *Identitet, frihet
och gemenskap: Politisk-filosofiska texter i urval av Harald Grimen*, ed.
C. Taylor (Gøteborg: Daidalos, 1995); C. Taylor, *Philosophical Arguments*
(Cambridge, MA: Harvard University Press, 1995); *Den politiske orden*,
ed. E.O. Eriksen (Bergen: TANO, 1994); J.G. March and J.P. Olsen, *Democratic Governance* (New York: Free Press, 1995); J.E. Fossum, "Group-
differentiated Citizenship – A Brief Evaluation," *LOS-senter Notat 9642*,
1996.
6 Taylor, *Philosophical Arguments*; Taylor, *Identitet, frihet och gemenskap*.
7 Rokkan, "Dimensions of State Formation and Nation-Building"; Taylor,
Philosophical Arguments; Taylor, *Identitet, frihet och gemenskap*; J.E.
Fossum and P. S. Robinson, "Regimes or Institutions? The Search for
Meaning in the Study of International Society," ARENA Working Paper 18
(1996); Marks, Scharpf, Schmitter, and Streeck, *Governance in the European Union*; C. Tilly, *The Formation of National States in Western Europe*
(Princeton: Princeton University Press, 1975).
8 Y. Soysal, *Limits of Citizenship: Migrants and Postnational Membership in
Europe* (Chicago: University of Chicago Press, 1994); A. Linklater, "Citizenship and Sovereignty in the Post-Westphalian State," *European Journal
of International Relations* 2, no. 1 (1996): 77–103; J. Weiler, "Does Europe
Need a Constitution? Demos, Telos and the German Maastricht Decision,"
European Law Journal 1, no. 3 (November 1995): 219–58; Held, *Prospects
for Democracy*.
9 Conference of the Representatives of the Governments of the Member
States, *Consolidated version of the Treaty on European Union*, CONF
4007/97 ADD 1 (Luxembourg: Office for Official Publications of the European Union).
10 The EU lacks a clearly defined centre of authority. In fact, Joseph Weiler has
observed that there is a great discrepancy between what he terms the social
as opposed to the normative legitimacy of the EU. Until recently, at least, the
EU has enjoyed a high level of social legitimacy despite the lack of attention
to normative legitimacy. J. Weiler, "Legitimation and Democracy of Union
Governance: The 1996 International Agenda and Beyond," ARENA Working Paper 22, (1996). Phillip Schmitter has listed four possible outcomes for
the EU, which he has termed *Stato* (federation), *Confederatio* (confederation), *Consortio*, and *Condominio*. The last type, the Condominio, is
wholly unique, whereas the other three forms have contemporary or historical parallels. P. Schmitter, "Representation and the Future Euro-polity,"

Staatswissenschaft und Staatspraxis 3, no. 3 (1992): 379–405. See also Schmitter, P., "If the Nation-State Were to Wither Away in Europe, What Might Replace It," ARENA Working Paper, No. 11, April 1995. Schmitter, however, does not relate these to identity. Therefore, it is hard to tell which of the variants he lists will be the most likely outcome of the integration process.

11 Taylor, "The Politics of Recognition;" *Den politiske orden.*

12 Ibid., 13.

13 H. Grimen, "Starka värderingar och holistisk liberalism. Inledning till Charles Taylors filosofi", in *Identitet, frihet och gemenskap*, ed. C. Taylor.

14 Grimen, "Starka värderingar och holistisk liberalism," 22.

15 Ibid., 26.

16 Taylor, cited in Grimen, ibid., 37.

17 Taylor, "The Politics of Recognition," 27.

18 Ibid., 25, 35.

19 A. Honneth, *The Struggle for Recognition: The Moral Grammar of Social Conflicts* (Cambridge, UK: Polity Press, 1995); A. Honneth, *The Fragmented World of the Social: Essays in Social and Political Philosophy,* (Albany: State University of New York Press, 1995); C. Taylor, *Reconciling the Solitudes: Essays on Canadian Federalism and Nationalism,* ed. Guy Laforest (Montreal and Kingston: McGill-Queen's University Press, 1993); Taylor, "The Politics of Recognition;" Taylor, *Philosophical Arguments.*

20 J. Anderson, "Translator's Introduction," in Honneth, *The Struggle for Recognition*, xv.

21 Taylor, *Reconciling the Solitudes.*

22 One of the foremost proponents for group-differentiated citizenship is Will Kymlicka. To Kymlicka, group-based rights are required to rectify unchosen inequalities and as such are compatible with the basic tenets of a liberal perspective. See W. Kymlicka, *Liberalism, Community and Culture,* (Oxford: Clarendon Press, 1989); W. Kymlicka, *Multicultural Citizenship,* (Oxford: Oxford University Press, 1995); W. Kymlicka and W. Norman: "Return of the Citizen: A Survey of Recent Work on Citizenship Theory," in *Theorizing Citizenship*, ed. R. Beiner (Albany: State University of New York Press, 1995).

23 J. Fossum, "Group-differentiated Citizenship – A Brief Evaluation." Leadership, Organization and Management Centre, University of Bergen, Working Paper no. 42, 1996.

24 There are other dimensions of this debate on recognition. One such dimension relates to the tension between, on the one hand, the rights-based universalism of the modernity "optimists" such as Habermas and Honneth, and, on the other hand, those that contend that modernity is difference-blind and insensitive to structurally based sources of difference. I. Young,

Justice and the Politics of Difference (Princeton: Princeton University Press, 1990). Further, there is a debate as to whether the claims are individually based, are group based, or whether they are collectively based, i.e., anchored in nations and states/provinces.

25 J. Habermas, "Struggles for Recognition in Constitutional States," *European Journal of Philosophy* 1, no. 2 (1993): 136.

26 J. Habermas, "Citizenship and National Identity," in *Between Facts and Norms: Contributions to a Discourse Theory of Law and Democracy*, ed. J. Habermas (Cambridge, MA: MIT Press, 1996), Appendix II, 491–515; E. Meehan, *Citizenship and the European Community* (London: Sage, 1993), 4.

27 J. Cohen, and A. Arato, *Civil Society and Political Theory* (Cambridge, MA: MIT Press, 1994).

28 It is worthwhile here to note how much economic thinking has come to colour political science in recent years. The common denominator is the mode of rationality that is employed, i.e., instrumental and/or strategic, and the emphasis on actors as utility-maximisers. One of the best examples here is the neo-realist Kenneth Waltz.

29 E. Moxon-Brown, cited in B. Laffan, *Constitution-Building in the European Union* (Dublin: Institute for European Affairs, 1996), 89.

30 H. Wallace, "Deepening and Widening: Problems of Legitimacy for the EC", in *European Identity and the Search for Legitimacy*, ed. S. Garcia (London: Pinter Publishers, 1993), 95–105.

31 A. Hirschman, *Rival Views of Market Society and Other Recent Essays* (Cambridge, MA: Harvard University Press, 1992), 41–2.

32 Weiler, "Does Europe Need A Constitution?," 237.

33 Ibid., 219. See also J. Weiler, "The Reformation of European Constitutionalism," *Journal of Common Market Studies* 35, no. 1 (March 1997): 97–131.

34 Weiler, "Does Europe Need A Constitution?," 220.

35 Pascal Lamy, "Jacques Delors' *Chef de Cabinet*," cited in G. Ross, *Jacques Delors and European Integration* (Cambridge, UK: Polity Press, 1995), 194.

36 Linklater, "Citizenship and Sovereignty in the Post-Westphalian State," *passim*.

37 H. Bull, cited in Linklater, ibid., 78.

38 The Cosmopolitan Model of Democracy is based on the following elements:
   1. The global order consists of multiple and overlapping networks of power including the political, social and economic.
   2. All groups and associations are attributed rights of self-determination specified by a commitment to individual autonomy and a specific cluster of rights. The cluster is composed of rights within and across

each network of power. Together, these rights constitute the basis of an empowering legal order – a "democratic international law."

3. Law-making and law-enforcement can be developed within this framework at a variety of locations and levels, along with an expansion of the influence of regional and international courts to monitor and check political and social authority.

4. Legal principles are adopted which delimit the form and scope of individual and collective action within the organisations and associations of state *and* civil society. Certain standards are specified for the treatment of all, which no political regime or civil association can legitimately violate.

5. As a consequence, the principle of non-coercive relations governs the settlement of disputes, though the use of force remains a collective option in the last resort in the face of tyrannical attacks to eradicate democratic international law.

6. The defence of self-determination, the creation of a common structure of action and the preservation of the democratic good are the overall collective priorities.

7. Determinate principles of social justice follow: the *modus operandi* of the production, distribution and the exploitation of resources must be compatible with the democratic process and a common framework of action.

Held, *Prospects for Democracy*, 43.

39 Linklater, "Citizenship and Sovereignty in the Post-Westphalian State," 95.

40 Article 6.3 of the Amsterdam Treaty (a revised version of the former Article F.1 of the Maastricht Treaty) states that "The Union shall respect the national identities of its Member States." CONF 4007/97 ADD 1, 13.

41 But while the EU recognizes linguistic diversity, the commitment to multilingualism within each member state is not overly strong. The general pattern is national language and English.

42 Denmark issued a unilateral declaration on Union citizenship. Among the provisions listed were the following:

1. Citizenship of the Union is a political and legal concept which is entirely different from the concept of citizenship within the meaning of the Constitution of the Kingdom of Denmark and of the Danish legal system. Nothing in the Treaty on European Union implies or foresees an undertaking to create a citizenship of the Union in the sense of citizenship of a nation-state ...

2. Citizenship of the Union in no way in itself gives a national of another Member State the right to obtain Danish citizenship or any of the rights, duties, privileges or advantages that are inherent in Danish

citizenship by virtue of Denmark's constitutional, legal and administrative rules ... .
Council of the European Communities, *European Council in Edinburgh, 11–12 December, 1992: Conclusions of the Presidency*, Office for Official Publications of the European Communities, Annex 3, 12 December 1992, 1992, 57.

43 Meehan, *Citizenship and the European Community*, xi.

44 http: //europa.eu.int/inst-en.htm.

45 The Committee of the Regions is basically an advisory body made up of 222 mostly elected regional representatives. It has emerged as a strong champion of regional and local interests and defender of the principle of subsidiarity, in the sense that decisions "should be taken by those public authorities which stand as close to the citizen as possible." http: //europa.eu.int/inst/en/cdr.htm#intro

46 H. Bull, cited in Linklater, "Citizenship and Sovereignty in the Post-Westphalian State," 79.

47 L. Blichner and L. Sangolt, "The Concept of Subsidiarity and the Debate on European Cooperation: Pitfalls and Possibilities," *Governance* 7, no. 3 (1994): 289.

48 It is noteworthy that much of the original content of the principle of subsidiarity is highly consistent with the recommendations that Iris Young has set forth for how to address and reconcile competing claims for difference. She notes that: "a democratic public should provide mechanisms for the effective recognition and representation of the distinct voices and perspectives of those of its constituent groups that are oppressed or disadvantaged. Such group representation implies institutional mechanisms and public resources supporting 1) self-organization of group members so that they achieve collective empowerment and a reflective understanding of their collective experience and interests in the context of society; 2) group analysis and group generation of policy proposals in institutionalized contexts where decision makers are obliged to show that their deliberations have taken group perspectives into consideration; and 3) group veto power regarding specific policies that affect a group directly." Young, *Justice and the Politics of Difference*, 184.

49 The Protocol on the Application of the Principles of Subsidiarity and Proportionality annexed to the Amsterdam Treaty states that

1. In exercising the powers conferred to it, each institution shall ensure that the principle of subsidiarity is complied with ...

2. The application of the principles of subsidiarity and proportionality shall respect the general provisions and objectives of the Treaty, particularly as regards the maintaining in full of the *acquis communautaire* and the institutional balance; it shall not affect the principles

developed by the Court of Justice regarding the relationship between national and Community law ...

3. The principle of subsidiarity does not call into question the powers conferred on the European Community by the Treaty, as interpreted by the Court of Justice ...

50 The recent European Council Summit Meeting in Amsterdam illustrates this. Feminist and other international rights activists organized an "Alternative Summit" in Amsterdam just before the European Council Summit Meeting was held.

51 For a comprehensive overview of various incorporation regimes, see Soysal, *Limits of Citizenship*.

52 Meehan, *Citizenship and the European Community*, 123.

53 http: //europa.eu.int/abc/cit1_en.htm, copied 21 October 1997.

54 Soysal, *Limits of Citizenship*, 3.

55 Ibid., 154–5.

11 The Purchased Revolution in South Africa[1]

HERIBERT ADAM

The relatively peaceful changeover of political power in South Africa has been greatly facilitated by the vast resources of the state and by an economy led by the private sector. Many potential troublemakers were bought off by being put on the payroll of the public service or being absorbed into even more lucrative private business. Ideologues of the old regime were pacified with generous retrenchment packages. This purchased revolution has rapidly produced a new black elite whose lifestyle discredits the legitimacy of the liberation led by the African National Congress (ANC).

In this chapter, the embourgeoisement of the new power holders is critically analysed and the likely alienation of an impoverished constituency is assessed. However, it will be shown that government options to pursue a more radical economic policy of social justice are limited. Constrained by economic interdependence domestically, the semi-developed South African economy must adhere even more to a global neo-liberal consensus if it wishes to realize ambitious growth rates. The future of the ANC and of non-racial democracy hinges on an economic delivery that is lagging behind symbolic liberation.

I

General theories of nationalism and ethnocentric mobilization can be enriched and revised by the example of South Africa. An ethnic identity amounts to an awareness of culture in comparison with "others." The apartheid state mobilized culture for divide-and-rule purposes and thereby discredited ethnic identity among the disenfranchised. Mahmood Mamdani has aptly characterized the dual intentions of apartheid as follows: "to *unify* its *beneficiaries* around a racialist identity, and to *fragment* its *victims* through ethnicised identities."[2] Elsewhere the political use of a shared historical tradition (ethnicity) correlates with increased economic competition and downward mobility. Political insecurity, status anxieties, and doubts about individual identity are translated into a loss of collective worthiness. Nationalism promises to restore dignity and extinguish humiliation, according to specific group histories. Ethnic mobilizers develop myths in constructing scapegoats. The ascendancy to political power by the forces of liberation in the peaceful election in 1994 re-established dignity and identity for the colonized. It diminished the need for ethnonationalist mobilization, as apartheid could be blamed for all the misery.

It is generally recognized that ethnonationalist discourses serve symbolic (psychological) as well as instrumental (economic) ends. Ethnonationalism expresses claims to entitlement as well as identity needs. Nationalism appeals because it articulates belongingness and bestows meaning, but also because it aims at exclusionary power and monopoly control over scarce resources. The paradox to be explained is why people concerned with their misfortune and economic insecurity embrace nationalism, even if it entails greater sacrifices and material losses. During nationalist wars, whole armies march willingly to their deaths. Bathing in the glory of their collectivity compensates for real losses. Imagined group victories constitute the symbolic gratification that economic reality denies. The more individuals are demeaned, the more they need to borrow strength from victorious group membership, be it through identification with a sports team or by attaching themselves to "superior" religious or political causes. Those caught in the need to join are usually prone to denigrate and demonize non-believers.

In South Africa, a remarkable development in the opposite direction took place. Despite being demeaned by apartheid, blacks generally eschewed nationalism in favour of reconciliation with their oppressors. The oppressors in turn embraced their victims, whom they had demonized as terrorists. Given the ideological warfare and the real battles and atrocities that took place in the name of ethnoracialism during four decades of formal apartheid, this pragmatic reconciliation disproves the essentialist and primordialist notions of incompatible ethnic group relations.

At the same time, neither opponent cultivated a culture of revenge. Nor did they merge their ethnoracial identities in an assimilationist fashion. Everyone is aware of his or her "race" after decades of official racial classification. South Africa continues to be a "divided society" in the sense of phenotypical as well as cultural cleavages, reinforced by vast class differences. However, the apartheid emphasis on racial differ- ence made ethnoracial divisions increasingly controversial. The two sides can co-operate not only because they need each other for their mu- tual well-being, but also because they are secure in their self-definition and recognize each other as legitimate citizens with different identities.

This mutual reading of "race" in South Africa differs from the group perceptions in other ethnoracial or communal conflicts. Because the inter-group differences were so entrenched during apartheid, members of each group can transcend their group identity in the post-apartheid era without endangering their self-definitions. Serbs and Croats speak the same language and belong to a Christian tradition with minor dif- ferences of ritual. Yet Serbs and Croats have become mortal antagonists in their collective attitudes. In South Africa, the very real ethnoracial differences in a so-called divided society have facilitated the emergence of a common state.

II

The relatively peaceful South African transition was greatly facilitated by the vast resources at the disposal of the state and the private-sector- led economy. The "good surprise" would not have been possible with- out the security of pensions and the incentive of vast retrenchment pack- ages. The literature on transition has underrated the availability of options as a precondition for compromise by hard-liners in power. In many ways, the so-called South African miracle is better dubbed the "purchased revolution." The members of the liberation armies who were not incorporated into the official defence force receive a small pen- sion. Many other potential troublemakers were bought off by being put on the payroll of the public service or the even more lucrative private sector.

For example, when the budget for the intelligence services was drawn up in 1995, a 20% cut was envisaged. This amounted to a compara- tively minor reduction, given the absence of foes. However, the ultimate outcome was a "66 per cent increase from R427.5 million to R710 mil- lion – by far the biggest increase for any government department, and this at a time when health and teaching jobs were cut in the cause of the economy."[3] The increase resulted from the integration of over 900 ANC intelligence agents, the Pan Africanist Congress security service and three homeland spy agencies, so that in the end the National Intelli- gence Agency had almost three times as many staff members as the old security apparatus at the height of Afrikaner paranoia. The National Intelligence Agency is only one of five agencies that comprise South

Africa's "intelligence community." Similarly innovative job creation occurred in the South African Defence Force, although with greater transparency and public accountability. Yet, despite the money wasted on superfluous civil servants who now spy on each other, it is difficult to disagree with the Suzman Foundation: "If it was necessary to throw a lot of money at this key political problem of making the lamb lie down with the lion, the money was probably worth it."[4] However, only in comparatively wealthy South Africa could reconciliation be purchased. Buying off dissent also corrupts the newly co-opted, who know that their occupation and remuneration are not justified by the task at hand. How this consciousness of being pacified translates into job performance remains to be tested. Even purist Azapo and Pan Africanist Congress leaders did not prove immune from temptation. The fact that Cyril Ramaphosa could move from head of a militant mineworkers' union and secretary general of the ruling party to chief executive of a business conglomerate and main board member of the Anglo American Corporation indicated an atmosphere of non-ideological expediency, and was similar to the many shifts of principled ideologues to pragmatic profit-seekers in Eastern Europe. Only the need to justify private enrichment with black empowerment, which elevates corporate boardrooms to "new sites of struggles," is unique to South Africa.

It was legal continuity and a private sector economy that allowed key security bureaucrats from the old regimes to abandon control of the state peacefully for a golden handshake. Huge payouts were given to policy generals, who retired for "health reasons" or easily found alternative employment in the private sector. Peaceful change is greatly facilitated by such buy-out options. African military rulers and their underlings elsewhere who depend on the state as their main source of income cling to their power because they face not only loss of office, but economic insecurity (unless they have siphoned off revenue into foreign bank accounts). As Michael Holman has aptly observed: "Unlike South Africa's white minority which, when forced to surrender power, could derive compensation from control of the economy, the Nigerian regime and its supporters have no such safety net."[5]

III

At the ideological level, pragmatic co-operation is assisted by mutual group mythologies that avoid inferiorization. Blacks and whites constructed self-definitions of selected superiority that complement each other without indiscriminately inferiorizing the other. The image of whites as technically competent providers of vital goods and services is widely accepted in both camps. The image of moral superiority of blacks as victims of unjust discrimination holds equal currency on both sides. It did not instil in blacks a sense of personal or collective inferiority, since disadvantage could be attributed to "the system." Individual failure – debilitating self-hatred and racism against one's own group – was thereby minimized. With most whites accepting that amends had to be made for past injustices for which they, and not the blacks, had to be blamed, the ground was laid for the co-operation of equals. Blacks, on the other hand, perceived corrective policy measures not as charity for which they had to be grateful, but as rights long denied.

In these inter-group perceptions of mutual moral recognition, South Africa differs fundamentally from the United States and other countries where a relatively powerless minority remains at the mercy of a dominant majority, with all the psychological consequences that such an unequal relationship implies for members of both groups. South Africa also has little in common with Euro-fascist racism. Bosnian Serbs and Muslims no longer distinguish between members of the other side, but distrust each other as ethnic group members. Identification of white communists and liberals with the black cause and the need to find black collaborators for the white regime always militated against collective stereotyping on both sides. It blurred the boundaries of communalism.

Can a South African nation be built? The potential for ethnoracial polarization and mobilization is ever present. But it has been so for as long as South Africa has existed. Ethnic, racial, and cultural divisions and differences have been exploited, manipulated, and ideologized in the pursuit of power and domination. However, when the transition began in earnest in South Africa, these were not the dominant forces that determined the dynamic and pace of change.

The most formidable objective force against communal strife in South Africa has always been a thorough economic interdependence. Nonetheless, Donald Horowitz (among many other academic analysts) has explicitly doubted the significance of this bond for pragmatic accommodation: "The economic interdependence of South Africans is hardly different from the interdependence that characterized many societies later shattered by ethnic violence, among them Lebanon, Cyprus, Uganda and Sri Lanka."[6]

This is a questionable conclusion to draw. The interdependence of Lebanon, Cyprus, Sri Lanka, or Yugoslavia (not to mention an agrarian society such as Uganda, where the majority is still engaged in subsistence agriculture) differs from the interdependence in South Africa. In Lebanon and the former Yugoslavia, separate communal economies exist side by side. The civil war harmed the overall state economy, which relied on co-operation and the exchange of goods and services between the different ethnic regions and enclaves of the state. While the strife disrupted those intercommunal economic ties, it did not destroy the communal economies onto which nationalists could fall back in their own territory. Hence Croats employed only Croats, Sinhalese only Sinhalese, and Greeks only Greeks (in the territorially divided economy of Cyprus). Such exclusive communal economies lowered standards of living, but they still allowed for the indefinite survival of the ethnic group, albeit with a reduced or negative growth rate, inflated prices, soft currencies, and other indicators of long-term economic retardation.

In South Africa, on the other hand, there is no black or white economy. The number of blacks employed by black business remains negligible and there is hardly any white-owned business that does not rely heavily on black labour for its very existence and profits. This mutual dependency has always limited the potential ruthlessness of racial exploitation and dampened the militancy of the subordinates. When you know that you will go hungry or lose your only shelter in a hostile environment, you think twice about striking. Contrary to the Leninist immiserization theory – that radical actions increase with misery – impoverishment induces reluctant compliance. People struggling to survive from one day to the next do not have the energy to think about alternative strategies. Political consciousness of the militant kind remains the luxury of a privileged and unionized labour aristocracy. This is confirmed by South Africa's history of labour conflicts. The longest and most bitter strikes in South Africa's labour history occurred among the best paid and most secure segments: auto workers in Port Elizabeth and municipal employees in various towns. Conversely, corporate management had to take account of the grievances of its workforce well beyond the factory gates. As long as insecure transport, crime, unsafe housing, racial animosities, and general political discontent affected productivity and identification with the occupation, no sophisticated employer could ignore such factors for competitive advantage.

It was these mutual interests and constraints on pursuing confrontation that forged bonds of dependency and mutual recognition. The current social-democratic compromise in place of class or racial warfare owes its foundation less to the moral conviction or political will of the antagonists than to this structural interdependence. Notwithstanding the good will of the negotiating elites, the objective situation of their constituencies allowed them limited choice in pursuing ethnic mobilization for civil war. Even committed right-wing ideologues in rural town councils and school boards were quickly brought to heel when consumer boycotts by neighbouring black townships threatened their livelihood. Since neither side was economically viable on its own, the political reconciliation amounted not so much to a "good surprise," let alone a miracle, as to an act of collective rationality.

In the Nazi case, ideological obsessions clearly overrode economic logic. Despite the increased need for labour in the war effort, the Nazis killed rather than exploited their slaves. As Gordon Craig aptly remarked: "The Nazis operated officially designated work camps as if economic considerations were irrelevant, forcing their Jewish inmates to work at unproductive, repetitive and demeaning tasks with inadequate food and rest and under constant torture by brutal guards until they collapsed and died."[7] In contrast, South African racism constantly adjusted its ideological rationalizations to economic necessities. Implemented to provide a cost-effective labour force in the first place – although that was not the only rationale – apartheid ideology was bent and ultimately forfeited because it clashed with economic imperatives.

Some analysts of the South African situation have used the concept of an ideological state. In such an entity, political power is geared toward implementing a grand vision. The de facto administrative structure is subordinated to an overarching ideology or a set of ideas that determines all state actions, regardless of other implications. Cuba, North Korea, Israel, the Vatican, and Nazi Germany are examples of ideological states in which the ruling elite is or was legitimized with the myth of a mission extending beyond normal pragmatic state interests. In its heyday, apartheid South Africa flirted with the notion of an ideological state but could never implement it fully because of economic counterforces as well as the controversial nature of a racial state within the white minority itself. Industrial interdependence reduced the conflict over land and other non-negotiable issues that bedevil other communal conflicts. In the Middle East, the economic aspect of the conflict is clearly about land and water. Although space diminished as a security issue with the use of long-range rockets, fertile land is scarce and overcrowded. Redistribution of land is also said to be of crucial concern to South African blacks. The Pan Africanist Congress made the return of the conquered land to the colonized indigenous people a central issue of its election platform. Not only did the poor showing of the Congress in the 1994 election expose the issue as a myth, but the number of blacks who are eagerly waiting to become subsistence farmers is generally overrated. Most unemployed people in rural areas would rather move to the city, if work were available, than till the soil. Blacks strive to improve their living conditions, but whether this is by peasant farming or by wage labour depends on availability and prospects. Land hunger *per se* is not the burning desire it is made out to be. In all opinion surveys, land hardly figures as a high priority among black expectations. This reflects the basic industrial character of South African society, where farming is associated with rural backwardness and the city is seen as the venue for upward mobility.

Commentators have almost unanimously identified inflated expectations as the inevitable cause of mass disappointment and future instability. However, the concern over frustrated expectations may well stem
from a European experience of relative deprivation that does not necessarily apply to Africa. Some observers have argued with good evidence
that black South African people actually display low expectations. As
Moeletsi Mbeki points out: "They're willing to accept low standards,
live off subsistence agriculture, wear the same sets of clothes for weeks
on end and walk instead of riding a bicycle or motorbike. I would
argue that we should in fact encourage expectations in South Africa."[8]
While this description fits the traditional peasants in Zimbabwe or
Tanzania more than the urban proletariat in Soweto or Kwa Mashu,
few ordinary black South Africans compare themselves with their
white counterparts in the sense of measuring their satisfaction by having achieved consumerist affluence. With modest expectations, most
hope for gradual improvement in the basic necessities of life rather
than instant utopia. This colonized mindset by which people compare
themselves to the members of their own group cushions the ANC from
its inability to deliver on vast promises.

IV

The group that benefits most from the post-apartheid order is a fledg-
ling black middle class. It consists of a growing number of independent
entrepreneurs, a managerial aristocracy in high demand, and a new
political bourgeoisie eager to join in the consumerism of their former
oppressors. Gandhi associated political liberation with an alternative
lifestyle. Most ANC officials measure equality by comparison with the
affluence of their predecessors. On top of the vast discrepancies in
wealth, a thorough Americanization has penetrated all segments of
society. American habits and ostentatious consumption have become
the desired yardstick by which South African progress is measured.

When the state broadcasting corporation launched its revamped
television schedule in February 1996, it presented a glitzy show of
flown-in African–American entertainers (as well as O.J. Simpson's
lawyer, Johnny Cochran). With no mention of world-renowned South
African literary or arts talents, the new cosmopolitan image of an
alleged Africanized service was confined to recycled black Hollywood
entertainers. The emulation of Hollywood lifestyles by a new *Ebony*
elite resembles the silly glorification of royal titles, quaint British country culture, or English dress codes by the old colonizers. It should be of
no concern were it not for the squandering of public money amidst a
sea of poverty.

At the beginning of 1996, the ANC caucus decided to halve compulsory contributions to the party. At the same time the ANC whip complained about the monotonous subsidized fools in Parliament. Most impartial observers would agree with Tom Lodge's judgement that "Nelson Mandela's cabinet is excessively well paid for a relatively poor country, as are most senior civil servants, whose numbers were considerably enlarged with the creation of nine regional governments each with dozens of director generals."[9] Although pay scales were derived from the Melamat Commission's comparisons between private- and public-sector salaries, Lodge is also right "that it is most unlikely there would have been serious discord in the Government of National Unity" had the ANC caucus turned down the recommendation. For many years members of parliament and their spouses or nominated companions have also each been entitled to fifty-four single airline tickets a year to anywhere in South Africa. Once the flights were used up, they could buy tickets at 20% of normal prices. However, the 20% privilege was so widely abused that Speaker Frene Ginwala suspended it in February 1997. While several new office holders were embarrassed, few said so publicly. Venal self-justification of the importance of public office, laments about financial sacrifices during the apartheid years, and a pseudo-racist "blacks must be as well paid as whites" mentality all combined to spread the impression that the new state should be used rather than serviced.

When the same politicians later began a moral crusade against rent and service boycotts they were inevitably ignored. Moral renewal lacked role models at the top. Although most new office holders worked tirelessly for the common good, they were not widely perceived as immune to self-enrichment. Although the amounts are small, and corrupt self-enrichment among the new elite is still rare compared with the plundering of the state resources by the previous regime, the writing is on the wall and ever-fewer of the former idealists seem to care about their deteriorating image. The old elite, on the other hand, adores the new-found disciples. White businessmen even gloat that the African masses love their rulers to display their superior status. In any case, it is said, a little bit of capitalist temptation oils the state machinery by providing influence that fanatical ideologues would deny.

Lack of Gandhian austerity would not be worth criticizing were it not for the superior moral claims of the ANC to represent all the people and particularly the downtrodden. While half of the constituency cannot afford a used bicycle, can their representatives afford to wave at them from German luxury cars? As half of the electorate struggle to buy enough food for the next day, can legislators allocate themselves salaries that are justified by the profit making of the private sector? Should politicians be expected to be more altruistic than business people in working for the public interest?

According to a falsely maligned Institute for Democracy in South Africa (IDASA) survey,[10] 56% of South Africa's voters feel that people in government work in their own self-interest rather than for the public good; 60% feel that parliamentary salaries are too high; and a staggering 84% perceive some level of corruption in government. Half of those consider the corruption to be worse than in the old regime. It is an explosive situation when 85% of voters believe that people elected to govern should be "more honest" than ordinary citizens, while a sizeable number (34%) feel that, in reality, elected officials are less honest than the average person.

While concerned democrats worry unduly about weak opposition institutions, they neglect a much more immediate danger of elite pacting, namely the coinciding interest of common financial rip-offs. The new order is less undermined by timid party competition than it is discredited by the common legitimization of high salaries and perks for its functionaries. In addition, a new provision for cabinet ministers to hire special advisers from outside the civil service at monthly salaries of up to R28 000 opened the door to corruption and nepotism. When the vast majority of the black electorate earns less in a year than its parliamentary representatives make in a month, it would be a miracle if disenchantment with the ANC leadership emerges only in the distant future. At present, the relatively high salaries of politicians, senior civil servants, consultants, and members of statutory committees also lure talents from less rewarded occupations, particularly university teaching and public medicine. Other appointments are frequently made as a reward for past services or personal relationships with officials.

V

Comparative extreme inequality remains South Africa's ticking bomb. The wealthiest 10% of households receive fully 50% of the nation's income, while the bottom 20% capture a mere 1.5%, according to a report by the Labour Market Commission.[11] Moreover, this skewed income distribution overlaps with race, although the white–black income gap is narrowing. Still, 85% of the poor are black and 65% of blacks are poor. Only 0.7% of whites are classified as poor. At the same time, the internal stratification among blacks is widening with the emergence of a new bureaucratic bourgeoisie far removed from the lifestyle of "the masses."

There is still a widespread belief that the ANC administration is pursuing the economic interests of the poorer half of South African society. In his reply to Mandela's opening speech of the 1997 Parliament, Democratic Party Leader Tony Leon accused the ANC of "socialist schemes and revolutionary romanticism." Similarly, F.W. de Klerk insists that his National Party articulates "the true mainstream alternative to the ANC's inherently socialist direction."[12] Even Wilmot James writes, "Since 1994, South Africa's approach to economic growth and development has been mass-oriented, in the sense that it has always been tied to the interests and needs of the poor and previously disadvantaged."[13]

However, such an orientation has existed in rhetoric only. Taking the self-image for reality means believing in fairy tales. In reality, a liberation aristocracy has emerged. New office-holders allocate themselves disproportionate spoils while their constituency is ignored. The often-cited masses merely serve as a legitimating backdrop for the necessary radical adjustment to the new world economic order.

The government's macro-economic blueprint, Growth Employment and Redistribution (GEAR), represents the very opposite of socialist vision or revolutionary romanticism. Guided by the World Bank and warmly embraced by South African business, the ANC is constantly exhorted to implement its neo-liberal GEAR. Cabinet ministers have promised to deliver on privatization, wage flexibility, deficit reduction, and massive public service cutbacks. Finance Minister Trevor Manuel described this as a "deep transformation" in his 1997 budget speech. It amounts to transformation indeed, but it means free-market transformation rather than the redistributive transformation popularized during the anti-apartheid struggle. There can be both left-wing and right-wing transformation. The popularity of transformation discourse in South Africa results from everybody being able to project contradictory visions onto the radical-sounding term.

A similar confusion is reflected in the large number of business people who consider "union activity" an obstacle to growth. In reality, a recalcitrant union leadership has been co-opted, cajoled, and silenced for fear of being marginalized. Weakened by global corporate legitimacy and structural unemployment, socialist unionists will soon become an endangered species. Even with a history of politicized independence from the powers that be, the South African labour movement is toeing the line and not rocking the boat of export-driven growth. With the exception of public service unions, union membership is stagnating or declining worldwide. South Africa is no exception despite its different history of labour politicization. How little influence trade unions now exercise on government policy can best be demonstrated by the catalogue of measures that the general secretary of the Confederation of South African Trade Union (COSATU) demanded from the 1997 budget: "If [Finance Minister] Trevor Manuel wants to reduce inequalities he must introduce a capital gains tax, set a tax rate of 55 per cent on the super-rich, tax luxury goods at a higher rate, have more zero VAT [value-added tax] ratings on basic necessities – water, medicines and basic foodstuffs – increase levels of corporate taxation and close the loopholes used by the wealthy to reduce tax liabilities." Since these suggestions would send the wrong signal to the new investors on which GEAR depends, none of the union proposals was included in the budget.

In the end, the rump of a bread-and-butter oriented labour movement will be dominated by a few powerful labour bosses who cooperate with the ruling political class, as in the United States – or, more likely, who are part of the revolutionary establishment, as in Mexico. There, powerless but militant "unofficial" unions have split from the mainstream official unions, which still deliver most of the votes for the ruling party and are rewarded with patronage in return. Unlike the dependent unions in the former Communist bloc, which were mere transmission belts for the party in power, the new South African union leaders increasingly command their own economic empire. Already several former socialist union organizers in South Africa have joined the corporate system at the head of huge union investment funds. Making profits for provident funds is marketed as a legitimate union activity, although the private "fixing fees" that the comrades in business receive on the side are not publicized.

Joining the once much-maligned capitalist system does more than create tension between the concepts of private gain versus collective benefits. Union democracy and grassroots input are inevitably sacrificed when takeovers and financial transactions require secrecy. Hierarchical orders dominate in the corporate world, quite apart from the difficulties ordinary workers would encounter in making intelligent investment decisions. On the crucial decision as to whether unions should set up their own investment companies, the much celebrated internal COSATU democracy did not produce a single discussion paper. It just happened. Nor is it much contested with whom the union billions should be invested, so that the funds often end up with union-hostile companies.

Furthermore, even the South African Communist Party has considered the establishment of investment arm among a number of options intended to make the party financially self-sufficient or "to trade its way out of the red,"[14] to quote a clever headline. Although the general secretary is anxious to assure a bewildered following that the party "would definitely not compromise our principled position and become a capitalist party," the reliance on capitalist principles for financial survival speaks louder. Will a "socialist" union mobilize a strike against a firm on which it depends for vital income? Will a communist party still want to replace a capitalist system in which its functionaries have vested interests? In reality, the official Marxist-Leninist Party long ago adopted reformist social-democratic policies, although to be called a social democrat still amounts to a slur for an orthodox socialist of the Leninist variety. Social democrats are accused of having accommodated themselves within the capitalist system, having sold out or having been co-opted into giving an exploitative order a humanitarian veneer, thereby strengthening capitalism rather than overthrowing it.

Such revolutionary fantasies may have had some hope of being realized as long as an example of actual "socialism" existed in Moscow. With the disappearance of this last colonial empire, the Marxist vision of greater equality and non-alienated labour has changed into a pipe dream. Even the Chinese Communist Party exhorts the official slogan: "Enrich yourself." Globalized capitalism has indeed triumphed everywhere, starving North Korea and Cuba's bankrupt regime notwithstanding. However, the growing inequality and misery that Marx first addressed remains on the agenda, particularly in South Africa with its large contingent of outsiders.

Does the disappearance of official socialism mean that the 40% of the South African population who are "outside" the capitalist system are satisfied with the crumbs they may pick up? Who is representing the interests of the downtrodden in the political system or at NEDLAC (the National Economic Development Labour Council)? While unions and the ANC claim to look after the poor, everyone knows that they champion their own middle class and employees' interests first. Will it be left to a populist yet to emerge or a revived Pan Africanist Congress to mobilize the underclass? What will the ideological platform be, if not a refurbished socialism under another name? It is a mistaken belief that the forgotten poor simply adopt a lethargic, apolitical apathy, incapable of organized opposition.

VI

South African politics, like the politics of other Western democracies, is increasingly devoid of ideological divisions. The ideological thrusts of all parties broadly resemble each other. They all advocate market-oriented economies within a liberal human rights constitution. Differences emerge with regard to the implementation, style, and effectiveness of generally agreed-upon policy goals. Cultural traditions and the ethnoracial makeup of political parties then substitute for the lack of ideological distinctiveness. In other words, the more policy programs are similar, the more ethnic differences and historical mythologies gain importance in shaping a distinct image of the contenders.

Since no ideologically creditable alternatives to global economic imperatives exist, the danger lies in the racialization of heightened competition. How long the ANC's professed non-racialism can contain and dilute the demands for racial empowerment by both the underclass and the newly emerging black bourgeoisie remains to be seen. While the self-enrichment of sections of a liberation aristocracy and its dubious allies in the empowerment lobby can be delegitimized more easily, the claims of the neglected underclass will carry far more weight, regardless of the form in which they are expressed.

The ANC is engaged in a delicate balancing act. It must adhere to the broad dictates of the market unless it is willing to risk being heavily penalized. On the other hand, it cannot afford to be perceived as having abandoned its concern for the masses and the unions. As an editorialist commented, "The last thing that the ANC needs in this sensitive period is a perception of itself and business ganging up against COSATU."[15] Yet adhering to the "Washington consensus" of the market means objectively sidelining the unions. The ANC resolves its dilemma by pursuing neo-conservative economic policies but obfuscating them with an occasional dose of socialist lip service to redistribution and the desires of the masses. To be sure, the party also genuinely prioritizes the less privileged, who are after all its main reservoir of voters. However, the ANC is so constrained by unfavourable repercussions both locally and internationally that it cannot translate an ideological commitment into practical policy if it clashes with vital business interests. Wavering between pleasing free-market and privatization lobbyists and alienating its left, the ANC is frequently paralysed. In this dilemma the leadership has concentrated on winning over COSATU leaders without incorporating the social agenda of labour in its economic policy. All strong democratic nations thrive on an economically secure and politically involved bourgeoisie. On the other hand, the greed of a parasitic elite could further reinforce the alienation of the marginalized underclass.

Profiteering has united former ideological foes in a common search for new opportunities. "So strong has the lure of capitalism been," writes Thabo Leshilo, "that former political enemies from the African National Congress, Azanian People's Organization, the Pan African Congress of Azania and the Inkatha Freedom Party have abandoned their ideological differences. Even former socialists and Communists have united under the new concept of the patriotic bourgeoisie!"[16]

Above all, the patriotic bourgeoisie eyes the state assets yet to be privatized. Already 10% of the parastatal telecommunications company, Telkom, has been earmarked for black empowerment groups. The lobby clamours for more preferential treatment, particularly in state tender procedures. While affirmative action for disadvantaged minorities is generally accepted worldwide, what is highly contested is the extent to which a state should favour one rich consortium over another on the basis of skin colour. Capitalizing on past restrictions, the "patriotic bourgeoisie" plays on colour to reap advantage. Even Thabo Mbeki has warned the new black elite to avoid being perceived as a parasitic class that thrives only on pillaging state resources.

Black embourgeoisement could nonetheless be supported if it were to trickle down to the poor. However, most black empowerment deals are limited to existing economic activities and do not create new employment. A few black entrepreneurs enter the market through asset acquisition and financial engineering but neglect the training required to equip a functioning bourgeoisie. There is also the danger that some empowerment deals will go sour and then need to be bailed out in the public interest. The 1996–97 buyouts took place at a time of inflated stock prices and unusually high real interest rates. Even if properly managed, performance above the debt load is not guaranteed and enthusiastic new companies could face financial difficulties later.

The new South African elite banks on unlimited economic growth. While its infectious optimism may be unfounded, it is not out of line with world trends of expanding globalized growth. The former colonial outpost and relic of institutionalized racism has joined its competitors for its share of the market regardless of ideological hang-ups of the past. South Africa's international trade with some of the world's leading violators of human rights (Iran, Nigeria, Indonesia, and China) is soaring. While this does not distinguish the country from its Western counterparts, even they raise eyebrows when a senior official suggests that certain criminals resemble animals that should be locked up in disused mine shafts never to see daylight again. When South Africa is selling small arms to Rwanda, helicopters to Malaysia, or considering supplying Syria with sophisticated tank technology, the country has become a "normal" national entity, deprived of its former moral glory. Once its idealized president has left the political stage, the country will further resemble its competitors. Whether the ANC has squandered a moral high ground by its own faults or whether the South African government merely complied with global imperatives will be debated endlessly. After all, who says that one can survive on a moral diet of liberation purity once the routine of political office in an interdependent world squeezes seeming options into one-way solutions?

NOTES

1 This analysis draws from and is further elaborated in: Heribert Adam, F. van Zyl Slabbert, and Kogila Moodley, *Comrades in Business: Post-Liberation Politics in South Africa* (Cape Town: Tafelberg, 1997).
2 Mahmood Mamdani, *Mail & Guardian* [Johannesburg], 17–23 October 1997.
3 *Focus Letter*, February 1996.
4 *Focus Letter*, February 1996.
5 Michael Holman, *Frontiers of Freedom*, 2 (1996): 18.
6 Donald Horowitz, *A Democratic South Africa?* (Berkeley: University of California Press, 1991), 137.
7 Gordon Craig, "How Hell Worked," *New York Review of Books*, 18 April 1996.
8 Moeletsi Mbeki, "Development and Democracy," 9 December 1994.
9 Tom Lodge, "A Year in the New S.A.," *Indicator S.A.*, 12, no. 12 (Autumn 1995): 7–10.
10 IDASA, "Parliamentary Ethics and Government Corruption: Playing with Public Trust," *Public Opinion Service Reports* no. 3, (February 1996).
11 Labour Market Commission, "Report of the Presidential Commission to Investigate Labour Market Policy," *Restructuring the South African Labour Market* (Pretoria: The Commission, 1996), 5.
12 *Sunday Times* [Johannesburg], 2 March 1997.
13 Wilmot James, *Cape Times* [Cape Town], 10 February 1997.
14 *Business Day* [Johannesburg], 18 February 1997.
15 *Business Day* [Johannesburg], 25 March 1997.
16 Thabo Leshilo, *Sunday Independent* [Johannesburg], 23 March 1997.

12 Citizenship, Human Rights, and Diversity

VIRGINIA LEARY

Since the time of the Greek and Roman civilizations, the concept of "citizenship" has defined rights and obligations in the Western world. Roman citizens were protected from scourging as punishment for crimes and had other rights in the Roman state; we know from Christian scripture that St Paul considered his Roman citizenship of importance when he was detained and demanded his rights as a citizen.[1] The concept of "citizenship" has long acquired the connotation of a bundle of rights – primarily, political participation in the life of a community, the right to vote, and the right to receive certain protection from the community – as well as obligations. During the French Revolution, the concept of "citizen" also implied a rejection of the special privileges and honours claimed by the aristocracy and nobility. Citizenship connoted that all men (!) were free and equal. The French Declaration was entitled "The Declaration of the Rights of Man and Citizen."

Viewed from the perspective of the long history of the concept of "citizenship," the concept of "human rights" is relatively new, but it has had great rhetorical, political, legal, and ethical impact. Does the newer concept of human rights have implications for the notion of citizenship and for the bundle of rights traditionally attached to citizenship? How important are the rights of citizens from a human rights perspective? Does international human rights law consider issues relating to citizenship?

Although the concept of citizenship remains of major importance in the modern world, I suggest in this chapter that the rights and obligations linked to citizenship are being modified and eroded by the international movement for the protection of the human rights of *all* persons. A transition is occurring: the concept of the "person" with human rights, whatever his or her political affiliation – first enunciated most clearly in the French Declaration of the Rights of Man and Citizen – is gaining on the concept of "citizenship" as the main purveyor of rights.

The concepts of "citizenship" and "universal human rights" raise issues of exclusion and diversity. The concept of the citizen as a bearer of significant rights also implies exclusion: non-citizens are denied rights, particularly rights of political participation, thus perpetuating an essential inequality based on whether one is or is not a citizen. Persons with no citizenship – "stateless persons" – are without protection or rights from any state, and treaties have been adopted under the auspices of the United Nations to address the problems of that stateless persons face.

A basic dilemma relating to cultural diversity is implicit in the concept of *universal* human rights. This concept posits a fundamental equality of all persons simply because they are "persons" and considers that human rights norms apply equally to all countries and all cultures. The United Nations General Assembly adopted the Universal Declaration of Human Rights in 1948, but, given the diversity among cultures in the world, can it be claimed that human rights concepts are truly universal? In recent years, increasing criticism has been directed at the contention that human rights are universal, raising serious challenges to the international movement for the protection of human rights.

These two issues form the main themes of this chapter: (1) the impact of international human rights law on the bundle of rights traditionally identified with citizenship, and (2) the challenge to the universality of human rights posed by the diversity among the cultures of the world.[2]

I begin by tracing the historical development of the concept of human rights and the development of the international law of human rights. Subsequent sections of the chapter describe the manner in which political rights linked to citizenship are addressed in major international human rights instruments and the problems presented to the international human rights movement by cultural diversity. In the final section I refer briefly to some current problems in international human rights law relating to citizenship issues.

CITIZENSHIP AND THE ORIGIN OF THE CONCEPT OF HUMAN RIGHTS

The French Declaration of the Rights of Man and Citizen, the American Declaration of Independence and the Declaration of Rights in the Constitution of the State of Virginia are hailed as major signposts in

the development of the concept of human rights. They are the forerun-
ners of the later international human rights instruments.

These declarations of rights did not appear simultaneously by
chance. The way to the great declarations of rights had been prepared
by a long intellectual history: by the Enlightenment philosophers of the
eighteenth century, by the Reformation, by medieval natural law scholars, and, even before, by Roman and Greek stoicism and jurisprudence.
The influence of Enlightenment philosophy was most significant, given
its emphases on individualism, the right to property, an original state of
nature in which men were free before they entered a social contract, the
overthrow of established privileges and of the feudal and semi-feudal
structure of society, the importance of religious tolerance, a concept of
men as free and equal, and the concept of natural rights. Many of these
notions were revolutionary and have profoundly affected political life
since the time of the American and French Revolutions.

These ringing declarations of rights, however, did not truly mean that
all people were considered free and equal. The landless classes in France
could not profit from the concept of the right to property, and in the
United States slaves were not granted equal rights with other citizens.
The American Constitution provided that slaves should be counted as
only three fifths of a person for the purposes of proportional representation. If the concept that all men were created "free and equal" did not
apply to slaves and serfs, what about women? It was not until the
women's movement of the early twentieth century that equal rights for
women were strongly asserted.

The French Declaration of Rights of Man and Citizen was limited in
its purview. Condorcet remarked that it should have been called "The
Declaration of the Rights of *White* Man,"[3] since little was done at the
Revolution to end the slave trade or to give civic rights to blacks. Citizenship with its complement of rights was limited, and the incipient
notions of human rights made no fundamental changes. It was not
intended to relate to the rights of women.

But even the incipient development of the "rights of man" was criti-
cized. Edmund Burke understood the rights of Englishman – that is, the
rights of citizens – but not the abstract notion of the rights of man.
Thus, in his mind, rights resulted from participation in political society
and not from an abstract entitlement to human rights.[4] It has also been
noted that the American Constitution did not recognize the rights of all
men to freedom and equality, but rather the rights of all to live under
constitutional government.[5]

In the United States, the Bill of Rights, the first ten amendments to
the Constitution, were largely limitations on the powers of the government rather than ringing endorsements of the rights of all men. It was
the thirteenth, fourteenth and fifteenth amendments, which followed

the Civil War (100 years after the founding of the Republic) that extended full citizenship rights to black men – but not to women, white or black.

Until the civil rights movement of the 1960s, a number of American states effectively managed to undermine the right to vote of black Americans, despite the post Civil War constitutional amendments, by imposing poll taxes or literacy requirements for voting. And only in 1920 did the Nineteenth Amendment extend full citizenship rights to women: "The rights of citizens of the United States to vote shall not be denied or abridged by the United States or by any State on account of sex."

The rights of citizenship have been extended in most parts of the world to women and others previously excluded from full participation as citizens, but many states – probably most – have many residents who are not citizens. What are the rights of these non-citizens, and what are the sources of their rights? Human rights norms adopted by the international community apply to *all* persons, not only to citizens. How these general human rights norms relate to the rights of non-citizens is the subject of the following sections.

THE ORIGINS OF AN INTERNATIONAL SYSTEM FOR THE PROTECTION OF HUMAN RIGHTS

A forerunner of the later development of international human rights law was the international law doctrine of "diplomatic protection" developed in the nineteenth century. Under this doctrine, states were required to guarantee a certain minimum level of human rights to aliens (citizens of another country) within their borders, even though international law at the time imposed no standards as to how a state should treat its own citizens. The doctrine of "diplomatic protection" was devised to protect the rights of the foreign government concerned rather than the rights of aliens. To deprive a citizen of another state of his or her rights was considered an attack on that state. Reparations received from the offending state belonged to the state that had invoked the diplomatic protection of its citizen and might or might not be handed over to the injured citizen.

However, the seeds of the future international law of human rights were contained in this doctrine of diplomatic protection. Arbitrators and international tribunals referred to minimum standards of "justice which all civilized nations hold in common"[6] in investigating and punishing criminal offences.

The obligation of a State to protect the rights of its own citizens as a requirement of international law had a hesitant beginning in the doctrine of humanitarian intervention. Edwin Borchard wrote in 1915 that

where a state under exceptional circumstances disregards certain rights of its own citizens, over whom presumably it has absolute sovereignty, the other states of the family of nations are authorized by international law to intervene on the grounds of humanity. When these "human rights" are habitually violated, one or more states may intervene in the name of the society of nations and may take such measures as to substitute at least temporarily, if not permanently, its own sovereignty for that of the state thus controlled.[7]

The doctrines of diplomatic protection and of humanitarian intervention were subject to gross abuse. Diplomatic protection was exercised primarily by strong states against weak states and came to be used primarily to protect property rights rather than individual human rights. Humanitarian intervention was also exercised by powerful states against weak states; it was employed arbitrarily, usually only when there was a link of religion or ethnicity between the intervening state and the individuals whose rights were being violated. Intervention often occurred for political reasons under the guise of humanitarian intervention.[8]

Another direct antecedent of present human rights law were the treaties protecting minorities adopted by European powers after the First World War. Ratifying states were committed to protect the linguistic, religious, and educational rights of specific minority groups within their borders. Other states (normally adjacent states with a population of the same ethnicity as the minority protected under the treaty) were entitled to protest and take actions permitted under international law if the treaty was violated. These treaties resulted from the perception that the violation of the rights of minorities had been a contributing cause to the outbreak of the war.

While the doctrines of diplomatic protection and humanitarian intervention, together with treaties protecting minorities, contained an incipient notion of the protection of human rights in international law, the fuller development of international human rights law did not occur until the creation of the United Nations.

THE DEVELOPMENT OF INTERNATIONAL HUMAN RIGHTS LAW AFTER THE SECOND WORLD WAR

In 1948 The Universal Declaration of Human Rights was drafted as a "common standard of achievement for all peoples and all nations."[9] For the first time a major international instrument – albeit a non-binding declaration and not a treaty subject to ratification – spoke in terms of the rights of "everyone." Article 2 of the Declaration provided that: "Everyone is entitled to all the rights and freedoms set forth in this Declaration without distinction of any kind, such as race, colour, sex, language, religion, political or other opinion, *national* or social origin, property, birth or other status" [emphasis added].

The Declaration has had an enormous influence, and most of its provisions are now considered binding international customary law. Twenty-eight articles detail the rights of "everyone." Following the adoption of the Declaration, two major international covenants on human rights were drafted: the International Covenant on Civil and Political Rights (ICCPR) and the International Covenant on Economic, Social and Cultural Rights (ICESCR). These are international treaties that become binding on states when ratified and their drafting was lengthy and difficult. They both entered into force in 1976; each has now been ratified by more than 100 countries. Monitoring committees composed of independent experts supervise the implementation of the Covenants.

The setting of standards for the protection of human rights in international treaties has proliferated; there are now more than 100 international and regional treaties concerned with human rights. International conventions have been adopted on the prohibition of discrimination on the grounds of gender or race, on statelessness, on the rights of children, on refugees, on migrant workers, and on the rights of many others. A number of these conventions are monitored by a committee of independent experts. Regional human rights conventions have been adopted in the Americas, Europe, and Africa.

While these treaties generally accord rights to *all* persons simply because they are human beings, they have not ignored the rights associated with citizenship. References to citizenship and political rights were included in the Universal Declaration, in the Covenants, and well as many other conventions. Treaties concerning stateless persons, refugees, and migrant workers have a direct bearing on the rights of non-citizens.

The implications and limitations of citizenship rights arising under international human rights law are discussed in the following section.

HUMAN RIGHTS STANDARDS AND CITIZENSHIP ISSUES

Sovereignty and Citizenship

A fundamental tension exists between the development of the international law of human rights and the desire of states to protect their national sovereignty. International human rights law necessarily circumscribes the realm of national sovereignty, creating a tension that is particularly evident in issues concerning citizenship. Decisions concerning citizenship remain largely the province of a state's sovereign power. States may accord their nationality and issue passports to whomever they wish.[10] Within their national boundaries, they may grant political rights to whomever they wish. But arbitrariness and discrimination in according citizenship and the treatment of non-citizens have been increasingly perceived as human rights issues. International human rights law has thus necessarily begun to be concerned with issues of citizenship. While many rights are accorded to "everyone" by international human rights law, some important rights, particularly political rights, are still dependent on citizenship. Citizenship provides privileges and protection; thus nationality and citizenship remain important sources of rights.

In 1923, the Permanent Court of International Justice declared that the question of nationality was a matter within the reserved domain of domestic jurisdiction.[11] But a contemporary commentator has noted the evolution in international law that took place sixty years later: [T]he Inter-American Court of Human Rights declared that nationality was an inherent right of all human beings; the manners in which States regulate matters bearing on nationality could no longer be deemed within their sole jurisdiction, but are circumscribed by their obligations to ensure the full protection of human rights.[12]

STATELESSNESS: IS THERE A RIGHT TO A NATIONALITY?

A person who lacks a nationality may lack many important rights: the right to protection by a state, the right to a passport permitting travel, and the right of political participation in a community. Even aliens who have long resided in a particular State may lack many rights and are almost never accorded rights of political participation. Nationality remains important for individuals in many contexts: tax laws, residency laws, laws relating to testamentary disposition, extradition laws, and laws relating to marital status are often based on or governed by nationality. It is not surprising then that attempts have been made to address statelessness or the situation of aliens systematically through international human rights instruments. But, as will be seen from the treaty provisions detailed in the following, while many steps have been taken and some treaties provide for a "right to a nationality," they stop short of imposing on states the obligation to grant nationality to particular individuals. Article 15 of the Universal Declaration provides that: (1) Everyone has the right to a nationality; and (2) No one shall be arbitrarily deprived of his nationality nor denied the right to change his nationality.

Although the Declaration is non-binding, its recognition of the right to a nationality provides a moral benchmark;[13] Article 15 has been invoked in the decisions of a number of national courts.[14]

In 1954 and 1961, two international conventions dealing with statelessness were adopted by the United Nations. They have been ratified by few states, however, and their effect has thus been limited. The 1954 Convention relating to the Status of Stateless Persons[15] provided for stateless persons to be accorded, in their country of residence, treatment equal to that of nationals with regard to certain rights. The Convention on the Reduction of Statelessness, adopted in 1961, came into force in 1975 and has received even fewer ratifications than the earlier Convention. It stipulates, among other things, that a contracting State should grant its nationality to a person born in its territory who would otherwise be stateless and that a state should not deprive a person of its nationality if the deprivation would render him stateless. During the drafting of these two conventions there was strong opposition from many states on the grounds that nationality was within the exclusive jurisdiction of states.[16] This continued opposition is evidenced by the few ratifications that the more ambitious 1961 Convention has received.

Article 24(3) of the ICCPR provides that "Every child has the right to acquire a nationality." During the drafting of this Article, agreement was reached that every effort should be made to prevent statelessness among children, but no agreement could be reached to reaffirm in a binding instrument the concept contained in the Universal Declaration that there is a "right to a nationality" in general. One commentator has pointed out that

[w]hile Article 24(3) protects the right of every child to acquire a nationality, it does not *necessarily* make it an obligation for States to give their nationality to every child born in their territory. States are required to adopt every appropriate measure, both internally and in cooperation with other States, to ensure that every child has a nationality when born. The purpose of the provision is to prevent a child from being afforded less protection by society and the State because he is stateless.[17]

The widely ratified Convention on the Rights of the Child[18] also guarantees the right of a child to acquire a nationality, but does not state which nationality nor does it guarantee the right of a child to acquire a nationality at the time of birth.

A regional convention, the American Convention on Human Rights, contains the strongest provision concerning the granting of nationality in a binding instrument. Article 20(1) guarantees the right of every person to a nationality and Article 20(2) provides that "Every person has the right to a nationality of the state in whose territory he was born if he does not have the right to any other nationality." Nearly every country in the Americas bases its nationality legislation primarily on the *jus soli* principle that birth on a given state territory is the decisive factor in the acquisition of nationality, hence facilitating the implementation of the provisions of the American Convention.[19]

Neither the African Charter on Human and Peoples' Rights nor the European Convention on Human Rights contain provisions on nationality. The countries of Africa and Europe have diverse provisions concerning the granting of nationality: some adopt the *jus soli* principle and others the *jus sanguinis* principle. The Council of Europe has recently adopted a new convention on nationality that includes general principles and lays down various conditions for attribution and loss of nationality.

In summary, problems associated with statelessness and the right to a nationality have been recognized as serious human rights problems, and international human rights instruments have attempted to limit and reduce statelessness. Yet such efforts have been strongly contested by some states on the grounds of their exclusive sovereignty in issues regarding nationality. It cannot be said that international standards concerning acquisition of a nationality are entirely satisfactory. In addition, problems of implementation remain for such standards as exist, as for all human rights standards. Nevertheless, as Johannes Chan has pointed out:

[I]t can safely be concluded that there is a clear trend in international law towards a gradual recognition of an individual's right to a nationality ... . The right to nationality, though not yet firmly secured in international law, includes three distinct aspects: the right to have a nationality, or in the negative form, the right to be protected from statelessness, the right to change one's nationality, and the right not to be arbitrarily deprived of one's nationality.[20]

Political Rights

The right of all citizens to participate actively in political life is a right of major importance. Yet, as Henry Steiner has pointed out:

For a right regarded as foundational, political participation suffers from serious infirmities. The norms defining it are either vague or, when explicit, bear sharply disputed meanings. Within the framework of human rights law, the right expresses less a vital concept meant to universalize certain practices than a bundle of concepts, sometimes complementary but sometimes antagonistic. On occasion this human right serves as a universal rallying cry against a friendless outlaw nation. But more often it becomes another weapon of rhetorical battle, a convenient, even authoritative concept through which each of the world's ideological blocs, infusing the right with its own understandings, attacks the other for violating those understandings.[21]

Article 21 of the Universal Declaration provides that:

1. Everyone has the right to take part in the government of his country, directly or through freely chosen representatives.
2. Everyone has the right to equal access to public service in his country.
3. The will of the people shall be the basis of the authority of government; this will shall be expressed in periodic and genuine elections which shall be by universal and equal suffrage and shall be held by secret vote or by equivalent free voting procedures.

Article 25 of the ICCPR states that:

Every citizen shall have the right and opportunity, without any of the distinctions mentioned in Article 2 and without unreasonable restrictions:
   a. to take part in the conduct of public affairs, directly or through freely chosen representatives;
   b. to vote and be elected at genuine periodic elections which shall be by universal and equal suffrage and shall be held by secret ballot, guaranteeing the free expression of the will of the electors;
   c. to have access, on general terms of equality, to public service in his country.

Article 25 is the only article of the Covenant that restricts rights to citizens. Thus, it is clear that aliens may be denied the right to vote. And despite the reference to every citizen, international human rights law permits a state to restrict the right to vote and participate in political life on certain accepted grounds. Most countries have provisions prohibiting persons convicted of serious crimes and mentally incompetent individuals from voting. Age requirements for voting are universal. The use of the terminology "without unreasonable restrictions" in the first paragraph of Article 25 is interpreted as permitting many such restrictions.

Article 2 of the ICCPR provides that states undertake to respect the rights recognized in the Covenant without distinction of race, colour, sex, language, religion, political or other opinion, national or social origin, property, birth, or other status. The first paragraph of Article 25 read together with Article 2 would prohibit contracting states from restricting the suffrage on any of the grounds mentioned in Article 2. It is important to remember that only recently in many countries were women accorded the right to vote (for example, in Switzerland, a Western democracy, it was not granted until the 1970s). In 1953, a Convention on the Political Rights of Women was adopted by the United Nations to ensure full political rights for women.[22] It has been widely ratified.

Article 25 does not indicate any preference for a particular form of government so long as citizens have the right to take part in the conduct of public affairs and to vote. Read alone, the Article is scarcely sufficient to guarantee a democratic form of government. Rights to freedom of speech, freedom of the press, and freedom of association are all important – even necessary – aspects of the democratic process and are laid down in other articles of the Covenant.[23]

Since political rights are limited to citizens, aliens have no Covenant right to participate in political life. Aliens often reside for many years in a particular country and abide by obligations such as the payment of taxes without acquiring the right to vote. To date, human rights law does not require that aliens be given the right to participate in political life. In some European countries, aliens are now given the right to vote in local elections. When substantial numbers of residents in a given country are denied political rights, it cannot be said that full democracy has been achieved in that country.

A requirement of a reasonable period of residence for voting is justifiable, but denying the vote to aliens who have lived many years in a country – and may not have a reasonable possibility of naturalization – is unreasonable, but not yet prohibited by human rights law.

There are many means by which an electoral system can be constructed so as to limit even the equal rights of all *citizens* to participate in political life. There may be gerrymandering of electoral districts, and a minority ethnic group may not be able to make its views heard if a proportional system of representation is not instituted. Article 25 does not address these concerns. Thus, Henry Steiner's view that the right to political participation addressed in human rights law "suffers serious infirmities" seems clearly supported.

Aliens

In the previous section, I pointed out that aliens are expressly not accorded political rights under human rights law. However, certain provisions of the two major Covenants and other human rights instruments concern the rights of aliens. Article 13 of the ICCPR provides:

An alien lawfully in the territory of a State Party to the present Covenant may be expelled therefrom only in pursuance of a decision reached in accordance with law and shall, except where compelling reasons of national security otherwise require, be allowed to submit the reasons against his expulsion and to have his case reviewed by, and be represented for the purpose before the competent authority or a person or persons especially designated by competent authority.

Aliens have no general right to enter a country, nor to reside in a country. Entry and residence of aliens remains a prerogative of the sovereign rights of states. Article 13 provides for procedural guarantees against expulsion, but it does not prohibit the expulsion of aliens, assuming procedures are complied with. The expulsion of aliens remains a common practice.[24]

The laws of many countries make distinctions between the rights accorded citizens and those accorded to aliens, particularly economic and social rights as defined by laws on social security, on participation in labor unions, and on the ownership of certain key industries.

The ICECSR provides that all rights shall be accorded to "everyone," with one exception. Article 2(3) provides that "Developing countries, with due regard to human rights and their national economy, may determine to what extent they would guarantee the economic rights recognized in the present Covenant to non-nationals." This Article relates to issues concerning nationalization or expropriation of foreign property. Since the right to property is not protected in the ICESCR it does not seem to have significant practical relevance, although it has resulted in political reactions.

Individual members of the Committee on Economic, Social and Cultural Rights have expressed their opinion that the Covenant was violated in particular countries that did not accord economic and social rights to aliens. The Committee as a whole has not generally taken a common position with regard to such situations; on one occasion it expressed concern about foreign workers being barred from holding trade union office in Senegal.[25]

In addition to the two major Covenants, a number of international human rights instruments are concerned with the rights of non-nationals in particular situations: the International Convention on the Protection of the Rights of All Migrant Workers and their Families, 1990 (not yet in force); the Convention Relating to the Status of Refugees, 1951; the Protocol Relating to the Status of Refugees, 1966; and several international labour conventions relating to migrant workers and social security.

CONTEMPORARY ISSUES CONCERNING CITIZENSHIP

While international law has been slowly – and as yet somewhat inadequately – attempting to focus attention on human rights issues relating to the rights of non-nationals, violations of the dignity and rights of non-citizens continue throughout the world.

In the United States, serious discrimination against undocumented non-nationals (illegal aliens) is threatened by proposed laws in California and elsewhere. In November 1994, California voters approved Proposition 187, which would deny basic social services, in particular health care and education, to persons determined to be in violation of federal immigration laws.

If enforced, this law would mean that children of undocumented parents would not be permitted to remain in school and that undocumented persons would be denied even the most basic health care. Such denials would be in flagrant violation of the most fundamental human rights to health care and education contained in human rights instruments.[26] An examination of the legality of Proposition 187 under American constitutional law and international law is now pending in American courts; it is to be hoped that it will never enter into effect.

In 1996, the United States Congress passed a law that eliminated public assistance for many legal immigrants. George Soros, writing in the *International Herald Tribune*, reported that:

Elderly and disabled legal immigrants panicked when they learned that they could lose their Medicare or Supplemental Security Income. They fear that they would be kicked out of nursing homes and hospitals. For most of these immigrants, these benefits are the difference between having a place to live and being homeless. Because of a public outcry, Congress, in the recently passed balanced budget legislation restored Supplemental Security Income and Medicaid benefits for those elderly and disabled legal immigrants who lived in the US before the welfare reform bill was passed.[27]

George Soros, Chairman of the Open Society Institute, has long been active in promoting human rights in Eastern Europe. His Institute has now turned its attention to the impoverished and poor, including immigrants, in the United States and is providing substantial sums to assist vulnerable populations in that country.

On the other side of the globe, similar problems are arising. In 1997, a Conference in Melbourne, Australia, on "Globalization and Citizenship: Guaranteeing Rights in a Multi-Cultural Society" focused on difficult citizenship issues in the Asia and Pacific region. A summary report on the Conference stated:

At a time when migration throughout the Asian and Pacific area is quickening, multi-culturalism is also a challenge in many other countries of the region. "Who belongs" in each society, and who does not, is a subject of increasing debate. The terms on which citizenship is granted, and the rights of foreigners working and living within various countries are undergoing revision. Frequently this occurs within an atmosphere of increasing inter-cultural tension and suspicion ... . Of course, citizenship debates often centre not on cultural but on social and economic questions. What rights should members of a specific political community enjoy to basic social services and protection from destitution? What corresponding obligations must they accept?[28]

HUMAN RIGHTS AND DIVERSITY

The apparent conflict between the contention that human rights are universal and the extent of cultural diversity in the world has been referred to in the Introduction. The issue is often phrased as one of cultural relativism versus universal human rights. I want to suggest that the concept of universal human rights is not incompatible with an appreciation of the extent of cultural diversity in the world.

In international forums, statements attacking the universality of human rights have come primarily from some Asian governments – and the term "governments" should be stressed, since Asian non-governmental organizations have distanced themselves from these criticisms. Prior to the Vienna Conference on Human Rights in 1994, Asian non-governmental organizations, following governmental attacks against the universality of human rights, issued the "Bangkok statement" to strongly affirming their support of the universality of human rights.

At the Vienna Conference, discussions concerning the universality of human rights became a major issue and were resolved by an agreed statement of the governments attending the Conference that reaffirmed the universality of human rights. Controversy over universality has continued, however. Recently, Prime Minister Mahathir of Malaysia argued for the removal of the term "Universal" from the Universal Declaration of Human Rights.

It appears from comments by governments that this controversy has less to do with cultural diversity than with political and economic concerns. The Asian governments in question have objected to normative rights such as freedom of speech and of association and the right to form free labour unions on the grounds that, in their countries, they would lead to political and economic instability. They have not generally cited cultural differences that make these rights unacceptable, but rather the need for political and economic stability. The economic and political arguments against according such rights have not been accepted in international forums or by the international human rights movement in general.

There are legitimate issues of interpretation of particular human rights norms, such as the extent to which freedom of speech may be limited in particular instances (e.g., speech that incites hatred or poses a threat to public security during periods of emergency). To affirm the universality of human rights is not to deny that there are problems of interpretation and application regarding particular human rights included in international instruments. In every legal system, conflicts arise over the precise interpretation of laws; human rights norms, like all legal standards, need interpretation and are subject to opposing claims about their meaning. Differing interpretations are seldom based on contentions of cultural differences, but more generally result from the particular political situation in countries applying the norms.

Nevertheless, some human rights standards included in international instruments are rejected by particular states, most frequently on the basis of religious views. A number of human rights instruments contain references to equality between the spouses in marriage and dissolution of marriage. The Universal Declaration contains a provision stating that everyone has the right to change his religion. Human rights treaties normally permit ratifying states to make reservations to particular provisions, and Islamic countries have made reservations to these provisions when ratifying the treaties.

The subject of abortion is not generally referred to in human rights treaties, given the lack of agreement among states concerning whether or not it is a violation of the right to life. Human rights instruments are understood as requiring protection of life from the moment of birth, without reference to whether life should be protected from the time of conception. Each state is thus left free to enact its own laws on the matter of abortion. The American Convention on Human Rights is an exception to this general rule. It contains a provision stating that the right to life should, in general, be protected from the moment of conception. While this is in accord with the religious beliefs of most Latin American nations, the United States, in the event of ratification, would certainly make a reservation to this provision.

The possibility of making reservations to particular provisions in treaties thus makes it possible for states to accept the overwhelming majority of provisions of these treaties, without accepting particular provisions to which they object. Reservations may not be made if they are contrary to the objects and purposes of the treaty in question, but are usually permitted to a number of particular provisions. Built into the system of international protection of human rights is a certain degree of permissiveness for religious, political, and cultural differences among states. For example, the African Convention on Human and Peoples' Rights has attempted to incorporate particular aspects of African culture in the Convention by emphasizing collective rights as well as individual rights and stressing duties as well as rights.

The list of human rights in the Universal Declaration of Human Rights is not exhaustive. New human rights have been added to the corpus of internationally accepted human rights since that time. Two groups – women and indigenous peoples – have pointed out that the rights contained in the Universal Declaration are not exhaustive. The Convention on the Elimination of All Forms of Discrimination against Women and the recent Declaration on Violence against Women have established additional rights for women. International Labour Convention No. 169 on Indigenous and Tribal Peoples and the United Nations Draft Declaration on the Rights of Indigenous Peoples respond, in part, to the demands of indigenous peoples for rights that protect their lands and their cultures.

The concept that all people have basic human rights is founded on the principle of the equal dignity of each individual regardless of race, colour, nationality, or ethnic origin. As a principle, it is, and must remain, in my view, a universal and protected principle of the international community. At the same time, it must be recognized that rights important to particular individuals or groups that have not yet been recognized internationally may be added to the list of internationally recognized human rights over time. The list of internationally protected human rights will not remain static. Moreover, conflicting interpretations of particular international standards will always exist without undermining the basic conception of the universality of human rights.

CONCLUSION

The Preamble to the Universal Declaration of Human Rights begins with the statement that "recognition of the inherent dignity and of the equal and inalienable rights of all members of the human family is the foundation of freedom, justice and peace in the world." But violations of the inherent dignity of persons occur continually, simply because such persons do not have political citizenship in the country in which they reside. While the effort to develop standards in various human rights instruments to protect non-nationals is to be applauded, it remains rudimentary, inadequate, and not yet complete. We have not yet arrived at the point where international human rights law, even "on the books," truly protects "all persons."

The slogan of "cultural relativism" has frequently been used as an attack on the universality of human rights. Developments in international human rights law have taken account of legitimate demands for divergent interpretations of particular norms, and the international community is increasingly recognizing the violations of the previously ignored human rights, of, among other groups, women and indigenous peoples, and is adopting new norms for their protection. These developments do not reflect a conviction that human rights are relative and not universal, but rather a recognition of the importance of the concept of human rights and the need to perceive violations of human dignity previously unrecognized. Diversity among the peoples of the world must be recognized by the international human rights movement, but the universality of the concept that all human beings, whatever their culture or nationality, are free and equal in dignity must remain the fundamental basis of human rights protection.

NOTES

1 "Paul said to the centurion who was standing by, 'Is it lawful for you to scourge a man who is a Roman citizen, and uncondemned?' When the centurion heard that, he went to the tribune and said to him, 'What are you about to do? For this man is a Roman citizen.' So the tribune came and said to him, 'Tell me, are you a Roman citizen?' And he said, 'Yes.' ... So those who were about to examine him withdrew from him instantly; and the tribune also was afraid, for he realised that Paul was a Roman citizen and that he had bound him." *Acts* 22, v. 25–9. See also *Acts* 16, v. 17; 23, v. 26.

2 I have generally used the term "nationality" in this chapter as synonymous with "citizenship," although the two terms are distinguishable. The term "nationality" is frequently used to refer not to membership in a state but to membership in a particular ethnic or linguistic community. The term "citizenship" usually refers to membership in a state with corresponding political rights in that state, although it may sometimes refer to membership in a smaller community, such as a town or other political unit. In general, international human rights law uses the terms interchangeably, with some exceptions. Given the diverse usages of the two terms, I will attempt to clarify in my discussion the precise sense in which they are used in international human rights instruments.

3 Elizabeth Badinter and Robert Badinter, *Condorcet* (Paris: Fayard, 1988), 304–5.

4 Edmund Burke, *Reflections on the Revolution in France* (Chicago: H. Regnery Company Gateway Edition, 1968), 44.

5 Hannah Arendt, *On Revolution* (New York: Viking Press Compass Edition, 1965), 147.

6 Cutting Case, Claim by the United States against Mexico, 1886–88. 2 J.B. Moore, A Digest of International Law 228–42 (1906). Note from US Secretary of State (Bayard) to the US Minister to Mexico (Jackson), 20 July 1886, reproduced in Louis B. Sohn and Thomas Buergenthal, *International Protection of Human Rights* (Indianapolis: Bobbs-Merrill, 1973),73–4.

7 Edwin M. Borchard, *The Diplomatic Protection of Citizens Abroad* (1915), reproduced in Sohn and Buergenthal, *International Protection of Human Rights*, 139.

8 See Ibid., 137–211.

9 Adopted and proclaimed by United Nations General Assembly resolution 217 A (III) on 10 December 1948.
10 With a limited exception relating to the law of "diplomatic protection." While states may accord their citizenship to whomever they wish, such a grant may not be opposable to another state under the doctrine of "diplomatic protection" unless a "genuine link" exists between the state granting the nationality and the individual concerned.
11 *Tunis and Morocco Nationality Decrees Case*, (1923) P.C.I.J., Ser. B, No. 4, 4.
12 Johannes M.M. Chan, "The Right to Nationality as a Human Right: The Current Trend Towards Recognition," *Human Rights Law Journal* 12, nos. 1–2 (1991): 1.
13 R. De Groot, "The Acquisition and Loss of Nationality and the African Charter on Human and Peoples' Rights: Lessons from the European Experience," *Africa Legal Aid Quarterly* (July–September 1996): 16.
14 Chan, 3, "The Right to Nationality as a Human Right," note 20.
15 United Nations Treaty Series, vol. 360: 117.
16 Chan, "The Right to Nationality as a Human Right," 4.
17 Ibid., 5.
18 United Nations Document A/44/25, (1989).
19 De Groot, "The Acquisition and Loss of Nationality," 18.
20 Chan, "The Right to Nationality as a Human Right," 13.
21 Henry Steiner, "Political Participation as a Human Right," *Harvard Human Rights Yearbook* 1 (Spring 1988): 77.
22 United Nations Treaty Series, vol. 193: 135.
23 See Manfred Nowak, *United Nations Covenant on Civil and Political Rights: CCPR Commentary* (Arlington, VA: N.P. Engel, 1993, 435–57 for an extensive discussion of the drafting of Article 25 and a discussion of the interpretation by the Human Rights Committee of the Article.
24 See Nowak, *United Nations Covenant on Civil and Political Rights*, 222–32 for a discussion of the drafting and implementation of this provision.
25 Ibid., 173.
26 For a human rights critique of Proposition 187, see Stephen Knight, "Proposition 187 and International Human Rights Law: Illegal Discrimination in the Right to Education," *Hastings International and Comparative Law Review* 19, no. 1 (Fall 1995): 183.
27 George Soros, "Restoring the Immigrants' Hopes," *International Herald Tribune*, 23–4 August 1997.
28 *UNRISD* [United Nations Research Institute on Social Development (Geneva)] *News*, no. 16 (Spring–Summer 1997): 24.

13 Democratic Exclusion (and Its Remedies?)
The John Ambrose Stack Memorial Lecture

CHARLES TAYLOR

Democracy, particularly liberal democracy, is a great philosophy of inclusion. Rule of the people – by the people, for the people – and where "people" is supposed to mean, unlike in earlier days, everybody, without the unspoken restrictions of yesteryear against peasants, women, slaves, etc. – this offers the prospect of the most inclusive politics in human history.

And yet there is also something in the dynamic of democracy that pushes to exclusion. This was allowed full rein in earlier forms of this regime, as among the ancient poleis and republics, but today it is a great cause of malaise. In this chapter, I want first to explore this dynamic and then to look at various ways of compensating for it, or minimizing it.

I

What makes the thrust to exclusion? We might put it this way: what makes democracy inclusive is that it is the government of all the people; what makes for exclusion is that it is the government of all the people. The exclusion is a by-product of something else: the need, in self-governing societies, for a high degree of cohesion. Democratic states need something like a common identity.

We can see why as soon as we ponder what is involved in self-government, and what is implied in the basic mode of legitimation of democratic states: that they are founded on popular sovereignty. For a people to be sovereign, it needs to form an entity and to have a personality.

The revolutions that ushered in regimes of popular sovereignty trans-ferred the ruling power from a king to a "nation" or a "people." In the process, they invented a new kind of collective agency. These terms ex-isted before, but the thing they now indicated, this new kind of agency, was something unprecedented, at least in the immediate context of early modern Europe. Thus the notion of a "people" could certainly be applied to the ensemble of subjects of the kingdom, or to the non-elite strata of society, but prior to the turnover it had not indicated an entity that could decide and act together, to whom one could attribute a will.

Why does this new kind of entity need a strong form of cohesion? Is not the notion of popular sovereignty simply that of majority will, more or less restrained by the respect of liberty and rights? But this kind of rule can be adopted by all sorts of bodies, even the loosest aggregations. Suppose that during a public lecture some members of the audience find the heat oppressive and ask that the windows be opened; others demur. One might easily decide this by a show of hands, and those present would accept this as legitimate. And yet the audience might be the most disparate congeries of individuals, unknown to one another, without mutual concern, brought together simply by that event.

This example shows, by way of contrast, what democratic societies need. It seems intuitively clear that they have to be bonded more pow-erfully than this chance grouping. But how can we understand this necessity?

One way to see it is to push a bit farther the logic of popular sov-ereignty. This logic not only recommends a certain class of decision-making procedures – those that are grounded ultimately in the majority (with restrictions) – but also offers a particular justification. Under a re-gime of popular sovereignty we are free in a way that we would not be under an absolute monarch or an entrenched aristocracy, for instance.

Now suppose we see this from the standpoint of some individual. Let us say I am outvoted on an important issue. I am forced to abide by a rule I oppose. My will is not being done. Why should I consider myself free? Does it matter that I am overridden by the majority of my fellow citizens rather than by the decision of a monarch? Why should that be decisive? We can even imagine that a potential monarch, waiting to return to power in a coup, agrees with me on this question against the majority. Would I not be freer after the counter-revolution? After all, my will on this matter would then be put into effect.

We can recognize that this kind of question is not merely theoretical. It is rarely put on behalf of individuals, but it regularly arises on behalf of subgroups, e.g., national minorities, who see themselves as op-pressed. Perhaps no answer can satisfy them. Whatever one says, they cannot see themselves as part of this larger sovereign people. And therefore they see its rule as illegitimate, and this according to the logic of popular sovereignty itself.

We see here the inner link between popular sovereignty and the idea of the people as a collective agency in some stronger sense than the lecture audience. This agency is something one can be included in without really belonging to, which makes no sense for a member of the audience. We can see the nature of this belonging if we ask what answer we can give to those who are outvoted and are tempted by the argument that they are therefore not free.

Of course, some extreme philosophical individualists believe that there is no valid answer and that appeals to some greater collective is just so much humbug designed to make contrary voters accept voluntary servitude. But without deciding this ultimate philosophical issue, we can ask: What is the feature of our "imagined communities" by which people accept that they are free under a democratic regime, even when their will is overridden on important issues?

The answer runs something like this: You, like the rest of us, are free by virtue of the fact that we are ruling ourselves in common and are not being ruled by some agency that need take no account of us. Your freedom consists in the fact that you have a guaranteed voice in the sovereign, that you can be heard, and that you have some part in making the decision. You enjoy this freedom by virtue of a law that enfranchises all of us, and so we enjoy this together. Your freedom is realized and defended by this law, and this whether or not you win or lose in any particular decision. This law defines a community of those whose freedom it realizes and defends together. It defines a collective agency, a people, whose acting together by the law preserves their freedom.

Such is the answer, valid or not, that people have come to accept in democratic societies. We can see right away that it involves their accepting a kind of belonging much stronger than that of the people in the lecture hall. It is an ongoing collective agency, one in which the membership realizes something very important, a kind of freedom. Insofar as this good is crucial to their identity, they identify strongly with this agency and hence feel a bond with their co-participants. It is only an appeal to this kind of membership that can answer the challenge of our imagined individual above, who is pondering whether to support the monarch's (or general's) coup in the name of his or her freedom.

The crucial point is that, whoever is ultimately right philosophically, it is only insofar as people accept some such answer that the legitimacy principle of popular sovereignty can work to secure their consent. The principle is only effective via this appeal to a strong collective agency. If the identification with this is rejected, the rule of the government seems illegitimate in the eyes of the rejecters, as we see in countless cases with disaffected national minorities. Rule by the people, all right; but we cannot accept rule by this lot, because we are not part of their people. This is the inner link between democracy and strong common agency. It follows the logic of the legitimacy principle that underlies democratic regimes. A regime that fails to generate this identity does so at its peril.

This last example points to an important modulation of the appeal to popular sovereignty. In the version I have just given the appeal was to what we might call "republican freedom." It is the one inspired by ancient republics, and which was invoked in the American and French Revolutions. But, very soon after, the appeal began to take on a nationalist form. Attempts to spread the principles of the French Revolution through the force of French arms created a reaction in Germany, Italy, and elsewhere: a sense of not being part of that which was represented by the sovereign people and in the name of which the revolution was being made and defended. It came to be accepted in many circles that to have the unity necessary for collective agency, a sovereign people had to have an antecedent unity of culture, history, or (more often in Europe) language. And so behind the political nation there had to stand a pre-existing cultural (and sometimes ethnic) nation.

Nationalism, in this sense, was born out of democracy, as a (benign or malignant) growth. In early nineteenth-century Europe, as peoples struggled for emancipation from the multinational, despotic empires joined in the Holy Alliance, there seemed to be no opposition between the two. For a Mazzini, they were perfectly converging goals.[1] Only later did certain forms of nationalism throw off the allegiance to human rights and democracy in the name of self-assertion.

But even before this stage, nationalism lent another modulation to popular sovereignty. The answer to the objector above – something essential to your identity is bound up in our common laws – now refers not just to republican freedom, but also to something of the order of cultural identity. What is defended and realized in the national state is not just your freedom as a human being, but the expression of a common cultural identity.

We can speak therefore of a "republican" variant and a "national" variant of the appeal to popular sovereignty, though in practice the two often run together and often lie undistinguished in the rhetoric and imagination of democratic societies.

(And, in fact, a kind of nationalism has developed even in the societies that issued from the original "republican" pre-nationalist revolutions, the American and the French. The point of these revolutions was the universal good of freedom, whatever the mental exclusions that the revolutionaries in fact accepted and even cherished. Their patriotic allegiance was to the particular historical project of realizing freedom – in America, and in France. Their very universalism became the basis of a fierce national pride in the "last, best hope for mankind," in the republic that was bearer of "the rights of man." That is why freedom, at least in the French case, could become a project of conquest, with fateful results in reactive nationalism elsewhere.)

And so we have a new kind of collective agency, with which its members identify as the realization and bulwark of their freedom and the locus of their national and cultural expression. Of course, even in premodern societies people often "identified" with the regime, with sacred kings, or with hierarchical orders. They were often willing subjects. But in the democratic age we identify as free agents. That is why the notion of a popular will plays a crucial role in the legitimating idea.[2]

This means that the modern democratic state has generally accepted common purposes or reference points, the features whereby it can lay claim to being the bulwark of freedom and locus of expression of its citizens. Whether or not these claims are actually well founded, the state must be so imagined by its citizens if it is to be legitimate.

So a question can arise for the modern state for which there is no analogue in most pre-modern forms: What or whom is this state for? Whose freedom? Whose expression? The question seems to make no sense applied to, say, the Austrian or Turkish Empires – unless one were to answer the "For whom?" question by referring to the Habsburg or Ottoman dynasties; and this would hardly give you their legitimating ideas.

This is the sense in which a modern state has what I want to call a political identity defined as the generally accepted answer to the "What for?" or "For whom?" question. This is distinct from the identities of its members, that is, the reference points, many and varied, that for each of these defines what is important in their lives. There had better be some overlap, of course, if these members are to feel strongly identified with the state; but the identities of individuals and constituent groups will generally be richer and more complex, as well as often being quite different from each other.[3]

The recent constitutional struggles in Canada provide a good example of political identity as a source of contention. No one in Quebec doubts that its own "What for?" question must be answered in part by something like: "to promote and protect Quebec's distinct character," paraphrasing the Meech Lake amendment. The major point at issue was whether Canada could take this goal as a component of its own answer to this question. The rejection of the Meech Lake Accord was widely read in Quebec as a negative answer to this question, and this predictably gave an immense lift to the Independentist movement. Whether this will be enough to carry it over the top is still uncertain.[4]

The close connection between popular sovereignty, strong cohesion and political identity can be shown in another way: the people are supposed to rule. This means that the members of this "people" make up a decision-making unit, a body that takes joint decisions. Moreover, it is supposed to take its decisions through a consensus, or at least a majority, of agents who are deemed equal and autonomous. It is not "democratic" for some citizens to be under the control of others. It might facilitate decision-making, but it is not democratically legitimate.

In addition, to form a decision-making unit of the type demanded here it is not enough for a vote to record the fully formed opinions of all the members. These units must not only decide together, but must deliberate together. A democratic state is constantly facing new questions, and in addition aspires to form a consensus on the questions that it has to decide, not merely to reflect the outcome of diffuse opinions. However, a decision emerging from joint deliberation does not merely require everybody to vote according to his or her opinion. It is also necessary that each person's opinion should have been able to take shape or be reformed in the light of discussion – that is to say, by exchange with others.

This necessarily implies a degree of cohesion. To some extent, the members must know one another, listen to one another, and understand one another. If they are not acquainted, or if they cannot really understand one another, how can they engage in joint deliberation? This is a matter that concerns the very conditions of legitimacy of democratic states.

If, for example, a subgroup of the "nation" considers that it is not being listened to by the rest, or that they are unable to understand its point of view, it will immediately consider itself excluded from joint deliberation. Popular sovereignty demands that we should live under laws that derive from such deliberation. Anyone who is excluded can have no part in the decisions that emerge, and these consequently lose their legitimacy. A subgroup that is not listened to is in some respects excluded from the "nation" but, by this same token, it is no longer bound by the will of that nation.

For it to function legitimately, a people must thus be so constituted that its members are capable of listening to one another and effectively do so; or at least it should come close enough to that condition to ward off possible challenges to its democratic legitimacy from subgroups. In practice, more than that is normally required. It is not enough nowadays for us to be able to listen to one another. Our states aim to last, so we want an assurance that we shall continue to be able to listen to one another. This demands a certain reciprocal commitment. In practice, a nation can only ensure the stability of its legitimacy if its members are strongly committed to one another by means of their common allegiance to the political community. Moreover, it is the shared consciousness of this commitment that creates confidence in the various subgroups that they will indeed be heard, despite the possible causes for suspicion that are implicit in the differences between these subgroups.

In other words, a modern democratic state demands a "people" with a strong collective identity. Democracy obliges us to show much more solidarity and much more commitment to one another in our joint political project than was demanded by the hierarchical and authoritarian societies of yesteryear. In the good old days of the Austro-Hungarian Empire, the Polish peasant in Galicia could be altogether oblivious of the Hungarian country squire, the bourgeois of Prague, or the Viennese worker, without this in the slightest threatening the stability of the state. This condition of things only becomes untenable when ideas about popular government start to circulate. This is the moment when subgroups that will not or cannot be bound together start to demand their own states. This is the era of nationalism, of the breakup of empires.

I have been discussing the political necessity of a strong common identity for modern democratic states in terms of the requirement of forming a people, a deliberative unit. But this is also evident in a number of other ways. Thinkers in the civic humanist tradition from Aristotle to Arendt have noted that free societies require a higher level of commitment and participation than despotic or authoritarian ones. Citizens have to do for themselves, as it were, what otherwise their rulers would do for them. But this will happen only if these citizens feel a strong bond of identification with their political community, and hence with those who share with them in this.

From another angle, because these societies require strong commitment to do the common work, and because a situation in which some carried the burdens of participation and others just enjoyed the benefits would be intolerable, free societies require a high level of mutual trust. In other words, they are extremely vulnerable to mistrust on the part of some citizens that others are not really assuming their commitments: e.g., that they are not paying their taxes, or are cheating on welfare, or as employers are benefiting from a good labour market without assuming any of the social costs. This kind of mistrust creates extreme tension and threatens to unravel the whole skein of the mores of commitment that democratic societies need to operate. A continuing and constantly renewed mutual commitment is an essential basis for renewing this trust.

The relation between nation and state is often considered from a unilateral point of view, as if it were always the nation that sought to provide itself with a state. But there is also the opposite process. To remain viable, states sometimes seek to create a feeling of common belonging. This is an important theme in the history of Canada, for example. To form a state in the democratic era, a society is forced to undertake the difficult and never-to-be-completed task of defining its collective identity.

II

So there is a need for common identity. How does this generate exclusion? In a host of possible ways, which we can see illustrated in three different circumstances.

(1) The most tragic of these circumstances is also the most obvious: a group that cannot be assimilated to the reigning cohesion is brutally extruded by means of what we have come to call "ethnic cleansing."

But there are other cases in which, although it does not come to such drastic expedients, exclusion works all the same against those whose difference threatens the dominant identity. I would class forced inclusion as a kind of exclusion, which might seem a logical sleight of hand. Thus the Hungarian national movement in the nineteenth century tried forcefully to assimilate Slovaks and Romanians, and the Turks today are reluctant to concede that there is a Kurdish minority in their eastern borderlands. This may not seem to constitute exclusion to the minority, but in another clear sense it does. It is saying in effect: as you are, or consider yourselves to be, you have no place here; that is why we are going to make you over. Or exclusion may take the form of chicanery, as in the old apartheid South Africa, where millions of blacks were denied citizenship on the grounds that they were really citizens of "homelands," external to the state.

All these modes of exclusion are motivated by the threat that others represent to the dominant political identity. But this threat depends on the fact that popular sovereignty is the regnant legitimacy idea of our time. It is hard to sustain a frankly hierarchical society in which groups are ranged in tiers, with some overtly marked as inferior or subject, as with the millet system of the Ottoman Empire.

Hence the paradox that earlier conquering people were quite happy to coexist with vast numbers of subjects who were very different from them. The more the better. The early Muslim conquerors of the Umayyad empire did not press for conversion of their Christian subjects and even mildly discouraged it. Within the bounds of this unequal disposition, earlier empires very often had a very good record of "multicultural" tolerance and coexistence. Famous cases come down to us, like that of the Mughals under Akbar, that seem strikingly enlightened and humane compared to much of what goes on today in that part of the world and elsewhere.

It is no accident that the twentieth century is the age of ethnic cleansing, starting with the Balkan Wars, extending in that area through the aftermath of the First World War, and reaching epic proportions in the Second World War, and still continuing – to speak only of Europe. The democratic age poses new obstacles to coexistence because it opens a new set of issues concerning the political identity of the state that may deeply divide people. In many parts of the Indian subcontinent, for instance, Hindus and Muslims coexisted in conditions of civility, and even with a certain degree of syncretism, where later they would fight bitterly. What happened? The explanations often given include the British attempt to divide and rule, or even the British mania for census figures, which first made an issue of who was a majority where.

These factors may have their importance, but clearly what makes them vital is the surrounding situation, in which political identity becomes an issue. As the movement grows to throw off the alien, multinational empire and to set up a democratic state, the question arises of its political identity. Will it simply be that of the majority? Are we heading for a Hindu Raj? Muslims ask for reassurance. Gandhi's and Nehru's proposals for a pan-Indian identity did not satisfy Jinnah. Suspicion grows, guarantees are demanded, and ultimately separation ensues.

Each side is mobilized to see the other as a threat to political identity. This fear can then sometimes be transposed, through mechanisms we have yet to understand, into a threat to life; to this the response is savagery and counter-savagery, and we descend into the spiral that has become terribly familiar. Census figures can then be charged with ominous significance, but only because, in the age of democracy, being in the majority has decisive importance.

(2) Then there is the phenomenon we sometimes see in immigrant societies with a high degree of historic ethnic unity. The sense of a common bond and a common commitment has been bound up for so long with a common language, culture, history, ancestry, and so on, that it is difficult to adjust to a situation where the citizen body includes lots of people of other origins. People feel a certain discomfort with this situation, and this can be reflected in a number of ways.

In one kind of case, the homogeneous society is reluctant to concede citizenship to the outsiders. Germany is the best known example of this, with its third generation Turkish *Gastarbeiter*, whose only fluent language may be German, whose only familiar home is in Frankfurt, but who are still resident aliens.

But there are subtler and more ambivalent ways in which this discomfort can play out. Perhaps the outsiders automatically acquire citizenship after a standard period of waiting. There even may be an official policy of integrating them, widely agreed on by the members of the "old stock" population. But these are still so used to functioning politically among themselves that they find it difficult to adjust. Perhaps one might better put it that they do not quite know how to adjust yet; the new reflexes are difficult to find. For instance, they still discuss policy questions among themselves, in their electronic media and newspapers, as though immigrants were not a party to the debate. They discuss, for instance, how to gain the best advantage for their society of the new arrivals, or how to avoid certain possible negative consequences, but the newcomers are spoken of as "them," as though they were not potential partners in the debate.

You will have guessed that the example I am thinking of here is my native Quebec. I do not mean to exaggerate the phenomenon. It is changing, and I have great hopes that it will go on improving. It has taken time to learn the reflexes of inclusion, but they *are* being learned. Moreover, the problem is somewhat worse among extreme nationalists; it is not a universal phenomenon. It is worse among them because nationalists cherish a dream – of independence – that virtually no one who is not a *Québécois de souche* shares, for understandable psychological-historical reasons. It is only natural that this strand of the Quebec ideological spectrum should have more difficulty opening itself to outsiders, as the catastrophic speech of our ex-premier after the last referendum showed.

This example helps to illustrate just what is at stake here. I do not want to claim that democracy unfailingly leads to exclusion. That would be a counsel of despair, and the situation is far from desperate. I do want to say that there is a drive in modern democracy toward inclusion in the fact that government should be by all the people. But my point is that, alongside this, there is a standing temptation to exclusion, which arises from the fact that democracies work well when people know each other, trust each other, and feel a sense of commitment toward each other.

The coming of new kinds of people into a country or into active citizenship poses a challenge. The exact content of the mutual understanding, the bases of the mutual trust, and the shape of the mutual commitment all have to be redefined, reinvented. This is not easy, and there is an understandable temptation to fall back on the old ways and deny the problem, either by frank exclusion from citizenship (as in

Germany) or by the perpetuation of "us and them" ways of talking, thinking, and doing politics.

And the temptation is the stronger in transitional periods in which the traditional society may have to forgo certain advantages that came from the tighter cohesion of yore. Quebec clearly illustrates this. During the recent agonizing attempts by the government to cut back the galloping budget deficits, the premier organized "summits" of decision-makers from business, labour, and other segments of society. All of these – the fact that this seemed worth trying, in addition to the atmosphere of consensus, or at least the earnest striving toward an agreement – reflected the extremely tightly-knit nature of Quebec society as it has come down to us. The decision-makers still are disproportionately drawn from old-stock Quebeckers – quite naturally, at this stage of development. The operation might not be as easy to repeat twenty years from now.

So much for historically ethnically homogeneous societies. But we have analogous phenomena in mixed societies. Think of the history of the United States: how successive waves of immigrants were perceived by many Americans of longer standing as a threat to democracy and the American way of life. This was first of all the fate of the Irish in the 1840s. Then immigrants from southern and eastern Europe were looked askance at in the last decades of the century. And, of course, an old-established population, the blacks, when they were given citizen rights for the first time after the Civil War, were in effect excluded from voting through much of the Old South until the civil rights legislation of our time.

Some of this was blind prejudice. But not all. In fact, the early Irish and later European immigrants could not integrate at once into American White Anglo-Saxon Protestant political culture. The new immigrants often formed "vote banks" for bosses and political machines in the cities; this was strongly resented and opposed by progressives and others who were concerned for what they understood to be citizen democracy.

Here again, a transition was successfully navigated, and a new democracy emerged in which a fairly high level of mutual understanding, trust, and commitment (alas, with the tragic exception, still, of the black/white divide) was recreated, although arguably at the price of the fading of the early ideals of a citizen republic and the triumph of the "procedural republic," in Michael Sandel's language.[5] But the temptation to exclusion was very strong for a time, and some of it was motivated by the commitment to democracy itself.

(3) The cases I have been looking at are characterized by the arrival from abroad, or the entry into active citizenship, of people who have

not shared the ethnolinguistic culture or else the political culture. But
exclusion can operate along another axis. Just because of the importance of cohesion, and of a common understanding of political culture,
democracies have sometimes attempted to force their citizens into a
single mould. The "Jacobin" tradition of the French Republic provides
the best-known example of this.

Here the strategy is, from the very beginning, to make people over in
a rigorous and uncompromising way. Common understanding is
reached, and supposedly forever maintained, by a clear definition of
what politics is about and what citizenship entails, and these together
define the primary allegiance of citizens. This complex is then vigorously defended against all comers, ideological enemies, slackers, and,
when the case arises, immigrants.

The exclusion operates here, not in the first place against certain
people already defined as outsiders, but against other ways of being.
This formula forbids other ways of living modern citizenship; it casti-
gated as unpatriotic a way of living that would not subordinate other
facets of identity to citizenship. In the particular case of France, for
instance, a certain solution to the problem of religion in public life was
adopted by radical Republicans – one of extrusion – and they have had
immense difficulty even imagining that there might be other ways to
safeguard the neutrality and comprehensiveness of the French state.
Hence the overreaction to Muslim adolescents who wore headscaves
to school.

But the strength of this formula is that it managed for a long time to
avoid or at least minimize the other kind of exclusion, that of new
arrivals. It still surprises Frenchmen, and others, when they learn from
Gérard Noiriel[6] that one French person in four today has at least one
grandparent born outside the country. France in this century has been
an immigrant country without thinking of itself as such. The policy of
assimilation has hit a barrier with recent waves of Maghrébains, but it
worked totally with the Italians, Poles, and Czechs who came between
the two world wars. These people were never offered the choice, and
became indistinguishable from les Français de souche.

It has been argued that another dimension of this kind of inner
exclusion has operated along gender lines; and this not only in Jacobin
societies, but in all liberal democracies, where without exception
women received voting rights later than men. The argument is that the
style of politics, the modes and tone of public debate, and the like, have
been set by a political society that was exclusively male, and that this
has still to be modified to include women. If one looks at the behaviour
of some of our male-dominated legislatures at question time, resembling as they sometimes do, a boisterous boys' school at recreation, it is

clear that there is some truth to this point. The culture of politics could not fully include women without changing somewhat, even though we may be uncertain just how.

III

I hope I have made somewhat clear what I mean by the dynamic of exclusion in democracy. We might describe it as a temptation to exclude, beyond that which people may feel because of narrow sympathies or historic prejudice; a temptation that arises from the requirement of democratic rule itself for a high degree of mutual understanding, trust, and commitment. This can make it hard to integrate outsiders, and tempt us to draw a line around the original community. But it can also tempt us to what I have called "inner exclusion," the creation of a common identity around a rigid formula of politics and citizenship, which refuses to accommodate any alternatives and imperiously demands the subordination of other aspects of citizens' identities.

It is clear that these two modes are not mutually exclusive. Societies based on inner exclusion may come to turn away outsiders as well (as the strength of the Front National in France, alas, so well illustrates) while societies whose main historical challenge has been the integration of outsiders may have recourse to inner exclusion in an attempt to create some unity amid all the diversity.

The present drama of English Canada (or Canada outside Quebec) illustrates this only too well. Partly because of a sense of fragmentation that some Canadians feel in face of the rapid diversification of Canada's population, partly because this sense of fragmentation is often intensified rather than diminished by Quebec's affirmation of difference, partly because of time-honoured Canadian angst about national identity in face of the seemingly traditional security on this score of the United States, attitudes have become steadily more rigid in English Canada toward any possible accommodation of Quebec's difference during the last ten years. Canada's tragedy is that, at the moment where it is becoming more and more necessary to do something about Quebec's status in the federation, it is also becoming politically less and less possible to do anything meaningful.

Quite specifically, there is a growing rigidity around the political formula; this is visible for instance, in the insistence that all provinces must be treated identically, subsumed into uniformity under the principle of citizen equality. This kind of uniformity is, in fact, very foreign to our history. It is very doubtful if the federation could ever have got going if we had tried to operate like this in the past. But it comes forward now because it seems to many people to be the only way to recreate trust and common understanding between diverse regions, some of whom bear a grudge against others. This rigidity will make it difficult not only to accommodate Quebec, but also to make space for Aboriginal groups who are calling for new modes of self-rule.

The obvious facts about our era are that, first, the challenge of the new arrival is becoming generalized and multiplied in all democratic societies; the scope and rate of international migration is making all societies increasingly "multicultural." Second, the response to this challenge of the Jacobin sort, a rigorous assimilation to a formula involving fairly intense inner exclusion, is becoming less and less sustainable.

This last point is not easy to explain, but it seems to me to be undeniable. There has been a subtle switch in mind-set in our civilization, probably coinciding with the 1960s. The idea that one ought to suppress one's difference for the sake of fitting into a dominant mould, defined as the established way in one's society, has been considerably eroded. Feminists, cultural minorities, homosexuals, and religious groups all demand that the reigning formula be modified to accommodate them, rather than the other way around.

At the same time, possibly connected to this first change, but certainly with its own roots, has come another. This is an equally subtle change, and one that is hard to pin down. Migrants no longer feel the imperative to assimilate in the same way. One must not misidentify the switch. Most of them want to assimilate substantively to the societies they have entered, and they certainly want to be accepted as full members. But they frequently want now to do so at their own pace, and in their own way, and, in the process, they reserve the right to alter the society even as they assimilate to it.

The case of Hispanics in the United States is very telling in this regard. It is not that they do not want to become anglophone Americans. They see obvious advantages in doing so they have no intention of depriving themselves of these. But they frequently demand schools and services in Spanish because they want to make this process as painless as they can for themselves, and because they welcome such retention of the original culture as may fall out of this process. And something like this is obviously in the cards. They will all eventually learn English, but they will also alter somewhat the going sense of what it means to be an American, even as earlier waves of immigrants have. The difference with earlier waves is that Hispanics seem to be operating now with the sense of their eventual role in co-determining the culture, rather than this arising only retrospectively, as with earlier immigrants.

The difference between the earlier near-total success of France in assimilating East Europeans and others (who ever thought of Yves Montand as Italian?) and the present great difficulty with Maghrébains, while it reflects a whole lot of other factors – e.g., greater cultural-religious difference, and the collapse of full employment – nevertheless must also reflect, I believe, the new attitude among migrants. The earlier sense of unalloyed gratitude toward the new countries of refuge and opportunity, which seemed to make any revendication of difference quite unjustified and out of place, has been replaced by something harder to define. One is almost tempted to say, by something resembling the old doctrine that is central to many religions, that the earth has been given to the human species in common. A given space does not just unqualifiedly belong to the people born in it, and so it is not simply theirs to give. In return for entry, one is not morally bound to accept just any condition that is imposed.

Two new features arise from this shift. First, the notion I attributed to Hispanics in the United States has become widespread, namely, the idea that the culture they are joining is something in continual evolution, and that they have a chance to co-determine it in the future. This, instead of simple one-way assimilation, is more and more becoming the (often unspoken) understanding behind the act of migration.

Secondly, we have an intensification of a long-established phenomenon, which now seems fully "normal": that is, where certain immigrant groups still function morally, culturally, and politically as a "diaspora" in relation to their home country. This has been going on for a long time – think, for instance, of the "Polonia" in all the countries of exile. But whereas it was frowned on, or looked askance at, by many people in the receiving society, or where toleration for it depended on sympathy for the cause of the home country (the Poles were lucky in this respect) and whereas people muttered darkly in the past about "double allegiance," I believe now that this kind of behaviour is coming to be seen as normal. Of course, there are still extreme variants that arouse strong opposition, as when terrorists use the receiving countries as a base for their operations. But that is because these manifestations shock the dominant political ethic, and not because of the intense involvement in the country of origin. It is becoming more and more normal and un-challenged to think of oneself and be thought of as, say, a Canadian in good standing, while being heavily involved in the fate of some country of origin.

IV

The upshot of this discussion could be expressed this way: democracies are in a standing dilemma. They need strong cohesion around a political identity, and precisely this provides a strong temptation to exclude those who cannot or will not fit easily into the identity with which the majority feels comfortable, or believes alone can hold them together. And yet exclusion, besides being profoundly objectionable on moral grounds, also goes against the legitimacy idea of popular sovereignty, which is to realize the government of all the people. The need to form a people as a collective agent runs against the demand for inclusion of all who have a legitimate claim on citizenship.

This is the source of the malady; what are the remedies? These are a lot harder to find. But I believe that an important first step is to recognize the dilemma. For this allows us to see that it can very often only be dealt with by struggle toward a creative redefinition of our political identity. The dilemma, after all, arises because some often historically hallowed definition cannot accommodate all who have a moral claim to citizenship. And yet the reaction is all too often to render this original identity even more absolute and unchallengeable, as though it somehow belonged essentially to a certain people with its territory and history that it be organized under this and no other identity.

This appeal to origins can occur in both "republican" and "national" registers. In the first case, the particular features of our republican constitution are made absolute and sacrosanct, in face of all evidence that they may be impeding the search for a new common ground. Thus there is a certain Jacobin fundamentalism that comes to the surface in France, in reaction to certain demands to accommodate the growing Muslim minority. The wearing of headscarves in school by Muslim teenagers is judged to infringe the principles of "laïcité," as laid down in the French republican tradition. The general principle of state neutrality, indispensable in a modern diverse democracy, is metaphysically fused with a particular historical way of realizing it, and the latter is rendered as non-negotiable as the former.

As a panic reaction, this is understandable even if disastrous. Faced with the unfamiliar and disturbing, one reaches for the age-old sources of common identity. But the reaction is facilitated by the belief that this original constitution was meant to resolve the issue of political identity once and for all, that somehow it precluded in advance any need for illegitimate exclusion.

This amounts to a denial that the potential for the dilemma is built into democracy itself. It cannot be conjured once and for all by the ideal constitutional settlement. Even if this perfectly suits the population at the time of founding (and what constitution ever has?), the shifts in personal identity over time, through migration and moral or cultural change, can bring the established political identity out of true with the people who are supposed to live within it. This kind of fundamentalism attempts to deny history.

We are more familiar with this reaching back to sources in the national register; its destructive consequences are more immediately evident. The claim is that a certain territory belongs by right to a certain historical ethnic, or cultural, or linguistic, or religious identity, regardless of who else is living there, even if they have been there for centuries. And so Hungarian nationalists laid claim to the lands of the Crown of St Stephen in the nineteenth century, and the Bharatiya Janata Party feels it can and must impose a "Hindutva" identity on all the immense diversity of India today. Even more gruesome examples of the working out of this kind of claim have been visible in recent years in the territory of the former Yugoslavia.

The reflex of many people in liberal societies to this kind of thing is to blame "nationalism" and not democracy. But this is to take too quick a way with it. To start with, nationalism has many senses. The original idea, for instance in its Herderian form, was liberating and highly consonant with democracy. We do not have to force ourselves into an artificial homogeneity in order to live together in peace. We can recognize different "national" (*Volk*) identities, and even give them political expression, because each in this act of recognition acknowledges that it is not universal, that it has to coexist with others that are equally legitimate. Herderian nationalism is a universalist idea, all *Völker* are equally worthy of respect; it can be used (and was so used by Herder) to defend Slavic people against German encroachment, as well as to defend German culture against the hegemonic claims of French. You do not have to accept French as a universal language to live in freedom with guaranteed rights. The political identity under which you live can reflect you, too. This demand allows of an impeccably democratic justification.

What this pushes us toward is the idea that I believe is the key to facing the dilemma of exclusion creatively: the idea of sharing identity space. Political identities have to be worked out, negotiated, and creatively compromised between peoples who have to or want to live together under the same political roof (and this coexistence is always grounded in some mixture of necessity and choice). Moreover, these solutions are never meant to last for ever, but have to be discovered or invented anew by succeeding generations.

The idea of nationalism that creates bitter trouble is that defined by Ernest Gellner: the "political principle, which holds that the political and national unit should be congruent."[7] According to this idea, the problem of how to share identity space can be solved by giving each nation its territory on which it can erect its sovereign state. The utopian, even absurd, nature of the proposal immediately strikes the eye. Quite apart from the thousands of groups that can claim the status of "nation," even giving each its parcel of land would still leave each pocket-handkerchief state with national minorities, so inextricably mixed are the world's peoples. The utopian scheme could only be carried through by massive ethnic cleansing.

It is clear that this idea will only "work" by making certain nations more equal than others. These are to get their states, and the rest are to live in their shadow as minorities, if they are allowed to live at all. This idea of nationalism can be applied only by negating its own universalist ethical basis.

It is this distorted idea that justifies the claim by historical national identities to monopoly control over "their" territory. In the worst cases, this ends in a Yugoslav scenario. In the best cases, as with the Parti Québécois, and the more liberal wing of the Bharatiya Janata Party, minorities are to be guaranteed their rights, but the idea of sharing identity space and actually negotiating some compromise political identity is vigorously rejected.

Just as with "republican" forms of constitutionalism, the unreal idea of a definitive solution to the problem of democratic coexistence blinds people to the situation on the ground in almost all democratic states. The hope is once again to arrest history, to fix it in some original moment when our people attached themselves to this territory. And, similarly, what offers itself as a solution to the democratic dilemma can only exacerbate it to the point of bitter conflict.

But the belief that the problem here is "nationalism" can accredit another utopian solution, that of a political identity grounded purely in "republican" elements, without any reference to national or cultural identities.

In face of the prospect of having to bring together so many differences of culture, origin, political experience, and identity, the temptation is natural to define the common understanding more and more in terms of "liberalism," rather than by reference to the identities of citizens. The focus should be totally on individual rights and democratic and legal procedures, rather than on the historical-cultural reference points, or the ideas of the good life by which citizens define their own identities. In short, the temptation is to go for what Sandel calls the "procedural republic."

Already this has been evident in the Canadian case. I mentioned earlier that there has been a tendency in English Canada, in face of growing cultural diversity, to make certain aspects of the political culture central to the national identity. The main element that has been chosen for this has, not surprisingly, been the Charter of Rights, introduced into the Constitution in 1982. The underlying idea is that, whatever other differences distinguish us, as Canadians we can share a certain schedule of rights and certain procedures for enforcing them.

What does the procedural republic have going for it? A number of things, some of them tendencies in our philosophical tradition. I have discussed this elsewhere,[8] but I think we can both see and understand the drift away from ethics of the good life toward ethics based on something else, allegedly less contentious, and more apt to carry general agreement. This partly explains the popularity of both utilitarianism and of Kantian-derived deontological theories. Both manage to abstract from issues of what kind of life is more worthy, more admirable, and more human, and to fall back on what seems more solid ground. In one case, we count all the preferences, regardless of the supposed quality of the goals sought. In the other, we can abstract from the preferences, and focus on the rights of the preferring agent.

The act of abstraction here benefits from three important considerations. First, in an age of (at least menacing, if not actual) skepticism about moral views, it retreats from the terrain where the arguments seem the most dependent on our interpretations, the most contentious and incapable of winning universal assent; whereas we can presumably all agree that, other things being equal, it is better to let people have what they want, or to respect their freedom to choose. Second, this refusal to adopt a particular view of the good life leaves it to the individual to make the choice, and hence it fits with the anti-paternalism of the modern age. It enshrines a kind of freedom. Third, in face of the tremendous differences of outlook in modern society, utilitarianism and Kantian deontology seem to promise a way of deciding the issues we face in common without having to espouse the views of some against others.

Now the first two considerations are based on philosophical arguments about what can and cannot be known and proved, and about the nature of freedom, respectively. They have been much discussed, debated, and (often) refuted by philosophers. But the third is a political argument. Regardless of who is ultimately right in the battle between procedural ethics and those of the good life, we could conceivably be convinced on political grounds that the best formula for democratic government of a complex society is a kind of neutral liberalism. And this, mainly, is where the argument has gone today. The shift between Rawls I and Rawls II is a clear example of this. His theory of justice is now presented as "political, not metaphysical." This shift perhaps comes in part from the difficulties that the purely philosophical arguments run into. But it also corresponds to the universal perception that diversity is a more important and crucial dimension of contemporary society. This comes, as I argued earlier, partly from the actual growth in diversity in the population through, say, international migration; and partly from the growing demand that age-old diversities be taken seriously, as has been put forward by feminists, for instance.

So the issue now could be: What conception of freedom, of equality, of fairness, and of the basis for social coexistence are not right in the abstract, but feasible for modern democratic societies? How can people live together in difference, granted that this will be in a democratic regime, under conditions of fairness and equality.

The procedural republic starts off with a big advantage. If in your understanding of the citizen's roles and rights, you abstract from any view of the good life, then you avoid endorsing the views of some at the expense of others. Moreover, you find an immediate common terrain on which all can gather. Respect me, and accord me rights, just in virtue of my being a citizen, not in virtue of my character, outlook, or the ends I espouse, not to speak of my gender, race, sexual orientation, etc.

No one in their right mind would deny that this is an important dimension of any liberal society. The right to vote, for instance, is indeed accorded unconditionally; or on condition of certain bases of citizenship, but certainly in a way that is blind to differences of the range just quoted. The question we have to ask is whether this can be the only basis for living together in a democratic state, whether this is the valid approach in all contexts, whether our liberalism approaches perfection the more we can treat people in ways that abstract from what they stand for and others do not.

Now it can appear that whatever other reasons there might be for treating people this way, at least it facilitates our coming together and feeling ourselves to be part of a common enterprise. What we all have in common is that we make choices, opt for some things rather than others, and want to be helped and not hindered in pursuing the ends that flow from these options. So an enterprise that promises to further everyone's plan on some fair basis seems to be the ideal common ground. Indeed, some people find it hard to imagine what else could be. But this retreat to the procedural is no solution to the democratic dilemma. On the contrary, it very often itself helps to activate it. We can readily see this in two ways.

First, the condition of a viable political identity is that people must actually be able to relate to it, to find themselves reflected in it. But, in some cases, the preservation of an historical cultural identity is so important to a certain group that suppressing all mention of it in our answer to the "What for?" question cannot but alienate that group. The protection and promotion of its "distinct society" cannot but figure in the common identity of Quebec as a political entity, whether in the Canadian federation or outside. Refusing all mention of this in the canonical definitions of the Canadian identity can only increase the feeling of many Quebeckers that they have no place in the federation. This is not a solution to the conundrum of a common Canadian political identity; it is rather the source of the greatest contemporary threat to it.

Second, the procedural route supposes that we can uncontroversially distinguish neutral procedures from substantive goals. But it is in fact very difficult to devise a procedure that everyone perceives to be neutral. The point about procedures, or charters of rights, or distributive principles, is that they are meant not to enter into the knotty terrain of substantive differences in way of life. But, in practice, there is no way of ensuring that this will be so.

The case of the Muslim teenagers wearing headscarves in school in France is eloquent in this regard. "Laïcité" is supposedly a neutral principle, not favouring one religion or world view over another. On this basis the headscarves were refused, but other French girls often wear, for example, a cross around their necks, and this was unchallenged. In a "secular" society, this is presumably often just a "decoration." The presumption is valid enough, but the religious "invisibility" of the cross reflects France as a "post-Christian" society that follows upon centuries of Christian culture. How can one expect to convince Muslims that this combination of rulings is neutral?

The mistake here is to believe that there can be some decision whose neutrality is guaranteed by its emerging from some principle or procedure. This breeds the illusion that there is no need to negotiate the place of these symbols, and hence to confront the actual substantive differences of religious allegiance in the public square. But no procedure can dispense with the need to share identity space.

Something similar holds of the American case. What is meant to be a procedural move, neutral between all parties – the separation of church and state – turns out to be open to different interpretations, and some of these are seen as very far from neutral by some of the important actors in the society. The school prayer dispute is a case in point. One could argue that insistence on a procedural solution – in this case, a winner-take-all constitutional adjudication – is exactly what will maximally inflame the division; which indeed, it seems, to have done.

Moreover, as against a political solution, based on negotiation and compromise between competing demands, this provides no opportunity for people on each side to look into the substance of the other's case. Worse, by having their demand declared unconstitutional, the losers' programme is delegitimated in a way that has deep resonance in American society. Not only can we not give you what you want, but you are primitive and unAmerican to want it.

In short, I would argue that the current American *Kulturkampf* has been exacerbated rather than reconciled by the heavy recourse in that polity to judicial resolution on the basis of the constitution.

V

My argument has been that a full understanding of the dilemma of democratic exclusion shows that there is no alternative to what I have called sharing identity space. This means negotiating a commonly acceptable political identity between the different personal or group identities that want to or have to live in the polity. Some things will, of course, have to be non-negotiable, the basic principles of republican constitutions, democracy itself, and human rights among them. But this firmness has to be accompanied by a recognition that these principles can be realized in a number of different ways and can never be applied neutrally without some confronting of the substantive religious-ethnic-cultural differences in societies. Historic identities cannot simply be abstracted from. Nor can their claims to monopoly status merely be *received*. There are no exclusive claims to a given territory by historic right.

What does this mean in practice? Fortunately, I do not have space to go into this here. But also there are not too many things that one can say in utter generality. Solutions have to be tailored to particular situations. Some of the political mechanisms of this sharing are already well known, e.g., various brands of federalism as well as the design of forms of special status for minority societies, such we see today in Scotland and Catalonia. But many other modalities remain to be devised for the still more diverse democratic societies of the twenty-first century.

In the meantime, it will have helped, I believe, if we can perceive more clearly and starkly the nature of our democratic dilemma, since the hold of unreal and ahistorical solutions over our minds and imagination is still crippling our efforts to deal with the growing conflicts that arise from it. If this chapter contributes a little to this end, it will have been worth the writing.

NOTES

1 And, in fact, the drive to democracy took a predominantly "national" form. Logically, it is perfectly possible that the democratic challenge to a multinational authoritarian regime, e.g., Austria or Turkey, should take the

form of a multinational citizenship in a pan-imperial "people." But, in fact, attempts at this usually fail, and the peoples take their own road into freedom. So the Czechs declined being part of a democratized Empire in the Paulskirche in 1848; and the Young Turk attempt at an Ottoman citizenship foundered and made way for a fierce Turkish nationalism.

2 Rousseau, who laid bare very early the logic of this idea, saw that a democratic sovereign could not just be an "aggregation," as with our lecture audience above; it has to be an "association," that is, a strong collective agency, a "corps moral et collectif" with "son unité, son commun, sa vie, et sa volonté." This last term is the key one, because what gives this body its personality is a "volonté générale." *Contrat Social*, book 1, ch. 6.

3 I have discussed this in "Les Sources de l'identité moderne," in *Les Frontières de l'identité: Modernité et postmodernisme Au Québec*, ed. Mikhaël Elbaz, Andrée Fortin, and Guy Laforest (Sainte-Foy: Presses de l'Université Laval, 1996), 347–64.

4 I have looked at this issue in *Reconciling the Solitudes*, ed. Guy Laforest, (Montreal and Kingston: McGill-Queen's University Press, 1993). See especially "Shared and Divergent Values," 155–86.

5 Michael Sandel, *Democracy's Discontents* (Cambridge, MA: Harvard University Press, 1996).

6 Gérard Noiriel, *Le Creuset français* (Paris: Le Seuil, 1989).

7 Ernest Gellner, *Nations and Nationalism* (Ithaca: Cornell University Press, 1983), 1.

8 Charles Taylor, *The Sources of the Self: The Making of Modern Identity* (Cambridge, MA: Harvard University Press, 1989), ch. 3.